MONARCHS

mascotbooks.com

Monarchs: Bud Metheny, Old Dominion Baseball,
and the Foundational 1960s Championship Teams

For more information, please contact:
Mascot Books, an imprint of Amplify Publishing Group
620 Herndon Parkway #320
Herndon, VA 20170
info@mascotbooks.com

CPSIA Code: PRV0722A
Library of Congress Control Number: 2021923302
ISBN-13: 978-1-63755-152-3

Printed in the United States

This work is dedicated to the memory of my father, John Akers Ingram Jr., a pitcher on the 1964 Old Dominion Monarch baseball team, who passed away on October 16, 2020.

Dad taught me about life, work ethic, respect, integrity—and baseball. I cannot imagine a better father and mentor. You will be missed, in eternity.

One hundred percent of proceeds from the sale of this book will go to a scholarship fund that the family endowed at Old Dominion shortly before Dad's passing. For anyone who might be inspired by this work to assist the Old Dominion baseball cause, donations to this scholarship fund are welcomed. Income from the endowment is to be awarded annually to an Old Dominion student athlete who participates on the baseball team, as chosen by the director of athletics. Donations can be made by filling the check memo field with "John A. Jr. and Arlene Ingram Scholarship," and sending to: Old Dominion Athletic Foundation, 4417 Monarch Way, 4th Floor, Norfolk, Virginia 23529.

Jay Ingram

MONARCHS

BUD METHENY,
OLD DOMINION BASEBALL, AND
THE FOUNDATIONAL 1960s
CHAMPIONSHIP TEAMS

JAY INGRAM

TABLE OF CONTENTS

FOREWORD

One of my nephew Jay Ingram's closing comments in the first draft of this book is that there is something special about baseball. Special, indeed! But maybe nothing is so special as a college team, with no athletic scholarships to offer, whose players all hail from the community where their institution is located, whose coach has been widely admired within the city for much of his adult life, a team that plays its home games not in a modern-day scaled-down version of a major league park, but on a dirt field located behind an elementary school. This, as far as it goes, is not an inaccurate summary of the early days of Old Dominion University baseball.

For many of us Norfolkians of middle-class means, ODU was a natural choice of where to continue your education. "The Division," as it was more familiarly known ("Where ya going after high school?" "The Division, I guess."), offered a solid education at a cost that we could manage and no room and board to pay, if you lived at home, as almost all of us did. Although enrollment was small in those days, say 4,000–5,000, it seemed like most, or at least many, of the kids you went to high school with went there. On our block alone in Commodore Park in Norfolk, there were four of us attending all at the same time, including my sister, who went on be the president of the class of 1964. We could have carpooled, but, of course, no one had a car (or a pool).

The Division during my student days, the late 1950s to the early 1960s (by which time it had become Old Dominion College), covered an area about one-eighth of the size, or less, of its current footprint, extending south down Hampton Boulevard a few blocks, from the Old Arts Building (a former elementary school) at the corner of Bolling Avenue, to about 48th Street. The academic complex comprised only a few structures. The facilities were so modest that the university administrative offices, library (until Hughes Library, which is now a faculty office building and has a new name, opened its doors in 1959), gymnasium, and swimming pool were all located in the same building. There were no dorms; consequently, there was no campus life after classes were over for the day. The few fraternities and sororities had houses off-campus in adjacent neighborhoods. The perfervid contemporary issues, such as race relations (conforming to Virginia laws of the time, there were no black students or faculty), the developing Vietnam War, and the military draft, did not occasion campus demonstrations or emotional discussions, except maybe at the meetings of the Political Science Club. The most overwrought student issue on campus was the lack of a football program. Many a petition promoting the creation of a football team was circulated and presented to the administration, which publicly responded with all the reasons why we could not have football. Certainly, the fact that there was not a football program was a factor in the strong student support for the baseball team.

I would estimate that about 90 percent of the students were from the immediate Hampton Roads area, with a few from more distant regions who rented rooms in the spacious neighboring homes or lived with relatives. The Old Dominion of that era was in many respects what would today be classified as a community college. The atmosphere was comfortable and unintimidating, and as mentioned, a lot of your fellow students were ones you had gone to high school with.

So it was with the ballplayers. In those years, essentially 100 percent of them came from Norfolk, Portsmouth, Chesapeake, and Virginia Beach (in their earlier identities as Norfolk County and Princess Anne County, respectively), or from the peninsula cities of Newport News and Hampton. Contrast this with a look at the 2019 ODU baseball team, which shows only seven from the Tidewater area, out of a thirty-six-man roster. The players came from the community that the college served, and the community appreciated their play and their success. Now the players from those days and the population that supported and encouraged them can reflect on those days and take pride in knowing that their accomplishments have been recognized and preserved for all of us to enjoy.

Bill Palmer
Old Dominion College Class of 1963

PREFACE

This work began with the intention of telling the story of the 1964 Old Dominion Monarchs baseball team, which was the most successful to that point, and instrumental, in my thesis, to the future success of the college as a whole. Driving my personal interest in this story, 1964 was also my father's senior year at Old Dominion College. As I learned more about the subject matter, I also realized that the singular story of that year is intertwined with the history of the school itself, the history of its baseball program, other social and political forces that shaped the national and regional culture, and perhaps most importantly, the personal influence of Old Dominion's legendary coach, Arthur "Bud" Metheny. As such, the scope of the work expanded to include all these elements, and while my original thesis still holds, the focus of the work shifted from sole attention on the 1964 team to a spotlight shared between the several championship teams of that era, and the coach personally.

I began research with personal phone interviews with fourteen members of the late-1950s and early-1960s teams, starting with my father, a pitcher on that 1964 team. Those interviews and personal reflections really influenced the direction of this work—What was your experience while locked out of your Norfolk high school? What was it like to play in Yankee Stadium? What kind of coach was Bud Metheny? These recordings and transcriptions, incidentally, have been donated to ODU as part of their Oral History project and will hopefully soon be available on the school's digital archives.

As far as I know, this history hasn't been fully treated and published before. Tony Zontini authored a history of Old Dominion baseball for his master's thesis in 1978, and it's available in the Old Dominion Library, and the Old Dominion Baseball Media Guide also contains some program history, but neither work attempts to tie the baseball program to the City of Norfolk, or to national events, or to extrapolate success on the baseball diamond to success as a growing institution of higher learning.

There is a wealth of contemporary information available to help write the story. Bud Metheny's papers, including all his old scorebooks, are available in Old Dominion's Patricia W. and J. Douglas Perry Library Special Collections, and the library also has all available yearbooks and editions of the school newspaper, dating back to the school's founding in 1930. Newport News' *Daily Press*, which covered the college's athletic program extensively, is available and searchable online. Norfolk's *Virginian-Pilot* is not online, but it's available on microfilm, and I paid a genealogical researcher to find all articles relating to Old Dominion baseball through 1964 (or, in its earlier incarnation, the Norfolk Division of the College of William & Mary). That cache of digital clippings has also been donated to ODU.

Baseball is a game measured statistically like no other, and statistics are necessarily a key element in this work. Sources of information for the statistical analyses contained here, however, are not always perfectly aligned with each other, or always complete. I have used these sources primarily: Coach Bud Metheny's own scorebooks, and accounts in the *Daily Press* of Newport News, the *Virginian-Pilot* of Norfolk, and the school newspaper (*The High Hat*, and later, the *Mace and Crown*). As secondary and confirming sources, I have used yearbook accounts, Mr. Zontini's thesis, and other material available in Coach Metheny's papers at ODU.

Coach Metheny's firsthand, real-time scorekeeping records are treated as the primary source. In general, they are meticulous, and a great resource for a historian fifty-plus years later. However, even these are not 100 percent complete and consistent, and so in some instances, the other sources are relied on more heavily. In this writing, I have tried to make clear the source data for my analyses, where appropriate. Further, the sometimes-inconsistent availability of authoritative historical information also introduces some possibility of error, and yields statistical conclusions in this work that, in some cases, do contain differences (relatively minor) from ODU's annual baseball media guide.

As a final note, in some cases the newspaper articles embedded within the text have been digitally manipulated to combine continuations on a later page into a single image, or to turn a single long column into an image with two side-by-side columns. These are probably obvious, and in these few cases, they have only been manipulated in order to display the entire article in the space available. The written integrity of all such articles is maintained throughout.

INTRODUCTION

The 1964 Old Dominion Monarch baseball team achieved everything they could have possibly hoped to achieve, both from a team perspective and an individual one. The team had a legendary coach in former New York Yankee "Bud" Metheny, a man for his time at the peak of his influence. The team had Fred Kovner, who went on to play professional baseball, and one who made the major leagues, in pitcher Denny Riddleberger. The 1964 team featured three of the pitchers who make up the top four in ODU's career ERA list, in Bill Yeargan, Fred Edmonds Jr., and Bob Walton. The team had seven past or current all-conference performers in its lineup. It had All-Americans, and it had the national Coach of the Year. As a team, this unit played in the NCAA College Division East Region tournament in Yankee Stadium and ultimately stood as 1964 champions.

Old Dominion College had served Norfolk since 1930 but was still in its relatively early growth stages in 1964. In fact, Old Dominion had only become an independent institution two years before—with separation from the College of William & Mary system, the Norfolk Division of the College of William & Mary had become Old Dominion College, a name initially known primarily only locally, to the Tidewater students it intended to serve. At the time, the school was still small enough that it was exclusively a commuter school, with no dorms on campus. The 1964 championship baseball team provided more regional and national visibility for the newly named school, and that visibility has certainly played a part in the still-developing success story that is Old Dominion University.

Baseball success did not happen overnight, and the Norfolk Division spent its initial seasons playing primarily against high school teams and non-four-year institutions, and later, Navy-affiliated teams. The World War II years were particularly lean ones for the baseball program, but the team's fortunes changed with the hiring of ex-Yankee Bud Metheny as the coach. While not an unqualified immediate success, Metheny continued to drive the program forward relentlessly, overseeing the Norfolk Division's inclusion in the mythical "Little Eight" circuit in Virginia and membership in the NCAA, and later, Old Dominion's inclusion in the Mason-Dixon Conference.

The name recognition that these advancements gained for the college helped provide Metheny with a fertile recruiting ground locally and helped create the environment in which he could gather such an assemblage of talent on his home field in Larchmont. Success follows success, and as his assemblage of talent started winning championships, so too did the institution itself reap the rewards. The successes of the baseball team created local interest in the school and led to more coverage in local newspapers, but also took the name of the school to all fifty states, as championships were announced, as All-Americans were announced, as national coaches of the year were announced, and as major league baseball drafts happened. While clearly not the single factor in the rise of Old Dominion University, Bud Metheny's championship baseball teams of 1964 and before certainly had foundational impact.

BEGINNINGS

"**D**uring the '20s the city of Norfolk had the dubious distinction of being the largest city in the English-speaking world without an institution of higher learning," Dr. James R. Sweeney begins his book, *Old Dominion University: A Half Century of Service.* This lack of local opportunity didn't sit well with all in the community, and as Dr. Sweeney recounts, the decade of the 1920s began to see several prominent citizens of the city (namely William Holmes Davis, A. H. Foreman, and Robert Morton Hughes) beginning to develop thoughts, ideas, and plans to introduce a formal college to Norfolk.

Williamsburg's venerable College of William & Mary, approximately forty miles from the heart of downtown Norfolk, had begun offering some classes in Norfolk in 1919. In such close proximity to Norfolk's barren educational landscape, William & Mary was, and remains, iconic—"William and Mary is famous for its firsts," the school's website notes. "The first U. S. institution with a royal charter, the first Greek-letter society (Phi Beta Kappa, founded in 1776), the first student honor code, the first college to become a university and the first law school in America." In the United States, only Harvard is an older institution of higher learning, although, as William & Mary points out in a somewhat competitive-sounding passage, "While our original plans date back to 1618—decades before Harvard—William & Mary was officially chartered in 1693."[1]

Instructors leading these extension classes commuted to Norfolk from Williamsburg, although travel from the Peninsula to the South Side in the 1920s was not quite as simple as today and certainly required timeliness on the part of the traveler. The Hampton Roads Bridge-Tunnel (connecting Norfolk to Hampton) was not open until 1957, and the Monitor-Merrimac Memorial Bridge Tunnel (between Suffolk and Newport News) not until 1992. A 1921 map of Norfolk demonstrates the means of commuting in the 1920s: the Old Point Ferry (from the tip of Willoughby Spit in Norfolk to the Fort Monroe area of Hampton) and the Newport News Ferry (from Sewell's Point in Norfolk to Newport News).[2] Commuting instructors had evidently begun to find a willing audience in Norfolk, as Dr. Sweeney notes that by 1929–30—the year before the extension classes officially became the Norfolk Division of the College of William & Mary—356 students availed themselves of this opportunity in Norfolk.[3]

In 1930, William & Mary leadership encountered some unwelcome competition for dominion over South Side Tidewater's higher education, and this competition likely sped the formal creation of the Norfolk Division. In that year, it was announced that a new college, Atlantic University, would open at Virginia Beach in the fall.[4] The new institution at the oceanfront had a grand vision and enlisted William Moseley Brown, a former Virginia gubernatorial candidate and professor of psychology at Washington and Lee University, to serve as school president. Also on the new school's board were New York businessmen, a Chicago executive, and Edgar Cayce, a local Virginia Beach psychic and spiritualist upon whose work the new university proposed to expound.

Atlantic University had a relatively spectacular rise, followed by an equally spectacular demise. During the week of April 13, 1930, newspapers across the country heralded the plans for the new school; residents in cities such as Atlanta, Green Bay, Indianapolis, Baltimore, Louisville, and St. Louis could read about the new Virginia Beach university, its wealthy financiers, and its vision for future expansion. Throughout that summer, Atlantic University continued to build its impressive faculty by raiding other institutions; in fact, a May 31st *Daily Press* (Newport News) article announced that three members of the William & Mary faculty had resigned their posts to sign on with Atlantic.[5] Under a headline of somewhat smaller font, and further down the very same page, the paper also announced that "Final action on the establishment of a junior college at Norfolk by the College of William & Mary will be taken at the meeting of the board of visitors here next Saturday. With the approval of the proposed transfer of the old Larchmont School Building on Hampton Boulevard given by the City Council recently, the action of the college board of visitors is all that remains to make the plans definite."[6]

In the deepening Depression, Atlantic University's promising future lasted approximately one semester. On January 4, 1931, brothers Morton and Edwin Blumenthal, who had invested a reported $60,000 in the venture, pulled out, citing the "alleged failure of Dr. William Moseley Brown . . . to live up to the budget of operating expenses authorized by the board," as the *Chicago Tribune*, and many other national outlets, reported.[7] The school continued operations, but more trouble followed in November of that year when Edgar Cayce was arrested in New York City on charges of "pretending to tell fortunes"[8]—a charge he successfully contested. But a month later, on December 14, Atlantic again made national news, as papers were submitted to appoint a receiver for the school, allegedly insolvent by that time, indebted by $21,000 and still owing $65,000 in staff salaries. By the end of 1931, on the recommendation of receiver Percy S. Stephenson, Atlantic University ceased operations (although the charter was still valid, and it did reopen in Virginia Beach in 1985 as a "spiritually centered and mindfully focused institution" still affiliated with Cayce's Association for Research and Enlightenment).

Despite the failure, Atlantic University provided motivation for William & Mary President Dr. J. A. C. Chandler to take action on the concept that had been discussed for several years—the establishment of a permanent junior college in Norfolk, affiliated with the college in Williamsburg, and providing a conduit for students wishing to continue their academic careers at William & Mary after two years of instruction in Norfolk. The threat to William & Mary's interests in Norfolk that Atlantic University had posed prompted Norfolk lawyer (and William & Mary alumnus) Robert Morton Hughes to write to Chandler in early 1930, advising him to "act promptly on your junior college plan if you intend to act at all."[9]

Norfolk attorney A. H. Foreman, chairman of the Norfolk School Board and a member of William & Mary's Board of Visitors, was in the perfect position to help make the idea of a junior college a reality. The City of Norfolk was replacing the Larchmont School, constructed in 1912, with a new building nearby, and Foreman helped broker a deal between the Norfolk City Council and the College of William & Mary: Norfolk would turn the old school building over to the College of William & Mary for use as the new junior college, William & Mary would provide ten scholarships to worthy Norfolk students selected by the recommendations of Maury High School Principal A. B. Bristow, and the property would be returned to Norfolk should William & Mary cease operations there.[10]

In the spring of 1930, the Norfolk City Council approved the proposal, and in short order, William & Mary's Board of Visitors concurred, prompting a flurry of activity that summer to ready the site for operations in the fall. Sweeney recounts a "dramatic" visit to the site in June, which ended in instructions from Chandler to Joseph Healy, director of the extension classes that had been in offered in Norfolk: "Healy, employ a secretary, install a telephone, and prepare a catalog for me to be on my desk by next Saturday." As the Norfolk Division of the College of William & Mary, Old Dominion University was born.

While the building was readied to open as a college, William & Mary leadership was also finalizing the administrative details, and sought to establish the new school as an integral part of Norfolk life. One means to the end of marriage of school and city was the selection of the Board of Directors of the new Division, and the *Daily Press* reported Dr. Chandler's selections on June 15:

> Announcement has been made by Dr. J. A. C. Chandler, president of William and Mary, that the Board of Directors of the college division will be composed of the following:
>
> A. H. Foreman, prominent Norfolk attorney and chairman of the Norfolk School Board, and a member of the Board of Visitors of the college; C. W. Mason, superintendent of the Norfolk city schools; H. A. Hunt, superintendent of the Portsmouth city schools; James Hurst, superintendent of the Norfolk County schools. All of the above have accepted the positions on the board. In addition to the above, S. Heth Tyler, Mayor of the City of Norfolk, has been asked to serve on the board, but is absent in Europe at the present time and has not accepted.
>
> The plan is to open the Norfolk division on September the tenth with a faculty of 25 to 30 trained university professors. The school will offer a complete two-year college course, upon the completion of which a student can continue his studies in Williamsburg or elsewhere. About 12 of the professors will be resident in Norfolk and the school will be in charge of a director whose identity has not yet been announced.
>
> Fees in the new college division will amount to $100 a year or $50 a semester.[11]

The Norfolk Division of the College of William & Mary, in the Larchmont School building. Courtesy of Special Collections and University Archives, Patricia W. and J. Douglas Perry Library, Old Dominion University Libraries, Norfolk, Virginia.

Less than three weeks before the start of school, Chandler announced his new permanent director: H. Edgar Timmerman, a World War I veteran, holder of AB and MA degrees from Columbia University, and recently an instructor at New York University. In published comments to the *Daily Press* on September 5, Timmerman noted his view of the importance of the new school, saying that "it is very evident that the junior college fills a long-wanted need, not only in Norfolk but within this general area." At this time, however, he was also specifically noncommittal about athletics at the Norfolk Division: "Mr. Timmerman said that a physical education program will be followed during the first year, but that it would be impossible to have a complete program of sports. He added that he did not see why freshmen basketball would not be feasible during the first year, but that it would be impossible to follow a football schedule until later."[12]

The student body, starved for the opportunities that come with a college environment, ensured almost immediately that opportunities available at other schools were available in Norfolk, too. The initial printing of the school newspaper, *The High Hat*, was released in November 1930 and offers a fascinating look at the beginnings of the college. The first edition includes a letter to students from the director, announcements of the formations of the "TIGA" fraternity, the "Imp" fraternity, a monogram club, a girls' cotillion club, a dramatic club ("Student interest has been aroused to the point of wholesome enthusiasm"), an orchestra ("Fines will be instituted for unexcused absences of members from either the rehearsals or meetings"), and a women's student government association ("A very strict account is kept of the absentees and they are fined a sum of 50 cents for every absence"). The new college's honor system was introduced and explained; the terms were simple yet draconian, and with lifelong consequences for those discovered to be in violation: "The Honor Code of this institution is very simple and consists merely of this: A man or woman shall not be a liar, thief, or a cheat. If he is, he must leave college and go in disgrace throughout his life."[13]

Most importantly for this work, the beginnings of the Norfolk Division athletic programs also drew extensive coverage in the first *High Hat*—in fact, the very first headline of the school newspaper read "BANG! Basketball Season Starts Off With A Crash . . . ". The basketball schedule, slated to begin on December 12, showed twenty-five contests, primarily against local high school teams and freshman teams from Virginia colleges such as William & Mary, Washington and Lee, and VMI. Despite Director Timmerman's early projections, the school had indeed fielded a football team, and with some amount of success. Coach Tommy Scott, it was reported, had "injected some unfathomable 'vim' and power into his teams, hence impressive victories were scored over such teams as Oceana High, South Norfolk High, Hertford High and our brothers, the William and Mary Freshman

[sic], of Williamsburg."[14] Timmerman evidently was supportive of this initial football edition, as the newspaper, in a section entitled "Scholarly Musings," acknowledged his attendance at contests, although not without some amount of accusatory wording: "Dame Rumor hath it that a certain college director known as Mr. H. Edgar Timmerman—we mention no names—has been of late attending football games free of charge by the ingenious strategem [sic] of going disguised as a member of the band . . . The disguise is simple; he can pass any gatekeeper as a saxophone player merely by carrying along his pipe." Along with coverage of football and basketball, the initial *High Hat* covered progress on the development of women's sports programs at the new school, as well.[15]

To the Students of The Norfolk Division College of William and Mary

It is indeed a rare opportunity that a college administrator has the privilege of officially welcoming a new class and at the same time offering his congratulations to them for the establishment of a new publication.

What has been done in this new division of an old and honored institution during the past two months is now history, and to say what we are going to do in the future - would require a special gift of prophesy. Yet, there are so many things that one can do to make the Norfolk Division of the College of William and Mary an institution to which not only the City of Norfolk, but all of Vrginia and the whole South, may look to with pride. It is especially important that during this formation period that the faculty and the student body co-operate in the highest degree in order that the institution may pass through its really "critical" period. I

am sure that all are desirous of seeing the Norfolk Division of the College of William and Mary expand and develop to meet the fullest educational needs of the City of Norfolk, and to this end may I ask your help?

With the establishment of this publication of the student body, I feel that a much needed want in our school has been fulfilled. The High Hat can be of so much service to our division of the college that it is hard for us to realize its potentialites. It should boost our athletic, literary, dramatic and musical activities, and at the same time stand for the highest in scholastic attainment. I know that will prove to be an expression of the latent talents of our student body.

I bid the students of the Norfolk Division, College of William and Mary, and The High Hat a welcome.

H. EDGAR TIMMERMAN.

Letter from Director Timmerman to students, from the first edition of The High Hat.
Courtesy of Special Collections and University Archives, Old Dominion University.

From a single vacated elementary school on Hampton Boulevard, Old Dominion has grown to a school of 24,176 students in 2021; from a school that was founded to serve the Norfolk and Tidewater community, Old Dominion has grown to an institution with eighty-nine countries represented in its student body.[16] From its birth in that single building, the campus itself has grown to 335 acres and 148 buildings. Old Dominion University has become deeply enmeshed as a major player in the fabric of the regional economy, and by the school's own reckoning, ODU's initiatives contribute an incredible $2.6 billion to Virginia's economy.[17]

How does a school grow from such a relatively humble beginning to become what Old Dominion University is today? Certainly, it takes a confluence of many factors for a fledgling institution of higher learning to achieve this level of success. It takes a population eager for such opportunity, and William & Mary extension courses in Norfolk were already well-attended before the permanent college was established. It takes the support of influential community and business leaders, such as the new school had with A. H. Foreman and Robert M. Hughes, one of whom was honored later with his name on the football stadium (Foreman Field), and one who was honored with the naming of the Robert M. Hughes Memorial Library on campus in 1959. It takes support from, and relationships with, local government, such as was offered by Norfolk with the initial transfer of the Larchmont School Building. It takes being in the right place at the right time, too; during the Depression years, a cost of fifty dollars per semester could keep prospective students at home in Norfolk, when in more prosperous times they may have gone elsewhere. Certainly, the closing of Atlantic University also increased the number of prospective students searching for educational opportunities in Norfolk.

Success requires dedicated and lifelong stewards of the school's mission, and the Norfolk Division had several in its early decades. Former director of the Norfolk Division, and then subsequently president of Old Dominion College, Lewis Webb ("The Father of Old Dominion") probably shines brightest in that regard, as he served the school for over thirty years, overseeing its transition from a division of the College of William & Mary to an independent institution. But the Norfolk Division also had William W. Seward Jr., anchoring the English Department for over thirty years beginning in 1945, and W. Gerald Akers, chairing the Foreign Language Department and heading the Division of Humanities in a career that started in 1931 and lasted over forty years. The Division had Edgar Kovner, another veteran of over forty years, who led the Technical Institute for a time and coached the lacrosse team. The school had J. C. "Scrap" Chandler, a former star athlete at William & Mary, who came to the Division in 1942 and served the school for nearly thirty years as athletic director and coach of four sports; his name graces Old Dominion's natatorium. And, luckily, the Norfolk Division of the College of William & Mary, Old Dominion College, and then Old Dominion University had Arthur Beauregard "Bud" Metheny, who retired from professional baseball to serve in Norfolk for over thirty years as athletic director, baseball coach, basketball coach, instructor, trainer, mentor, team bus driver, school representative, and, as needed, gym floor sander.

Success also takes an ability to galvanize a population, to create interest in the school, and to bond alumni to their alma mater, and very little does that the way a successful athletic program can. As an example, Davidson president David G. Martin was quoted in the February 27, 1964, *Virginian-Pilot* saying, "The [basketball] team has created more expressed enthusiasm than anything that's ever happened at Davidson. It's caused more excitement than the 14 Rhodes Scholars we have turned out or a bequest of a million dollars which we received last year. The impact has been greater." Certainly, the fairly recent growth and expansion at Virginia Tech, which followed Coach Frank Beamer's success with the football team, can be viewed as a similar modern example. The Norfolk Division of William & Mary employed a similar blueprint for success, notably including the baseball program of the 1950s and early 1960s. The Norfolk Division began a sports program in its very first semester by fielding a football team; basketball and baseball teams followed in their respective seasons, and over the course of years, the college has won NCAA titles in baseball, women's basketball, and field hockey, and can boast many athletes who went on from Norfolk to success in the professional arena.

The football team, in its original incarnation, lasted eleven years, but due to debt and other issues, ceased functioning in the early 1940s. The basketball team had some early successes, but in the early decades of the school, it was the baseball team that was able to bring athletic prominence to the Norfolk Division. Unlike the basketball team, the baseball team had a natural ability to upgrade its annual competition beyond the high school and military teams it played in the earliest years, since northern schools would travel south in the spring in search of baseball competition in warmer climates. When Coach Bud Metheny took the reins of the baseball program in 1948, he exploited that opportunity, as well as his connections as a former New York Yankee, to create better schedules and more visibility for his Norfolk Division baseball program. In terms of wins and losses, Coach Metheny was willing to sacrifice the short term, to a degree, for his long-range vision; as he continually upgraded the level of competition his baseball charges faced, his program became better and brought more name recognition to the school. In 1958, his team made news around Virginia as "Little Eight" champions for the first time; in 1963, his team brought the school's brand-new name, Old Dominion College, to newspapers across both Virginia and Maryland by winning the Mason-Dixon Conference title in ODC's first year in the league, and then brought greater prominence to the name of the college along the Eastern Seaboard by winning the NCAA regional title at Hampden-Sydney College. In 1964, Coach Metheny and his team achieved the pinnacle of team and personal success, winning the NCAA Eastern Region tournament on the hallowed grounds of Yankee Stadium. The program gained further recognition when outfielder Fred Kovner was named as a first-team All-American and pitcher Bob Walton as second-team, and again when Metheny was named national Coach of the Year. Multiple factors certainly have played into the success of Old Dominion University, but the national visibility created by this 1964 baseball team, the ability of the team to create local and regional interest in the small commuter school, and the lasting impact of Coach Bud Metheny played an integral, and inestimable, part.

CHAPTER ONE

The 1930s

*We must remember that students have many
ambitions for college outside of academics, and of
course athletics has always been one of those. And so they
tried to fill that need of the student body. Of course,
we operated on a shoestring, and so any and all efforts
were made with a minimum of capital outlay.*

—DEAN EDWARD WHITE, *Old Dominion 1932–1974,*
on early Norfolk Division athletics

Baseball at the newly formed Norfolk Division of William & Mary began with Coach Tommy Scott's 1931 call for ballplayers—the typical way of constituting the team in Norfolk for many years, at a time long before any athletic scholarships were available. As reported by *The High Hat*, thirty-five candidates presented themselves that year for Coach Scott's review.[1] Viewed from 2019, that seems like

BASEBALL TEAM ORGANIZED

Thirty-five men responded to the call issued for basball candidates by Coach Scott.

The team will practice Mondays, Wednesdays and Fridays on diamond two, City Park.

So far the team has not been able to have a complete work-out due to the unfavorable weather conditions.

A schedule of thirty games is being arranged. Most of the games will be played at the City Park, with the most important games transfered to Bain Field.

From The High Hat, March 21, 1931. Courtesy of Special Collections and University Archives, Old Dominion University.

a reasonable number of hopefuls to make up a ball team, as the current NCAA rules on Division I baseball scholarships allow the parceling of 11.7 full scholarships to a maximum of twenty-seven ballplayers per team.[2] However, the Norfolk Division had opened its first semester in September 1930 with 125 male students, and on February 6, 1931, The High Hat published the names of forty new students for the second semester. Assuming no attrition of first-semester students, and assuming all initial-only first names (such as V. J. and M. L.) and all gender-indeterminate first names (such as Andred and Elfrain) published in the February list of new students were all male, then the Norfolk Division boasted a total of 153 male students in March 1931, meaning that a full 22.9 percent of the male student body tried out for the first edition of the school baseball team!

Coach Tommy Scott, already a legendary athlete in the state, had attended Norfolk's Maury High School and had been part of a basketball team that had gone 25–0 during the 1925–26 season and advanced to play in the National High School Tournament in Chicago. Scott also lettered in track and football at Maury, and had continued his athletic career at Virginia Military Institute, where he had lettered in football, baseball, and basketball. As his biography in the Virginia Sports Hall of Fame describes it, his VMI football career netted All-State,

All-Southern, and honorable mention All-America commendations, as well as a somewhat backhanded compliment from Georgia Tech coach Bobby Dodd, who evidently called Scott the "greatest 165-pound end I ever saw."[3] For his accomplishments on the field, Scott has been named to Maury's Sports Hall of Fame, to the Virginia Sports Hall of Fame, and, as a charter member, to VMI's Sports Hall of Fame.

In 1931, Coach Scott was just beginning on the path that would make him a charter member of Old Dominion University's Sports Hall of Fame, as well—although the school's early baseball teams may not have been his main focus, since his 1980 induction into the ODU Hall of Fame is as "Football/Basketball Coach." During his career at the Norfolk Division, however, he also coached the baseball and track teams and served as the first athletic director during the critical formative years of the institution.

An account of the Norfolk Division's first recorded baseball contest was offered in the April 2, 1931, edition of *The High Hat* under the headline, "Braves Trim Deep Creek by 8–3 Score." Division pitcher Rufus Tonelson had been "hit quite freely but tightened up in the pinches," although if the published box score is to be believed, he also somehow gave up six hits in four at-bats to Deep Creek pitcher P. Hewitt.[4] In the same edition, it was reported that the Norfolk Division had also won their second game, an 18–6 triumph over Norview High School, on the strength of a strong pitching performance by "Buckwheat" Stewart.

The first Norfolk Division baseball team played local high school teams almost exclusively, including Deep Creek, Maury, Kempsville, Cape Charles, Norview, South Norfolk, Wilson, and Hertford. Although the schedule published in the school paper on April 17, 1931, does also include Campbell College and the William & Mary freshmen, the paper also notes that "These games are subject to alteration, so we advise anyone intending to really follow the team to keep in touch with the manager." According to available records, the only collegiate competition the Norfolk Division Braves faced in their first season turned out to be the William & Mary freshmen, who defeated their junior institution by a score of 7–6. Still, the season was a success; as former three-sport Old Dominion College star Tony Zontini recorded in his 1978 master's thesis about the history of baseball at Old Dominion, the Norfolk Division earned a winning mark in their first run, as they chalked up eight wins against five losses.

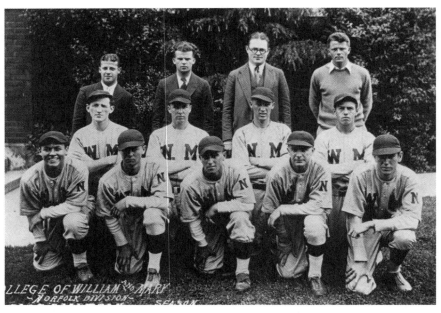

The 1931 Norfolk Division of William & Mary baseball team. Front row, left to right: Joseph Schnitzer, Al Wilson, Richard Bacchus, Rufus Tonelson, Marion Kelley. Second row, right to left: Dave Nesson, Nathaniel Parks, Fred Stewart, Philip Stroud. Back row, left to right: Bernard Rosenfeld, Francis Morrisette, H. Edgar Timmerman, Coach Tommy Scott. Not pictured: Terry Maxey, William Abrams, Harry Hamburger, Truman Baxter, and Joseph Berman. Courtesy of Special Collections and University Archives, Patricia W. and J. Douglas Perry Library, Old Dominion University Libraries, Norfolk, Virginia.

Either the initial success led to a high level of anticipation for the sophomore season, or the school paper needed something to write about, as *The High Hat* reported on the 1932 baseball squad no fewer than eight times on the front page, with three of those articles coming before any games were even played. An interesting note came on March 4, when it was reported that hometown boy Dave Robertson, a former major leaguer who had twice tied for the league lead in home runs and who had won a World Series with the New York Giants, would "assist Scott in whipping the Baby Indians into shape." Robertson's major league career had ended in 1922, and more recently, he had spent the 1925–1927 seasons managing the minor league Norfolk Tars. There also appears to have been some ambiguity regarding his nickname: *The High Hat* refers to him as "Demon Dave" in the headline, but "Dangerous Dave" in the article text.[5] In an interesting historical side note, Robertson was not the only former major leaguer who would assist Coach Scott. In the mid-1930s, Norfolk policeman Allie Watt, a former Washington Senator (as well as Norfolk Tar), would also help with coaching duties. Since Watt was a Norfolk resident, that fact alone may be neither surprising nor interesting, until one looks at Watt's major league career stats: one game played for the Senators in 1920, one at-bat, one double, and one RBI, for a career batting average of 1.000, and a career slugging percentage of 2.000. Additionally, Watt, a second baseman, has the distinction of being one of very few players named correctly in comedians Abbott and Costello's "Who's on First?" routine, popularized in the late 1930s. "What" was on second.

"Demon" Dave Robertson's professional background, combined with Coach Scott's talents, may have provided the lift the Braves needed in their sophomore year of 1932, as they played to a .706 winning percentage, finishing with a 12–5 overall mark against primarily high school competition, but also against Campbell College, Louisburg College, and East Carolina Teacher's College. In an important move for the fledgling college, they also gained standing in the local sports scene by affiliating with the Tidewater Scholastic League, a circuit that was made up of the Norfolk Division, Suffolk High School, Maury High School, Wilson High School, and South Norfolk High School. Although playing local high school competition doesn't seem like an ambitious beginning for a collegiate program, it must also be remembered that the Norfolk Division was still a junior college that offered classes for only two years beyond high school, and in the second semester of 1931, the enrollment was approximately 246 total students. Maury High School's 1931 yearbook, by contrast, pictures more than twice that number in the senior class alone and lists a total of 2,027 students in the sophomore through senior years. Portsmouth's Wilson High School enrolled 757 students, according to the 1931 yearbook—still three times that of the Norfolk Division.

Joining the Tidewater Scholastic League in 1932 was an important first step for the Division, as it gave the school regional name recognition. The league also offered the Braves strong competition, since the high schools had such a large pool of potential players; in one 1933 early-season account, Maury had one hundred hopefuls for their baseball team and Wilson had seventy-five, while the Division had a sixteen-man squad.[6] Over a five-year association, the Norfolk Division did win Scholastic League titles in 1932 and 1934, but historically struggled the most against Maury, which to this day can still claim an 6–5 advantage in the series (and, for emphasis, also point to a resounding 23–7 win against the Norfolk Division's inaugural team).

But as the baseball team began to outgrow the Scholastic League, so too did the school itself continue to grow quickly and to deepen its roots in the fabric of Norfolk. In the fall of 1931, the Division's second year, Virginia Polytechnic Institute (familiarly Virginia Tech today) began offering engineering classes at the Norfolk Division; by its third year of operation, the school began offering some third-year classes, and enrollment had grown to 410 students. With help from the Depression-era Works Progress Administration, in 1936 a $150,000 classroom/gymnasium building opened, as did the $350,000 Foreman Field—an 18,000-seat stadium described as the only such athletic bowl in the state, which served the college and the community until its demolition and reconstruction in 2018. By the end of the 1930s, enrollment had risen to approximately 500 students.

On March 13, 1937, *The High Hat* signaled the next step in the evolution of the Norfolk Division baseball program, stating in a preview article about the upcoming season that "The college will follow the policy established during the past basketball season of playing only Freshman or small college teams."[7] According to the schedule published a week later, thirteen contests had been arranged, but almost half were against various US Navy or Navy-affiliated teams, some of which would rise to much prominence a few short years later. Of these pre-war Navy teams, authors Clay Shampoe and Thomas Garrett wrote, "In the past,

Coach Scott said that he expected to list 20 games and thus far he has scheduled the 13 games listed below:

April 2, Savage School (New York) at Division.
April 7, Navy Yard Apprentices at Division.
April 10, Newport News Apprentices at Division.
April 14, Division at Training Station.
April 17, William and Mary Frosh at Division.
April 29, Division at Carolina Teachers.
April 21, Division at Louisburg College.
April 26, Training Station at Division.
April 28, Division at Navy Yard Apprentices.
May 1, Louisburg at Division.
May 2, Division at William and Mary Frosh.
May 5, Carolina Teachers at Division.
May 10, Division at Newport News Apprentices.

From The High Hat, *March 20, 1937. Courtesy of Special Collections and University Archives, Old Dominion University.*

baseball teams at the Norfolk Naval facility were formed to give sailors a diversion from training. Little attention was given to these teams until the Navy brass decided to promote the newly enlisted major league players to Chief Specialist Athletic and add their talents to the station's baseball team."[8] It would be fair to assume that the Navy teams of the late 1930s were more advanced than local high school squads, but in five recorded 1937 games against Navy or Apprentice squads, the Braves won three.

In the 1938 and 1939 seasons, the Norfolk Division put together one break-even and one losing season, with a combined mark of nine wins, nineteen losses, and one tie.[9] Against service teams, the team recorded four wins against six defeats in those two seasons, and against collegiate competition, the Braves went 4–13. Still, progress was evident, as the pre-war 1939 Braves played eleven contests against collegiate-level opponents, five more than in any year prior. The 1939 team, in fact, also had the opportunity to test themselves against professional talent, including future major leaguers Russ Derry and Ken Sears, when they faced the Norfolk Tars at Bain Field on April 4. Unfortunately, the 21–2 shellacking delivered by Manager Ray White's Tars demonstrated that there was still a pretty significant talent gap between the two squads, and the loss probably didn't do much for the Division's athletic pride.[10]

Still, considering the decade of the 1930s as a whole, the baseball team should be considered as a limited success, and a further means by which the developing institution integrated itself into Norfolk life. Although the won-lost ledger shows fifty-seven wins, sixty-eight losses, and two ties, five of the nine seasons were either winning or break-even seasons, and the decade included two Tidewater Scholastic League championships. And more importantly, as the size of the student body of the new school had begun to steadily increase, so too had the caliber of baseball competition the Braves scheduled.

CHAPTER TWO

The 1940s

Everything went to war, at that time.

—DOROTHY PIERCE LADD, *Norfolk Division librarian during the war years*

f the 1930s can be viewed as a steady rise in the baseball fortunes of the Norfolk Division, the 1940s cannot. The decade began with the dissolution of the program due to what *The High Hat* termed "heavy expenses incurred by past ball teams, the lack of playing facilities, and lack of suitable opponents."[1] The last two reasons may have been excuses made to an eager student reporter simply to bolster the logic of the decision, since the Braves had managed to schedule nineteen contests the season before, and since they had a baseball diamond in Larchmont that they could use. The first stated reason is likely the primary culprit; the country was starting to emerge from the Great Depression, but the athletic budget had been a problem since the school's beginning, and to such an extent that consideration had been given to canceling spring sports as far back as the 1935 season.[2]

In fact, even football, a fairly popular campus sport—and one which had its own five-year-old, 18,000-seat facility—would fall victim to the budgetary ax following the 1940 season, not to return until 2009. On August 3, 1941, the *Daily Press* of Newport News reported that Charles A. Duke, "director of the Norfolk division following a series of unpleasantries between Dean W. T. Hodges and President John Stewart Bryan in Williamsburg," had sent a letter requesting that opponents abandon their scheduled 1941 contests, while making it clear that the Norfolk Division would still honor their contract if necessary.[3] The reporter noted that "Football hasn't paid in several years at the Norfolk division. Tommy Scott, formerly head coach and athletic director, operated his set-up on a shoestring several years."[4] In the previous day's edition, Duke also mentioned an additional reason for abandoning football: a Southern Conference requirement that

Baseball May Be Curbed By High Costs

Softball Tournament For This Spring

Men of the college today face the prospect of the most extensive intra-mural spring sports program in the history of this institution.

According to present plans, a softball tournament in which clubs and independent teams will participate will be held to supplant baseball, which is being abolished for this spring.

The softball tourney in mind now would embrace nearly every athletic-minded student here, for members of the three social clubs, Phi Sigma, the V.P.I. Club, the Aeronautics Club, the Monogram Club and any men who wish to form a team may compete for top honors.

The clubs entered will form a league. Trophies will be awarded winners of the circuit.

The abolition of the diamond sport for this year came about as the result of the heavy expenses incurred by past ball teams, the lack of playing facilities and the lack of suitable opponents.

From The High Hat, *February 16, 1940. Courtesy of Special Collections and University Archives, Old Dominion University.*

tied Norfolk Division athletics to William & Mary athletics, and, therefore, disallowed freshman participation, creating an impossible hurdle for a junior college. As Duke stated, "There you are, added to the fact that football has not paid its way at the division in recent years."

Baseball resumed in 1941, but legendary coach Tommy Scott had left for other opportunities, and George Gregory, an English professor at the Division, assumed the reins of the program for the next two years. The revived team struggled in the first year of its return to the diamond, losing all seven games it played: two to East Carolina Teacher's College by an average score of 17–4.5, three to the Naval Training Station by an average score of 12.0–1.7, and then, in the closest game of the year, one to the USS *New York* by a 6–1 margin.[5]

Baseball results paled into insignificance on December 7, 1941. For the baseball team, the school, and the city, the Japanese attack on Pearl Harbor was a life-altering event. Throughout the 1930s, *The High Hat* had published occasional pieces on German and Japanese aggression, including a March 10, 1933, commentary by M. Doyle on Adolf Hitler's rise to power: "Imperialistic tendencies have again been emphasized by the swift ascension of an ex-jailbird to a position of highest authority in the government of that country. Hitler heads the German government today for reasons which indeed would rack [sic] the soul of the holiest of democratic bodies."[6] Nearly a year later, M. Kruger, in a letter to the editor, would pose the prescient question, "What I want to know is has it ever occurred to the student body of this institution that the attempt of Germany to carry out any of these campaigns will embroil the world into another World War?"[7]

When the United States entered World War II, the Norfolk Division of William & Mary and its athletic teams did, too. As Dr. Sweeney writes, "During the war the Norfolk Division did more than its share. The college was divided into three units: the day college, offering the first two years of regular college work; the night college, providing the same courses for working students; the war-training and vocational courses . . . Edward White directed the war-training courses and Lee Klinefelter, who later became director of the Technical Institute, was in charge of the vocational program. The war-training courses were grouped in four areas: aircraft aeronautics, general engineering science and management, civil engineering, and drafting or graphics. Training women to do work traditionally performed by men was a primary objective of these courses."[8] As an offshoot of these wartime efforts, the Division's Technical Institute continued to offer courses even after the conflict.

During the war years, numerous articles referring to student efforts could also be found in *The High Hat*, exemplified by, but not limited to, the following:

- In 1942, the school newspaper sponsored a "War Bond Queen" drive (one bond purchased entitled the purchaser to one vote).
- In 1943, the Di Gamma sorority sponsored a blood drive for American troops.
- In 1943, the Tri Kappa sorority led a clothing drive to provide war relief to Russia, devastated by fighting with Nazi Germany.
- In 1943, *The High Hat* sponsored a cigarette drive for the troops— a donation of five cents for a single pack, or of twenty-five dollars for 500 packs, delivered to the troops.

Most of all, however, the Norfolk Division gave its men. *The High Hat* played a key role in recruitment efforts, as the newspaper in 1942 and 1943 focused on themes of patriotism and the career benefits of military service, and included regular series of cartoons such as "Super-men of the U. S. Army" as well as "Stars in Service," featuring such well-known athletes as Bob Feller and Joe Louis. Even advertisements for products such as Chesterfield cigarettes ("There's satisfaction in knowing that the 6½¢ revenue tax you pay on every pack of twenty cigarettes is doing its bit for Uncle Sam.") and Coca-Cola ("'Gimme a

Coca-Cola' is the watchword for refreshment with every branch of the service.") aligned themselves with patriotic themes.

The student body responded to the American war effort. On May 19, 1943, *The High Hat* printed the names of sixty-two former Norfolk Division students in military service, noting that "during the past nine months the Armed Forces have taken the majority of the Division's enrollment."[9] Whether or not "majority" was truly mathematically correct, it is certainly true that the published sixty-two of approximately five hundred students is a very high percentage, and it is also true that during the war years, the service of the Norfolk Division's men turned the school into one attended overwhelmingly by females. The baseball team had not been exempted from this attrition either, and at a minimum, the 1943 baseball edition had lost first baseman Walter Hambury (Army Air Corps), pitcher Bill Longworth (Merchant Marines), and shortstop Bud Whitney (US Navy).[10]

April 17, 1942

February 9, 1943

Army Is Seeking 215,000 College Men For Forces

October 27, 1942

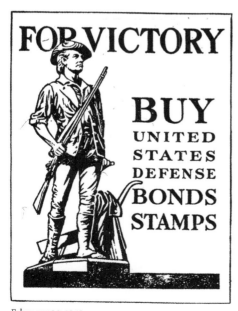

February 20, 1942

November 7, 1944

Despite the ongoing war, baseball at the Norfolk Division somehow managed to survive with only one lost season for the duration of the hostilities. The 1942 season opened in a bad way, as the Braves were no-hit and struck out sixteen times in a loss to the Naval Air Station.[11]

Luckily, however, Coach George Gregory didn't have the Naval Training Station on his baseball schedule in 1942. The series had been a regular since 1935, with the Braves holding their own by winning their share of games prior to 1940. But with the advent of the war, professional baseball talent from all over the nation had congregated in Norfolk in service of the US Navy, creating a unique situation that saw major leaguers Bob Feller of the Cleveland Indians, Fred Hutchinson of the Detroit Tigers, and Sam Chapman of the Philadelphia A's, among other professional talent (including local boy and former major leaguer Ace Parker), all suiting up for the N.T.S. "Bluejackets." The Bluejackets had already been good; they had won sixty-six of seventy-eight games in 1941, including three over the Norfolk Division by a combined score of 36–5. But with the arrival of the pros, the team was even better, playing to an incredible 92–8 won-loss record. Yet, the Naval Air Station "Flyers" were getting similar talent (such as Dodger Pee Wee Reese) by 1943, and authors Shampoe and Garrett note that "The advent of the Korean War saw several major leaguers don the Navy flannels but the teams never attained the legendary status of the World War II years, when Norfolk truly had two of the most powerful teams in all of baseball."[12] After the 1942 season, these two teams were not part of the Norfolk Division's schedule for the duration of the war years.

According to available records, the 1942 season didn't get much better for the Braves, as they lost the only other six games they played, marking two straight years in which the team couldn't pull out a victory for skipper Gregory. The 1942 team had been outscored by a combined eighty-seven runs against twenty-three and had given up no fewer than eight runs in any game. Despite these results, and despite the loss of manpower to the war effort, *The High Hat* somehow found a way to be optimistic at the start of 1943, and not even cautiously so: "With a little effort we should have a baseball team worth bragging about this year," the paper claimed on March 16. A week later: "With the prospect of having one of the most successful baseball seasons in the history of the Division, [new] Coach Chandler and his boys went through their first week of practice last week."

If winning percentage is the yardstick, then the 1943 team's 28.6 percent win rate over seven games was indeed a success, as it included the only two recorded wins by the Division between 1939 and 1946. New Coach Joseph "Scrap" Chandler was a legend who followed the model of Tommy Scott, and from his post at William & Mary, Chandler moved to Norfolk in 1942 to take the athletic director position, as well as to teach and coach. Like Tommy Scott before him, Chandler brought impeccable athletic qualifications, as he would become a charter member of his alma mater William & Mary's Athletics Hall of Fame (oddly enough, for swimming and for track and field, although his induction picture shows him in his baseball uniform), a charter member of Old Dominion's Hall of Fame (as a swimming coach), and a member of the Virginia Sports Hall of Fame. Swimming was where he made his most enduring impact at the Norfolk Division, and the Old Dominion swimming facility is today the J. C. "Scrap" Chandler Pool.

During his three seasons as baseball coach, Chandler guided the Braves to a record of seven wins and eighteen losses. In fairness, however, in only one of those seasons (1946) did he really have any available manpower, and his 1943 team did post the first victory for the Division in four years. Of his 1944 team, which went winless in five tries against various Navy teams, one must wonder who his team manager was, as "Martha and Johnny" had some tough words for the holder of that position in the *High Hat* edition of May 23, 1944: "This year's baseball manager seems to have been very unpopular with the players. We can hardly blame the players though, because he seldom appeared at practice and didn't take his work in general very seriously.

Players had to wear the same dirty equipment for weeks at a time and use the same dirty towels day after day. Several times the coach had to pass out equipment just because the manager couldn't find time to supply the team. No gripping [sic] has been heard of late. We wonder if this is the 'calm before the storm.'"[13]

The school began to return to gender-balanced life in 1946, with the return of war veterans. In the Division's 1946 *Voyager* yearbook, fifty-two of sixty-six pictured sophomores are female, and most of the listed freshman student names were female. *The High Hat* staff is listed as entirely female except for the lucky George Bacon, a "Co-Sports Editor" with Liz Seelinger. Fraternity Delta Omega Phi "was the only active men's club on the campus. Though members drifted off to the Army and Navy periodically, the club survived, and by the end of the first semester [of the 1945–46 school year] it boasted eighteen members."[14]

But on page 34, the yearbook also brought happy news for the college, listing an incredible 216 names behind the following entry:

> On the first day of the new term, the Veterans, full of high hopes and lofty ambitions, invaded the college in vast numbers. It was an almost unbelievable sight to see so many men strolling across the campus. The formerly empty booths in Bud's were crowded with men for a change, and the book lines reminded one of the Army and Navy chow lines. Classrooms were jammed at all hours of the day with Vets eager for learning. Former officers rubbed shoulders with former privates, and remnants of uniforms were the last tangible evidences of their G. I. days.
>
> Now they are full-fledged civilians, taking up their education where they had left off. The Voyager dofts [sic] its hat to these veterans whose desire for higher learning brought them back to W&M-V.P.I.

In the spring of 1946, the Brown- and Harvard-educated Dr. Ernest Gray, chairman of the faculty at the Norfolk Division, wrote that "Classes have suddenly become predominantly masculine, to the dismay of the instructors, who for the past four years have been playing up to feminine tastes . . . As a matter of fact, there are just a little more than two hundred veterans now in college. There are about three hundred students who are not veterans. Thus, there are over five hundred students, nearly two hundred more than last semester. The crowded classes and halls bear witness to the fact that more students are now in attendance than ever before in the history of the Division."[15]

By the fall semester of 1946, that number would balloon again, up to a record-shattering 830 students,[16] with additional numbers turned away and directed to Saint Helena in the Berkley section of Norfolk, a newly created extension that was housed in a wartime naval facility purchased by William & Mary. Twenty-three additional instructors brought the 1946 total up to forty-two, a 700 percent increase over the original six that had served the college in its first year.

Baseball success, unfortunately, did not immediately follow the influx of available manpower. The 1947 squad was initially coached by former Brave Everett Tolson, who was replaced on May 5 by Woody Gray, the Maury football coach and a former low-level professional baseball player; Gray's tenure at the helm was so brief that his name doesn't even appear in the Old Dominion University baseball "History and Records" media guide.[17] Combined, the 1947 team and Coach Jack Callahan's 1948 squad compiled a 5–19 won-lost record, including four losses to new cross-town rival Saint Helena, in what certainly must have been galling defeats. If there were any cause at all for optimism at this time, it could only have been in the fact that the Norfolk Division had at least returned to playing games at a collegiate level, as approximately half of the games in 1947 and 1948 were against collegiate-level opponents (including St. Helena), and half were against Navy squads.

By the extant records, then (which are surely not complete), the Norfolk Division had accumulated an overall record of sixty-nine wins against one hundred and nineteen defeats and two ties prior to 1949. While the 1930s were generally successful for the growing school's baseball team, results from the years 1940 to 1948 were certainly not a continuance of that trend. Aggregated records from these years show that:

- In two years, 1940 and 1945, the school did not field a team.
- In three years that the school did field a team, the team recorded no wins.
- There were five different coaches in the seven years that the Division had a team.
- After the team's last win in 1939, another win was not recorded until 1943. After 1943, not again until 1946.
- The 1944 team was outscored 55–3 in the five recorded games they played.
- The 1942 team gave up 12.4 runs per game, meaning the pitching and defense had managed to regress from the previous year, when the team had only given up 11.7 runs per game.
- The 1942 team lost to an American Legion team, and the 1946 team lost to a team known as "Clyde's Cardinals"—a team so obscure that even the internet can't find reference to them today, although a contemporary *Virginian-Pilot* article refers to them as a "City Recreation League" team.[18]
- The 1942 team was no-hit twice and one-hit once by the Naval Air Station.
- The team's recorded won-loss record was 12–51 between 1940 and 1948.

Prior to 1949, The Norfolk Division's record competing against high schools stood at 34–24–2; against service teams, 19–43; against American Legion teams, 0–1; against Clyde's Cardinals, 0–1; and against college-level competition (including freshman teams), just nineteen wins against forty-three defeats, and just two wins in the entire decade of the 1940s.

With the team mired in a decade of such relative futility, and having had five different coaches manage the last seven teams the school had fielded, Athletic Director Scrap Chandler was doubtlessly looking for more stability at that position, as well as improved on-field results, when he placed a call in the summer of 1948 to Arthur Beauregard "Bud" Metheny, former New York Yankee outfielder, and former 1935 opponent of the Norfolk Division squad while a member of the William & Mary College freshman team.[19]

CHAPTER THREE

Bud Metheny

He was a gentleman right from here, from the core.
Bud was one of the most honest people I've met in my life.

—**RUFUS TONELSON,** *original Norfolk Division student and athlete*

Arthur Beauregard Metheny was born in Saint Louis, Missouri, on June 1, 1915, the son of James Arthur "Art" Metheny and Laura Lee Godfrey. According to census records, Art was a native Iowan, but by 1900 appears to have relocated to the District of Columbia, where eighteen-year-old Art was enumerated (along with various other siblings, in-laws, and nephews) in the home of his forty-one-year-old uncle, Charles Knoble, at 23 O Street NE, Washington, DC. Laura Lee was born in 1888 in Fauquier County, Virginia, and in 1900 she and the Godfrey family resided in the Cedar Run district of Fauquier, which was (and remains) very rural, despite its proximity to Washington. Laura Lee was more or less a "middle child" of Beauregard Davis Godfrey and Sommerville Robinson—but there were fourteen "middle children" of this union! Giving some glimpse into his heritage (in possibly offensive terms), an article from Bud Metheny's player file at the Baseball Hall of Fame, likely penned in 1943, states that his ancestry was "Scotch-Irish-English and Indian. On his maternal side his great-grandmother was a full-blooded descendant of Pocahontas or some such upper-crust Virginia Indian. He gets his middle name of Beauregard because his [maternal] grandfather was named in honor of the Confederate leader who fired the first shot on Fort Sumter."[1]

In 1904, twenty-two-year-old Art and sixteen-year-old Laura Lee were married in Rockville, Maryland, only a few months after their respective siblings, Clifford Clyde Metheny and Learah Roberta Godfrey, had also tied the knot. For a time, the newly married Art and Laura Lee stayed in the Northern Virginia area, at least long enough for daughter Violet Lola Metheny to be born there in 1906, but by 1910, they had relocated to St. Louis, Missouri—likely with their respective siblings, since Learah Godfrey Metheny died in St. Louis in 1909. It was in St. Louis that Art and Laura Lee introduced Arthur Beauregard to the world. Art, employed by the Chicago, Burlington, and Quincy railroad as an electrician, had eventually settled the family in the College Hill section of the city. That neighborhood endures harder times today, but according to census records of 1920 and 1930, it was home at that time to a population that was almost entirely literate and entirely employed, typically at such blue-collar occupations as clerk, barber, carpenter, butcher, and grocer.[2] Young "Bud" attended Bryan Hill Elementary School, an eight-minute walk from their home at 1502 De Soto Avenue, for his early education, and then Beaumont High School. At an early age, Bud Metheny caught the baseball bug; in fact, as he recalled in 1979, "My sister launched my career. She gave me my first baseball glove when I was 10 years old, an authentic Bill Doak model, the epitome of baseball gloves."[3] A lifelong love was born, and as *St. Louis Post-Dispatch* writer Bob Broeg put it in 1966, at an early age Bud "used to frequent old Sportsman's Park as a Knothole Gang member smitten by the Cardinals' early championship clubs and by pot-bellied Babe Ruth."[4] St. Louis is credited as among the first to have such a program to let kids into games; in Metheny's youth, kids would have actual "Knothole Gang" membership cards and would travel to the park by streetcar, get into the games for free, and even have no restriction on getting on the field when the game was done.

As his own baseball career began to develop, Metheny began to distinguish himself, even at an early age. Of his early baseball career in St. Louis, Broeg wrote: "Prof. Metheny, as a high school freshman, played right field for Vic Kirk's Public High [sic] League champions at Beaumont in 1930. He also played for the Aubuchon-Dennison American Legion team run by Grover Resinger's father." Broeg went on to note that "The Methenys moved to Calverton, Va., when Bud was 15. He played semipro ball in the Shenandoah Valley League and then accepted college scholarship money from the Yankees in exchange for the promise to sign with them afterward."

Historically, however, it may not be entirely accurate to say that "the Methenys" moved to Calverton. Art and Laura Lee were enumerated together in the 1930 census in St. Louis, but the 1930s were the Depression years, and in 1940 Laura Lee was back in Fauquier County, Virginia, residing with her widowed mother, while records suggest Art was working in California. It must have been quite a culture shock for the young Bud Metheny to leave the excitement of the big city behind in favor of Virginia's farm country, but evidently he identified pretty strongly with his mother's side of the family, as he referred to himself as a "Virginian" in a 1975 interview.[5]

His play in the Shenandoah Valley League began to catch the eye of scouts. The Valley League, formed in 1897, remains a very well-respected circuit featuring some of the best college talent, and as recently as 2015, boasted thirty alumni playing Major League Baseball. Today, it is sanctioned by the NCAA and operates under not-for-profit status, completing an evolution from its past as an effective equivalent of today's minor league short-season Rookie Leagues.[6] Teams played (and still play) up and down the Shenandoah Valley, not far from Calverton, and the league afforded the young Bud the opportunity to hone his skills against top-level competition, under the watchful eye of major league scouts. The level of competition was such that five members of Metheny's Culpeper team eventually made the major leagues: Clarence "Soup" Campbell Jr. to the Cleveland Indians, Herb Hash and George Lacy to the Boston Red Sox, and Bud Metheny and Walter Beall to the New York Yankees.[7]

Metheny was signed to a professional contract with the Yankees when he was seventeen, but due to still being a minor, it was actually his mother who signed.[8] In a circumstance that would seem to violate today's NCAA standard of amateurism, he attended the College of William & Mary *after* the professional contract was signed, where he played baseball for four years and earned his degree. In 1975, he recalled that amateur status was defined differently at that time; as Metheny put it, "That was all right back in those days because they didn't turn in the contracts to the commissioner of baseball until you began playing professional baseball. And so, as a result, I was able to play at William and Mary for four years."[9]

As part of the agreement, the Yankees paid for his education. He recalled that they actually gave him three college choices—Duke, Holy Cross, or William & Mary. Metheny noted that "being a Virginian, I guess that's the reason I picked William and Mary because the other two schools did have much better baseball programs at that time. But William and Mary had such a fine name, and I wanted to go to school, and so they gave me this opportunity."[10]

Bud Metheny played both basketball and baseball at William & Mary, but distinguished himself to a much greater degree on the diamond than he did on the hardwood. A member of the varsity basketball team for the first time in his sophomore year of 1936, he was part of an Indians team (as they were known at the time) that started the season with six wins, but his collegiate basketball career went downhill from there. Of the remaining forty-one games in his varsity career, the Indians won only seven and lost thirty-four, a span which also included a twenty-three-game losing streak. Of his junior-season team, the 1937 *Colonial Echo* yearbook wrote, "Coach Tommy Dowler's Indian quintet closed their 1936–1937 season with the poorest record a Tri-Color squad has handed in for the last decade. When the final whistle blew the total stood at eighteen losses and no victories . . . The final game against the Virginia team brought out the inadequacy of the squad when the final quarter was played with only four men to a team due to the lack of W.-M. substitutes."[11] Despite the relative lack of hoops success, there was a silver lining; during his varsity career, Metheny's team won four of six games against every William & Mary student's most hated foe, the University of Virginia.

Between the chalk lines, it was a different matter. Metheny played for the freshman baseball team in 1935, and the nine games on the schedule consisted of seven games against high schools and two against the Norfolk Division, a team in just its fifth year. Recounting the Norfolk Division's 1935 baseball season in his thesis, Tony Zontini wrote, "'Lefty' Metheny of the William & Mary freshmen was cited [by Norfolk Division newspaper *The High Hat*] as being by far the best hitter faced by the Braves that year. Freddie Edmonds [Old Dominion Hall of Famer and father of pitcher Fred Edmonds Jr., who also excelled at Old Dominion College in the early 1960s] remembers 'Bud' Metheny as being a very hard out; 'Bud would always get his three or four hits against us when I pitched. I would handle the other guys, but Bud was some hitter.'" The teams split the two games in 1935, and Bud's freshman batting average was recorded by the William & Mary yearbook as .521.[12]

As a member of the varsity beginning in his sophomore season of 1936, the young Bud Metheny did not disappoint his Yankee scouts. His 1936 squad finished as co-champions of the state, with a 14–9 record;

the yearbook noted the "brilliant hitting of Captain Moore, Matheny [sic], Marable, and Harper."[13] As a junior in 1937, he co-captained a squad with Bob Adams that, at nine wins against eleven losses, was less successful than the year before, but the yearbook cited Metheny as one of only three to hit over .300. In 1938, Metheny captained a state champion team that won thirteen games and lost nine. The yearbook noted that "Metheny was a powerhouse at the bat with his .750 batting average on the northern trip," a swing that included six games against such opponents as Maryland, Vermont, Dartmouth, Rutgers, and Navy.[14]

During his four years of college, there were also a pair of events that altered the trajectory of Bud Metheny's life, both for the bad and for the good. The first was a knee injury, suffered while playing freshman football.[15] In an article obtained from his Cooperstown file, he is quoted as saying, "I could never really run after the injury. But Dr. Bennett, who was the Yankees surgeon at the time, operated on me at Johns Hopkins and made it possible for me to play. I could still hit pretty well." Despite the injury, he did make the major leagues, admittedly during the war years while many big leaguers were in the armed services, but also at a time when there were only sixteen teams, meaning that there were only approximately half as many places available to players competing for a roster spot as there are now. Even with the injury, he earned one of those few available spots; without the injury, it's impossible to know what heights he could have achieved in his major league career. So bad, in fact, was the knee on which he played major league baseball, that Metheny was classified as "4F" and rejected for military service by the draft board on November 16, 1943.[16]

A second life-changing event during his education at William & Mary was his introduction to his future wife, Norfolk's Frances Davis, a Gamma Phi Beta sister and member of the Library Science Club. Frances was a strong supporter of athletics, as a later article in the April 8, 1943 *Asbury Park Press* would attest to: "'We eat, sleep, drink, think, talk and live baseball,' asserted the former Norfolk, Va., school teacher,

Mrs. Metheny. 'The players talk it all winter and play it all summer,' she added in her pleasant southern accent."[17] For her part, she was a regular attendee at her husband's professional games, and in the best baseball tradition, even harbored her own superstitions. According to the same article, "Bud Metheny, promising young outfielder for the New York Yankees, may expect to see his wife in the same seats in the stands at every home game this season—providing the team is enjoying a winning streak. He knows Frances will be there, in the same seat at each game, because of baseball players' wives' superstitions. That the players themselves are extremely superstitious about their uniforms, bats, numbers, etc., is well known, but their wives are just as careful not to tempt fate."

Arthur B. Metheny, from the 1938 Colonial Echo. Courtesy of Special Collections Research Center, William & Mary Libraries.

Metheny had played some semi-pro ball in Vermont during his college years, and was lucky enough to begin his professional career close to home in Norfolk, playing for the Class-B Norfolk Tars of the Piedmont League in the 1938 season.

Frances Davis, from the 1938 Colonial Echo. Courtesy of Special Collections Research Center, William & Mary Libraries.

Over the next four seasons, Frances would have to adjust to her Bud spending three different stints with the Newark Bears of the International League and two with the Kansas City Blues of the American Association. But she stood with him, and during the 1942 off-season, the pair were married in Norfolk, on Valentine's Day—a union that would produce a son and a daughter and last nearly sixty-one years.

Metheny began his minor league career with the 1938 season, shortened by his tenure as William & Mary's baseball captain. Playing for the Norfolk Tars, he smacked twenty-one home runs in just eighty-nine contests (a pace for thirty-eight in a 162-game season), to go along with a .338 batting average. The big numbers earned him a quick promotion to Double-A for 1939, and between Kansas City and Newark, he batted .320 with ten home runs, but also injured his left knee in a slide, limiting his season to just ninety-six games and 300 at-bats. That fall, according to an article in his Cooperstown file, he underwent surgery at Johns Hopkins Hospital for knee repair, and as a result of the time off his feet, his weight rose to 200 pounds. Still, a successful 1940 season playing for Newark ensued, which saw Bud Metheny play a lead role in the Bears' Little World Series title run with 102 runs batted in and a .308 average. After the season, however, he was ordered back to Johns Hopkins to reduce his weight. Of stocky build anyway, his 200 pounds doesn't seem to be that far from "playing weight" for someone standing five foot eleven, but nonetheless, the strict Johns Hopkins regimen took him down to 170.[18]

Some contemporary writers attributed his lower power numbers in 1941 to the loss of weight; his 1941 season at Newark was the worst of his career to that point. Over 136 games, he launched only three home runs, knocked in only fifty-nine runners, and, at season's end, sported just a .240 average. Without question, this decreased power output delayed his promotion to the Yankees.

But in February of 1942, he married his college sweetheart. Whether it was that, or whether it was because he had stabilized his playing weight, or whether it was just that his knee was feeling healthy, in 1942 Metheny put himself squarely back on the Yankees' radar with the best season of his professional career: 148 games, eighteen home runs, ninety-four runs batted in, seventy-nine runs scored, a .296 batting average—and he even stole seven bases, his professional

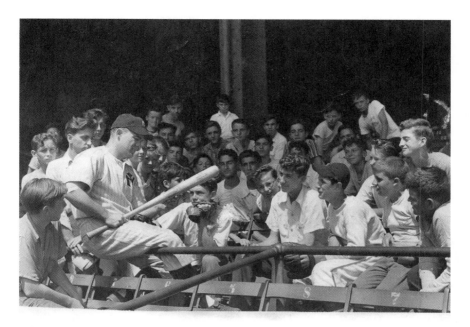

Published in the Circleville Herald *on August 3, 1945, this picture was captioned "Bud Metheny, outfielder of the New York Yankees, tells a group of youths in Yankee Stadium a few inside facts on playing baseball, all part of a drive to promote sandlot baseball."*

high point for seasons with complete records available. His masterful season earned him a shot in the 1943 Yankee outfield.

Replacing "Old Reliable," Tommy Henrich, in the Yankee outfield was the unenviable task for the rookie Bud Metheny in the spring of 1943. Henrich had hit thirty-one home runs in 1941, garnering some MVP votes, and had been an American League All-Star in 1942, before beginning the three-year military stint that left a hole in the Yankee lineup. Metheny made the club, and was expected to be a starter in the Yankee outfield along with Charlie "King Kong" Keller and Roy "Stormy" Weatherly, but that starting role took some time to develop. Uncertainty about his draft status, which would not lift until after the season, kept legendary manager Joe McCarthy from investing more playing time in him, and reserve outfielder Johnny Lindell was also hitting well, leading McCarthy to keep Lindell in the lineup. Metheny made his major league debut with a pinch-hit single in Boston's Fenway

Park on April 27, 1943, but it was not until a July injury to Charlie Keller that he began to start seeing significant playing time, and, in fact, he displaced Lindell (an All-Star that year) for most of the remainder of the season in right field, as Lindell increasingly patrolled center in place of Weatherly.[19]

Bud Metheny, cartooned in the Hagerstown (Maryland) Daily Mail on October 5, the day the World Series started. Copyrighted 1943–1965. Associated Press.

A slow start got better with more regular playing time. Batting under .200 into July, Metheny put together a ten-game hitting streak between July 10 and July 22 that raised his average to .268, and he also hit his first big-league home run against the Chicago White Sox on July 11. Now entrenched in the starting lineup, he played solidly through the months of August and September, to complete a very respectable rookie season with a .261 batting average, nine home runs, thirty-six runs batted in, and fifty-one runs scored in 103 games. And the Yankees won the pennant, advancing to the World Series to try to avenge the previous year's defeat at the hands of the Cardinals.

Metheny was the starting outfielder in Games Two and Five of the World Series, the first in Yankee Stadium and the second in St. Louis' Sportsman's Park, where a young Bud Metheny had learned to love baseball two decades before. In his first World Series appearance, he drew unfavorable comparisons to Tommy Henrich in the press, after a deep fly ball to right field in the fourth inning glanced off his glove and over the wall, giving the Cardinals a two-run home run and proving to be the difference in a 4–3 Yankee loss.

But that was the only loss for the Yankees in the series. In the deciding Game Five, a Bill Dickey home run plated Charlie Keller, and those were the only runs scored in the game. Metheny contributed a single in five trips to the plate, leaving his World Series average at .125—but perhaps more importantly, he earned a World Series ring in his hometown, in front of 33,872 fans.

The Yankees would not return to the World Series while Metheny was with the team, as they lost several more players from the 1943 squad to military service. His 1944 campaign was solid, however, and in fact, the best of his big-league career. Metheny played in 137 out of 154 games, and contributed fourteen home runs, sixty-seven runs batted in, seventy-two runs scored, and five stolen bases to the Yankee cause. To put the power numbers in perspective, fourteen home runs put him in tenth place in the American League; teammate Nick Etten led the league with only twenty-two. Defensively, the ten errors Metheny committed from the right field position tied Cleveland's Roy Cullenbine for the most from that position in all of Major League Baseball, but Metheny also had the eighth-most defensive chances in right field in baseball that year, with 229.[20]

In retrospect, the most interesting occurrence during Metheny's 1944 season may have been his June 13 dust-up with George Myatt of the Washington Senators. Several newspapers reported the incident, but perhaps none more colorfully than sportswriter Joe King. His account in the New York *World-Telegram* read: "The debate opened in the eighth when Myatt, fielding Ed Levy's grounder, tried for a tag-and-throw double play on Metheny, who was heading for second. The Yankee foiled the try by back-tracking, so that Myatt had to chase him to tag him. Metheny scuffed dirt on or near Myatt's person as he got up, and the two squared away and tossed a couple of punches, like hockey players—with no damage done. As the pair made their exist [sic] down the stairs adjoining the Washington dugout, an alarm was heard from without, and Senators piled down, too. [Umpire Eddie] Rommel plunged into the maelstrom, and the Yankees for the second time charged into battle. Eye-witnesses said Metheny and Myatt just gripped each other, but did not spar, and five minutes of rare excite-ment on the Potomac passed without an eye being blacked [sic]."[21] Metheny was fined fifty dollars, but in July, made a personal appeal to American League President Will Harridge, and somehow convinced Harridge to drop the fine, under the seemingly weak premise that he had not been at fault for the incident.[22]

Bud Metheny's Yankee years, incidentally, also provided one of the highlights of former American League umpire Red Jones' career, as recounted in 1962 by Arthur Daley of the *New York Times* News Service:

'One ball player who had great appeal for me was Bobo Newsome,' said the good-humored Red. '[Former supervisor of A.L. umpires and *working partner Cal] Hubbard didn't like him. He thought Bobo was a showboat who burlesqued the game. I thought his antics amusing.*

I'm working behind the plate one day when Bobo is pitching against the Yankees. The batter is Bud Metheny, who is strictly a hitch-hiker trying to get on base any way he can. The count reaches 3 and 2. Bobo throws one in and I lose the ball completely. I don't know what it is. So I give a call like this: strike-ball.

'What did you say?' asks Metheny.

'It's what I finished with,' I say. He trots to first. Now Bobo storms in.

'I heard you say strike,' he screams.

'It's what I finished with,' I say. 'Called it a ball.'

Bobo blows his top. He calls me every name he can think of, including a few I never heard before. He's screaming away. That big Hubbard moves in behind him and sticks his chin over Bobo's shoulder until it looks like Bobo has two heads. Hubbard has a message for me.

'Do you still think Bobo is funny?' he says.[23]

The 1945 season in New York was a fairly average one for the Yankee right fielder. In almost the same number of at-bats as the previous year, Metheny's power numbers regressed from fourteen home runs to eight, and his RBI total from sixty-seven to fifty-three, although his batting average did rise nine points, from .239 to .248. A total of fifty-three runs batted in from a right fielder may not seem like enough to hold the job, but for perspective, the average major league player that year, given the exact same number of plate appearances, could only be counted on for fifty-eight.[24] The highlight of the season on the field, without a doubt, was a doubleheader sweep of the Philadelphia Athletics in Yankee Stadium on June 24, barely weeks into Metheny's thirties, in which he contributed two home runs, eight runs batted in, and three runs scored, as part of his four-for-eight day.

For the year defensively, his .983 fielding percentage led all American League right fielders with more than sixty games played.[25]

In 1946, outfielders Joe DiMaggio and Tommy Henrich rejoined the club after their military service, and with holdover Charlie Keller still with the team, there was little room for additional outfielders. Metheny was good enough to make the team, but his playing time was spare, and by mid-May, he had only gotten three at-bats, the final of which came in New York on May 9 in pinch-hitting duty against the St. Louis Browns. Shortly thereafter, he was sent to Kansas City, and he played for another couple of years in the minors, including playing out the 1946 season in Kansas City, playing for Newark and Birmingham in 1947, and Birmingham again in 1948, where he received Scrap Chandler's welcome call offering stable employment in Norfolk. But before beginning his tenure with the Norfolk Division, Metheny made one last stop that season—in Baxley, Georgia, helping the Class-D team there as a player-manager, and adding seven home runs to his professional resume.[26]

In the 1966 *St. Louis Post-Dispatch* article, writer Bob Broeg quoted Bud Metheny as saying that the Yankees paid him $15,000 per year, but recent research by Dr. James Sweeney puts that figure closer to $4,500 per year. Dr. Sweeney notes for comparison that five-time Yankee All-Star Tommy Henrich only made $15,000 in 1946, and suggests the possibility that the writer misinterpreted the sum total of Metheny's career Yankee earnings as an annual salary. In either case, by the time Bud Metheny was playing professional baseball, the United States was pulling out of the Great Depression, but the national-average annual income gleaned from the 1940 US census was still only $1,368. Even though he was making at least three times that, his salary needed a supplement, and he always *worked*. During his playing career, Metheny had never taken the winters off, and always sought to improve himself in some way. According to the book *Who's on First: Replacement Players in World War II*, "During the offseason Metheny stayed in shape working as a fireman on a locomotive crane, picking up 60-ton loads at the naval base in Norfolk."[27] A 1943 blurb in the *Arizona Republic* noted that "Bud Metheny, Yankee outfielder, is spending the winter working as a ship rigger in Norfolk, Va."[28]

Beyond manual labor jobs that kept him in shape, Metheny also began pursuing his real passion of working with young people in his off-seasons, putting to good use the teaching certificate earned while at William & Mary. While still a Yankee regular, he began coaching basketball in the winter at Norfolk's Maury High School, and in the later 1940s, South Norfolk High School. Scrap Chandler, the Norfolk Division athletic director who had also been at William & Mary during Metheny's school years, could hardly fail to take notice. In a 1975 interview with Dr. Sweeney, Chandler recalled the recruitment of Bud Metheny to the Division: "Yes, Bud was one of my good friends up at William and Mary. He had been a student up there when I was teaching, and I taught him in gym classes. He took a major course in physical education. He was an outstanding baseball player, probably the only William and Mary baseball player who played in the big leagues. He was also a very good basketball player. He was teaching at Maury High School when I was struggling over here with myself doing all the work, and I went over to see him. He said he was going down to Birmingham to play baseball. Well, that spring we saw that a lot of boys were coming in, and so Mr. Webb and I said we ought to hire him. So I called him up on the telephone in Birmingham, Alabama, and told him that I had a job for him. He'd be his own boss. So he decided he'd take it and give up baseball and came on up here."[29]

Allow for one last glorious Yankee Stadium moment, though. On July 27, 1957, in a nationally televised affair that preceded a regularly scheduled game, Yankee Old-Timers squared off against Tiger Old-Timers, putting baseball legends such as Joe DiMaggio and Ty Cobb back on the field and in the dugout. Only one run was scored in the two-inning contest, as Joe DiMaggio "scored from second when Detroit Pitcher

Dizzy Trout and Catcher Mickey Cochrane bumped waistlines under Bud Metheny's pop fly between the plate and the mound." The writer who gleefully authored that line, appearing in newspapers all over the country the next day, clearly enjoyed the opportunity to comment on the physique of those two aging stars, and the article was headlined, at least in the *St. Louis Post-Dispatch*, "WELL-CUSHIONED COCHRANE, TROUT COLLIDE; DECIDE OLD-TIMERS' GAME."[30]

CHAPTER FOUR

Coach Bud Metheny—
The Early Years in Norfolk

All through my career I felt that you had to take those steps or you wouldn't get ahead. It's a slow process and sometimes it's a difficult process because sometimes the boys will get discouraged when they get beat, but later on in life, by playing this kind of competition, they found out that to be a competitor you have to be able to compete against the better ones, if you're going to be successful.

—BUD METHENY, 1975

LOCAL COACHING START

By 1945, Metheny began to spend his off-seasons in what would become a true calling, coaching, and he appears in that capacity that year in the *Commodore*, the yearbook of Norfolk's Matthew Fontaine Maury High School. Interestingly, and reflective of the times, this yearbook was printed in an atypical color; an editor's note stated that "War conditions account for the brown cover of the 1945 *Commodore*. The traditional blue was not available." Even while continuing his career at the highest level of professional baseball, Metheny also became enough of an integral part of the 1945 faculty at Maury to be pictured among them in the yearbook (as a physical education teacher and coach). The basketball pages of that book show that he led the varsity team to a 20–3 record (as well as the "Eastern Championship") and the JV squad to a 7–7 record.

In the several years to follow, Bud Metheny continued to spend his winters coaching basketball in Norfolk. In 1946, he returned to Maury and again led the boys' varsity squad, this time to a solid 15–8 record; he may have led the JV and girls' team as well, although the yearbook contains no record of that. In 1947, he moved to South Norfolk High School, where he appears to have done more than coach; his faculty picture credits him with both coaching and mathematics responsibilities. On the hardwood, Coach Metheny performed triple duty for the South Norfolk Tigers, as he led the boys' varsity, the boys' JV, and the girls' varsity to an amazing run of success, experiencing just five defeats among the three squads, and none from the girls. Still, the author of the 1947 *Tiger* yearbook wrung some drama out of the season, as the write-up for the JV squad noted that after a loss to Cradock, "Coach Metheny, humiliated by such a shellacking, silently vowed revenge in the next meeting of the teams. The Tiger J.V.'s advanced a great deal between that loss and the next contest with Cradock. Coach Metheny drilled his junior charges hard during the days preceding the Cradock clash. Result—the South Norfolk cubs completely out-classed the Cradock five and ended the game with the J. V. third team on the court."

In 1948, Bud Metheny again returned to South Norfolk High, and was again credited with both mathematics instruction and coaching. This may be partly due to the size of the faculty—in 1947, the *Tiger* showed a faculty of only twenty, and in 1948, only twenty-six (and

Bud Metheny was one of only five males in both years). Maury High School, by contrast, had boasted a faculty of eighty-three in 1946. While the 1948 *Tiger* doesn't mention the junior varsity coach, it is likely that Coach Metheny again pulled triple-duty, and the boys' varsity record of 10–10 may have been some his best coaching, since the yearbook commented that the team had lost eight varsity members to graduation. The 1948 girls' team again went undefeated under his tutelage, winning sixteen games and tying twice, but in a claim that wouldn't stand up to an engineer's review, the school's yearbook later asserted that the Tigerettes had amassed a total of "43 straight victories" dating to 1946.

In four years of coaching boys' high school varsity basketball, Bud Metheny had established a 65–24 record, good for a winning percentage of 73 percent. The opportunity to be a part of building something at the Norfolk Division of William & Mary, however, had appeal that he couldn't resist. In a 1975 interview, he recalled his decision in 1948 to join the Norfolk Division, noting, "I felt that coming here to the college that I could do the same work and have a more stable situation, and also I'd be dealing with young people. And I've always wanted to deal with young people and develop them. In professional baseball, you're moving all over the country. I had a family, and I didn't want to keep moving them, and so my wife was also a Norfolkian, and I wanted to just become established. And that's the reason I left professional baseball."[1]

FINALE FOR A BASKETBALL COACH

The day we have dreaded at last has arrived;
With gloom and despair we shall now be deprived
Of one of the greatest, most eminent men;
So let there be sorrow and weeping and wailing,
Although it's a waste, though it's all unavailing;
Man, woman and teacher, wise, average or fool,
Farewell to Metheny, the pride of the school.

The forwards, the guards and the boys on the bench
Will find this sad parting a heartbreaking wrench,
For it's to the coach that we owe such a lot,
Like the Rock of Gibraltar in every tough spot;
Now Liverman, Hardison, Mason and Jones,
And Butler and Hunter, give out with the groans,
For this is a foul past the referee's rule—
Farewell to Metheny, the pride of the school.

The girls who struck terror in every team's heart,
Ah, they will remember he gave them their start.
With Meacom and Burgess and Leggett all three,
Creef, Rountree and Williams, their hero is he;
They battled unbeaten through two hectic years
And on his departure will weep bitter tears;
He showed them the ropes, calm, collected and cool—
Farewell to Metheny, the pride of the school.

He goes to the diamond and leaves us behind.
His equal we'll never be able to find.
We bid him goodbye now, the Faculty first,
From Anderson (best), down to Caffrey (the worst),
Through all of the students at South Norfolk High,
The ones graded low and the ones graded high,
The girls who eat popcorn, the boys who shoot pool,
Farewell to Metheny, the pride of the school.

KATHARINE E. CAFFREY
March 3rd, 1948

METHENY AND CAFFREY BURY THE HATCHET

From the 1948 South Norfolk Tiger.

NEW BASKETBALL COACH AT "THE DIVISION"

Bud Metheny began his career at the Norfolk Division in the fall of 1948. As a former major leaguer, he could offer immediate name recognition and respectability to the Division's languishing baseball program. He would, however, serve in many roles in a career dedicated to the school; the first was that of head basketball coach.

At Metheny's hiring, the school itself was still a small junior college, affiliated with both William & Mary and Virginia Polytechnic Institute, but not offering a third year of study. In the 1949 Norfolk Division yearbook, *The Voyager*, only 131 sophomores and 187 freshmen sat for pictures, and only thirty-six faculty member photographs appear (although the yearbook acknowledges another twenty "faculty and staff" pictures missing). For a sense of the relative size and scale of the Division at that time, cross-town neighbor Maury High School had faculty and staff numbering eighty-eight, with another five committed specifically to veterans' programs, for a total that roughly approximated twice that of the Division's ranks. For a comparison of student body sizes, Maury pictured 500 graduating seniors (combining January, June, August, and Veteran), and 503 juniors.

The basketball program Coach Metheny inherited at the Division had followed much the same course as the baseball program, if with a bit more recent success. From its inception in the fall of 1930 and through its first decade, the program was led by legendary coach and ODU Hall-of-Famer Tommy Scott. In ten seasons, Coach Scott led the team to six winning campaigns and a respectable 92–83 overall record, against the same type of competition the baseball team was scheduling. In the first six Division basketball seasons, encompassing 102 total known contests, fifty-six were against high school teams, twelve were against William & Mary and VMI freshman teams, six against faculty or alumni teams, and five against military prep schools, among contests against some collegiate-level talent and others such as "Ravens," "Nachman's," and "Polygon Club."[2] High school competition dropped off the schedule for good after the 1936 season, leaving the school with a fixed lifetime basketball record of 1–7 against Maury High School, with average game scores of 24–29. Luckily, South Norfolk High School was also a frequent foe in those years, and the Braves fared much better in those contests, compiling a lifetime 10–0 won-loss record in that series, with an average score of 41–19.

Basketball schedules in the later 1930s began to show an increased level of competition, with Navy teams beginning to appear, along with several smaller colleges, such as squads from Bluefield, Elon, Shenandoah, and High Point Colleges. While the 1937–38 team had good success against an increased caliber of competition, Coach Scott's last two teams finished 8–14 and 4–16 respectively, before he retired in 1941 with a 53 percent winning percentage for his basketball tenure.

As they were for the baseball team and the school itself, the 1940s were a turbulent time for the basketball team, although it never suspended operations as the baseball program had. To replace the retiring Coach Scott for the 1940–41 season, as Thomas Garrett and Clay Shampoe wrote in *Old Dominion University Men's Basketball*:

> The new basketball coach that would replace Scott came from an unlikely source. During the summer of 1940, a young All-American halfback known as the 'Flying Dutchman' at the University of North Carolina declined an offer to play in the National Football League and instead signed a contract with the New York Yankees. His name was George Stirnweiss and this multi-talented athlete began his professional baseball career in Hampton Roads as a member of the Norfolk Tars, a minor league affiliate of the Yankees. As the Tars wrapped up their season, Stirnweiss remained in the area and served as a player-coach for the Norfolk Shamrocks of the Dixie League. When the semi-pro gridiron season ended, Stirnweiss found himself idled in Norfolk until baseball beckoned in the spring. With the Norfolk Division still on the lookout to fill the coaching position vacated by Scott,

*the school offered the leadership role to Stirnweiss, who, despite a lack
of experience on the hard court, took the job.*

*The new coach could count on only three returning lettermen
to headline the Norfolk Division Braves for the 1940–41 season. The
Stirnweiss 'Five' struggled all year and endured an embarrassing eight-
game losing streak and a disappointing overall campaign resulting in
a 4–15 record. Despite the scoring prowess of team captain Ed Kilgore,
1941–42 proved to be even more disheartening for the Norfolk cagers,
as they were unable to secure a single victory during the season.*

*With back-to-back disappointing seasons and baseball's spring
training taking priority, Stirnweiss gave his resignation and donned
Yankee pinstripes to begin a respectable 10-year major league career.[3]*

The 1941–42 team finished 0–14, giving "Snuffy" Stirnweiss a career
mark of 4–29 at the Norfolk Division, or a winning percentage of 12
percent, although one may suspect that the three World Series titles
he later won with the Yankees served to counteract the sting of that
mark. As the United States had begun to prepare for war, the basketball
schedules had also begun to reflect that. In Stirnweiss' first season, six
of nineteen opponents were military-affiliated; in his second and last
season, the number was ten of fourteen. This trend continued as J. C.
"Scrap" Chandler led the team for the next four seasons; of twenty-two
games in 1942–43, a large majority were against local military teams,
and by the 1944–45 and 1945–46 seasons, there were *no* contests scheduled
against anyone other than local military outfits. This may include 1943–44
as well, for which the ODU basketball media guide records a 1–7 won-loss
record, but says "Scores not available."[4]

The return of American servicemen from World War II, and the
accompanying swelling of the Norfolk Division's enrollment, benefited the basketball program more immediately than the baseball
team, and two successful seasons preceded Coach Bud Metheny's
arrival. The 1946–47 team won fourteen of its twenty-two games

and finished the year crowned as regional champions, winning the eight-team Tidewater Invitational Tournament. The 1947 *Voyager* yearbook offered glowing praise for both coach and team in its year-end summary:

> By far, the biggest sports attraction in the Division this year was the basketball team, which enjoyed a much greater degree of success than is indicated by their season's record of fourteen games won and eight losses . . .
>
> Julius Rubin, who had never coached before, was hired to tutor the cagers because of his own splendid record as a pre-war courtman. It took but a short while for Rubin to become a famous coach in the eyes of his players and followers in the school. The new mentor turned out to be a perfectionist; he greeted an almost entirely strange group of candidates and in a couple months time molded them into the most polished ball club ever to represent the Norfolk Division. Coach Rubin's ability didn't really become known until the last regularly scheduled game of the season, when his charges trampled the Saint Helena Extension, 63–32, while the sports editor of a local newspaper sat amazed at the classy brand of basketball taking place in front of him.[5]

The 1947–48 basketball team returned six lettermen, an unusual number for a two-year school. Among them was team captain Ted Bacalis, the future coach responsible for 296 Maury High School basketball wins, who led the Division team to its finest season to date. Under new coach Jack Callahan, a former Division player and a 1946 graduate of VPI, the Braves completed a 21–8 season against a schedule that still heavily favored local military outfits and some small-college competition. Still, the twenty-one-win total would not be surpassed by a team playing under the name "Norfolk Division," and would not be matched until Sonny Allen's 1968–69 team, the last team before the school was renamed Old Dominion University.

New Coach Former Yankee Baseball Player

Do we know our basketball coach like we should? For the benefit of the students who do not, let us look into his past which has led up to his present duties at the Division.

He is Mr. Metheny, and he hails from Norfolk, Virginia. He started playing pro-ball with the Norfolk Tars. Later he advanced to the Kansas City Blues and finally to the New York Yankees in 1943, '44, '45, '46, participating in the 1943 World Series in which the New York team emerged as World Champions. During his major league career he has faced great players such as Bobby Feller, Hal Newhouser, Dizzy Trout, Mort Cooper, and Al Brarle. Some of his teammates while with the Yankees were Joe Gordon, now with the World's Champion Cleveland Indians; "King Kong" Charlie Keller; the greatest catcher in the Major Leagues, Bill Dickey, and Johnny Lindell. He was not too, impressive at the plate, but with his ability of being a good fielder he managed to keep his name in the starting lineup. After baseball season with the Majors in 1943, '44, and '45, he coached the Maury basketball team. In 1946, '47, he was acquired by the South Norfolk school to coach the basketball team there. This year he has a hard time trying to fill Jack Callahan's shoes as basketball mentor. He tackles this task with playing support from Poteate, West, Roughton and and "Poochie" Bryant. We hope he is as successful as last year's team was.

What the team will need is student support, so let's give it to them. If you girls don't know anything about basketball, use that excuse to have some boy take you.

From The High Hat, *November 22, 1948.*
Courtesy of Special Collections and University Archives, Old Dominion University.

When Bud Metheny took over from Jack Callahan in 1948, he earned for the Norfolk Division what must certainly be a unique distinction, as Metheny became the second past or future New York Yankee to coach the same college's *basketball* team—and if that distinction isn't unique enough, then certainly no college basketball program has ever had two mentors that occasionally batted first and second in the same Yankees lineup, as Snuffy Stirnweiss and Metheny did. Garrett and Shampoe wrote in 2007 that "when Callahan's successor took the reigns [sic] in the fall of 1948, the Norfolk Division found one of its most charismatic, caring, and motivational leaders in Arthur Beauregard Metheny,"[6] but that story wasn't quite written yet in 1948. In fact, *The High Hat*, in its November 22, 1948, issue, did not gush with enthusiasm and excitement at the hiring of the new coach, despite his status as a former major leaguer, and his sterling athletic credentials from the parent institution. Rather, the author took a distinctly "wait-and-see" approach, opining that

Metheny had been "not too impressive at the plate" in his major league career, but had "managed to keep his name in the starting lineup." The writer noted that the new coach would have a "hard time trying to fill Jack Callahan's shoes as basketball mentor." The article's only high praise was reserved for those major league players that Bud Metheny had played with or against.

The 1948–49 Division basketball team only played sixteen recorded games; therefore, Metheny did not even have the possibility of matching Callahan's twenty-one-win squad of the previous year. However, the new coach did just fine with those sixteen games, recording wins in eleven of them, for a win ratio of 69 percent that was comparable to the 72 percent that had been recorded the year before. In this inaugural season for Metheny, the opponent schedule still had a heavy military presence, as five of sixteen recorded contests were played against such teams, although the percentage was down from the year before. An American Legion team (the Peninsula's Braxton-Perkins club) was the opponent on two occasions, and there was also a game against a "Gridiron Club." Still, Coach Metheny had collegiate-level talent on his schedule in six of his sixteen games, as his Division team faced the freshmen squads of Virginia, Richmond, and William & Mary. Metheny himself, in response to a question of whether it was difficult to schedule opponents in those early years, recalled in 1975 that "We did [have difficulty]. When I first came here, we started off playing city league teams, church league teams, service teams, and things of this type. And then we went from there to junior varsity teams and freshman teams, then four-year schools. And that was the progress. We had to start from nowhere and get going, and it takes time, especially when you don't have money."[7]

After the first five games of his collegiate coaching career, Bud Metheny was still undefeated, perhaps winning over the initially skeptical *High Hat* writer. After a two-point loss to Little Creek Amphibious Base, Metheny's charges then won another five games in a row, for an auspicious 10–1 start to the new coach's career. Losses in four of five games to close the year may have dampened the enthusiasm somewhat, but the season certainly started what would be a long career on a high note. In fact, Coach Metheny's basketball teams would not have a better winning percentage until superstar Leo Anthony's senior year of 1961, when the team won 80 percent of its games.

At season's end, the authors of the basketball write-up in the *Voyager* yearbook were prepared to offer some praise for the new coach: "The Braves can remember the season as being a very successful one. Coach Metheny molded the candidates into a well-balanced basketball team. . . . There were no glory boys in the group. Statistics would indicate that the boys took turns to be high scorer."[8] In the final analysis, did Metheny acceptably fill Jack Callahan's shoes? Bud Metheny never won a "Jack Callahan Award," but it was Jack Callahan who was the 1994 recipient of Old Dominion's "Bud Metheny Award," an annual honor given by Old Dominion since 1978 to recognize contributions to baseball in the Hampton Roads area.[9]

Bud Metheny's first Norfolk Division team. Front row, left to right: Edward Pelling III (11), Elmer Acey (9), Downs (16), Kalmon Markoe (14). Second row: John Vitasek (3), West, Nesbitt "Sack" Reviere (8), Bill Roughton (5), Bob Bedinger (13), Joe Agee (7). Third Row: Coach Bud Metheny, Bernard "Poochie" Bryant (10), McFarland (6), Wilmer Poteate (12), unknown. Courtesy of Special Collections and University Archives, Patricia W. and J. Douglas Perry Library, Old Dominion University Libraries, Norfolk, Virginia.

CHEERS

Pass It to the Center

Pass it to the center
Dribble down the floor
Put it in the basket
Raise that score!

A Tisket A Tasket

A tisket, a tasket
We want a basket
Don't get cold
Let's get bold
Come on boy
Let's make that goal!

Braves

B-R-A-V-E-S
B-R-A-V-E-S
B-R-A-V-E-S
Ray, rah, Braves!

Rickety, Rackety, Russ

Rickety, rackety, russ
We aren't allowed to cuss
But jam-it to jell
We gotta yell
For William and Mary or bust!

The 1948–49 Braves basketball team could expect to be serenaded by these treats from the cheerleading squad, according to the 1949 yearbook. Courtesy of Special Collections and University Archives, Old Dominion University.

FIRST BASEBALL TEAM

Coach Bud Metheny's first baseball team at the Norfolk Division took the field in the spring of 1949, looking forward to a schedule of games against the Naval Air Station, the Navy Plebes, the Newport News Apprentice school, the Norfolk Naval Base, the Little Creek Amphibious base, the University of Richmond freshman team, and Richmond Professional Institute. The Division baseball team had a very limited history of recent success, having only twelve recorded wins in the 1940s prior to Metheny's inaugural season, but the former Yankee did not shrink from the challenge of building the program from the ground up. Coach Metheny's 1949 squad, in general, was competitive

Bud Metheny's first Norfolk Division baseball team, 1949. Back row, left to right: Coach Bud Metheny, "Sack" Reviere, Bob Rawlings, Dick Windley, Blair Poteate, George Kiskinis. Middle row: "Pop" Ribling, John Vitasek, Larry Barnes, Miles Lacey, Joe Agee. Front row: Bill Ewell, Sonny Harrison, John Alexander, Rudy Simpson, Gene Cohen. Courtesy of Special Collections and University Archives, Patricia W. and J. Douglas Perry Library, Old Dominion University Libraries, Norfolk, Virginia.

with their opponents; in fact, removing two extreme outliers, the team outscored their opponents by a 57–51 count. However, there were also those outliers. The *Virginian-Pilot* described a May 10 defeat in violent terms, reporting that "The Naval Base unloaded a 14-hit barrage against the Norfolk Division yesterday for a 21–2 victory at the Naval Base. Mergler poled a homer and Breidt socked a double and triple to lead the assault."[10] Nine Division errors that day hurt the cause as well, and ten days later, another five errors and seventeen hits allowed resulted in a 16–1 defeat at the hands of the Norfolk Naval Air Station.[11] Despite these two bumps, the 1949 Norfolk Division squad recorded four wins against seven defeats, as they looked forward to putting the 1940s behind them.

CONTINUING PRO BALL

Even with his full-time employment at the Norfolk Division beginning in 1948, Metheny hadn't quite gotten the ball-playing bug out of his system. In the 1949 season, he still found time to suit up for the Portsmouth Cubs for 127 games, playing with the team during home night games until the school year was over, then full-time in the summer. At thirty-four years of age, he was the second-oldest player to take the field for Portsmouth that year, behind only player-manager Skeeter Scalzi, who checked in at thirty-six. In fact, with the Metheny/Scalzi duo on the roster, Portsmouth sported by far the oldest average age of position players in the six-team Class-B Piedmont League, at 29.1 years old, contrasted with 21.5 years old for the Roanoke Red Sox, the youngest.[12]

Even as only a Class-B team, the 1949 Portsmouth Cubs had enough talent that they could feature seven past and one future major league ballplayer on their roster. Besides Metheny, manager Skeeter Scalzi played in the 1939 season for the New York Giants, and has a Hall-of-Fame-worthy batting average of .333, although no other statistics would fairly qualify him, since that average is only over eighteen total major league at-bats. Outfielder Red Treadway, first baseman Reggie Otero, and pitcher George Eyrich had each made the majors during the war years, and catcher Ted "Porky" Pawelek recorded one hit in the four major league at-bats he took, all in 1946. Pitcher Lou Grasmick had pitched in the Majors the year before, but his career totals include only five innings pitched. In 1949, the only Portsmouth Cub to still have his major league career in front of him was right-handed pitcher Earl Mossor, who reached the big time in 1951, only to see his career totals stagnate at 1.2 innings pitched, with seven bases on balls issued, and a career earned run average of 32.40.

Still, while there were no past or future major league superstars on the 1949 Cubs roster, making the "Show" is something very few people can claim, and having eight on the same squad was an impressive array of talent for a Class-B team. Usually playing left field and batting in the middle of the order, Metheny hit the ball well all summer long, and on August 20, was named to the Piedmont League All-Star team, along with teammates Reggie Otero, Russell Kerns, and pitcher Angelo "Wimpy" Nardella. With only three weeks to go in the season at the time of this honor, Bud was batting at an impressive .343 clip, and ten days later his average still stood at .336, prompting at least some amount of national notice. A humorous item appearing in several newspapers across the country on August 31 and September 1 speculated that should the Yankees "get anyone else hurted [sic]," they may have a renewed interest in Metheny's services, although this prospect did not come to fruition.[13]

By season's end, the 1949 Cubs had played to a 74–66 won-lost record, finishing second behind the Lynchburg Cardinals, who would defeat the Cubs in the final

Sports Before Your Eyes

Bud Metheny, who played in two world series for the Yankees, has been hitting at a terrific clip this summer for the Portsmouth, Va., club of the Piedmont league. As a sideline, Bud coaches at the Norfolk division of William and Mary . . . If the Yanks get anyone else hurted, they may try to recall him

From the Lansing (MI) State Journal, September 1, 1949.

round of the Piedmont League's Shaughnessy playoffs. Bud Metheny finished with nine home runs and a .336 batting average that was good for second in the league, and marked his best average since batting .338 in his first season as a professional with the 1938 Norfolk Tars.

As the 1950 season dawned, Metheny continued to play with the Portsmouth club, even while in the early season he simultaneously led his Division charges to a four-win, five-loss campaign, the Division's best since 1937. The Portsmouth club looked primed to build on its successful 1949 campaign, with major league-caliber talents Earl Mossor, Reggie Otero, Red Treadway, and manager Skeeter Scalzi still in the fold. Additionally, former major leaguers Pep Rambert, Dummy Lynch, and Don Hasemeyer joined the group, as did future major league pitchers Duke Markell and Ralph Brickner.

The Cubs were predictably strong and would lead the league with an 83–54 record, on the strength of a combined thirty-nine wins and over 500 innings pitched by Mossor and Markell. Bud Metheny, however, wouldn't be around to enjoy the fruits of such a talent-laden roster, because on Thursday, July 20, he agreed to replace future Los Angeles Dodgers General Manager Al Campanis as the manager of the Newport News Dodgers. Newport News *Daily Press* sportswriter Charles Karmosky evidently wasn't convinced this was a plum position, as he wrote the next day that "Metheny . . . moves into a rather unenviable position with the Baby Brooks [for 'Brooklyn'] who have been rockin' and reelin' for the past month."[14]

Karmosky had good cause for his pessimism. At the time of Metheny's signing, the Dodgers' won-loss record stood at an unimpressive 28–55, leaving them 5½ games behind the hapless 32–48 Norfolk Tars just to get out of last place. And over the previous thirty-one games, the Dodgers had won only five.

The statistics for the 1950 Newport News Dodgers show that there were five future major leaguers on the squad at one time or another, including Charlie Coles, Ron Negray, Ed Roebuck, Gale Wade, and

GLAD TO HAVE YOU ABOARD, 'BUD'

Al Clarke (right), Business Manager of the Newport News Dodgers, gives the glad hand to Arthur "Bud" Metheny, former New York Yankee outfielder and William and Mary diamond star, who takes over the reins as manager of the Baby Bums tonight. Metheny replaces Al Campanis, who will return to scouting and field work for the parent club.

From the Daily Press, *July 21, 1950. ©Daily Press. All rights reserved. Distributed by Tribune Content Agency, LLC.*

future San Francisco Giant manager and split-finger fastball guru Roger Craig, in his first season of professional baseball.[15] However, all but one—Ron Negray—had moved on to different teams by July 21, compounding the work Bud Metheny had to do to make the team competitive, and to keep the fans coming out to the games.

At the Peninsula's War Memorial Stadium on Saturday night, July 22, a fireworks show greeted a crowd of 1,868 before a 7–5 Dodger win over the Richmond Colts, as new manager and first baseman Bud Metheny, hitting fifth in the lineup, went two-for-three with two runs batted in and raised his season average to .255.[16] A Hollywood storyline would have Bud Metheny, honing his skills as a leader of men, rise from this initial success and lead his team to an improbable championship. But that didn't happen, and in fact, the Dodgers never even overtook the Tars to climb out of the cellar. However, new manager Metheny did turn a struggling team that had lost much talent—not to mention twenty-six out of thirty-one games—into a respectable outfit. Before Metheny, and with several skilled ballplayers, the club had gone 28–55; after Metheny took the reins, the squad went 27–30 to close the year. The Dodgers' winning percentage during the games managed by Bud Metheny had increased from 33.7 percent to 47.3 percent, a significant improvement of 13.6 percent.[17]

Metheny was also continuing to learn the skill set that would serve him well as a leader, as he transitioned from star athlete to a coach who would ultimately receive many honors in that capacity. Despite his prominent positions as athlete and coach, those who knew him described Bud Metheny as a humble man, and his stint as Newport News manager certainly demonstrated his ability to subvert his own ego for the good of his unit. As the "Baby Bums" steadied their ship under him and played near .500 baseball, Bud Metheny the manager kept Bud Metheny the player's name off the lineup card more and more often until his final appearance in the box score as a professional baseball player: a zero-for-one with a walk in a 3–1 loss to his former teammates from the Portsmouth Cubs on August 30, taking his final season average down to .219. In fact, it was the fourth straight appearance in which he limited himself to pinch-hitting duty,[18] as he obviously recognized the decline in his own skill compared to the talented younger hitters in the league, who were on average 10.6 years younger than he.

"We had a very successful last half year, of which I was very proud. And that was the end of my professional career," Metheny summarized succinctly in an interview with Dr. James Sweeney in 1975.[19] As to his motivation, the advance of age and a .219 average playing for a Class-B minor league team would seem to be obvious drivers, but his "professional career" by this time also included a resume entry as a manager that could turn a team in the right direction—a skill certain to be in high demand at any level of professional baseball, and probably presenting much more lucrative opportunities than what the Norfolk Division could offer him to stay at the junior college as the basketball and baseball coach. For Bud Metheny, it wasn't about the money or the fame, though. His career as a dedicated member of the Norfolk Division staff had taken root with him, providing the chance to mentor young people, and a job satisfaction that few ever really achieve. He declined opportunities that came along that were surely tempting, such as a 1957 offer to scout for the New York Yankees.[20] Confirming his retirement from professional baseball, Metheny was quoted in the November 20, 1950, edition of the *Daily Press*, saying, "I like my work at the college. I like working with those kids and it's hard to combine both. In fact, I couldn't. That's my work and I'm going to stick to it."[21]

EARLY '50S DIVISION TEAMS

As the Norfolk Division entered the 1950s, the faculty of the Physical Education Department consisted solely of Bud Metheny, Joseph

C. "Scrap" Chandler, and Jane Gresham. By comparison, the Music Department at that time had four faculty members, the English Department had five, the Chemistry Department four, and the Economics Department either five or six, depending on one's interpretation of the 1950 *Echolalia* yearbook. The following year would see Emily Pittman replace Jane Gresham in the Physical Education Department, and the trio of Pittman, Metheny, and Chandler would completely represent the PE department (which also included the intercollegiate athletic program) for the next several years.[22]

The lack of personnel dedicated to the Norfolk Division's physical education and athletics, however, is not necessarily a true indicator of the relative importance of athletics at the school. Rather, the available budget that constrained the athletic program and the college itself was the primary driver. In two separate interviews conducted by Dr. James Sweeney in May of 1975, Bud Metheny mentioned budgetary constraints in no fewer than twenty-two of his responses. Still, characterizing school Director Lewis W. Webb Jr., Metheny recalled that "Mr. Webb was a great supporter of any facet of the college at that time, and, as a matter of fact, he and his family never missed a contest, if it was possible. So, he was very enthusiastic about our physical education and our athletic program. He backed us in every way, shape, or manner, and helped us when he could."[23]

The Norfolk Division's baseball program, however, did not even have its own field; Larchmont Field was leased from the City of Norfolk. Bud Metheny did not have an assistant coach, and so functioned as head coach, assistant coach, and trainer. There were certainly no funds for athletic scholarships through the school. These were simple realities in the career Bud Metheny had chosen, but if some of his motivation can be inferred from the words he chose in interviews, this very opportunity to build something from nothing was very likely a strong draw. "The conditions weren't the best, but it was a joy," he remarked later. "And we had the support of everybody.

It was a unique situation in that everybody knew that our kids were doing great under the conditions. And the faculty, the administration, everybody was behind our program."[24]

After his four-win, seven-loss maiden voyage in 1949, Coach Metheny's second baseball team entered the 1950 campaign after a *Virginian-Pilot* article headlined on March 22, "Pitching Talent No Problem to Division Head Coach." The question, according to *Pilot* writer Aubrey Mitchell, was "Where the heck can he find a first-string catcher?" The article referenced five pitchers immediately available, and even mentioned the possibility of converting George Kiskinis, who would become the starting catcher, to fill that role as well.[25]

Pitching talent in 1950 may have been no problem, but defense and holding leads certainly were problematic. In one fourteen-inning, 8–7 loss to the Apprentice School of Newport News, the Braves committed eleven errors, including five by Joe Agee, who later went on to an All-Southern Conference career at William & Mary. In a loss to Richmond Professional Institute, the team committed four errors and gave up a six-run rally in the bottom of the ninth, to lose 15–14. Errors, in fact, would be one of the hallmarks of the Division squads throughout the entire 1950s; other factors would contribute to the increasing success of the program, but in general, team defense was not one of them.

The field may have had something to do with the defensive lapses. "We played on old Larchmont Field, and there were a lot of rocks out there and bad bounces, and somehow you couldn't convince him [Coach Metheny] it had hit a rock, when it'd get through your legs," as Frank Zadell, a member of the 1964 team, recalled about the home field.[26] Boyd Nix, on the same team, remembered that "they had gopher holes out there."[27] Interestingly, though, the condition of the home field didn't appear to make much difference statistically. The Braves were playing their home games almost exclusively at Larchmont by 1952, and an analysis of Bud Metheny's scorebooks from that year through 1959 shows 237 Brave errors in sixty-four games at Larchmont, and 235 errors in sixty-five games at other fields. The Braves' fielders *did* make more errors at Larchmont in this period, but only by the slim average margin of 3.70 per game at home, as opposed to 3.62 per game at other venues.

The average Major League Baseball defense in the middle year of the 1950s committed .90 errors per game.[28] There is an obvious unfairness in comparing the small-college Norfolk Division Braves' defense to an average major-league caliber defense, but a rate around 3.6 errors per game by the Braves still led to a lot of unearned runs being scored, and games lost that could have, or should have, been won. While Bud Metheny did not always record in his scorebook the number of earned runs by each side in a game, he did so in the large majority of cases, and averaging all such games from 1952–1959 shows that the Braves allowed 2.86 unearned runs per game in that stretch; by comparison, the average 1955 major league team allowed .53 unearned runs per game.

	% OF DIVISION RUNS EARNED	% OF DIVISION OPPONENT'S RUNS EARNED	DIVISION ERRORS / GAME	UNEARNED RUNS ALLOWED BY DIVISION / GAME	DIVISION WINNING PERCENTAGE
1952	70.2	50.0	5.0	4.31	0.529
1953	63.4	50.4	4.8	5.91	0.353
1954	80.0	45.6	3.5	2.82	0.571
1955	75.0	60.0	5.6	2.33	0.500
1956	72.6	55.9	3.3	2.65	0.588
1957	55.9	47.4	3.5	3.53	0.471
1958	71.4	65.4	1.5	1.20	0.800
1959	69.1	62.9	2.8	1.64	0.773

In the chart above, which takes into account all games in Bud Metheny's scorebook between 1952 and 1959 except those few for which he did not record earned-run statistics in his scorebook, a clear relationship between unearned runs allowed versus team winning percentage emerges. In the year with the best winning percentage recorded at the school to that date (1958), the team allowed the fewest number of unearned runs per game; in the year with the worst winning percentage during that stretch (1953), the team allowed the most unearned runs, at a whopping rate of 5.91 per game. Whether the Division's 1950s team defensive statistics align with other small colleges of the time is a matter beyond the scope of this work, but as the defense began to show improvement in the late years of the decade, writer Bill Harrison noted in 1959 in his "Home of the Braves" column for the *Virginian-Pilot* that "The Braves were second to Washington (Md.) [College], Mason-Dixon runners-up to Hampden-Sydney last year, in team fielding percentage . . . Washington led the nation with .968, Norfolk W&M had .961."[29] Even in that year, with stars Leo Anthony and Kirkie Harrison in the defensive middle, the Braves allowed 1.20 unearned runs per game, and only 65.4 percent of opposing teams' runs were earned.

Luckily, however, the early 1950s teams could score. While the won-loss total for the years 1950–52 was still relatively mediocre as the developing program still faced many service teams and non-four-year schools, it was still a positive trend, as the Braves put the 1940s behind them. And while the team was giving up plenty of unearned runs, the Braves were also keeping the scorekeeper busy in their turn. In 1952, the Division was playing "Moneyball" a decade before Billy Beane was born. To go along with 8.6 hits per game, they also took 6.6 walks, and when an additional twelve hit batsmen are factored in, 16.1 Brave batters were reaching base per game, before the benefit of an average of more than four opponent errors per game is even considered. In that season, the Norfolk Division averaged 10.5 runs per contest to their opponents' 6.6 (including the three games not in Metheny's scorebook), and for the three-year span of 1950–52, the team scored in double digits almost 50 percent of the time, accomplishing the feat in twenty of forty-one contests.[30]

Despite the defensive struggles, the early 1950s showed continued slow but steady improvement for Coach Metheny's charges. Records show that nine contests were played in 1950, fifteen in 1951, and seventeen in 1952, as Metheny began scheduling more games. And in 1952, playing against more four-year institutions in any year than he had to that point (four), Metheny's Division baseball team won more than they lost for the first time, playing to a 9–8 record.[31] However, while the long-term trend of the baseball program was turning positive, the 1952 defensive statistics are still worthy of note. Although three games don't show up in Coach Metheny's 1952 scorebook, the fourteen that are in the book show seventy errors, or exactly five per game. The chart on the previous page uses only Metheny's scorebook, but if the *Virginian-Pilot* box scores of the other three games are to be believed (and Metheny's scorebook and the newspaper didn't always align), then an additional fourteen errors would have still kept that average high, at 4.94 per game. High error rates came from unusual positions, too. The catcher, Mel Gottlieb, contributed ten errors in the fourteen games in Metheny's scorebook (and Metheny did score passed balls separately), the outfield contributed thirteen errors, and there were six errors from the first base position. There was a game with ten errors made (by seven different players) and two games with nine errors. Third baseman Tommy Downing contributed five in a single contest; shortstop Tommy Wyszatycki contributed six in one. In a description that probably fit several other games over the course of the 1952 season, the *Pilot* described the Division's April 26 win over RPI by saying, "Pushing over a marker in the ninth inning yesterday, the Norfolk Division Braves edged the Richmond Professional Institute, 12–11, in a battle of miscues." The moral victory for RPI, one must assume, is that even though they lost, they only committed six errors to the Division's eight!

The 1953 season was a relative low ebb in Metheny's early baseball coaching tenure. His team won only six games while losing eleven against the scheduled variety of Navy and junior college teams, and that mark ultimately represented the fourth-worst winning percentage in his thirty-one-year career. Starting with a 23–5 spanking at the hands of the Little Creek Amphibious Force "Gators" on March 31, the team would go on to be outscored by a total of 193–115 over seventeen games—or an average of 11.4–8.1 per contest. In ten of the seventeen contests, the Braves gave up double-digit runs; in all but two, they gave up at least six runs. For those who believed in the analyses of *High Hat* sportswriter Bernie Weiss, these results weren't really all that unpredictable. On March 13, 1953, Weiss had written, "Pitching will be the big question mark of the 1953 William and Mary-VPI baseball team . . . Only one member of last year's nine will be returning for action this season on the mound. He is right-hander Harvey Saks. Outside of Saks, coach Bud Metheny has no one upon whom he can rely to any extent . . . Probably the strongest point of the squad will be the hitting."[32]

Of the six wins recorded by the 1953 Braves, one stands out clearly as a key moment in Old Dominion baseball history. On April 2, Bud Metheny's junior college Norfolk Division Braves went head-to-head in a meaningful baseball game with a major four-year college for the first time, when Dartmouth visited Norfolk. As the *Virginian-Pilot* reported the next day, "The [Dartmouth] Indians have been making an annual trip to the Norfolk area, meeting the service teams, but it was the first game against the Division nine."[33]

Coach Metheny had a plan to advance his program, and by extension, his college, as he noted in 1975, "Everyone knew that we could be recognized nationally much quicker through the realm of athletics than we could with any other means. And not only would the

Division Plays Dartmouth Nine Here Today, 2:30

Bud Metheny's Norfolk Division Braves will go against a major college baseball team for the first time today when they meet Dartmouth College at the Larchmont Field at 2:30 o'clock.

Righthander Jack Smart, a 6-4, 225-pounder from Granby High, will o p p o s e the Ivy Leaguers on the mound. Melvin Gottlieb will be behind the plate for the Braves.

Other probable starters for the Division will be Walter Forbes, 1b; Sonny Howlett, 2b; Raymond Ellis, ss; Tommy Wilson, 3b; Tommy Downing, lf; Cecil Baecher or Billy Tyndall, cf, and Dick Butler, rf.

university benefit, the entire community would also."[34] The plan was to play the highest levels of competition possible, learn to compete successfully at those levels, earn name recognition for the school in doing so, and to repeat the process when a milestone goal was achieved. In the lengthy 1975 interviews with Dr. Sweeney, in fact, Bud Metheny refers to this general strategy more than a dozen times.

Metheny found the strategy much easier to pursue in baseball than he did in basketball. In the spring, many college teams from the North would travel to warmer climates in the South in search of baseball competition, while basketball provided no such obvious opportunity. Along with the natural geographical opportunity in baseball, getting Dartmouth on the Division schedule in 1953 may also have been assisted by the fact that Bud Metheny and Coach Bob Shawkey of Dartmouth were both former Yankees. Shawkey had been in a New York uniform between 1915 and 1927, racking up four twenty-win seasons and pitching in four different World Series for the Yankees. Metheny and Shawkey weren't contemporaries, but did share this connection, and the April 3, 1953, *Virginian-Pilot* noted that "Brave mentor Bud Metheny, who played with the Yankees in the early '40s, got a chance to talk over the Old Timers' Game that he and Shawkey played in together two years ago at the Stadium."[35]

Coach Metheny started Jack Smart and his creaky shoulder on the mound against the invaders from New Hampshire. "Jack Smart, who pitched for me, was a big-league prospect," Metheny recalled later. "But he had a very unusual physical makeup in his shoulder, and he'd pitch a game, and then he couldn't pick up a ball for almost a week . . . he had this little situation in his shoulder where the tendon always slipped out of its little groove, and it made him very, very sore. But he was a big-league prospect if it hadn't been for that, because he could throw hard."[36] After the season, Smart would undergo career-ending shoulder surgery,[37] but on April 2, 1953, he pitched a complete game against the Dartmouth Indians, allowing three runs while striking out six batters in leading the Braves to victory in their first test against a major college team. The series with Dartmouth wouldn't become an annual affair until 1960, but this first step in Metheny's broader plan was a success, and the strategy of making his program better by scheduling cold-weather teams in early spring would find such schools as Brown University, the University of Rochester, Colby College, and Ithaca College all coming to Norfolk before 1965.[38]

Bud Metheny continued to improve the level of competition on his baseball schedule for the 1954 season. Local Navy teams, which had provided the opposition in seven of seventeen contests in 1953, did not appear at all on the 1954 schedule, while freshman teams from four-year schools were much more well-represented. In 1953, only the Naval Academy "Plebes" could have counted in this category, while in 1954, six of fourteen contests were against the freshman teams from William & Mary, the University of Richmond, the University of Virginia, and Virginia Military Institute, with the Virginia and VMI teams appearing for the first time ever on the Division's schedule. Freshman teams didn't represent the varsity at those schools, but they did represent college-level talent from major schools, at a time when the Norfolk Division was still a junior college itself, enrolling athletes primarily only from local high schools and boasting a registration of only 996 "Day College" students in the 1954–55 school year.[39] Only Chowan Junior College and the Newport News Apprentice School were left on the Division's 1954 schedule to represent non-four-year schools, and they would also be the only two to appear over the next five years, until Bud Metheny eliminated that lower level of competition from his schedule for good with a 5–2 victory over the Apprentice School on April 28, 1959. Despite the upgrade, the 1954 team still did well against the scheduled competition, playing to an 8–6 record and reducing the number of runs they allowed per game from 11.4 in 1953 to 5.6, while outscoring opponents by an average of 1.5 runs per game.

Metheny's team continued its forward progress in 1955. Tony Zontini wrote of the 1955 baseball schedule that "Fourteen games made up the most attractive schedule in college history. Eight college varsity teams including University of Virginia, William and Mary, Washington and Lee, R.P.I. [Richmond Professional Institute], Hampden-Sydney, Bridgewater, Randolph-Macon, and Lynchburg were played. Two Junior College teams and two freshman teams rounded out the schedule."[40] This team finished with a mediocre 7–7 win-loss record, but, in effect, two different teams suited up for the Norfolk Division during this campaign—the first started the season by losing five out of six games, including an embarrassing 13–1 loss to the Naval Academy "Plebes," which featured so many Division errors that the *Virginian-Pilot*'s box score attributed errors to two players that weren't even in the lineup, as one "Tamhory" and one "Saranjow" were charged with two apiece.[41] The team righted the season on the strength of its offense, and a rejuvenated Braves squad won six out of eight games to close the year. The second half included a dominant five-game stretch sparked by the Division's first-ever win against the varsity of parent school William & Mary. After coming back from a five-run deficit and defeating William & Mary by a 13–7 score, the

Braves went on to crush Richmond Professional Institute (RPI) by a score of 19–0, the University of Virginia freshmen by 12–5, Chowan by 25–9, and then ended the stretch with a 10–0 shutout of Newport News Apprentice, for a gaudy five-game average score of 15.8–4.2 in the Braves' favor. The game against William & Mary marked only the second time the Division had competed against the parent school's varsity squad, both coming in the 1955 season. Prior to the six-run win, the Norfolk Division had a losing 7–8 lifetime record against the William & Mary *freshman* team, and had lost the early season match with the varsity.

In the first half of the 1950s, baseball box scores published in the *Virginian-Pilot* demonstrated an unclear school identity; the team was most commonly referred to as "Division" or "Norfolk Division," but at various times was also referred to as "W&M-VPI," "William and Mary," "VPI Braves," or "W. and M. Division." The years to follow would help define the school's identity, as the character of the institution underwent a major transformation. In December of 1951, the Norfolk Division had been accredited as a junior college, but Norfolk and school leadership envisioned much grander advancement in the future. In some of the biggest news to come from the college in the 1950s, in March 1954, the *Virginian-Pilot* gleefully headlined "4-year College to Start Next Year," noting that the advancement would come as the "result of the $375,000 for a library building wrested from tax credit funds with the aid of Norfolk members of the General Assembly."[42] Commenting for the story, Division Director Lewis Webb noted that the appropriation for the library building was the key to future accreditation, and that the initial plan would be to begin offering four-year courses of study in elementary education, business administration, and nursing. Funding for the library wasn't the only ongoing progressive change on campus; the 1954 *Chieftain* yearbook also described a new Science Building, representing the progress pictorially, along with a caption that included two memorable names:

"EYES TOWARD THE FUTURE . . . Evon Rasberry and 'Winkie' Wilgus watch the construction of the new Science Building, the first big step toward the future."

The Norfolk Division's 1956 *Chieftain* shows seniors for the first time in the history of the school, with fourteen "June Seniors" and two "August Seniors" pictured. The awarded degrees were in the specialties Webb mentioned in 1954, as eleven of those shown were BS (Business Administration), four were BA (Business Administration), and one was BS (Medical Technology).[43] Although the yearbook demonstrates the continuing growth of the school with forty Juniors pictured as well, it does not give as much insight into the character of the institution as the 1957 *Chieftain* yearbook, which provides not only the degrees granted, but also the hometowns of the students. In that year, sixty-four seniors were pictured, of whom 60.9 percent were male and 39.1 percent female, 17.2 percent were night school students, and a full 100 percent of whom listed hometowns in Hampton Roads—fifty-three (82.8 percent) from Norfolk, five (7.8 percent) from Portsmouth, and two each (3.1 percent) from Hampton, South Norfolk (which would later become part of the City of Chesapeake), and the area that would later become the City of Virginia Beach. At this time, not only was the school still only serving students from Hampton Roads, but even within that subset, it was nearly exclusively serving *southside* Hampton Roads students.

School growth continued throughout the latter years of the 1950s, and by 1959, 2,178 day students were enrolled in classes at the college,[44] and the original three baccalaureate-granting programs had expanded to twelve, including such courses of study as physical education, history, music, chemistry, economics, and sociology. However, despite the opening of the Hampton Roads Bridge-Tunnel in November 1957, the school was still primarily, although no longer almost exclusively, a provincial southside Hampton Roads institution. Of 129 seniors pictured in 1959, 66.7 percent were from Norfolk, 14.7 percent from Portsmouth, and 7.0 percent from areas such as "Lynnhaven," "Oceana," and "Bayside," which would later be part of the City of Virginia Beach. By the end of the decade, the character of the school was gradually, but clearly, becoming less provincial. Alexandria and Staunton were also now represented in the Norfolk Division's senior class, as were Peking, China; Cleveland, Ohio; and Hull, England. Still, the impact of these enrollment statistics on Norfolk Division athletics in the 1950s was, as Bud Metheny recalled, that "we had . . . some fine athletes, but we didn't have a whole lot, like we'd have one, maybe two, and then the rest were all local athletes . . . and they did well because this is a productive area, but naturally, being a junior college and on a very low scale athletically minded at that time, the top athletes were recruited by the bigger schools, and naturally they went away to school."[45]

The second half of the 1950s would bring significant forward steps in the Norfolk Division's athletic programs. Two new faculty members were added to the staff that already included "Scrap" Chandler, Bud Metheny, and Emily Pittman; Lou Plummer started in 1956 and took the reins of the track team, and Pete Robinson started in 1957 and did the same for the new wrestling team. The small staff of five was not broken into an athletic department that was separate from the academic structure of the institution; the head of the Department of Physical Education ("Scrap" Chandler, at the time) was also the athletic director. So ingrained, in fact, were the coaches into the academic realm of the college that when the school began awarding four-year Bachelor of Science degrees in Physical Education in 1958, it was the coaches who had developed the curriculum. As Metheny recalled, "This four-year program was formulated by Mr. Chandler and Miss Pittman and Lou Plummer and myself. We did most of the work on the program, and we wanted to get this program for the college at the time, and we were accepted the very first time that we handed our synopsis of our program in."[46]

316. (Men) **Theory of Coaching and Officiating.** *Second semester; four classes per week; two credits.*

Study of approved methods in coaching baseball, track (cross country), swimming, and tennis. Analysis of the rules, officiating techniques and problem solving in officiating team sports. A minimum of twelve contact hours of practical experience in supervised officiating in the intramural program is required.

318. **Tests and Measurements in Physical Education.** *Second semester; three classes per week; three credits.*

This course is designed to acquaint students with tests and measurements in the fields of health and physical education, test construction, scoring and methods of using results.

320. **Applied Anatomy and Kinesiology.** *Second semester; three classes per week; three credits.*

Prerequisites: Biology 105.

A study of the principles of human motion; anatomical and mechanical analysis of individual skills in Physical Education activities.

410. **Organization and Administration of Physical Education and Health Education.** *Second semester; three classes per week; three credits.*

This course includes principles, practices, and procedures of health education and physical education on both the elementary and secondary school level.

(96)

Example 300- and 400-level PE courses, from the 1957 "General Catalogue." Courtesy of Special Collections and University Archives, Old Dominion University.

THE LITTLE EIGHT

Bud Metheny knew the next step in the advancement of Norfolk Division athletics was to earn more name recognition and state-wide visibility for the program, while creating an attractive environment for athletes. Certainly, one way to do that was to affiliate the school with an athletic conference that had championships. The Mason-Dixon Conference, which included schools in Virginia and Maryland, seemed like a logical choice, and Metheny had begun scheduling baseball games against teams in this league with regularity in the spring of 1955. He doubled from four to eight the number of basketball games scheduled against Mason-Dixon opposition from the 1954–55 season to 1955–56. The Division had applied for full membership, but on March 28, 1955, the *Baltimore Sun* (and others) reported that "The Mason-Dixon Conference's board of directors today turned down the applications of the Norfolk Division of the College of William and Mary and Shepherd College for admission into the 15-member loop. However, the directors of the league left the door open for the two institutions to reapply at a future date ... 'The conference directors decided not to expand at this time,' Hugh Stephens of Randolph-Macon College, loop president, said. 'We feel that the conference is a somewhat unwieldy group now. However, we will review the situation from time to time ... If Norfolk Division and Shepherd are still interested in the future, they may seek admission once more, and their applications will be considered.'"[47] As Metheny recalled his interaction with conference leadership, the true reason for exclusion in 1955 was less the pre-existing "unwieldy" nature of the conference, and more the fact that the Norfolk Division was not yet an NCAA member, and continued to have too many junior colleges on its athletic schedules.[48]

During the 1955 season—the time of the Mason-Dixon Conference's initial consideration of their application—four of the Braves' fourteen baseball opponents were non-four-year schools, and one was the Naval Academy "Plebes." However, the Norfolk Division had also improved its schedule to face Mason-Dixon member schools Bridgewater College and Hampden-Sydney College for the first time, and saw Randolph-Macon ("the Yankees of the South," as Fred Edmonds Jr. recalled)[49] return to the schedule for the first time in nine years, and Lynchburg College for the first time in seven years. The gradual year-by-year changes in the nature of competition that had been taking place in his Norfolk Division baseball schedule exemplified Bud Metheny's long-term philosophy of building his programs by scheduling better competition with increasing frequency, and in the fall of 1955, even though Mason-Dixon membership had been denied earlier in the year, the Norfolk

Division nonetheless reaped the first real and measurable reward for Metheny's coaching efforts on both the baseball diamond and the basketball hardwood. In that year, the Norfolk Division was included as a member of Virginia's "Little Eight" (formerly, of course, the "Little Seven"). Contrasted to the "Big Six," which included the biggest schools in the state such as the University of Virginia and Virginia Tech, the Little Eight consisted of the smaller colleges around Virginia, namely Randolph-Macon College, Hampden-Sydney College, Roanoke College, Bridgewater College, Richmond Professional Institute, Lynchburg College, Emory and Henry College, and now, the Norfolk Division of the College of William & Mary.

The Little Eight was not a true athletic conference with a president, board members, and bylaws; it was a "bragging-rights" circuit. Words such as "mythical" and "imaginary" were often used by contemporary sportswriters to describe it, since it was such a loose grouping. Bud Metheny remembered that the term for the circuit was originated by a Richmond-area sportswriter, although he couldn't recall which newspaper employed him.[50] In any case, Metheny had the clear foresight to recognize the value in having his Braves included in the unofficial conference, and lobbied for the inclusion of his program. "I had spoken to them about what's the chance of us being included in the weekly rankings of the Little Eight, and they saw no reason why not because we were meeting all of the requirements of the other schools, even though it was mythical," Metheny noted. "It was a public interest situation, and it brought the schools from all over the state together."[51]

Metheny also knew well the benefits that the affiliation would bring to the Norfolk Division. Even though it was only a bragging-rights conference, playing for those bragging rights was enough to put the Norfolk Division on the sports map. Newspapers across the state published Little Eight standings in their sports sections, and Little Eight champions were named; for a regional school, the name recognition that goes with such affiliation is simply invaluable. Inclusion in the

Little Eight meant that the Division's sports programs, students, and prospective future athletes had a goal and a point of pride for the first time, and evidence of such can be found throughout school publications of the time. A hopeful April 13, 1956, *High Hat* article was headlined "Track Team Potential Power in 'Little 8.'" The 1956 *Chieftain* yearbook (the first edition since Little Eight membership) proudly captioned a picture "CHAMPIONS!! In their first season of Little Eight competition, the Brave Mermen captured the League championship."

The 1956 season was the first for the baseball Braves as Little Eight members. Whether it was the name recognition that Metheny had begun to generate for the school, the chase for a conference championship that he could now offer, the simple numerical inevitability as the college steadily increased its "Day College" enrollment by 219 percent between the 1954–55 session and the 1959–60 session, or just the obvious fact that it is fun to play baseball, *The High Hat* reported on March 15, 1956, that Bud Metheny had the enviable problem of nine returning lettermen to go with a record number of hopefuls. The author of the article went unnamed, and one wonders if that wasn't due to the likely unsanctioned liberties that he or she had taken with Metheny's nickname, referring to him in print as "Bud Bud."

Nine 1955 Lettermen To Be Nucleus of 1956 Baseball Braves

Baseball season begins on April 3 for the Braves, but for **Author Beauregard "Bud Bud" Metheny**, there is no break between seasons as the schedule indicates. After ending basketball season, Bud jumped into baseball within a week, and found the turnout to be the largest number of men ever to report for baseball.

From The High Hat, *March 15, 1956. Courtesy of Special Collections and University Archives, Old Dominion University.*

Although the win represented a personal victory to Blows, who had yielded four days earlier to Butt at Chowan, it nevertheless held a more important connotation. **For the Braves and their able coach, Bud Metheny, it marked the debut of the Norfolk William and Mary baseball squad into the Little Eight. The victory over the powerful hitting Tigers served to set the local diamondners up as a recognized power in league circles.**

Chas. "Turk" Hoofnagle's opinion after a victory over Hampden-Sydney, from the April 13, 1956, High Hat. *Courtesy of Special Collections and University Archives, Old Dominion University.*

On the field, results continued to be solid, even as the scheduled competition continued to improve. The seventeen baseball games scheduled for 1956 featured primarily four-year college varsity programs (by a 71 percent majority), and, as Metheny cast an eye to the future, also featured Mason-Dixon Conference member schools in eight of those games. In their inaugural year of Little Eight competition, the Braves held their own with a 5–5 record—good for third place—as part of an overall 10–7 year.

As the school had only recently started offering four-year degrees, Coach Metheny was blessed with several returning baseball lettermen in both 1956 and 1957. In 1956, the number had been nine; in 1957, it was an impressive eleven.[52] In an interesting demonstration of the changing nature of the regional college in the late 1950s, *The High Hat* noted in March 1957 that of several newcomers who were expected to make an impact in the coming season, only one of four was from "local high schools"; the other three were from North Carolina (Vance Pittman) and Hampton (Buddy DeRyder), and a transfer from Georgia (Randy Lee). Again Metheny had improved the schedule, and the 1957 ledger comprised games against four-year college varsity squads in fifteen of seventeen cases. Only two games against the Newport News Apprentice School, a longstanding rival which, along with the Richmond Professional Institute, were the only foes to have appeared on every baseball schedule in Bud Metheny's Norfolk Division career, kept the Braves from playing a schedule made up exclusively of four-year varsity clubs. Shrewdly, Metheny had also scheduled May dates at the home fields of the University of Baltimore and Mount St. Mary's, two Maryland schools that were not in Virginia's Little Eight but *were* in the Mason-Dixon Conference. The experience gained playing against the more challenging schedule in 1957 season was invaluable and paid off in the near future, but the Braves' 8–9 won-loss mark was certainly one that did not meet Coach Metheny's expectations. Nonetheless, an 0–2 start in Little Eight play turned into a 6–4 mark for the season, good for second place in the league, and continued steady improvement in the program.

LITTLE EIGHT CHAMPIONSHIP

The High Hat reported a whopping twelve returning lettermen for the Braves in 1958, and noted that "Coach Methany [*sic*] has a strong schedule this season and has added four new names to the list: Western Maryland, Catholic University, American University, and Towson College."[53] Through no accident of scheduling, each of these teams were also Mason-Dixon Conference members, as Metheny obviously knew the future value of scheduling competition against these teams. Weather caused the cancellation of the contests against Western Maryland and Towson, and in fact would prove to be such an issue in 1958 that Hampden-Sydney coach Claud Milam would be quoted as saying, "This is the worst baseball season, as far as weather is concerned, I've ever seen."[54] Metheny, however, had settled on his strategy to move his program forward, and was undeterred by a rainout or two as he continued to add Mason-Dixon opponents to his yearly schedules. In 1957, conference members University of Baltimore and Mount St. Mary's had appeared in the Norfolk Division scorebook for the first time. In 1958, American University and Catholic appeared for the first time. And, in 1960, the Braves would play Towson for the first time.

Simply scheduling the competition guaranteed no results, but the Braves had certainly held their own in two seasons of Little Eight baseball, finishing third in 1956, and second to the Tigers of Hampden-Sydney in 1957. Even with respectable past results and returning lettermen, however, Norfolk Division supporters weren't ready to call themselves the 1958 favorites. Writer Cal Rosenthal noted in his *High Hat* preseason report that the "Braves are scheduled to be in the top three this year."[55] Even by the May 1st edition of the newspaper, in which a seven-game winning streak was reported, the author wasn't ready to let go of the underdog mentality, noting that, "The Braves who had twelve returning lettermen from last year's second place winner in the Little Eight and predicted to do no better this year, are the 'Cinderella' team of Virginia, as they have proven all preseason's expectations to be wrong, by taking a commanding lead in the race."[56]

Newspaper coverage of the college baseball season brought the Norfolk Division's name into homes all across Virginia and into Tennessee, and the race for the Little Eight crown was contested well into May, despite all the rainouts. By the fifth of May, the *Daily Press* in Newport News reported that "only two teams—RPI, which is 0–5, and Emory and Henry, which doesn't play a State game—are out of the running for Little Eight Laurels."

The race soon thinned to defending champions Hampden-Sydney, Randolph-Macon, and the Norfolk Division (referred to in most newspapers as "Norfolk William and Mary"). On May 13, left-hander Willis Bell took the mound for the Braves in Norfolk against the Hampden-Sydney Tigers, with a chance to notch his fifth victory and effectively knock the Tigers out of the Little Eight race, as well as earn some payback for the Braves after an embarrassing 13–2 early-season loss to the Tigers. "Willis, he was a little boy . . . He only weighed about 145 pounds, but he was a fine competitor,"[57] his coach later recalled, and against the Tigers he impressed, delivering a six-hit shutout and earning the victory as the Braves won by an easy 9–0 margin.

Randolph-Macon set the stage for a winner-take-all clash with the Norfolk nine on May 17 by defeating Richmond Professional Institute 23–7 in their penultimate game. With this momentum behind them, and with the title on the line, the Yellow Jackets squared off with the Braves of Norfolk the following day on the Jackets' home field in Ashland. Randolph-Macon took an early lead by plating a run in the bottom of the second against Bell, but immediately gave it back in the top of the third. A single run in the seventh gave Randolph-Macon the lead heading into the last inning, but Yellow Jacket starter Jimmy Smith and his relief help, Cig Howerton, couldn't hold it. Norfolk's Matt Marshall, a .466 hitter for the year,[58] led off the top of the ninth with a deep triple, and the Braves unleashed a total of five hits that led to four runs in the inning, securing a 5–2 lead, and, for the first time, Virginia's Little Eight baseball championship.

News of the Norfolk Division's first Little Eight title filled the school newspaper and the *Virginian-Pilot* over the next week, and was reported statewide. Coach Metheny had spent a decade upgrading his teams' schedules to drive his program to where he wanted it to be and had all along been willing to overmatch his own squads, and suffer "character-building" losses, as part of the grander vision for school and team. In his third baseball season in the Little Eight, his team compiled the best record in the state and stood as champions. Aside from the accolades in the *Virginian-Pilot*, one particularly notable assessment appeared in *The High Hat* after the victory: "The Spring Sports have, without a doubt, put the College of William and Mary in Norfolk on the map."[59] The baseball championship was an achievement to be celebrated, but it didn't put the "Brave baseball team" or the "Norfolk Division's sports programs" on the map. To the *High Hat* writer, it put the school as a whole on the map, which was undoubtedly a point of pride for Coach Metheny.

The Virginian-Pilot and *The Portsmouth Star* **Sports & Business** Sunday, May 18, 1958

Big League Baseball .... Page 2
Brooks of the Game
Cage Tourney in Portsmouth ... Page 3
Thru-out Golf .... Page 4
My My Blacout .... Page 6
Boxing, Fishing News .... Page 6
Baseball Nicknames .... Page 7

Section B

Tim Tam Comes On to Beat Lincoln Road in Preakness; Baseball Title to Norfolk W-M; Wilson Trackmen 2nd

Big news in Norfolk, May 18, 1958 (above and top right of next page). ©Virginian-Pilot. All rights reserved. Distributed by Tribune Content Agency, LLC. Top right of next page, copyrighted 1943–1965. Associated Press.

Congratulations Braves...

The Spring Sports have, without a doubt, put the College of William and Mary in Norfolk on the map. The Sports page of the Virginian-Pilot carried the page one headline of: "Baseball Title to Norfolk W-M, . . ." on Sunday, May 18. Page two of the same issue showed the team picture of the Braves, in all their splendor. On the following morning, Monday, May 19, page two of the same section in the same paper re-echoed: "Norfolk W-M Celebrates First Little Eight Title", with a picture of Willis 'Iron Premier' Bell. The article goes on to say, in part: "As far as the Little Eight was concerned, Norfolk William and Mary was strictly a darkhorse with most of the mention going to the perennial powers, Hampden-Sydney and Randolph-Macon".

Joe Cox, the only senior on the

Portion of May 23, 1958, article from The High Hat. *Courtesy of Special Collections and University Archives, Old Dominion University.*

Braves Top Jackets in Ninth, 5-2

Marshall's Triple Launches Rally; Bell Goes Distance

ASHLAND ⁂—Norfolk William and Mary packed nearly half its hits into a four-run ninth inning here Saturday and came from behind to whip Randolph-Macon, 5-2, for the State Little Eight baseball championship.

Matt Marshall's triple to deep left center field lit the fuse for the Braves after they had entered the last inning trailing, 2-1. Jim Fant's sacrifice fly plated Marshall with the tying run, but for Jimmy Smith, Randolph-Macon righthander, trouble had just begun.

Bell Scores Zeb

Singles by John Zeb and Leo Anthony finished Smith. Sig Howerton, his relief, was greeted with a bunt safety by winning pitcher Willis Bell, which sent Zeb scurrying home with the go-ahead run.

Before Howerton finally got the side out, John Demma had singled home another Norfolk W&M marker and two walks had forced in the final Brave tally.

Bell limited Randolph-Macon to six hits in capturing his sixth victory of the season and contributed two hits to the Braves' 11-hit attack. Joe Cox, Marshall and Anthony also had two safeties.

The triumph enabled Norfolk W&M, which had never won a Little Eight championship in any sport previously in its two seasons in the league, to finish its campaign with a 6-2 Little Eight mark and 12-3 over-all. Randolph-Macon finished 6-4 and 10-6 for the season.

Bell, a little 138-pound southpaw who has lost only two games this season, yielded a run in the second inning. The Jackets loaded the bases on W. Cox's double, a walk and a hit batsman. Another walk forced in the run.

In the third the Braves tied it up at 1-1. Anthony singled but was thrown out attempting to steal. Bell and Hunt singled. A bunt hit by Cox sent Bell to third and Bell scored on an error.

Jackets Break Tie

Randolph-Macon broke the 1-1 tie with a run in the seventh on a single by Chick Crawford, two sacrifice bunts on which Norfolk W&M infielders tried to make plays but failed, and Tom Jones' sacrifice fly.

Coach Bud Metheny will have practically his entire crop of Braves back again next season. Catcher Joe Cox is the only senior on the squad.

Picture on Page 2

Norfolk W&M	ab	r	h	rbi		Randolph-Macon	ab	r	h	rbi
Hunt, 2b	5	1	1	0		Crawford, ss	5	0	1	0
J. Cox, c	4	0	2	0		Hughes, cf	4	1	0	0
Harrison, cf	3	0	1	0		Keeton, 2b	3	0	1	0
aDemma, cf	2	0	1	1		W. Cox, lf	3	1	1	0
Marshall, 3b	5	1	2	1		Jones, 3b	3	0	1	1
Butler, 1b	5	0	0	0		Goulder, rf	3	0	1	0
Fant, rf-cf	3	0	0	1		Colley, c	3	0	1	0
Zeb, lf	4	1	1	0		Bowles, 3b	2	0	0	0
Anthony, ss	4	1	2	0		J. Smith, p	2	0	1	1
Bell, p	4	1	2	1		Howerton, p	0	0	0	0
Totals	**37**	**5**	**11**	**4**		**Totals**	**33**	**2**	**6**	**2**

aStruck out for Harrison in 8th.

Norfolk W&M .... 001 000 004—5
Randolph-Macon .... 010 000 100—2

E—Bowles, J. Smith, Anthony, Bell. PO-A—William and Mary 27-11, Randolph-Macon 27-15. LOB—William and Mary 8, Randolph-Macon 12. 2B—W. Cox. 3B—Marshall. SB—J. Cox, Hunt. S—Keeton, Hughes, J. Smith. SF—Jones, Fant.

	IP	H	R	ER	BB	SO
Bell		9	6	2	1	4
J. Smith		8⅔		4	2	4	4
Howerton		⅓				

HBP—Bell (Colley). WP—Bell. U—Saunders and Williams. T—2:15.

The Braves began 1959 as defending Little Eight champions, but in typical coach-speak, Bud Metheny wasn't yet ready to predict similar results for the upcoming season. In Bill Harrison's "Home of the BRAVES" column in the *Virginian-Pilot's* March 16, 1959 issue, Metheny was quoted as saying, "We'll be in the race . . . But it's hard to know how tough we'll be because everyone else is as improved as we are. Hampden-Sydney and Bridgewater are always tough and the rest of the league is better."[60] While the Hampden-Sydney prediction would ring true, Harrison himself would be describing 0–8 Bridgewater as the "league patsy" by May 4. But Coach Metheny had room for plenty of optimism at the start of

1959, with a returning staff that Harrison's season preview described as "practically intact," and credited by the same author with a sparkling 2.52 ERA in 1958. Returning Willis Bell had led the mound corps with a 6–2 mark with a 1.96 ERA, but the 1958 offense had also been up to the task, hitting at a .284 clip, and the 1958 defense had been ranked second nationally among small colleges, with a .961 fielding percentage.

The 1959 squad entered the season with no player who had ever hit a collegiate home run, but Coach Metheny's early-season concerns about his team's power were alleviated in the first game, when co-captains John Zeb and Jim Fant both connected for long balls in a season-opening win over Newport News Apprentice. The 1959 Braves never really looked back from that first game. After its initial win, neither the team's overall winning percentage nor its "in-conference" Little Eight winning percentage ever dipped below 67 percent. By season's end, the Braves had rolled to a 16–5 mark, splitting a pair of games each with traditional powers Hampden-Sydney and Randolph-Macon, and compiling a team batting average of .296, including Don Palumbo (a team-leading .366) and co-captain Matt Marshall (.358) among six .300 hitters.[61]

The importance of Little Eight affiliation to the Norfolk Division's baseball program is very clear from a review of the *Virginian-Pilot*'s 1959 articles covering the team. In 1958, before the Braves baseball team won the conference championship, there was no "Home of the BRAVES" column, but during the 1959 season, this column appeared weekly, and routinely covered the Braves' quest for a repeat title. In published game accounts in 1959, the newspaper mentioned the Little Eight 83 percent of the time, even though only 50 percent of those articles covered contests against Little Eight foes. Combined with periodic publishing of the Little Eight standings, it is clear that Little Eight membership had a huge impact in bringing more widespread attention to the small college, and in giving local sports fans teams that they could follow and support.

By season's end, though, Hampden-Sydney had won the mythical title, with their lone conference loss coming in an 8–3 defeat to the

Norfolk Division. Norfolk's 9–2 mark was solid, but still percentage points behind the Tigers' league record. Then, something unusual happened. Washington and Lee was not able to make their season-ending game against Hampden-Sydney, and so the Tigers, in most sporting fashion, challenged the Norfolk Division to a rubber game. While the game was not exactly a playoff, Coach Bud Metheny clearly considered it to be, and was quoted to that effect in the May 7 and May 9 editions of the *Virginian-Pilot*.[62] *Pilot* writer Bill Harrison cleared everything up on May 11, though, by saying "Tonight's game at Hampden-Sydney is a benefit game for the Crewe Kiwanis Club and will not count in records or league standings. A misunderstanding on all parts had the game being billed as a 'playoff game for the Little Eight title' but the game is strictly a charitable affair."[63]

However, it is doubtful that the players took it that way. In front of 500 baseball fans in Crewe (a number equating to approximately 25 percent of Crewe's 1960 population of 2,012),[64] Hampden-Sydney raced out to a seemingly comfortable 9–2 lead after six innings. Things turned in the top of the seventh inning, however, as Norfolk's Ralph Wetherington got the offensive parade started with a home run. Pitcher Ed Woolwine singled but was erased on a fielder's choice off the bat of leadoff man Leo Anthony—and then Anthony, and each of the seven batters who followed him, all scored. Two hits, four walks, and two errors, and the Braves emerged from the top of the seventh inning having turned a 9–2 disadvantage into an 11–9 lead. The Tigers would plate one in the eighth on star pitcher Leon Hawker's home run, but the scoring would end there. So, who won the Little Eight in 1959? *The High Hat's* Bob Ainsworth wrote definitively on May 22 that "W&M's Braves defeated Hampden-Sydney 11–10, in an unofficial game at the season's end to give the Braves a 17–5 won-lost record which surpassed that of the Tigers. Hampden-Sydney was official champion with a better winning percentage in Little Eight competition."

What it looks like when fourteen batters come to the plate in one inning; from Bud Metheny's 1959 scorebook. Courtesy of Special Collections and University Archives, Patricia W. and J. Douglas Perry Library, Old Dominion University Libraries, Norfolk, Virginia.

NCAA MEMBERSHIP

During that 1959 season, on April 29, the *Virginian-Pilot* reported a major accomplishment for the Norfolk Division:

> *Norfolk William and Mary was given an important boost toward athletic prominence here Tuesday. The college was accepted as an associate member of the National Collegiate Athletic Assn. at a meeting of the NCAA executive committee. In Norfolk J.C. (Scrap) Chandler, athletic director of the college since 1942, hailed the decision as 'one of the finest things that has happened to us.' Application was made two weeks ago.*
>
> *Full membership in the NCAA is apparently less than a year away. The college began instituting a four-year degree program four years ago. At present bachelor's degrees go through William and Mary in*

Williamsburg. The Norfolk W-M library—the key to independent accreditation—is to be dedicated in June. Soon thereafter the Southern Assn. of Accreditation is expected to send appraisers to the college . . .

Should the expected favorable ruling be forthcoming the college will give degrees in its own right and be eligible for full membership in the NCAA. However, with associate membership comes eligibility for participation in NCAA sponsored events . . .

The college fields teams in cross-country, basketball, swimming, track, wrestling, baseball and golf. Since going on four-year status the college has adhered to all NCAA regulations. Minor scheduling changes may be necessary in the future, Chandler says. The NCAA teams may meet only four-year colleges in regularly scheduled games. At present the Navy Plebes are met in track and basketball.

The progress made by Norfolk W-M athletics has been especially noticeable in the last two years. The Braves won the Little Eight titles in swimming and baseball in 1958 . . . [65]

Ironically, the news was published side-by-side with the recap and box score of the final official game the baseball Braves would play against any opponent other than a four-year school, a 5–2 victory over Newport News Apprentice authored by starting pitcher Willis Bell. Bob Stanley, no doubt out to prove himself after being described in unflattering fashion by sportswriter George McClelland as a "husky right-hander" in the April 2 *Virginian-Pilot*, and then as a "chunky pitcher" on April 24 by Bill Harrison of the same paper, saved the game for the Braves with a single pitch.

EARLY 1960S TEAMS

Coming off a Little Eight title in 1958, and a "so-close" second place in 1959, *The High Hat's* Gary Wasserman was optimistic about the Braves' prospects to start the decade of the 1960s. "With 7 returning

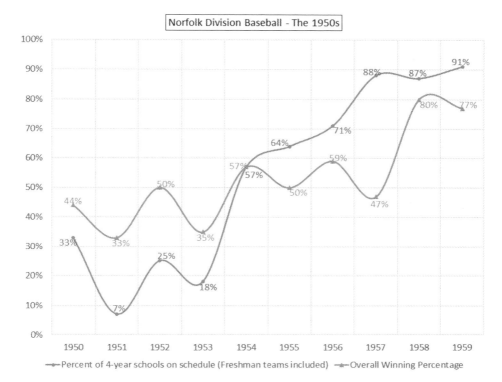

Norfolk Division Baseball - The 1950s

Percent of 4-year schools on schedule (Freshman teams included) — Overall Winning Percentage

lettermen and a total turnout of 25 men, Bud Metheny has initiated spring practice for the upcoming 1960 baseball season," Wasserman wrote in the March edition. "The Braves, who last year compiled a 17–5 season record and a 9–2 conference score, again are considered a top contender for the Little Eight baseball championship. Metheny feels that he will have difficulty with Hampden-Sydney, Bridgewater and Lynchburg. 'The Lynchburg field is nothing more than a band box, and I could throw a football over the right field fence,' said Metheny." The writer, however, offered no further insight as to why that might trouble the Braves, who had hit .302 as a team in 1959.

The *Virginian-Pilot* was somewhat more subdued in its March 19th season preview. "'We're only sure of a few starters,' Braves' coach Bud Metheny said Friday. 'The weather has restricted practice to indoors and I can't tell too much about the boys—particularly the newcomers.' . . . Only six veterans are assured of starting berths.

Pitchers Willis Bell and Ed Woolwine will start on the mound in the seven-inning contests [against Dartmouth]. Shortstop Leo Anthony, second baseman Kirkie Harrison, and outfielders Bert Harrell and Don Palumbo will be in the opening lineup."[66] Combined with a degree of lineup uncertainty, Metheny had also improved his schedule yet again. Permanently absent from the schedule were any opponents that were not four-year institutions. The Division's early-season contests were also significantly upgraded: Dartmouth returned to the schedule for March games, as did their Ivy League counterparts, the Bears of Brown University, as well as Maine state champions Colby College and Ithaca College from New York (although the scheduled March 28th game against Ithaca was not played).

Against this caliber of competition, the Braves got out to a decent, though unspectacular, start to the year. The Dartmouth series was limited to one game (and one loss) due to weather, but Norfolk won the series with Colby and took two out of three from Brown. Mixed in with a 7–2 victory over Washington and Lee, early returns left the team with a record of five wins against three losses and a tie. Unfortunately, this also marked the high-water point in the 1960 season, as the defense returned to early 1950s form, averaging 2.91 errors per game, despite the presence of noted double-play combination Leo Anthony and Kirkie Harrison up the middle. One loss during a seven-game losing streak prompted the *Virginian-Pilot* to comment that "Elon College came up from North Carolina Monday and handed Norfolk William and Mary one of its worst baseball defeats under Coach Bud Metheny [actually tied for fourth-worst, by run differential]. The score was 16–2 and Metheny couldn't recall a sadder afternoon 'for at least six or seven years.'"[67] On May 10, the paper offered this assessment, after a thirteen-run loss to Hampden-Sydney: "Norfolk William and Mary took a big step toward its worst baseball season Monday. About the only thing the Braves did right against Hampden-Sydney was show up for the game at the proper time. After the game started, Coach Bud Metheny's Braves did nothing right.

They committed nine errors and bowed, 19–6, at Larchmont." The situation was dire enough that entering the final game, the Braves had to win against league-leading Randolph-Macon just to stay out of last place in the Little Eight conference it had recently dominated. Throwing facts to the wind for the sake of a dramatic point, the *Pilot* noted prior to this game that "the Braves must win to avoid the Little Eight cellar for the first time since Bud Metheny began coaching the team 12 years ago. A loss would give the Braves a 3–7 league mark and drop them into the basement with RPI." Of course, for the first seven of Metheny's years, it would have been impossible to have been in the cellar of a league his team was not in, but perhaps due to the inspirational effect of this dramatic license, Metheny's team did go on to defeat Randolph-Macon by a 5–2 score, finishing with a 4–6 conference record and 9–12–1 overall mark.

Despite the mediocre 1960 results, the name recognition Coach Metheny was building for his program began to pay dividends in his ability to recruit players to the school. The ability to offer the chance to earn a four-year degree had doubtlessly enabled him to recruit better talent in the late 1950s, and on his 1960 roster he already had middle-infield stars in Leo Anthony and Kirkie Harrison, both of whom were future members of Old Dominion's Sports Hall of Fame, although Anthony is more celebrated for his basketball achievements. To the 1961 team, Metheny also added future ODU Hall of Famers Wayne "Sparky" Parks, a third baseman, and Bob Walton, a pitcher. Despite the lack of available scholarship help, Metheny's growing ability to recruit top baseball talent would continue, as success bred success. To the 1962 team he would add Fred Kovner and Billy Boyce, both of whom would later sign professional contracts; to the 1964 team, he would add Denny Riddleberger, who would go on to play in the major leagues. Beyond that, Metheny was also starting to be able to compete with the big schools and keep some of the best local talent local. Mel Renn, a member of the 1964 team, remembers turning down a scholarship offer to the University of Virginia before ultimately ending up in Norfolk.[68]

The 1961 squad was vastly improved over the previous year, in almost all statistical categories, although probably most notably in its defense. While the 1960 version had committed 2.91 errors per game, the 1961 team cut that by more than half, reducing the rate to 1.42 per game.[69] The pitching staff reduced the number of walks issued by 1.61 per game, and the combination of better pitching and better defense keeping runners off base produced the obvious result: fewer runs allowed. In total, the 1961 team only allowed 3.25 runs per game (including unearned runs), which was a dramatic improvement by almost 2.5 runs per game from the year before. As the pitching improved, the offense did the same, scoring almost two runs per game better than the year before.

Results in the scorebook were predictable. The team opened the year with the same Northern opponents in Dartmouth, Colby, and Brown, and won four games in six tries, splitting two each with Dartmouth and Brown, and sweeping two from Colby, while only giving up a total of seven runs in those six contests. This year, it only got better after the early-season games against Northern teams, as the Braves swept doubleheaders first from Towson State, and then Lynchburg to open the Little Eight season. Other than an April 17th home doubleheader loss to Guilford that saw Coach Metheny's team drop a pair of one-run games—one in extra innings, and one in which the Braves left the tying run on third in the bottom of the last inning—this team sailed through a twenty-four-game schedule, amassing eighteen wins and featuring some outstanding individual performances. Newcomer Wayne Parks batted .375 for the year, to lead the team. Sophomore pitcher Frank DeMille had a season that would be simply unheard-of in today's game, starting eight games, winning eight games, and completing every single one of them. On April 29, freshman Bob Mears threw a reported one-hitter against

Bridgewater on their home field, and the *Virginian-Pilot* noted the next day that "In the nightcap, the only hit off Mears came in the first inning. Phil Kincheloe slammed a hard-hit ball down the third-base line that bounced off the chest of Norfolk W&M third baseman Wayne Parks." Bud Metheny's scorebook, however, showed that play as an error, with no evidence of any post-game erasure to grant his pitcher some "home cooking."[70]

In Little Eight play, the Braves did not lose a single contest, starting with the doubleheader sweep of Lynchburg and ending with a statement win over Hampden-Sydney. Those same Tigers had kept the race close until the last two games, as the Norfolkians carried a 7-0 record against the Tigers' 7-2. Coach Metheny's 1961 team had already avenged 1960's 19-6 loss to Hampden-Sydney earlier in the season by a lopsided 9-2 score, and after a victory over Randolph-Macon put the Braves at 8-0 with no challengers still mathematically remaining, the only thing left was the icing—a 5-4 win over the Tigers, and the completion of an unblemished Little Eight season.

Virginian-Pilot sportswriter Bill Harrison wrote after the last game that "The Braves thus wrapped up the best season in the school's history with an 18-6 overall record and 9-0 in the league."[71] In terms of winning percentage, this wasn't true; the 1958 team had won 80 percent of its fifteen games, and the 1959 team had won 77 percent of its games, compared to the 75 percent won by the 1961 version. Those earlier teams still scheduled the Newport News Apprentices, however, and didn't face competition such as the established Ivy League schools. What *can* be said about the 1961 team is it certainly was the best team in terms of talent that Bud Metheny had ever put together on a baseball field, and the talent was still getting better.

The 1962 team returned many veterans, but still faced some changes. Frank DeMille transferred to study at East Carolina, and two key early-season freshman contributors were ruled academically ineligible on March 26, just nine days and six games into the schedule:[72]

Fred Edmonds Jr., who had already recorded two wins over twelve shutout innings pitched, and right fielder Jerry Hammer, who over six games was hitting at a .421 clip to go with six walks. The team was still laden with talent, however, and featured an incredible six future members of the Old Dominion Sports Hall of Fame—Kirkie Harrison, Wayne Parks, Bob Walton, and newcomers Fred Kovner and Jimmy Zadell, along with Edmonds. Walton, Kovner, and Zadell would also be first- or second-team All-Americans during their Norfolk tenure, and Kovner would go on to play professionally after college.

Adding to this stacked roster, Coach Metheny also had catcher Billy Boyce in the fold. Boyce would account for eight of the Norfolk Division's ten home runs in 1962, before signing with the New York Mets, who were likely looking for all the catching help they could find after their 40–120 maiden voyage in 1962 produced eight home runs, forty-five runs driven in, and a .242 batting average from that position.[73] Of Boyce's 1962 collegiate home runs, all came in Norfolk, and *Virginian-Pilot* writer Dan Richards wrote on May 12 that "Norfolk William and Mary is fortunate this year. Besides having a winning (15–3) baseball team, it has a 350-foot fence at its home diamond, Larchmont Field. And more important, the Monarchs have catcher Billy Boyce, who has cleared this fence eight times this year for a school record . . . Eight homers in 18 games is unusual for any baseball player—and Boyce is only a college freshman. NCAA statistics reveal that eight home runs were enough to lead the Atlantic Coast Conference last year. And the Southern Conference leader only had four . . . Billy has no home runs on the road, but he's hit a few high and far—right into an opponent's glove. 'Most of the teams we play have no fences,' explains a teammate. 'They just play Boyce about 400 feet back and let him hit away.'" Adding a dramatic flair that contrasts with almost everything ever written about Bud Metheny, Richards also recounted recent game activity by saying that " . . . On the second strikeout, Billy swung at a slow curve and looked so ridiculous that he stepped out of the box and laughed at himself. Norfolk W&M coach Bud Metheny turned red with anger. 'Get mad, Billy, don't stand there and take it,' he roared. Boyce just smiled. 'Gee whiz, coach, I can't get mad,' he replied."[74]

With this assortment of talent, the team, now playing as the Monarchs, recorded the best winning percentage in the school's history, at 84 percent. In many statistical categories, the 1962 team was actually slightly inferior to the 1961 team, but still outscored opponents by an average margin of 6.16–4.21, or almost two runs better. Atypically, Metheny continued to tinker all year with who would man his outfield positions and where they would hit in the lineup, and he spread the pitching duties around more than usual. The results, however, justified the maneuvers. After his team dropped the opening contest to Dartmouth, they lost only two more games, to Lynchburg and Randolph-Macon respectively, during the season. Had a scheduled April 13th doubleheader against Bridgewater not been rained out, there may have been some finality to the Little Eight race in 1962, but with two losses in conference play, the 1962 Monarchs had to settle for a tie with Bridgewater's Eagles, who matched their 6–2 circuit record.

	RUNS SCORED	EARNED RUNS SCORED	RUNS ALLOWED	EARNED RUNS ALLOWED	ERRORS	OPPONENT ERRORS	HR	SB	BB TAKEN	BB ALLOWED	STRIKEOUTS (BY DIVISION PITCHERS)
1960 (22 GAMES)	4.54	3.59	5.68	3.82	2.91	2.23	0.18	1.55	5.18	5.86	5.18
1961 (24 GAMES)	6.42	5.17	3.25	2.50	1.42	2.63	0.38	1.88	4.83	4.25	5.29
1962 (19 GAMES)	6.16	5.11	4.21	2.89	2.05	2.26	0.53	1.63	4.21	3.58	5.53

Early 1960s Norfolk Division per-game averages, compiled from Coach Bud Metheny's scorebooks.

1961 and 1962 Little Eight trophies. In possession of the family of ODC pitcher John Ingram.

CHANGES AT THE NORFOLK DIVISION

A name change to "Monarchs" for the 1962 season was just one change of many that the school experienced in the early 1960s, as the still-developing school fought for its identity. The loose conference affiliation with the Little Eight had helped with name recognition and given school supporters a point of pride, but the school's leadership also sought academic independence, especially as the Norfolk school became one of the largest institutions of higher learning in the state.

Although independence was not yet assured at the time, the pulse of student sentiment by 1960 can be taken from an April *High Hat* story of that year, gauging opinion as it pertained to the name of the institution. "With the possibility of the Norfolk Division of William and Mary becoming independent and having to make a name change, the Journalism class under Professor John F. West, as a special assignment, approached students and other people on campus with the following question: Do you think the name of the College should be changed? If

OLD DOMINION COLLEGE  Norfolk 8, Virginia

October 10, 1962

Dear Students:

It is my pleasure to welcome you, the student body, at the beginning of this new school year. This year is unusual in many ways, and I am sure that our freshmen will experience a greatly different emotion from the one experienced by our upperclassmen as they return to the campus. Our returning students have worked and played under the banner of Norfolk William and Mary for as long as three years; the revered name of William and Mary has become a part of them and cannot be discarded easily. Our faculty, of course, share this feeling of loss and will miss the tradition and other fine things associated with the name.

There comes, however, into the lives of all individuals and organizations a time when it is essential that their own identities be established and that they pursue on their own abilities the goals which are set for them. So be it with our College.

The name "Old Dominion College" has been selected by our Board of Visitors as a name which will give us an immediate identity with the great Commonwealth of Virginia and which will challenge us to our best endeavour to prove worthy of this historical name. The leadership supplied to our Nation by our State in the past is unexcelled. We of Old Dominion College proudly hope to continue to supply this type of leadership.

Our College is not "old" in terms of age as we were founded only thirty-two years ago. Neither was our Commonwealth "old" when given the name "Old Dominion." For the word "old" was used as a term of endearment and not age. When Charles II was restored to the throne of England he expressed his gratitude to Virginia for the steadfast loyalty and support given him by the Colony during his long period of banishment. In speaking of the Colony he expressed this feeling by referring to it as "my old [dear and loved] Dominion."

It is hoped that in the years ahead you will learn to love and appreciate your Old Dominion College as it can mean much to you in the happiness and success you derive from life. This should be a pact of mutual benefit. The success of your College will redound to your glory as will your own success reflect credit on your College. It is my sincere wish that each of you may profit from your stay on this campus and that you will always proudly support Old Dominion College as it grows in service and prestige through the years.

Very truly yours

Lewis W. Webb, Jr.
President

OLD DOMINION COLLEGE — FOUNDED 1930 — FORMERLY NORFOLK COLLEGE OF WILLIAM AND MARY

Letter to students in the October 1962 Mace and Crown, *announcing big changes. Courtesy of Special Collections and University Archives, Patricia W. and J. Douglas Perry Library, Old Dominion University Libraries, Norfolk, Virginia.*

not, why not? . . . The poll showed that the number of people wishing the College to keep the same named [*sic*] doubled the number wishing to change the name. Those who wished the name to remain the same felt that the prestige associated with the 'old' name could never be replaced. . . . Those who wished a change in name suggested Norfolk College, Tidewater University, Norfolk University and Chesapeake College as possibilities. Others said the name should be something that is identifying, but they had not heard one that they liked yet. Another name that was suggested and that received support among students interviewed was 'Webb College.'"[75]

MASON-DIXON CONFERENCE MEMBERSHIP

As inclusion in the Little Eight had helped raised the school's profile through its sports programs, so too did the mascot change and ultimate academic independence, both occurring in 1962. By November 1961, only five years since membership in Virginia's Little Eight had generated such excitement for the Norfolk Division's sports teams, one Charles Baldwin had already taken pen in hand and authored the following lines for the school newspaper, newly renamed for 1961 as the *Mace and Crown*: "It's about time we at the Norfolk College of William and Mary came out of the 'Dark Ages' in varsity sports in Virginia and saw the light. We've played in the Class 'D' Little Eight league for so long that fans at school and in the area have come to associate it with the Little League. This last point is rightly taken, for in fact, the Little '8' is not a sanctioned conference at all; rather it is a collection of small colleges in Virginia that have one thing in common, athletic teams . . . It seems to me that we have outgrown this 'Little' league and should at least try double A sports, namely the Mason-Dixon conference, which is a member of the National Collegiate Athletic Association . . . Coach Bud Metheny says, 'We'll be in it. It's something the school has needed for a long time.' He said further that 'it would bring recognition to the school and bring a better calibre [sic] of ball to the area."[76] Indeed, Bud Metheny had been angling toward that very goal since at least 1955.

The businessman in Metheny knew what had to be done after the Norfolk Division's failed 1955 bid to join the Mason-Dixon circuit: join the NCAA, obey the necessary regulations, and wait two years. He summarized the Norfolk Division's successful 1962 bid by simply saying that the Mason-Dixon Conference "sent an investigating team here, and they found out that everything they wanted we had abided by, and we had accomplished, and so as a result they let us join the Mason-Dixon Conference."[77] Metheny, the businessman, knew that a conference affiliation that stretched the school's sphere of influence into Washington, DC, and Maryland was advantageous for the growth and development of the school. Metheny, the sportsman, however, also liked what it could do for his athletes on the field. "Now we are in a conference, and in every sport we have a goal to shoot for, a conference championship," he recalled in 1975. "Also, it gave us the opportunity to get into the NCAA regionals and playoffs. So being in a conference was a big asset to our program."[78]

In 1940, the Mason-Dixon Collegiate Conference had taken the general shape it would retain into the early 1960s, by the combination of schools from two preexisting leagues: the Maryland College League and the Mason-Dixon Conference (a precursor loop that had begun primarily for track and field sometime around 1936). In its 1940 incarnation, the league consisted of nine member institutions, according to a report in the Wilmington, Delaware Morning News: the University of Delaware, American University, Catholic University, Johns Hopkins University, Mt. St. Mary's College, State Teachers' College (Towson State), Washington College, Western Maryland College, and Loyola College.[79] By late 1941, the league was beginning to see some success, and an article in the Baltimore Sun on December 7—the same date of the Japanese attack on Pearl Harbor—noted that "basket ball [sic] and baseball competitions of this expanded group have become well-established. In the basket-ball playoff, as a matter of fact, the conference was able to earn funds to help in its organizational and promotion work. There is a trophy at stake for this event and a baseball prize is also awarded." At the time of this reporting, potential Mason-Dixon football and tennis competitions were under discussion among member schools, as well.[80]

Despite the optimism in that report, the World War II years were lean for the conference (as they were for many intercollegiate leagues), but the Mason-Dixon continued operations, and by 1943, was awarding championships in basketball, baseball, wrestling, cross-country, track and field, and soccer, although at least in baseball, no champions would be named between the years of 1944 through 1946. But as the league gained some amount of prestige, it also began to grow in membership. In 1941, the year after its inception, the conference had expanded into Virginia and added Randolph-Macon College in January, and Bridgewater College in March. By 1955, when it rejected the application of the Norfolk Division, membership had grown to fifteen schools.[81]

The landscape of intercollegiate athletics in the early decades of the Mason-Dixon Conference was much different than that of 2021. Several schools also retained membership in other conferences, such as Lynchburg College, which was also a member of the Dixie Conference. As such, the Mason-Dixon policy on scheduling league games was to leave it to member institutions, while the conference only mandated minimums, as a September 1963 article in the *Gettysburg Times*, in reference to the conference basketball tournament, explained: "Teams which do not meet tournament qualification requirements of nine games against six different opponents will have no opportunity for postseason berths, but games against these teams will count in league standings. A new requirement passed last spring demands that tourney games be played with personnel eligible for NCAA postseason play."[82] Demonstrating some of the scheduling quirks that came with the loose conference policies, in 1963 (Old Dominion's first year of baseball competition in the Mason-Dixon), American University only played seven conference baseball games, while Loyola College and the University of Baltimore both played fourteen. Old Dominion played ten, but only competed against three of the other six teams in the South Division of the Mason-Dixon.[83]

This was a time before the NCAA had established full dominion over intercollegiate athletics. In March 1956, the Mason-Dixon Conference rejected a rule about transfer athletes that would have conformed to NCAA regulations, but the Danville *Bee* noted that, in the hopes of membership eligibility at future NCAA-sanctioned events, "All members of the Conference were urged to join the NCAA. Five of the league's 15 members do not belong at present."[84] The Norfolk Division joined the NCAA in 1959, and despite such seemingly loose and decentralized athletic governance at both the conference and national levels, in 1962 the Mason-Dixon Conference still offered a lot of advantages to the newly independent and renamed "Old Dominion College." The conference affiliation, for example, offered name recognition for ODC in such distant markets as Baltimore, Washington, DC, and Richmond. One might be inclined to think that conference membership might also have served to diminish the complaints of school sportswriter Charles Baldwin (who had referred to the Little Eight as "Class D" in November of 1961), but such was not the case. By the May 1962 issue of the *Mace and Crown*, Baldwin could be found with fresher complaints, this time regarding the difficulties associated with having to remember the new school name, new mascot name, and even the name of his own publication.[85]

In 1962, Old Dominion College was accepted by the conference, and the baseball team would begin 1963, its inaugural season in conference play, defending an overall 16–3 record from the season before. Familiar foes and Little Eight rivals such as Hampden-Sydney College and Randolph-Macon College—between them, winners of eight of the past twelve conference championships—would now stand as conference opponents in the way of Coach Bud Metheny's lofty goals for his newly named Monarch baseball team (now clad in Yankee pinstripes) and his college.

BUD METHENY'S "OTHER LIFE"—BASKETBALL

While making substantial progress on the baseball diamond, Coach Bud Metheny continued to stay busy in the service of his institution during the cold-weather months, as well. Since his inaugural season in the 1948–49 campaign, Metheny had continued to lead the Braves men's basketball team into the early 1960s. Of his early years at the Division, Metheny recalled that "it was easier to update the baseball because we could get these teams coming South. And they wanted to play. Whereas in basketball we had to play the teams that were located in the state or right outside the state, and they already had established schedules. It's very difficult to break in schedules once they get established. And so it was easier to schedule baseball than it was basketball."[86]

Nonetheless, similar to his schedule during baseball season, when he might be found playing professionally, managing a Norfolk City League team, or speaking at a local sports club, Coach Metheny didn't rest during his down time as the leader of

Chandler Says It's 'Big Help'

BALTIMORE (Special) — The Mason-Dixon Conference Sunday expanded its membership to 16 schools by approving the membership application of Norfolk William & Mary.

Although the Norfolk institution had been playing many Mason-Dixon Conference teams for the past few years and had sent representatives to previous meetings, this was the first time the school had applied for membership.

Norfolk W&M, which will sever its ties with William & Mary later this year and become a separate liberal arts school, will become eligible for M-D athletic competition on Sept. 1. The name of the college also will be changed.

SIX SPORTS

The newest league member is expected to compete in basketball, baseball, swimming, wrestling, cross country and track.

"It's wonderful," said J. C. (Scrap) Chandler, Norfolk William & Mary athletic director, when he heard the news. "This will help us a lot. We have been playing the six Mason-Dixon Conference teams in Virginia and now we hope to improve our schedules in all sports."

With the admission of Norfolk William & Mary, the executive committee of the conference was asked to study a possible realignment of the north and south divisions, and to make a report at the annual meeting in Washington Sept. 9.

An excerpt from the March 19, 1962, Virginian-Pilot, under the headline "Norfolk W&M Joins Mason-Dixon League." ©Virginian-Pilot. All rights reserved. Distributed by Tribune Content Agency, LLC.

the Norfolk Division's men's basketball team, either. Metheny was involved in the Virginia state high-school basketball tournament as committee chair for the Norfolk Sports Club in the early 1950s, and also refereed some local high school games, where he no doubt kept an eye on the upcoming local talent. In one particularly colorful example from his time as a referee, the *Daily Press* reported a contest between Hampton and Cradock High Schools on February 11, 1954, as a "nightmarish basketball game that included a fight, 60 personal fouls and a brief flare-up between the Admirals' coach and an official." The Cradock coach apparently took exception to Metheny's officiating, and the paper reported that "Henry 'Hank' Hambrecht, the Craddock [sic] coach, argued with ref Bud Metheny in one of their many verbal flurries of the night and the Admirals drew a technical foul . . . the only after-game action was another argument between the official and the Cradock coach on the floor."[87]

Coach Metheny also made time to coach the Amateur Athletic Union "Snow White" team, a local women's club. He never coached the women's team at the Division, but he recalled his AAU charges feeding that program, and so in this sense he contributed in another way to the Norfolk Division's progress, as he assisted in establishing a winning tradition in a program that would become a powerhouse in the 1970s and win a national championship in 1985. "I didn't coach the Norfolk Division William and Mary girls' basketball team," Metheny recalled in 1975. "But I had these same girls on an AAU team, and they were fine athletes. And we went on to national play at St. Joseph, Missouri, represented as the Snow White team. Now, that's when you could play outside the school as well as for the school. Now, girls' teams were not governed by this rule as the boys were. The boys could play for the school team, but they couldn't play outside. The girls could. So, the girls became very good. In their AAU play they won 125 and lost three. In national play they won five and lost three. And these same girls were playing for the college. So we had a fine team."[88]

His primary basketball coaching duty at the time, however, was still leading the Division men's program. After Metheny's initial 5–0 start and eventual 11–5 overall mark in 1948–49, success in terms of wins and losses was a little harder to come by in the early 1950s. In the eight succeeding seasons, Metheny's Division teams played to an overall 78–92 record. But in later interviews and in typical fashion, Coach Metheny rarely failed to discuss his strategy for the development of his program: Play better competition and let the results follow. While a 7–15 win-loss mark in the 1954–55 season, as an example, may not look like much progress when viewed on its own, seen through the wider lens of the entire decade (and the first part of the 1960s), that progress can be seen clearly in the graph below. The Braves' basketball winning percentage is plotted along with the percentage of collegiate-level talent they played in a given year. When Bud Metheny upgraded the competition on his schedule in his second year, his win percentage suffered. Another significant schedule upgrade in the 1954–55 season resulted in another dip in win percentage, but then in the seven years that followed, as the percent of

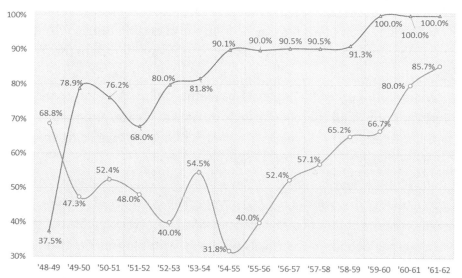

collegiate-level opponents stayed above 90 percent, the win percentage continued to increase in each of those seasons.[89]

Having no scholarship money to recruit specialized athletes, Coach Metheny's basketball players were often his baseball players, too. From Metheny's first basketball team in 1948–49, Joe Agee, "Sack" Reviere, and John Vitasek also all played baseball; using 1961–1962 as a random comparative example, so did Wayne Parks, Fred Edmonds Jr., and Billy Boyce.

In 1957, a two-sport athlete arrived on campus and immediately put the basketball program on the map. As Garrett and Shampoe recorded the events of that year, "For most of his early years at the Norfolk Division of William and Mary, Bud Metheny always seemed to be one player short in putting together his dream team. In the fall of 1957, a young freshman donned the No. 5 jersey for the Braves, and Metheny's prayers for a player to fill the role as team sharpshooter and leader were answered. Leo Anthony had arrived. . . . An all-sport star at Granby High, Anthony soon earned the respect and admiration of Metheny and his collegiate teammates. With veterans Holt Butt and Bob Johnson providing strong support, the Braves began the 'Anthony Era' with a record of twelve wins and nine losses. Over the next three seasons, Anthony and Bobby Hoffman guided the teams to records of 15–8, 12–6, and 16–4. In 1959, Anthony was named the school's first All-American and finished with 2,181 total points while averaging more than twenty-six points a game. In 1980, Leo Anthony was part of the inaugural group to be named to the Old Dominion Sports Hall of Fame."[90]

Such was Anthony's impact that the 1961 *Chieftain* yearbook devoted a full page to his achievements and a re-telling of the events of "Leo Night" in Norfolk, at which Anthony had received a watch, an inscribed cup, and the basketball he had used to score his 2,000th point. To top things off, Coach Metheny also retired his number "5" jersey at the ceremony. Recognizing Anthony's importance to the small school hungering for bigger things, the author of the yearbook article wrote that the "fans, coaches, and players will never forget him and will try their very best to keep alive the prestige Leo has helped our school attain."[91]

Success breeds success, and as Bud Metheny strove to build his school's profile and name recognition, his ability to add talents such as Leo Anthony had tremendous impact, as it contributed not only to on-field results, but also to regional, state-wide, and even national recognition. Leo Anthony's importance in this regard, coming at an inflection point in the school's trajectory, can hardly be overstated. His Hall of Fame entry with Old Dominion University notes the following achievements for the All-American who played for the little college in Norfolk:

> Leo Anthony, holding 11 of Old Dominion University's 13 cage records when he graduated in 1961 was the first basketball All-American to play for the University.
>
> The six-foot guard finished his ODU basketball career in February of 1961 by scoring 60 points against Lynchburg College and becoming the third highest scorer in the history of the State of Virginia.
>
> Besides Little All-American honors, Leo was named to the All-Virginia team four times and voted Player of the Year in the state twice.
>
> In the 1979–80 season Anthony's single career scoring mark of 2,181 points was broken by Ronnie Valentine. Anthony still owns the highest scoring average in a season at 31.0 and the highest career average at 26.6.
>
> Anthony had 29 30-point games during his career from 1957–61. Anthony averaged 24.1 as a freshman, 25.3 as a sophomore, 26.3 as a junior. He scored 35 or more points in a game 12 times.
>
> A player with unusual quick foot movement, Leo was known for his ability to get free for his shots and execute them. He developed innovative shooting methods against double-teaming and the many box-and-one defenses.[92]

The key to that unusually quick foot movement? Bud Metheny may have given away the secret to some of Anthony's success in a 1975 interview, when he offered the interesting fact that "to think about dedication, Leo, the four years that he was at the college here, he took dancing from Arthur Murray Studio all four years. And he was a beautiful dancer, but this gave him the poise on the floor and deception. It really made him great."[93]

After Anthony's career was complete, Coach Metheny actually improved his basketball team's winning percentage to 86 percent in the 1961–62 season, with an 18–3 record that represented the school's best-ever. The three seasons that followed resulted only in an even ledger of wins against losses, but these would represent the final seasons in Metheny's tenure as the Norfolk Division/Old Dominion basketball coach. As a longtime understudy to J.C. "Scrap" Chandler, Bud Metheny had to divest himself of some responsibilities when he received the well-earned opportunity to lead Old Dominion College's entire athletic department as its Director, when Chandler decided to retire in 1963.

Bud Metheny assumed his new duties as athletic director on July 1 of that year. After many years of coaching both baseball and basketball, as well as tending to his duties as an instructor and willingly performing community outreach for the school, Metheny realized that with the weight of new responsibility, it was time to find someone else to lead the basketball team. On May 26, 1964, the *Daily Press* of Newport News reported that the search was on: "Old Dominion's search for a basketball coach to replace Bud Metheny will end this week—one way or another. . . . Metheny who wants to restrict his activities to baseball and duties as athletic director, says the field has been sliced to three—'all out of this area.' If an agreement isn't made in the next several days, the ex-Yankee outfielder seems destined to one more year as the Monarchs' cage boss . . . "

No replacement was named in 1964, and Bud Metheny did, in fact, stay on for one more year. And in that time, he appears to have also developed an aura of invincibility, or benefited from short-term memories, such that many forgot some of the losing years he had experienced, and instead remembered them happily as winning years. On December 12, 1963, the *Mace and Crown* wrote that "Metheny came to this college in 1948 at a time when it was still the Norfolk Division of William and Mary. He has coached baseball and basketball ever since. He has never had a losing season in either sport. Not until last year when the Monarch cagers lost 12 games did any of Metheny's teams ever lose in double figures." A student following the program would have had to have been in school for six years to remember such lean years, but per the records in the ODU Basketball Media Guide, Metheny actually had five losing seasons between the span of 1949–50 to 1955–56. While his basketball teams were typically around the .500 mark in that period, they also experienced double-digit losing seasons in each season from 1949–50 to 1956–57.

Old Dominion Seeks Basketball Mentor

NORFOLK (AP)—Old Dominion College has launched a search for a basketball coach, Athletic Director Arthur (Bud) Metheny said Friday.

Metheny said that applications are now being accepted.

Appearing in the Daily Press, *February 8, 1964. Copyrighted 1943–1965. Associated Press.*

On February 28, 1964, as the 1963–64 season wound down, the *Mace and Crown* declared that "The chances were slim last December that the Monarchs would finish with a winning season. It was feared that this would be Bud Metheny's first losing cage season in his 15 years as coach." The 1964 *Troubadour* yearbook got into the act as well, noting at year's end that, "The Monarchs, faced with the possibility of having their first losing season under Bud Metheny in his 15 years as coach, found the winning way through the leadership of sophomore Randy Leddy and seniors Bob Shibley, Ronnie Byrd and Wayne

Parks." Garrett and Shampoe, too, in *Old Dominion University Men's Basketball*, credit Metheny with sixteen winning seasons between 1948 and 1965.[94]

Perception may be the better part of reality, and maybe the perception of a program with a winning tradition allowed Bud Metheny as athletic director to be able to pursue talents such as Cliff Hagan to replace himself as basketball coach. Hagan had been a member of a national championship team at the University of Kentucky, and in 1964 was still an impact player in the NBA, averaging 18.4 points for the St. Louis Hawks. That Metheny could interest Hagan in the Old Dominion job speaks to the school's rising profile, but ultimately it would be March of 1965 before Bud Metheny would name his basketball replacement, tabbing the twenty-nine-year-old Sonny Allen, who would continue to raise the basketball program to greater heights. As Metheny remembered his interview process:

> *Well, with [program supporters] Mr. Wilkins and Mr. Howard, I sat down and talked to them about it because I wanted to bring them into our program, too. Then we advertised that we were in the market for a new coach. And we had many applicants. And it was narrowed down to—well, first of all, we brought in Cliff Hagan the year before. And Cliff was very interested, but at the last minute he stayed with the pros. So, we had to wait a year. And during that time we did some more investigating and then it came down to two people, a high school coach out of Indiana and Coach Allen, who had been a freshman coach at Marshall University. And after we had interviewed them and compared their credentials, we felt that Coach Allen could do the best job for Old Dominion University. And so that's what it really boiled down to in the end was personal contact with Coach Allen, which we were impressed with.[95]*

While Bud Metheny's record of success and progress as a basketball coach at the Norfolk Division is not as clearly demonstrable in terms of NCAA titles as it is for baseball, the basketball foundation that he built at the Division, and then Old Dominion College, still stands on its own as an incredible achievement. Metheny led the baseball team for thirty-one seasons; no other coach is within two decades of that level of service. Metheny, however, is also the longest-tenured *basketball* coach the school has ever had, logging seventeen seasons at the helm, five years more than Blaine Taylor, who is the next closest at twelve years.[96]

One could view Metheny's overall 198–163 basketball won-loss mark as somewhat pedestrian, since a winning percentage of 54.8 percent in today's collegiate environment probably wouldn't permit a coach to stay on the sidelines for seventeen years. But the true measure of success is not obvious in those numbers. Before Coach Metheny, the program did not have a winning history, and had played to an exactly even 159–159 record, according to the school's media guide. 1948 to 1963 was a time of significant changes at the school, and a period in which Metheny also continuously upgraded his schedule every year with an eye to the future benefits. It was a time that saw the school go from basketball schedules heavily dependent on military and club teams, to freshman and JV teams, and finally to four-year institutions. The same period saw the school's inclusion in the "Little Eight," the Mason-Dixon Conference, and the NCAA, and as Bud Metheny led that advance, he won many more basketball games than he lost. The true measure of success must include legacy. Bud Metheny won 54.8 percent of his games, but the coaches that inherited the program also benefited from the foundation he laid. While the program was 159–159 before Bud Metheny, after his tenure it has gone 1,028–627 through the 2018–2019 season, good for a winning percentage of 62.1 percent. The coaches that immediately followed Metheny—Sonny Allen and Paul Webb—stayed for a decade apiece and led teams that won 65.8 percent and 66.4 percent of their games, respectively. Allen led his team to an appearance in the 1970–71 Division II national title game and a 1974–75 Division II national championship. Bud Metheny certainly can't be credited with the success these coaches enjoyed, but, along with his substantial baseball accomplishments, he can certainly be credited with laying the groundwork that made possible such progress at Old Dominion University.

CHAPTER FIVE

Fields, Jerseys, and the Norfolk City League

THE BASEBALL FIELD

Home field for the Braves in Coach Metheny's inaugural 1949 baseball campaign was Larchmont Field, a symmetrical field with 350-foot fences all around, similar to several other diamonds around Norfolk that the city owned and maintained, such as at Lafayette Park. By the time Bud Metheny arrived, the Division's baseball teams had established some home-field consistency, in that they had called Larchmont home for more than a decade. Earlier squads, however, hadn't had it as easy, and had to earn a place to play with their own blood, sweat, and possibly even tears, although it does seem somewhat unlikely that Coach Tommy Scott would have permitted that.

When the Norfolk Division had opened its doors in 1930, academic facilities had been at a premium and athletic facilities even more so. Dr. James Sweeney noted that the first baseball team didn't have the benefit of a ballfield on campus, and so practices were held two miles away at Lafayette Park[1] (which also appears to have still gone by its previous name, "City Park").[2] City Park had at least two ballfields at that time; *The High Hat* mentioned in March of 1931 that "the team will practice Mondays, Wednesdays, and Fridays on diamond two, City Park."

Rufus "Poofball" Tonelson, the starting and winning pitcher in the Norfolk Division's first baseball game, was also arguably the first student at the Norfolk Division. To his own recollection, he was the first to register for classes at the Norfolk Division's administration building in 1930, and the secretary accepting his paperwork had commented as such to him. Sweeney, however, gives the distinction of being first to Albert E. Wilson, who registered around the same time at a different location; in either case, Tonelson was certainly among the very first, and had insight into those first lean years at the Division. In December of 1975, he recalled how the lack of athletic facilities affected the initial Norfolk Division students. "I remember that many times a Physical Education class consisted of running down to the waterfront along Bolling Avenue and then running back," Tonelson noted. "We probably had two showers at best for those who were in the gym classes, so it was not unusual on the hot spring and summer days to have those of us in the Phys. Ed. class just keep on going and plunge in. I guess this may have been the beginning of a swimming team, which followed."[3]

Sweeney notes that the first home baseball games were played either at City Park or occasionally at Bain Field, which was located two and a half miles away, near the intersection of East 20th Street and Church Street. Bain Field was home to the Norfolk Tars, and as authors Shampoe and Garrett describe, the name had changed from League Park to Bain Field in 1931, and upgrades such as "removal of the high outfield fences, increased seating for 'Negro patrons,' and a partially covered bleacher section down the first base line"[4] had accompanied the name change that year. The Tars, who would be affiliated with the New York Yankees in 1934, played in the Class-A

Eastern League in 1931, and so the early editions of the Norfolk Division Braves had the occasional good fortune to be able to use the field of a professional team such as the 1931 edition of the Tars that featured fifteen future or past major leaguers, and included such colorful names as Blackie Carter and Snake Henry, as well as the same Dave Robertson who would help Coach Scott with his Division charges the following spring.[5]

Bain Field in 1939. Courtesy Sargeant Memorial Collection, Norfolk Public Library.

The 1932 Division team built their own field on a property south of Bolling Avenue, and over the next few years it came to be known as Scott Field, or Scott Stadium. Asked in 1976 to pinpoint the site of Scott Field, Coach Tommy Scott's widow interestingly chose to define it as a concept rather than a specific place: "They had no facilities for bleachers or chairs. It was just—I have heard that when the boys came out for their first baseball team, as they came in to sign up, Tommy gave them all a shovel and they had to go make their own diamonds . . . I don't know we had anything called Scott's Field, but I think that in our minds, anywhere Tommy's boys were on the field, it was Scott's boys, Scott's men or Scott's field, whether it was on a street in Larchmont in the area where our stadium is today. If Tommy was there and Tommy's boys were there, it was Scott's field."[6]

Norfolk Division baseball teams used the field for four years, although also continued to use City Park and Bain Field. Scott Field clearly left something to be desired as a home field, as illustrated by an April 1934 *High Hat* article that was headlined "Game With

This 1935 aerial photograph was taken looking west. The structure in the center of the picture is the "new" Larchmont School of the time (now demolished); Bolling Avenue is to the right of it, and Hampton Boulevard runs horizontally through the center of the picture. To the right in the picture is the "Old" Larchmont School, where the Norfolk Division began. Across Hampton Boulevard is the site of S. B. Ballard Stadium now, but was "Scott Field" in 1935. Courtesy of Special Collections and University Archives, Patricia W. and J. Douglas Perry Library, Old Dominion University Libraries, Norfolk, Virginia.

Cape Charles Postponed Because of Local Diamond; Scott Field Not In Shape."[7] With the impending construction of Foreman Field "almost assured,"[8] the Athletic Board also refused in May 1934 to make any immediate improvements on that ground, which would become part of the new stadium in 1936.

In 1936, a new baseball diamond was built again, with the help of the Division's Physical Education classes and the National Youth Administration, a Depression-era New Deal agency. As *The High Hat* reported on March 13, 1936, "The Division physical education classes have finally found something to do, and coach Tommy Scott has put them to work making a new baseball diamond in back of the Larchmont grammar school. The work on the new stadium has completely demolished last year's diamond and it is necessary to build an entirely new field . . . The gym classes and all available NYA students have been put to work and the field should be in fair condition in several weeks. The new location for the diamond is ideal with a vast expanse of outfield and a smooth, clean infield. The old bleachers will probably be moved to the new site."

Some consideration was given by the administration in 1937 to adding a baseball diamond within Foreman Field,[9] but that never materialized, and the field behind the Larchmont grammar school, while not actually owned by the Norfolk Division, would generally become its baseball home for almost fifty years. Asked about the facilities in his early days at the Norfolk Division, Bud Metheny remembered, "Well, the facilities here were what we called the Old Administration building, which was a high school size gym and then a much smaller gym and then a twenty-five-yard, four-lane pool. Outside of that we had no outside facilities. The stadium [Foreman Field] was rented to the city, so we were only able to use that in the spring of the year, and it isn't large enough to put a baseball field in . . . The [baseball] facilities that we have used ever since 1948 were provided by the city of Norfolk, which is Larchmont Field. And they kept it up for us; they were very good to us."[10]

The Braves' baseball residence at Larchmont Field led to at least one interesting exchange between town and gown. Available parking at Larchmont was not that close to the field, and after Coach Bud Metheny evidently received a ticket for his parking practices in the spring of 1954, Division Director Lewis Webb Jr. went to bat for him. Webb wrote to Norfolk Director of Public Safety Calvin H. Dalby: "Each Spring our baseball team practices and holds its home games on the baseball diamond directly south of the Larchmont Apartments. This diamond is one of the City Recreation Program's athletic fields, and we have received permission to use the field . . . It has been the practice of our coach to park his car, and one of the cars of the visiting team, during the games on a grassy plot about twenty feet from the curb . . . The reason for this is that it is necessary for the coach to bring all of the equipment—bats, bases, etc. and his large first-aid kit to the field. Since there is generally no room along the curb very close to the field he has been parking his car on the grass plot in order to have the vehicle available in case of emergency due to injury to one of his players ... We have been following this practice but recently one of the City policemen objected and gave our coach and the coach of the Richmond Professional Institute a ticket for improper parking." Dalby responded by acknowledging receipt of the correspondence, but getting it off his

Aerial view of Larchmont Field in the 1960s. Courtesy of Special Collections and University Archives, Patricia W. and J. Douglas Perry Library, Old Dominion University Libraries, Norfolk, Virginia.

desk as quickly as he could, said that he would forward the matter to the Police Chief "for his investigation and advices." No further mention of this matter is to be found among Metheny's papers.[11]

Today, the field used by so many Norfolk Division and Old Dominion teams no longer exists as a baseball diamond, and the two pictures below highlight the difference fifty years can make. The first is a 1960s

Aerial view of the former site of Larchmont Field, 2021 (from Google Maps™ Mapping Service).

aerial picture from the ODU Library's Digital Collections, showing the Monarchs' longtime home field, with bleacher seats behind home plate, and spectator fences around the infield. The second, taken from Google Earth, shows the same area, with the tennis courts and smaller ballfield as good reference points. Today, the ground that was the home field of several championship college baseball teams is part of the new Larchmont Elementary School.

EVOLUTION OF THE UNIFORM: BRAVES TO MONARCHS

The baseball team uniform changed every year for three consecutive years through 1963 at the Norfolk Division/Old Dominion College. In the picture at left, Coach Bud Metheny (top) and Bob Walton don "Braves" jerseys with William & Mary caps, in the 1961 team picture.

Team pictures courtesy of Special Collections and University Archives, Patricia W. and J. Douglas Perry Library, Old Dominion University Libraries, Norfolk, Virginia.

In the picture at right, Kirkie Harrison (top) and Wayne Parks are shown in new uniforms in 1962—a simple "N" for Norfolk on the caps, "Monarchs" across the jerseys. The jerseys were the exact same ones as the year before, but with the "Braves" insignia removed and "Monarchs" added instead. In the middle picture, Ronnie Evans has the modernized uniform of 1963 and 1964: the "OD" logo on both cap and jersey, with Yankee pinstripes.

NORFOLK CITY LEAGUE

As the Norfolk Division, and then Old Dominion College, began to lay the foundation for its athletic development and success by joining conferences such as Virginia's unofficial Little Eight and then the Mason-Dixon Conference, Bud Metheny was also getting some summer help from the Norfolk City League, a semi-pro circuit that had its beginning in the 1940s. The Tidewater Summer League, a contemporary collegiate wooden-bat league claiming ancestry to the City League, summarizes the early history on its website: "The Tidewater Summer League traces its origins back to the mid 1940's. In the midst of WWII, a group of local baseball teams, including some Military teams, organized by Harry Postove, begin [sic] playing in what eventually became known as the Norfolk City League. The inaugural season of the Norfolk City League is listed at [sic] 1946, with the 1946 City League All Star game drawing over 3,000 fans to Norfolk's Lakewood Park, as reported by the *Virginian*."[12]

For Bud Metheny, the City League was an excellent chance for his current college players to play against a high caliber of competition outside of the college season. Clyde "Ducky" Davis Jr., longtime member of the Chesapeake Athletic Club (a City League sponsor) and a winner of the 2013 Bud Metheny Award (given in recognition of contributions to local baseball), remembers watching City League games as a child in the 1940s and 1950s, and to his estimation, 90 percent of the players had played some professional baseball.[13] While there are no specific histories written or official league archives, one name that everyone involved with the league in the early 1960s recalls is Al Gettel, a Tidewater native who pitched for six major league teams between the years 1945 and 1955. According to Gettel's 2005 obituary in the New York *Sun*, "He also began appearing in bit parts in Westerns, taking advantage of his horsemanship. On Al Gettel Day at the Oakland [Oaks] stadium one year, he galloped onto the field on horseback sporting Western gear, a stunt for which he was branded 'Two Gun' for the rest of his career."[14] Coincidentally, Bud Metheny's final major league at-bat would be pinch-hitting in the ninth spot in the Yankee lineup, an inning after Yankee starting pitcher Al Gettel had left the game and vacated that spot.

Bruce Howard, former White Sox pitcher and contemporary and friend of many members of the 1964 Old Dominion College team, was another major league talent in the Norfolk City League, although his participation was somewhat atypical, since it was prior to his professional career instead of on the back end of it. As Old Dominion pitcher Fred Edmonds recalled in 2017, "I think Bruce's record in the City League before he went to the White Sox was like 1–3, and mine was like 5–0. I always kid him about that."[15]

The City League teams were sponsored by local clubs or businesses such as the Chesapeake Athletic Club, Colonial Chevrolet, Cavalier Coin, Wisco Storm Windows and Doors, Zoby Plumbing, and Gray's Pharmacy, and played a majority of games at Norfolk's City Park and Lakewood Park. Former players from the early to mid-1960s remember it as a "semi-pro" league, in that some of the noncollegiate players might be paid a stipend to play, although that was not necessarily the norm. The team makeups consisted of a range of ages from the best high-school talent to college level to "Two Gun" Gettel pitching into his late forties, but the caliber of competition top-to-bottom was considered excellent. Some participants from the early 1960s equate it to minor league baseball at the B or C level, although as Ducky Davis recalls, "Some of those teams were just as good as a Single-A team."[16]

The league was popular, too, giving Bud Metheny's ballplayers not only the chance to develop their skills against high-quality competition, but also while under the pressure of playing before good-sized crowds. As Davis remembers, "On any given Sunday afternoon, say, at City Park, there'd be a thousand people or more there watching them play, even though you had the Norfolk Tars, the Portsmouth Cubs, and the Newport News Dodgers playing in the Piedmont League."

Since the collegiate season typically ended in May, Bud Metheny was also able to help his own cause by taking an active role in the City League during the summer, both as league commissioner for a time, and as manager of the Gray's Pharmacy team. For Metheny, the benefit of the league was really two-fold. Not only did it provide an additional development stage for his college players, but the City League, along with American Legion ballfields, also provided him an opportunity to scout the top high-school talent. In fact, John Zeb, a former Division ballplayer from the late 1950s, recalls of his time in the City League that "I was there for my sophomore and junior year, but in my senior year, Bud . . . requested that I not play since I was graduating from college. He said because that's what he used to try to get players to come play with them in the City League, then hopefully, he or they would make a mutual agreement for them to come to [the Norfolk Division of] William and Mary, or Old Dominion, to play."[17]

The April 23, 1964, City League season preview published in the *Virginian-Pilot* makes obvious the important tie that existed between the Norfolk City League and Old Dominion College baseball. In late April, City League teams were still forming as the high school and college seasons neared an end, and this article noted that during the team-formation process, "especially sought after are the covey of outstanding prospects under Bud Metheny's wing at Old Dominion."[18] Of the thirty-four names specifically mentioned on individual teams in the article, more than 20 percent were former, current, or future Monarchs—and those specifically named did not include Mel Renn, Frank and Jimmy Zadell, Wayne Parks, John Ingram, or Tom Harrell, each members of the 1964 Old Dominion team who also played in the Norfolk City League.

CHAPTER SIX

1963
Pinnacle . . . and Prelude

You're as good as the league you're in. It's just the same in the business world. If you work for a shoddy concern that doesn't stress perfection you won't be a success.

—BUD METHENY, *at the Peninsula Sports Club's "Spring Sports Night," June 12, 1962*

1963—THE SEASON

The baseball team came into the 1963 season representing their "new" school on the baseball field for the first time, with brand-new uniforms, and with a new conference affiliation as members of the Mason-Dixon. Yet despite the seemingly clean slate, Metheny's diamond men still had to live up to high standards. Over the previous two seasons, the team had gone a combined 34–9 (a winning percentage of 79 percent), had won the Little Eight in consecutive years (although the 1962 title was shared with Bridgewater), and entered the season on a nine-game winning streak.

The roster was relatively youthful but loaded with local baseball talent. Bud Metheny, by this time a fifteen-year-veteran basketball and baseball coach at Old Dominion, had gotten to know the area. As Jimmy Zadell recalls, "Playing baseball in town, having Bud in town with the Norfolk College of William and Mary, in the papers and so forth. He knew everybody in town. He knew everybody in town since they were probably ten years old! Things were different. Norfolk was a pretty significant city even in the mid-fifties; it was a fairly big area, but everybody played baseball in the city of Norfolk surrounding the Dunn Field, Lakewood area, and so forth—Shoop Park, Bluebird Park. Everybody from Ocean View, we all played in that central area—around the Larchmont area, Dunn Field. So he knew everybody!"[1] In 1963, Coach Metheny also had the benefit of a fairly captive and noncompetitive college market for ballplayers—today's Christopher Newport University in Newport News was only a two-year extension of William & Mary at the time, and had no baseball team. Virginia Wesleyan College in Norfolk did not open for classes until 1966. Norfolk State College had no baseball program until 1964.

Financial considerations, too, limited the educational choices of many of the Monarch athletes. John Ingram recalls, "We stayed local because of the money. I mean, it was cheap to go there in relation to going away to school. I don't remember any rich kids on the team."[2] Jimmy Zadell remembers of the time, "For most of the people who grew up in Norfolk and, really, middle-class to low-middle-class people, the opportunity to go UVA or someplace like that was usually economically out of bounds for us."[3] Fred Kovner's father headed the Technical Institute at Old Dominion, and Fred recalls a similar financial consideration in the Kovner household: "Let's see, my dad taught over there, and 'that's the only place you're going, because I'm not spending money sending you anywhere else.' How about that?"[4]

With his personal connections, the ability to scout American Legion and City League games, the relative lack of other local collegiate options for baseball players, and the affordable education Old Dominion provided, the ground in the early 1960s was fertile for Bud Metheny to build an All-Star cast of ballplayers at the school. Metheny recruited Wayne Parks after seeing him play in American Legion and City League contests. He recruited John Ingram after seeing him play an American Legion game, and then convincing Ingram's father that Old Dominion would be a better choice for college than East Carolina. The Methenys had known Tom Harrell since his seventh-grade year, when Bud's wife, Frances, had taught Tom at Holy Trinity School. Coach Metheny had known Fred Kovner since Fred was a boy, because Fred's father, Edgar, was also an Old Dominion coach (of the club lacrosse team). Metheny had also known Fred Edmonds Jr.'s father from the time the elder Edmonds was a star athlete at the Division, and the two had competed against each other when Metheny was on the William & Mary freshman team. Mel Renn, captain of the Warwick High School baseball team, remembers working in the shipyard immediately after high school, and contacting Bud Metheny about the possibility of coming to Old Dominion and playing ball, and hearing in response, "Yeah, come on over here, I know all about you."[5]

Bud Metheny used all his available options, too, including the local papers. Probably the best recruitment story from the time comes from catcher Jimmy Walker: "I didn't go anywhere after I graduated from high school. I got a good summer job, and I worked for a year. I was an IBM computer operator in the shipyard, which was pretty much in the infancy of the computer operations—pretty good job. Then everything's fine, I'm reading in the paper and it said 'Bud Metheny's looking for Jim Walker from Newport News, he wants him to come catch.' So, I called him, and that's how I got there."[6]

Bud Metheny assembled the talent, but he was also the lone coach of the team. As with other Old Dominion sports of the time, there was no assistant coach. Metheny actually served triple duty: as head recruiter, head coach, *and* head trainer. Interviewed more than fifty years later, most of his players remember Metheny and his omnipresent medicine kit. John Ingram remembers his coach's in-game demeanor: "He sat on the end of the bench with his foot on the medicine kit and the scorebook in his lap. He would give his signals using things like the scorebook. The one I remember is if you saw the back of the scorebook, the clipboard, [it] was the steal signal. Players, usually the pitchers, coached the bases."[7] The simplicity of Coach Metheny's signals led Jimmy Zadell to facetiously recall in 2016, "Simple?? I thought the man was a simpleton! I mean, it was so simple, no one figured them out!"[8]

As the only coach of the team, Bud Metheny wasn't as able to focus on specific instruction as a modern coach. He did teach Fred Kovner how to grip a ball when Fred was twelve years old. Tom Harrell recalls Metheny teaching the first-and-third play, an offensive maneuver in which a runner on first draws a throw to create an opportunity for a runner on third to score. When asked in 2020 for more specifics about how the play was taught, John Ingram recalled, "Wayne [Parks] could tell you more about that, because I was never going to try that . . . that was for guys who could run."[9] For the most part, though, Old Dominion baseball players of the early 1960s don't recall an inordinate amount of practice time devoted to technical instruction. Coach Metheny brought something else to the game as a coach, something less tangible. Metheny was a *Yankee*—not in a braggadocious, vocal, or cocky way, but in a professional way that commanded respect on and off the field, and that demanded the best out of his players. "His experience in professional baseball; he brought lots of things to the table," Fred Kovner recalls. "Bud brought a different maturity to the game."[10] Wayne Parks remembers the specific non-baseball lessons he received under Metheny's tutelage: "the right way to play, and respecting the other team, and giving your best always."[11]

The array of talent and character that Coach Metheny assembled on the 1963 Old Dominion team caught the eye of at least one Associated Press reporter, who published his impression of the Monarchs' 1963 edition in the Newport News *Daily Press* on April 1, 1963:

This year, he [Bud Metheny] is again building character—and a winning baseball team. Currently, the Monarchs are 7–0 and have a 17-game winning streak since a 10–8 loss last April 18 to Randolph-Macon.

But not only does the ODC baseball team have character—it also has characters; characters who would warm the heart of a Ring Lardner—or even a less humorous sportswriter.

Take freshman catcher Frazier O'Leary for example. And some people would say, you take him, I don't want him. This pink-cheeked Irishman, a Bostonian by origin (what else?) is the freshest of freshmen.

When practice opened indoors in March, O'Leary was seen walking around the gym carrying a portable home plate. Asked what he was doing, he said: 'Oh, I'm just going to be the first guy this year to steal home.'

Last week, Metheny told O'Leary to get a glove and warm up a relief pitcher. Fearless Frazier, sometimes known as Cassius after a certain loquacious boxer, calmly asked: 'Do I need a ball, too?'

NO EGGHEAD

O'Leary isn't the only nutty squirrel in the Old Dominion forest. Pitching ace Fred Edmonds is another.

Edmonds, unbeaten in two years of college competition, admits that he isn't the greatest scholar who ever entered a college classroom. Told that members of the freshman class could play for a whole year regardless of grades, Edmonds said: 'I guess I'll be around for four years, then.'

In centerfield for the Monarchs is Fred Kovner, one of the few ball players ever to play second fiddle in a symphony orchestra. But this speedy sophomore is strictly first fiddle as a leadoff man and outfielder. He's not nicknamed Piersall just for his hot temper.

Kovner's hot temper had him in continual trouble at Granby High School. Metheny is the first coach for whom Kovner has played a full season.

At second base is a William and Mary 'castoff,' Ronnie Killmon of Onancock, Va. This 23-year old, formerly a football player at William and Mary, lost his scholarship two years ago after an injury and transferred to Old Dominion. His experience steadies the Old Dominion infield, which includes Jerry Hammer—a natural outfielder—at shortstop and freshman Fred Balmer at first.

LUCKY TO BE ALIVE

A reserve outfielder, John Cooke, is lucky to be alive. After leaving Great Bridge High, Cooke played football at VMI. There, he was injured (a broken neck) in an automobile accident and his life was despaired of for some time.

Freshman pitcher Bill Yeargan is nearsighted, a la Rhyne Duren of the Angels. But Yeargan pitches without glasses, hardly an encouragement for opposing batsmen to dig in.

In Wilson, N.C., last week, a rabid Atlantic Christian fan 'rode' Metheny and his players from behind the ODC dugout. 'Typical State school—all you have to do is go out and buy 'em.'

Metheny and his players had a good laugh at that one. Only Wayne Parks, his third baseman, received scholarship aid—the princely sum of $180 per year. Everyone else is on his own.

On the road, Old Dominion's athletes always make a favorable impression with their coats and ties off the field and with their sportsmanship on it. Ex-Yankee Metheny—the last man to wear Babe Ruth's *number three—says, 'I was so bad, they had to retire that uniform.' Metheny may not have been the greatest of Yankees, but he has taught his teams two Yankee traits—class off the field and victory on it.*[12]

Already riding a nine-game winning streak at the end of the 1962 season, the 1963 team began its first year in the Mason-Dixon Conference by winning another fourteen straight games. They defeated Dartmouth four times in the early going, and won five games against new Mason-Dixon Conference foes in these first fourteen, including a 6–1 spanking of defending champion Randolph-Macon College. The team was also putting up some particularly eye-popping offensive numbers in the early season. The 1963 cumulative team batting average was never out of the .300s; in fact, after the sixth game, when there is enough of a representative sample size to eliminate statistical anomalies, the team batting average never dropped below .315 or went above .331! By year's end, as a *team*, the average stood at .322, good enough for sixth-best nationally in the College Division.[13]

There were also plenty of standout individual performances within that .322. Left fielder Frank Zadell knocked in thirty-six runs over the twenty-seven-game 1963 schedule—a pace for an incredible 216 RBI, if extrapolated to a 162-game season. But four other batters on the team would have also extrapolated to more than 100 RBI: freshman first baseman Fred Balmer (132), third baseman Wayne Parks, right fielder Jimmy Zadell (both 108), and center fielder Fred Kovner (102). A team with five batters maintaining a 100-RBI pace is impressive, but this team also had *seven* that maintained a pace to score more than 100 runs! Led by Wayne Parks' twenty-eight runs (a pace for 168, if extrapolated over 162 games), Fred Kovner (156), Fred Balmer (144), second baseman Ron Killmon (126), shortstop and sometimes right fielder Jerry Hammer (120), Frank Zadell (114), and Jimmy Zadell (108), the 1963 Monarchs averaged 7.4 runs scored per contest.

For a comparison to a major league team that offered similarly dominant firepower, the 1999 Colorado Rockies put an offensive machine on the field, scoring 5.6 runs per game. The problem was that they also gave up 6.3 runs per game, on their way to a 72–90 win-loss record. Could the 1963 Monarchs' pitching match the offensive prowess? The short answer, statistically, was "yes." Through the winning streak of the first fourteen games, the staff had a 1.93 ERA and allowed 1.24 baserunners per inning by hit or walk. Bob Walton, the team's innings leader, had accounted for only one of those walks, and would walk only *five batters* all year. At season's end, the team's ERA stood at 2.59, 23rd nationally in the College Division.[14]

The 1963 Monarchs had the statistics, the confidence, and the skills to play the "Yankee Way" for Coach Metheny. The team, however, lacked depth. Of eighteen hitters to get at-bats during the season, the top seven averaged more than three at-bats per game, and everyone else averaged fewer than two. In fact, if players who got fewer than ten total at-bats on the season are removed from the list, there are only thirteen players remaining who received appreciable chances to contribute at the plate for the entire twenty-seven-game season. Monarch pitching was even more reliant on the arms of a few, perhaps contributing to the rise in team ERA from 1.93 after fourteen games to 2.59 at season's end. Only *six pitchers* contributed to the 1963 Monarch cause—and the full season stat line for one of those pitchers includes just one batter faced, and one walk issued.

The young team was also still developing maturity, the trait that would serve the 1964 edition so well. The 1963 defense allowed thirty-nine unearned runs over twenty-seven games (or an additional 1.4 runs allowed per contest), while the team would cut that number by more than half (to nineteen unearned runs) the following year. The team was still learning how to win the close ones, too. When the twenty-three-game win streak that included fourteen in the current year was broken, a three-game losing streak on a Baltimore road trip followed: one loss to Loyola, when Loyola scored the winning run in their last at-bat, and two losses to Baltimore in the exact same fashion, as Baltimore pitcher Ron Mather beat the Monarchs in both games of a doubleheader. In the first game of their first Mason-Dixon Conference championship series later in the year, Loyola scored three runs in their last two innings to secure a one-run victory over Old Dominion. To be fair, the ability of the 1963 Old Dominion team to win the close games was not altogether lacking; the team did win an equal number of games in their last at-bat (four) as they lost. That maturity and mentality was still developing, however; the 1964 team would go 10–1 in games won in the victorious team's final at-bat.

MASON-DIXON CONFERENCE CHAMPIONSHIP SERIES

Old Dominion easily rolled to the bragging-rights Little Eight title in 1963, without losing a single contest to in-state foes. And in their first year in the Mason-Dixon Conference, Old Dominion compiled a 7–3 conference record, with the only three losses in the conference schedule coming by a total of three runs in a bad two days in Baltimore on April 19 and 20. The Monarchs' .700 winning percentage was enough to eliminate defending champion Randolph-Macon (with an 8–4 record and .667 win percentage) from championship consideration, and give Old Dominion first place in the Mason-Dixon South Division.

Representing the North Division in the 1963 championship series was Loyola College of Baltimore, setting up a clash that pitted the Mason-Dixon "old guard"—one of the founding institutions of the conference, with five baseball titles to its credit—against first-year upstart Old Dominion. In fact, since 1941, the first year of recorded Mason-Dixon baseball championships, only Randolph-Macon had won as many championships as Loyola, and Loyola had also won the North Division in a couple of other years without winning the overall championship. The Greyhounds entered the championship series on a roll, as winners of nine of their previous ten games—a streak that included their first-ever game against Old Dominion, decided in Loyola's favor in the bottom of the tenth inning by a leadoff home run.

Loyola had several noteworthy players, too, including six who earned Mason-Dixon All-Star honors. On the first team, the Greyhounds were represented by second baseman Bob Rossi, who (along with Old Dominion's Wayne Parks) was nearly a unanimous selection, and who was also drafted by the Cubs in 1965 and went on to play a few seasons of minor league ball. Joining Rossi on the Mason-Dixon first-team All-Stars was Loyola's shortstop, Michael Elliott. Freshman pitcher Howie Murray made the second team, and pitcher Rel VanDaniker, third baseman John Campbell, and outfielder Charley O'Donnell all merited honorable mention as well.

Completing the portrait of Loyola as an "old guard" Mason-Dixon power, the Greyhounds were also coached by Loyola legend Emil G. Reitz. "Lefty" Reitz had been with the school since 1938 in various capacities such as athletic director, baseball coach, and basketball coach, although his services were interrupted during the World War II years, when he had enlisted for military service. Reitz was also instrumental within the conference itself; during the 1940s, he served at various times as Mason-Dixon treasurer, president, and secretary-treasurer. In his 1992 obituary, it is noted that he also coached lacrosse, cross-country, and soccer,[15] and that he was survived by a wife and three children, although one wonders how he had time for family life!

The same obituary notes Reitz's career baseball coaching record as 290–245–2 over thirty-two seasons, and coming into the 1963 Mason-Dixon championship, he had five conference titles already to his credit, and one win in one try against Old Dominion. But the Monarchs had their share of Mason-Dixon All-Stars, too, and in the five games since the three mid-April losses in Baltimore, had been averaging 10.8 runs per contest. The championship series, a best-of-three, was to begin on Loyola's home field starting with a doubleheader of seven-inning games on Friday, May 17.

On a humid, seventy-degree day in Baltimore, Old Dominion coach Bud Metheny elected to start Bob Walton, with a 6–1 record and 1.69 ERA to this point in the season, in the first game. Reitz chose freshman starter Howie Murray, whose season stat line ended with a 5–1 record, a 1.73 ERA and one no-hitter thrown.[16] After a coin flip, Loyola batted as the visiting team and started quietly in the first two innings, registering only a single by right fielder Charley O'Donnell that led off the game. For the Monarchs, leadoff hitter Fred Kovner got things going immediately with a single and a steal of second, scoring on cleanup hitter Jerry Hammer's two-out single.

In the third, Howie Murray helped his own cause and tied the score at one with a home run off Walton. So it would stay until the fifth inning, when left fielder Frank Zadell hit a solo home run of his own to take back the lead, which the Monarchs followed with some insurance in the sixth, when Fred Balmer plated Wayne Parks with a sacrifice fly.

Up by a score of 3–1 and with Bob Walton on the hill and only three outs to go to take Game One, the Monarchs' chances looked good. But Bob Rossi led off the seventh inning with a home run to halve the lead, and then a single by John Campbell was followed, incredibly, by consecutive errors by Walton, both allowing Campbell to score and putting catcher Joe Kernan on second base with no one out. After a successful sacrifice by first baseman Bill Falkenhan moved Kernan to third, Walton was able to escape without further damage, and the game went to the bottom of the seventh tied.

Murray was doing just enough. He only struck out two batters on the day, but checked the Monarch offense enough to give his team a chance. In the bottom of the seventh, he let a runner get into scoring position, but allowed no runs, and the game went to extra innings tied at three. Greyhound center fielder Ed Burchell took it from there, homering to lead off the top of the eighth to give Loyola a 4–3 lead. In Old Dominion's last chance, Bud Metheny tried a desperation move of inserting powerful infielder Lee McDaniel into right fielder Jimmy Zadell's batting spot, but ultimately the Monarchs could only muster a harmless single by Jerry Hammer in their frame, and dropped Game One.

The pitching matchup in Game Two featured Loyola's Phil Potter, whose final season line totaled four wins against two losses and a 2.24 ERA,[17] against Old Dominion's Fred Edmonds Jr., who came into the game with a 6–0 record and a 3.46 ERA. Edmonds was a much different pitcher than Walton, relying more on power than pinpoint control. For the 1963 season, Edmonds averaged 8.73 strikeouts per nine innings, but 4.64 walks as well, while Walton averaged 5.56 strikeouts per nine to go with just 0.65 walks. The different styles worked in Coach Metheny's favor; in a scenario that would repeat in 1964, the pair had won both ends of a doubleheader twice in 1963.

"The Hound nine featured some lusty hitting during the 1963 season," claimed Loyola's 1963 yearbook, and, in fact, they had earned their overall 14–3 won-loss record coming into this series by outscoring their opponents by a 5.8–4.1 score, on average.[18] But whether or not Walton's pitching style had softened the ground for a power pitcher in Game Two, Edmonds certainly kept all the "lusty hitting" under control in the second game. Only one unearned run would cross the plate against Edmonds in this game, when Game One hero Ed Burchell reached on an Edmonds error, later advanced to third on a passed ball by Old Dominion catcher Frazier O'Leary, and ultimately scored on a sacrifice fly.

That run scored in the first, however, and since it was a seven-inning game, the score started to put pressure on Old Dominion bats, as the number of outs that they had to work with began to dwindle. Potter navigated a relatively quiet first inning for the Greyhounds, and then a second. But in the third, he opened by hitting his counterpart,

Fred Edmonds, with a pitched ball, and then followed that by hitting Fred Kovner as well. With none out, Wayne Parks hit into a fielder's choice, erasing Edmonds from the basepaths for the first out. Jimmy Zadell got the next chance for the Monarchs, and he made the most of it, tripling to right field and giving his team a 2–1 lead.

Second baseman Ron Killmon provided insurance with a home run in the top of the fourth, giving Old Dominion the same 3–1 lead that they had given away in the first game. For Edmonds' part, though, all he had really needed was Zadell's big hit. For his seven innings of work, Edmonds allowed only two hits in twenty-two official Greyhound at-bats (an .091 average) and struck out five, while issuing only two free passes. The game ended with the same 3–1 score, with the Monarch victory forcing a deciding Game Three, a nine-inning game to be played the following day with the conference title at stake.

"THE GAME"

"The day that I pitched in the conference championship in Baltimore, he [Bud Metheny] gave me the ball the morning of the game. I didn't have any idea that I would be pitching in the final game,"[19] Old Dominion starter John Ingram recalls. Bob Walton and Fred Edmonds, who had both pitched complete games the day before, weren't available options, and between the two of them, they had accounted for an incredible 62 percent of all Monarch innings pitched in 1963, with 69⅔ and 66 innings pitched, respectively. The remaining 38 percent was made up by Ingram (31 innings pitched), Bill Yeargan (27⅓ innings), and Donnie Bradshaw (24⅔ innings). Metheny settled on the lefthanded Ingram—possibly the morning of the game, given the timing of naming his starter.

The day was again warm and humid, the temperature reaching about seventy-five degrees for the 2 p.m. start. Ingram, 2–0 with a 3.68

ERA coming into the game, was opposed on the mound by Loyola's Rel VanDaniker, whose 1963 final stats were reported by the Loyola yearbook as 5–2 with a 3.23 ERA, meaning that his ERA was probably much better than that coming into this game.

Ingram was shaky to start the top of the first inning, as was the Old Dominion defense. Greyhound leadoff hitter Charley O'Donnell led off with a walk, and after a fielder's choice and a strikeout, an error by Monarch third baseman Wayne Parks allowed shortstop Michael Elliott to reach first base and O'Donnell to score. Consecutive two-out singles by Bob Rossi and then John Campbell drove Elliott home, and a walk to catcher and team captain Al Schroeder loaded the bases. Already down 2–0, with runners on all bases, and with a pitcher on the mound who had the highest walk rate on the 1963 team (5.23 per nine innings for the season), the game was dangerously close to getting away in the top of the first inning.

Metheny, however, stuck with his junior left-hander, and Ingram, who also owned the staff's second-highest strikeout rate at 7.26 per nine innings, responded with a crucial strikeout of Loyola first baseman Bill Falkenhan to keep the game close.

VanDaniker was a little shaky to start the bottom half, too. He was good for one batter, as he retired leadoff man Fred Kovner on a grounder to second, but then Wayne Parks doubled and was followed by consecutive walks to Jimmy Zadell and Jerry Hammer to load the bases. Fred Balmer tied the score by knocking in two runs with a single, and two batters later Frank Zadell put the Monarchs up by two by singling home Hammer and Balmer.

While Ingram settled down for the Monarchs, VanDaniker continued to struggle. He allowed Ingram's first hit of the year, and then, with two outs, had a four-batter stretch in which he walked three men and hit Jimmy Zadell. The last of the two walks, to Jerry Hammer and Fred Balmer, forced in the fifth and sixth Monarch runs, and knocked VanDaniker out of the game. Despite seven innings pitched the day before, Phil Potter came in as relief help, and ended the bases-loaded threat by getting Ron Killmon to hit into a fielder's choice. After two innings of play, though, the score was already 6–2 in favor of Old Dominion, and Loyola had given the game over to a tired bullpen.

After the first, Ingram put in steady work, both issuing walks and striking batters out at the rate that his statistics would generally predict, totaling six of each for the game. Not until the fifth did he have a three-up, three-down inning, but despite baserunners in most innings, runs weren't scoring. The Old Dominion bats added a pair of runs to the lead in the bottom of the fifth inning on consecutive singles by Hammer, Balmer, and Killmon, and excitement was high as the Monarchs led 8–2 going into the late innings.

Ingram gave one back in the top of the sixth, as his own error allowed Al Schroeder to reach base and ultimately come around to score. But thereafter, the Greyhounds offered a real threat only in the eighth, when they started the inning with a walk and a single. Ingram retired the next three men in order—two by strikeout—to extinguish the developing rally.

Ingram, zero-for-nine on the season at the plate coming into the game, still had more to prove, however. Eighth-inning singles by Frank Zadell and Frazier O'Leary put two men on base with one out for the pitcher's spot in the lineup, and Ingram responded with a double—his only double of the year, and his only RBI of the year. Additionally, the two-for-four performance at the plate raised his average 154 points—from .000 to .154 for the season.

Ingram worked a three-up, three-down top of the ninth to complete a game in which he gave up no earned runs, and Old Dominion College's baseball team, in their first try, left Baltimore as Mason-Dixon champions. The victory registered across the Mason-Dixon's geographical footprint, as papers such as the *Baltimore Sun*, the *Progress-Index* of Petersburg, Virginia, and the *Daily Press* of Newport News, Virginia, all carried reporting of the event.

1963 Mason-Dixon Conference Championship game ball, with signatures. In possession of the family of winning pitcher John Ingram.

NCAA EAST REGIONAL TOURNAMENT

After the conference championship, Bud Metheny had another decision to make. Adding to his duties as recruiter, coach, and head trainer, he had also added significantly more responsibility around the beginning of the 1963 baseball season. J. C. "Scrap" Chandler announced his retirement as Old Dominion College's athletic director on April 8, and Metheny had on July 1 assumed the reins as both athletic director and head of the physical education department. In that new role, he had to decide whether to accept an offer for his 1963 baseball team to play in the NCAA's College Division East Regional tournament, which, at the time, was the only postseason tournament available to College Division teams. In fact, it was the only tournament of its kind anywhere, since the other regions had no tournament, and there was nothing held at the national level.

Interviewed twelve years later by James Sweeney, Coach Metheny recalled a pretty easy decision:

Sweeney: *In 1963, you accepted an invitation to the NCAA Atlantic Coast Regional College Division Tournament. Before this, you had indicated that the invitation would be turned down because freshmen would be ineligible. I wonder why you changed your mind?*

Metheny: *The best I can recall on that is that we didn't have too many freshmen, if any. I can't recall any on there right now—probably was one or two. So, we accepted because we didn't get hurt because of this. And that's when we went on and won the whole thing.*[20]

Possibly buoyed by the happy recollection of the Monarchs' performance in the tournament, this memory paints a little bit rosier picture than the true fact. Fred Balmer, Frazier O'Leary, Lee McDaniel, and Bill Yeargan were all freshmen and ineligible for the competition. The loss of the three hitters, to a team without a great deal of depth anyway, meant the unavailability of significant run-scoring and run-producing contributors. Combined, Balmer, O'Leary, and McDaniel had accounted for a total of thirty-nine runs scored (1.6 per game), thirty-nine runs knocked in (1.6 per game), fifty-six hits (2.24 per game), and a significant 174 at-bats (6.96 per game). The ineligibility of Bill Yeargan meant that the Monarchs also lost 20 percent of their five-man pitching staff.

Part of Metheny's consideration of the NCAA invitation must certainly have also rested on catcher John Ward's availability. In the fourth inning of an April 24th contest against Randolph-Macon College, Ward had been struck in the face by a pitched ball from Macon relief pitcher Earl Johnson. So horrific was the beaning that spectator Arlene Palmer Ingram recalls it even fifty-four years later: "I thought the pitcher killed him. He crumpled at the plate and lay there motionless. I can still hear and feel it."[21] The *Mace and Crown* reported that Ward's nose and cheek were broken, and Coach Metheny installed freshman Frazier O'Leary behind the plate for the rest of the regular season and the conference championship. But O'Leary wasn't eligible for the NCAA tournament, leaving Bud Metheny without a catcher if Ward wasn't available in time. Luckily for the Monarchs, just five weeks after pitcher John Ingram remembers paying a hospital visit to Ward when he "really looked awful" with broken facial bones, John Ward was ready to get back behind the plate.

Without the availability of his freshman contributors, Metheny still had a difficult choice. Consistent with his philosophy of attempting to raise the profile of his program and his school by accepting such challenges, however, he decided to accept the tournament bid, to be played that year on May 30 and 31 at Hampden-Sydney College's "Death Valley" in Farmville, Virginia.

Semifinals: *Old Dominion College vs. Coast Guard Academy*

The Monarchs faced the Coast Guard Academy of New London, Connecticut, in the first semifinal, beginning at 10 a.m. on Thursday, May 30, 1963. The Bears were led by Coach Carl Selin, a Navy veteran, former baseball and football player at Northern Illinois University, future member of the Coast Guard's athletic Hall of Fame, and a coach who had molded a program that had won zero games the year before his arrival into a legitimate contender for the NCAA's College Division Regional tournament. But Coast Guard's athletic director was the Bear with the real name recognition: Coast Guard sports were led by no less than Otto Graham, NFL champion quarterback and Hall of Famer, Washington Redskins head coach, and even a 5.2-points-per-game scorer on the champion 1945–46 Rochester Royals of the National Basketball League, a precursor to the NBA.

The 1963 edition of the Coast Guard yearbook, *Tide Rips* (written and published before spring sports seasons were complete) stated that "The Bear nine is the team to beat in New England in 1963. With the loss of only two starters from last year's squad which posted the finest record in Academy history, the outlook for this year seems even brighter."[22] Interviewed around the time of his 2004 induction into the Coast Guard Academy Hall of Fame, Coach Selin also remembered his 1963 team fondly, recalling "That year we could have played with anybody. All the big schools."[23] And the Bears had lived up to the hype on the diamond, posting a 13-6 overall record coming into the tournament, and scoring more runs than any of the other thirteen varsity programs in Connecticut, while only two of those schools had allowed fewer runs. The offensive leaders were leadoff man and shortstop Johnny Craven, described by the yearbook as a .400 hitter, and Bill "Thunder" Thompson, the cleanup man and first baseman, described as "the r.b.i. artist."[24]

Senior Bob Leggett led the mound corps and had posted a 0.89 ERA for the 1963 season coming into the game, allowing only three earned runs on 30⅓ innings pitched, while striking out twenty-four.[25] Coach Selin tabbed Leggett as his starter in the NCAA semifinal, to oppose Old Dominion's Fred Edmonds Jr. Missing Fred Balmer, Lee McDaniel, and Frazier O'Leary, Coach Metheny's offensive lineup looked a little different than any of the twenty-five previous lineups he had used during the season, although it was buoyed by the return of catcher John Ward after a five-week absence. In this game, Bob Walton started at first base, a position that had been the exclusive territory of Fred Balmer all season, and hit seventh in the lineup; left fielder Frank Zadell, who had hit exclusively in the seventh spot in the lineup all year, moved up to take the fifth spot, typically occupied by Balmer.

Batting as the visiting team, Old Dominion got off to a good start, as center fielder Fred Kovner singled and stole second. A one-out single by Jimmy Zadell pushed him to third and put runners on the corners, but cleanup batter Jerry Hammer followed by hitting into a 6-4-3 double play to end the threat. Old Dominion's defense made and escaped its own trouble in the bottom half, as leadoff man Johnny Craven reached on an error but was caught stealing by catcher Ward, and Bear center fielder Donnie Polk also reached on an error, but was erased at third on an assist by left fielder Frank Zadell.

The scoring opened in the bottom of the second, as the Bears pushed an unearned run across on the strength of a single by left fielder Larry Hyde. Edmonds, however, started to settle in, and worked around four Monarch errors, partly by striking out nine over seven effective innings. On the offensive side, Old Dominion immediately responded to Coast Guard's single run in the bottom of the second with two of their own in the top of the third, as Jimmy Zadell tripled home Wayne Parks, and was immediately driven home himself by a Jerry Hammer single. In the sixth, pitcher Fred Edmonds helped his own cause with a solo home run; in the seventh, a single by Hammer scored Wayne Parks, and a Frank Zadell triple plated one more, knocking Leggett from the game and leaving the score at 5–1 in favor of Old Dominion.

But the Bears showed signs of life in the eighth, as the first four batters reached base against Edmonds, scoring two runs and putting the tying runs on first and second, with no one out. Metheny brought Bob Walton in for relief, and Coach Carl Selin immediately had second baseman "Tater" Livingston execute a successful sacrifice that moved the tying runs into scoring position with one out for Coast Guard. Walton, however, rose to the high-pressure late-inning situation, notching the critical second out by striking out Larry Hyde, and then retiring a pinch hitter on a ball to Ron Killmon at second base.

The Bears would stir again in the ninth with a pair of one-out singles, but the scoring was done. Old Dominion was playing for the NCAA Regional title.

Finals: *Old Dominion College vs. State University of New York at Buffalo*

The final game of the 1963 NCAA tournament essentially became a grudge match, at least for the Monarchs. Prior to the game, the Buffalo coach, Jim Peelle, made a remark that was picked up by Monarch ears. Recalling that 1963 game twelve years later, Bud Metheny noted, "And then a funny thing happened there against the University of Buffalo. Just before the game started, a coach made a comment that our team didn't even look like ball players. And he said something to our pitcher, Bobby Walton, and he came over to me and he said, 'Coach,' he said, 'what's wrong with that coach?' And I said, 'Well, don't worry about it; just forget it.' And Bobby said, 'Well, we're going to beat them but good.'"[26] In 1977, Tony Zontini interviewed Coach Metheny again as part of the research for Zontini's master's thesis, and Metheny offered a further elaboration: "Freddie Edmonds Sr. was in the stands and heard the Buffalo coach comment that Old Dominion didn't even look like a ballclub. He quickly replied, 'They may not, but they will beat the [expletive] out of Buffalo.'"[27] For some extra bulletin-board material, the Old Dominion ballplayers may have also been aware of the Associated Press preview of the game, which ran in at least the Petersburg *Progress-Index* and the Danville *Bee* the day before the tournament, and stated, "If it weren't for this [freshman ineligibility], Old Dominion's Mason-Dixon Conference champions probably would be the favorites for the regional title. Instead, Buffalo gets the nod."[28]

The 1963 Bulls came into tournament play with plenty of confidence, and with good cause. 1963 was the team's ninth consecutive winning season, and in that time frame (including the current year to that point), Buffalo's winning percentage was 70.1 percent. According to the school's 2015 Media Guide, the team had opened 1963 by winning thirteen straight games (which is tied for the all-time school record in one season), and still holds the school's all-time record win streak of fifteen games, if two games from 1962 are carried over. As a team, the 1963 squad batted .309. But to cap it off, the 1963 Bulls featured a one-two pitching combination that still represents two of the three best career ERAs ever at the school: Jim Krawczyk to this day is credited with Buffalo's all-time single-season ERA title with his 0.43 in 1963, and his career number of 1.37 is the second-best ever. Gerald "Larry" Gergley was the second half of this 1963 combo, and is credited with a career 1.39 ERA, just behind Krawczyk.[29]

But Krawczyk had pitched a complete game in the semifinals, as the Bulls had beaten Hampden-Sydney by ten runs in an easy 12–2 win, leaving the task of earning the championship against Old Dominion to Gergley. To oppose him, Bud Metheny unsurprisingly went with Bob Walton, despite Walton having thrown two innings the day before. In a likely attempt to create some consistency, Metheny stayed with the same batting order as the day before, although once again players were necessarily out of defensive position. Jerry Hammer, a shortstop and very occasional right fielder in 1963, started the game at first, and Fred Edmonds started the game at shortstop, batting ninth. Neither had played either of those positions the entire year. Edmonds, in fact, had only pitched during the 1963 Monarch season, and had not otherwise manned *any* defensive position.

Old Dominion again batted as the visiting team, and the game was quiet for the first three innings. Gergley faced the minimum nine batters through the first three with the help of one double play, and inducing ground balls that led to seven assists by his middle infielders on the first nine Old Dominion hitters. Walton, too, was in control, allowing only a harmless single to right fielder John Stofa in the second. The Monarchs even got solid early play from Fred Edmonds at short, who assisted on outs by the very first two Buffalo batters, on his way to successful conversion of all eight defensive chances that would come his way in the game.

Old Dominion opened the scoring in the fourth inning, as Fred Kovner and Wayne Parks led off with back-to-back singles, and came around to score when Buffalo shortstop Steve Wasula booted a ball off the bat of Ron Killmon. In the fifth, the Monarchs broke it wide open. John Ward—who contributed significantly in his return to action in this two-game tournament, going two-for-seven with two walks, two runs scored and a .444 on-base percentage—led off with a single and scored on Fred Kovner's home run. Jimmy Zadell knocked in Wayne Parks with a triple. Jerry Hammer walked, Ron Killmon reached on another error, and Frank Zadell pushed another run across with a single. By the time it was done, ten batters had come to the plate, Old Dominion had a 7–0 lead—and Peelle still had Gergley in the game.

Walton had not slowed. For the game, he would only strike out five batters, but he walked none, and the defense was stout behind him, as just one runner reached by error, only to be erased in the next at-bat as part of a double play turned by Fred Edmonds at short. As Edmonds played out of position and handled all eight chances that came his way, so too did Jerry Hammer successfully convert the eleven chances he got at first base. The strong defense helped Walton on his way to facing only thirty-one batters in the game, just four more than the minimum.

Old Dominion added single, but ultimately meaningless, runs in the eighth and ninth, as John Ward and Ron Killmon respectively walked and scored. Walton had pitched a complete game, and as Bud Metheny noted in the 1975 interview, "Bobby went out, and he set a record at the time that has since been broken. He threw seventy-two pitches in a nine-inning game, and we beat them 9–0. And so that's the kind of team they were, real competitors."[30] Gergley, too, had pitched a complete game, but with ten Monarch base hits, six walks allowed, and two batters reaching by error, Gergley's pitch count must have been much higher than seventy-two, although Metheny's scorebook does not provide that count.

While available sources suggest that news of Old Dominion's Mason-Dixon Conference championship had been largely confined to the conference's home states of Virginia and Maryland, coverage of the NCAA victory spread further along the Mid-Atlantic and New England states. Newspapers in places such as Kingsport, Tennessee, and Bridgeport, Connecticut, provided coverage of the championship game with sportswriters' articles, but the score of the game was reported by papers much further removed, getting Old Dominion College's name in newspapers in places such as Oakland, Des Moines, Kansas City, and Rapid City, South Dakota.

After the season, predictably, accolades flowed. For their inaugural work in the conference, the Monarchs garnered five of the available ten first-team Mason-Dixon All-Star spots, as Wayne Parks, Frank Zadell, Jimmy Zadell, Fred Edmonds, and Bob Walton all were honored. How Old Dominion center fielder Fred Kovner was overlooked for the same honor is mystifying, since his twenty-seven-game season, extrapolated to a 162-game schedule, would have included a .330 average, forty-two home runs, forty-two stolen bases, 156 runs scored, and 102 RBI. Inexplicably, these numbers didn't even merit honorable mention to the Mason-Dixon voters.

Bob Walton, with a 1.42 ERA and an average of less than one baserunner per inning permitted, was also subsequently named as a first-team All-American by *Collegiate Baseball*. Right fielder Jimmy Zadell was named as a second-team All-American on the strength of his outstanding .422 batting average. Yet despite such nationally recognized performers on the team, it was Frank Zadell, with thirty-six runs batted in over twenty-seven games, who was voted by the team as the Most Valuable Player. As Jimmy Zadell recalled in 2016, "In Bud's memoirs, he makes a statement regarding All-Americans. And he says, 'Well, Frank Zadell was All-American in 1963.' *I* was the All-American in 1963! But you know something? In the back of Bud's mind, he *knew* who should have been the All-American. I think Bud made a slip of the tongue, but he always knew Frank was the best. Frank was the most valuable player on the team, and he didn't get All-American, and I think Bud knew that—that it was the wrong decision."[31] For his own part in guiding the team, former New York Yankee Bud Metheny had his name in the national news again, as he was named by the American Association of College Baseball Coaches as "Coach of the Year" for District III of the College Division, which included the states of Virginia, Maryland, West Virginia, North Carolina, and South Carolina.

Monarchs Grab Regional Crown

HAMPDEN-SYDNEY (AP)—Old Dominion's Bob Walton gave up four hits Friday in blanking Buffalo, 9-0, as the Monarchs won the NCAA small college Atlantic Coast regional baseball title.

Hampden - Sydney topped the Coast Guard Academy, 4-3, in a morning game to win third place.

Walton and Buffalo's Larry Gergley pitched to a scoreless standoff the first three innings before Old Dominion's Fred Kovner opened up with a single which led to the first two runs in the fourth inning.

The fifth inning was a wild af-

See Walton, Page 15, Col. 1

Old Dominion	000 250 011—9	10 1
Buffalo	000 000 000—0	4 3

Walton and Ward. Gergley and Dulucia, Haut. (7). Home run, Oold Dominion Kovner.

Walton Sparkles In Monarch Win

Continued From Page Fourteen

fair for Old Dominion, which batted around. Fred Kovner banged a homer with one on and John Zadell socked a triple to get two RBIs.

Kovner and Zadell's hits were the only extra-base whacks of the game.

Walton pitched to 31 batters, struck out five and didn't give a walk.

It was the second top-notch performance for Walton in two days. It was Walton who came on in the eighth to stop a Coast Guard Academy rally Thursday and preserve a 5-3 win which boosted Old Dominion into Friday's finals.

The win lifted Old Dominion's season record to 22-5. Buffalo closed out with a 15-3 mark.

Reporting in the Newport News Daily Press, *June 1, 1963. Copyrighted 1943–1965. Associated Press.*

The 1963 baseball Monarchs, from the 1964 Troubadour yearbook. Top row, left to right: Coach Bud Metheny, Boyd Nix, Lee McDaniel, Fred Edmonds Jr., Jerry Hammer, John Young. Middle row: Ron Killmon, John Ward, John Ingram, Frazier O'Leary, Fred Kovner, Bill Yeargan. Bottom row: Frank Zadell, Ronnie Evans, Bob Walton, Wayne Parks, John Cooke, Jim Zadell, Fred Balmer. Seated at front: batboy Joe Grandy. Courtesy of Special Collections and University Archives, Old Dominion University.

1963 OLD DOMINION MONARCHS TEAM LEADERS

(Collated from records in Bud Metheny's scorebook, including postseason)

	AB		R		RBI		2B	
1.	KOVNER	106	PARKS	28	F ZADELL	36	BALMER	8
2.	PARKS	103	KOVNER	26	BALMER	22	PARKS	8
3.	F ZADELL	93	BALMER	24	PARKS	18	F ZADELL	8
4.	BALMER	89	KILLMON	21	J ZADELL	18	KILLMON	7
5.	HAMMER	85	HAMMER	20	KOVNER	17	KOVNER	6
6.	J ZADELL	83	F ZADELL	19	HAMMER	15	J ZADELL	4
7.	KILLMON	82	J ZADELL	18	McDANIEL	11	HAMMER	3
8.	O'LEARY	48	McDANIEL	11	KILLMON	10	McDANIEL	2
9.	WARD	44	EDMONDS	7	WALTON	7	O'LEARY	2
10.	McDANIEL	37	WALTON	6	2 tied with	6	3 tied with	1

	3B		HR		SB		AVG	
1.	J ZADELL	4	KOVNER	7	KOVNER	7	COOKE	0.500
2.	F ZADELL	4	F ZADELL	3	PARKS	5	J ZADELL	0.422
3.	HAMMER	2	BALMER	2	BALMER	4	F ZADELL	0.398
4.	KILLMON	2	HAMMER	2	HAMMER	4	BALMER	0.371
5.	KOVNER	2	EDMONDS	1	F ZADELL	4	EDMONDS	0.367
6.	BALMER	1	KILLMON	1	KILLMON	4	KOVNER	0.330
7.	PARKS	1	McDANIEL	1	COOKE	3	PARKS	0.330
8.	11 tied with	0	PARKS	1	O'LEARY	2	KILLMON	0.317
9.			10 tied with	0	J ZADELL	2	McDANIEL	0.297
10.					2 tied with	1	HAMMER	0.282

	IP		K		K/9	
1.	WALTON	69.67	EDMONDS	64	EDMONDS	8.73
2.	EDMONDS	66	WALTON	43	INGRAM	7.26
3.	INGRAM	31	INGRAM	25	YEARGAN	5.93
4.	YEARGAN	27.33	YEARGAN	18	WALTON	5.56
5.	BRADSHAW	24.67	BRADSHAW	11	BRADSHAW	4.01

	BB		BB/9		W	
1.	EDMONDS	34	WALTON	0.65	EDMONDS	8
2.	INGRAM	18	YEARGAN	1.98	WALTON	7
3.	BRADSHAW	11	BRADSHAW	4.01	INGRAM	3
4.	YEARGAN	6	EDMONDS	4.64	BRADSHAW	2
5.	WALTON	5	INGRAM	5.23	YEARGAN	2

	L		ERA		WHIP	
1.	WALTON	2	WALTON	1.42	WALTON	0.95
2.	BRADSHAW	2	YEARGAN	1.98	YEARGAN	1.17
3.	YEARGAN	1	INGRAM	2.61	INGRAM	1.42
4.			EDMONDS	3.00	EDMONDS	1.45
5.			BRADSHAW	5.47	BRADSHAW	1.58

Plaque recognizing the three championships won by the Monarchs. In possession of the family of John Ingram.

CHAPTER SEVEN

Changing Times

At present, we are in an era of transformation.

—BUD METHENY, *in the* Mace and Crown, *January 15, 1965*

THE ASSASSINATION OF JFK

The year 1964 ushered in a different time for Old Dominion College and the baseball Monarchs. Cold War hostilities with Russia, and the concern over the Communist threat, had become a real and ever-present part of life, beginning with the Korean conflict in 1950. More recently, the failed 1961 "Bay of Pigs" CIA coup attempt against Fidel Castro's Communist government, and the Cuban Missile Crisis standoff in October of 1962, had heightened these concerns, leaving many in fear of nuclear war with Russia. But against this backdrop, the American home front in the post-World War II years prior to 1964 was relatively peaceful and prosperous. The national economy was good, and the worst of the scandals rocking the nation may have been the wiggling of Elvis Presley's pelvis. This was "Camelot" in the United States, as former First Lady Jackie Kennedy famously opined after her husband's death, coining a phrase so appropriately representative of the times that it has endured to the present day as the descriptor for the era.[1]

Camelot ended in Dallas, Texas, on November 22, 1963, as bullets from an assassin's gun took the life of President John Fitzgerald Kennedy. With those bullets, the idealized innocence of the 1950s came to an end, and symbolically opened the door to the turbulence of the 1960s in America. It may be impossible to gauge the true effect of this seminal event on the national psyche, but one measure is certainly that no American alive at the time forgets it, or where they were at the time.

Old Dominion pitcher John Ingram, a junior at the time, recalls receiving the terrible news while in an anatomy class at Old Dominion. Old Dominion outfielder and pitcher Tom Harrell, not in school at the time, remembers getting the news while traveling with his wife to Chowan, North Carolina. Old Dominion left fielder Frank Zadell recalls specifically that he was going into the library on campus at the time and was informed by people standing out front.

Colonel Boyd Nix, USAF (Ret.), a pitcher on the 1963 Old Dominion team, recalls, "Our president was assassinated on November 22, 1963, and I don't believe there was a dry eye on campus that day. Also, we all attended and played for Old Dominion during this time. In fact, I was pledging a fraternity and me and a couple of my buddies captured a brother but released him when we heard of the assassination because we were all devastated."[2]

Fred Kovner, the star center fielder of the Old Dominion teams in the early 1960s, recalls the shock, but with a slightly different take: "I was walking in the fraternity house because it was a Friday afternoon, and we had a keg party. We were there, and then somebody came in and said, 'The President's been shot and we're closing down the keg.' And I'm thinking, 'Why? Why are we stopping the party?' That was exactly . . . right around two o'clock, or something like that. I was out of class, I was headed to the fraternity party, or fraternity house, to start our happy hour. The keg was going, and then they closed the keg down. I don't know what the timing was, someone said he was shot, and soon thereafter somebody said he had died. Yes, I remember exactly where I was on that particular day."[3]

Arlene Palmer Ingram, Old Dominion 1964 Senior Class President and wife of John Ingram, also provides succinct perspective on the event and its historical importance: "I was student teaching at a school in Norfolk that was a pretty deprived school called Coleman Place Elementary, and I was way in the back, and about one o'clock in the afternoon, I came in and heard the shocking news, and you just . . . there were no words that could express how I felt or how everyone else felt. It was like 9/11, it was like when the Challenger crashed. It was just—there were no words that could explain how you really felt—just speechless, shocking."[4]

MUSIC

The true effect of the assassination of the president on the course of history is certainly one that is impossible to judge, but at the beginning of 1964, there were still other new, or simmering, forces conspiring to shape the character of an American generation. In 1963, popular music was still generally an extension of the 1950s, as bubble-gum balladry or beach music dominated the airwaves. The style of music popular at the time focused less on lyrical content and intensity than it did on establishing a recognizable and identifiable hook: "He's So Fine," "Hey Paula," "Surfin' USA," "Wipeout," and the fraternity-rock standard "Louie Louie" were among the biggest hits for the year.

But on February 9, 1964, the Beatles made their first American television appearance on the Ed Sullivan Show, an event watched by almost *half* of all Americans with televisions, as described by edsullivan.com: "At 8 o'clock on February 9th 1964, America tuned in to CBS and *The Ed Sullivan Show*. But this night was different. Seventy-three million people gathered in front their TV sets to see The Beatles' first live performance on US soil. The television rating was a record-setting 45.3, meaning that 45.3 percent of households with televisions were watching. That figure reflected a total of 23,240,000 American homes television's [sic]. The show garnered a 60 share, meaning 60 percent of the television's turned on were tuned in to Ed Sullivan and The Beatles."[5]

And so began a generational battle between American fathers and American sons regarding the appropriate length of hair. The music that was popular with American audiences didn't change overnight, though. In fact, the Beatles had performed such innocuous hits as "All My Loving" and "I Want to Hold Your Hand" on Sullivan's show, and the biggest hits of 1964 still included beach-music favorites by The Beach Boys and Jan and Dean, and songs such as "My Guy," "Under the Boardwalk," and "Chapel of Love" by the Dixie Cups. But a full five of the top sixteen biggest hits of 1964 were authored by The Beatles, beginning an influence that would be profound in the second half of the 1960s. With The Beatles began the ideas of change—artists that wanted to change the world with their music and lyrics, not merely reflect it. The Beatles' appearance (like "eels after an explosion in a wig factory" . . . "long, monstrous, shaggy haircuts," according to at least one writer)[6] also represented freedom to some and change from the conformity of the day.

Reaction to The Beatles' initial American television performance wasn't universally favorable, despite the numbers of people who tuned in to watch it. The *Virginian-Pilot*'s Warner Twyford, a long-time veteran of the paper, reported in the February 11 edition that the "Beatles have infested our land, and so far I have heard nothing about a [now-banned pesticide] dieldrin counter-attack from the agriculture department." After a review of their music as "strictly routine," featuring "voices innocuous but inoffensive," Twyford concluded that he could not identify the reason for the mass hysteria surrounding the Beatles, and ended his account with an evaluation of their hairstyles: "Then mindful of Samson, bring on Delilah!"[7] For generational context, Mr. Twyford was in his mid-fifties when he wrote this review, and his article also compared the Beatles unfavorably to Frank Sinatra. For stylistic context, it should be further noted that fellow long-time *Virginian-Pilot* writer (and one-time assistant to Twyford) Mal Vincent recalled in 2017 that Twyford "wrote lines like: 'This person belongs on the stage—the next stage to Tucson' and 'the Norfolk Symphony played Beethoven last night. Beethoven lost.'"[8]

A representative account from VMI's *The VMI Cadet* appears on the following page, and refers to the group as having hair so long that "we can't see their faces, but maybe this is a blessing," and in musical terms, John Lennon, Paul McCartney, and George Harrison as the "grinning cronies" of Ringo Starr, who just "stand in front and wail."[9] Richmond Professional Institute's *Proscript* referred to the group as "unkempt," and even questioned the band's very hygiene, opining that "cleanliness is not next to godliness any more."[10]

The articles drew some predictable reaction, and one in particular in the edition of RPI's *Proscript* that followed. In a letter to the newspaper, Karol Linthicum wrote succinctly for many of her generation when she noted, "Then you make fun of their hair style which dates back to the late Gothic and early Renaissance England, according to Lucy Barton's 'Historic Costume for the Stage.' I infer that, basically, you object to their hair style because it doesn't conform to the masses. How can anyone attending RPI condemn originality? Worst of all, you make fun of their style of singing. You clamor for your stereotypes, Doris Day and Yul Brynner, while turning your back on the Beatle's [sic] special charm. What is their drawing power? I can't define it, but when I hear a Beatle record, it makes me feel 'happy inside' like nothing else can."[11]

The Beatles, for all their power to effect generational changes across their home country and abroad, don't seem to have had a tremendous effect on the baseball Monarchs. Left fielder Frank Zadell recalls, "Well, I saw it on TV. I mean, I saw them going on the Ed Sullivan Show . . . I'm more of, like, American rock and roll . . . it wasn't really my style

The Beatles Invade:

Insecticides Useless

Never have so few meant so much to so many. We speak, of course, of the Beatles, the hottest thing since the hula hoops and Elizabeth Taylor. These youngsters—we use this term after rejecting other things to call them —have descended on America in what must be the most grandiose attack four insects have ever made. We must admit they have snowed our women and bolstered Ed Sullivan's Trendex rating so we must give them credit.

Now that we have given them credit, let's look at them (ever examined a bug?). Their performance is quite long-hair—so long, in fact, we can't see their faces, but maybe this is a blessing. When (sigh!) we do see their faces we are treated to grins so toothy as to make J. Fred Muggs envious. The best grinner is Ringo who also beats the drums. It is difficult however, to judge his percussion talent because it is drowned out by his three grinning cronies— Paul, George, and John (sorry girls, he's married) who just stand in front and wail.

The overall result (soundwise) is really not unpleasant, especially the first 400 times it's heard. And the lyrics are super: "She loves you, yeah, yeah, yeah, she loves you, yeah, yeah, yeah, she loves . . . ." and so on into the night. About the only thing the Beatles lack is variety and talent.

Alas, like all fads, the Beatles may fade out like hula hoops; or, they may last forever like Elizabeth Taylor. But someday their star is bound to decline. Twenty years from now they might become bald and that could end it all.

Or they just might be appointed to the British Foreign Ministry Then England could just sing her enemies to death.

What a horrible way to die!

From The VMI Cadet, *February 14, 1964. Courtesy of Virginia Military Institute Archives.*

of music. I liked the more rock and roll stuff."[12] Infielder Mel Renn recalls, "I was pretty much a Beatle fan . . . but I always was a country music fan. Of course, country music is very popular today, and I'm still hanging with them."[13]

But to catcher Jimmy Walker, a freshman in 1964, the popularity of the Beatles' music took a much darker turn, leading directly to a chewing-out from his coach: "One time when we were playing at VMI, we were in their—they looked like barracks—cots everywhere, all over the place. We were waiting for time to get up and go get dressed. We were laying on the cots, he [Coach Metheny] walked in, and I was singing that Beatles song 'That Boy.' I don't know if you've ever even heard that, but that was a hit then. He thought I said 'Fat Boy' when he walked in. Man, he jumped all over me! I didn't do anything wrong. I never thought he was fat. He was burly, he was, you know, a big man."[14]

RACE

The simmering issues of race in America may not have been particularly visible to the boys of the Monarch baseball teams in the early 1960s. After all, no black students attended Old Dominion College. In fact, in the entire 1964 *Troubadour* yearbook, there is only a single African-American face: on page 128, a black man is shown tending bar at a "TIGA" fraternity party, under a ticking Old Milwaukee clock—a scene captured on film and published in the yearbook somewhat ironically, since the initials TIGA stood for Tolerance, Integrity, Gentility, and *Abstinence*.

Some members of the Old Dominion team had never attended school at any level with black children and had never competed on the field of play against black athletes. Pitcher John Ingram, a senior in 1964, was one of the few players from Virginia Beach (or what was then Princess Anne County, before it became the city of Virginia Beach in 1963), and had attended Princess Anne High School. Black students didn't attend high school with white students in Virginia Beach; they attended the Princess Anne County Training School, which became Union-Kempsville High School in 1962. Younger African-American children in 1950s Virginia Beach also had their own elementary schools—Seatack and Seaboard. Ingram did not recall from his experience anything akin to the iconic pictures of the segregated South that so imprint the American national consciousness—no "Whites" and "Colored" signs, no separate bathrooms. Simply, he recalls of the races, "They just didn't mix."[15] Reflecting on his athletic career in 2017, in fact, Ingram recalls only a single occasion when he shared a baseball diamond with an African-American competitor: one game, during his Old Dominion college career, against a black pitcher who played for the Marines of Camp Lejeune.

Several Old Dominion ballplayers who attended high school in Norfolk (which comprised ten out of the sixteen players on the 1964 non-freshman roster) had a much different high-school experience. Public school segregation had legally ended in 1954 with the United States Supreme Court's *Brown vs. Board of Education* decision, which declared segregation by race unconstitutional. In practice, segregation still existed, but by September 1958, federal judges in Virginia were ordering an end to separate schools. Governor J. Lindsay Almond Jr., however, acting under the so-called "Massive Resistance" laws enacted by the Virginia General Assembly in 1956, ordered public schools in Warren County, Charlottesville, and Norfolk to close before the 1958 school year, rather than integrate. As a result, Norfolk's Maury, Norview, and Granby High Schools, as well as Northside, Norview, and Blair Junior High Schools, were all closed, keeping seventeen prospective black students and an approximate 10,000 white students out of school, and leaving their parents to try to find alternate means of education. Many of these students were educated in church basements, some found "tutoring groups," some moved to areas where schools were open, and certainly some received no education at all.

Among thousands of other students, schools closed on future Old Dominion ballplayers Fred Kovner at Granby High School, Wayne Parks at Maury High School, and Tom Harrell at Northside Junior High. Parks, a junior at the start of 1958, recalls attending a makeshift school at a church with several other students from Maury,[16] and Harrell recalls attending the start of his ninth grade year at a Baptist church on Bayview Boulevard.[17] While the schools were closed, from September 27, 1958, until February 2, 1959, the "Norfolk Seventeen" (the African-American schoolchildren who would attend the six closed and formerly all-white schools) also attended a makeshift school, in the basement of the First Baptist Church on Bute Street in Norfolk.[18]

Sophomore Fred Kovner, as the son of Norfolk Division faculty member Edgar Kovner, had a different, somewhat more positive experience while locked out of Granby:

> *My education was, my father was the Dean at Old Dominion . . . all the professors at Old Dominion that had high school kids that were locked out of the schools, they opened up a little school at Old Dominion. That's who my teachers were — the head of the English Department, the head of the Math Department, the head of the Science Department, a Latin scholar, all that stuff. We didn't have any study hall, or any gym. We just went to class.*
>
> *We started probably six weeks into the first semester. But these guys said, 'We've got to do the whole first semester's work in a short period of time.' So, we covered the first semester's work in all those subjects in two six-weeks rather than three. And then when the schools didn't open in January, my dad pulled a string and I wound up going to Wilson High School for a week. Then when school was opened, I came back to Granby.*
>
> *In other words, you've got a [college] math teacher that's got his regular load and says, OK, we'll have geometry class three days a*

week or four days a week on a varying schedule, whenever he could make it. They built a schedule, and they would come over, teach for an hour, and walk back to their classes at Old Dominion. We got a great education.

The kids, different churches had what they called 'tutoring groups' and different kids went to the different places and got an education of some type. When we got back to Granby the teachers would say, 'OK, how far did you get?' Most people probably got a quarter of the way through the book. We all backed up to where they were, to cover that material. In a sense, it was almost a waste for me, since I already covered it.

A number of kids, like if you had an uncle who lived in Georgia, maybe your parents sent you down there to Georgia to go to school, to live with your uncle. A number of kids went out of state. A number of kids went to South Norfolk to go to Oscar Smith. I'm sure some kids went to Virginia Beach, and went to those high schools. And I guess some at the last minute could get into Norfolk Academy, or schools like that. The rest of them had tutoring groups. I ran into one kid that I knew, within the last two or three years when they were doing all this stuff, he said he just went to Gray's Pharmacy and read comic books for a semester.

I remember there was a kid that was a sophomore in our class that was shipped off to Georgia. He won a state wrestling championship in Georgia. And then as a junior, came back to Granby and wrestled JV. He couldn't make Billy Martin's varsity. I remember it as nineteen out of twenty [state championships for Billy Martin's Granby High School wrestling team], and the year they didn't win it was when we opened the schools in January, and the states were in February. So Billy Martin had his kids for a month. They came in second . . . that's all he needed, a month. If they'd have had six weeks they would have won the whole thing. That's the only year they lost in that streak. Now, my recollection is nineteen out of twenty years, but hey, stories get better as *we get older.*[19] [In fact, the story is even better than the memory—Martin's teams actually won twenty-one out of twenty-two state championships.]

Parochial schools in the city, such as Norfolk Catholic High School, were not affected by *Brown vs. Board of Education*, as the ruling pertained to public schools. But as Frank Zadell recalls, Norfolk Catholic was already integrated when he attended in the late 1950s, and he remembers several black students in his grade. "I had some good friends, I thought nothing of it. And when I would ride the [Norfolk city] bus to grade school when I was seven, eight, nine, ten years old or something like that, I mean there were black people on the bus, and I would sit right with them. It didn't bother me at all. I didn't see much prejudice—any, really. I know the school, the public schools, they shut them down, kids went to different schools at churches and stuff like that, but I wasn't really impacted by it."[20]

That perspective of indifference to race, and to the emotional legacies left by years of race-based injustices, summarizes well the viewpoint of so many schoolchildren of the time. Old Dominion outfielder and sometimes-pitcher Tom Harrell went to St. Mary's Academy, a parochial school in Norfolk, for his first eight years, and recalls some of his first experiences: "I was a kid that was in like the third grade, but I would go to those [black-owned] stores. Little white kid with a uniform on. I would go to the store and buy some marbles or baseball cards—you know, you'd buy bubblegum and you'd get five baseball cards or something like that in a package. If I had some money, I would go buy some baseball cards for a nickel or whatever. But I was treated fine. I never knew anything about the race problem or anything, and I don't think any of the kids did. It was all adults, and, like the government, they think they know what's best for you."[21]

Arlene Palmer Ingram was locked out of Granby High School before her junior year in 1958. When asked about it in 2016, she summarized the experience in a similar way: "A lot of it didn't seem like reality . . . my lasting image is one of sort of disruption and stupidity by the people who know that education is the most important thing that you can give to a child, or one of the most important things, and to impede that was just stupid."[22]

Even Bud Metheny himself was not exempted from issues of race. On January 11, 1957, it was erroneously reported by several newspapers that Norfolk Division basketball coach Metheny had informed Shepherd College coach Jess Riggleman that Shepherd's two black basketball players, Bill Grant and Paul Williams, would not be permitted to take the floor in a contest in Norfolk. In fact, Shepherd's players were *not* permitted to play, but in the Newport News *Daily Press* account of January 12, Norfolk Division Athletic Director J. C. "Scrap" Chandler acknowledged that he had broken the news to Riggleman, acting on the guidance of Norfolk Division Director Lewis Webb.[23] Webb himself was acting in accordance with a "higher authority," namely the William & Mary Board of Visitors' interpretation of an

Two Negro Cagers Barred From Playing In College Clash

Norfolk, Va. (AP) — Shepherd college of Shepherdstown, W. Va., dropped a 78-70 basketball decision last night to Norfolk William and Mary in a game in which the losers were not permitted to play two Negroes.

Jess Riggelman, Shepherd coach, was informed early yesterday afternoon by Coach Bud Metheny of Norfolk W&M that the two Negro members of the visiting Rams' team would not be allowed to play.

The Shepherd coach was ready to leave the decision to his squad whether to go ahead with the game, but the Negro players suggested the team play. The Negroes are William Grant, regular center, and Paul Williams, a freshman.

The Virginia general assembly last year prohibited integrated athletics in the state's public high schools, but the law does not apply to colleges. Norfolk W&M is a state-supported institution.

From the Gazette and Daily, York, PA, January 11, 1957. Copyrighted 1943–1965. Associated Press.

unwritten policy of the state of Virginia, barring interracial competition at the collegiate level.

Metheny recalled this incident in a May 1975 interview:

Dr. James Sweeney: *In January of 1957 a serious controversy arose over the Division's refusal to allow Shepherd College of West Virginia to use two black players in its basketball game with the Division at Norfolk. Coach Jess Riggleman of Shepherd declared that, if he had had his black players, the game, which was won by the Division 78–70, would not 'have been much of a contest.' The newspapers saw the action by the Norfolk Division as arbitrary because the General Assembly resolution prohibiting integrated athletics in state public schools did not apply to colleges. Reference to college athletics was stricken from the resolution before it was adopted. Also one black had played the previous night against the Apprentice School at Newport News, and blacks had appeared on visiting basketball and football squads previously in Virginia. There are two questions about this incident. I wonder if you could supply your recollections about and your reaction to it, and did the incident cause a rupture in our athletic competition with Shepherd College?*

Metheny: *Back in those days, being a state institution, we did not have integrated schools. And Apprentice School is not a state institution. But this was blown up by a mistaken thing that was said by the newspapers and by television. And we had no qualms against playing against blacks except from the state government—nothing written, but implied—that they would request that this didn't happen. Now I was accused of stopping this, but I wasn't the one that stopped this. And I went to the newspapers and the television, and they retracted and apologized to me for saying that I was responsible for this.*[24]

The Norfolk schools reopened, and Coach Metheny was vindicated personally, but to think that the 1959 integration of six schools in Norfolk had the effect of settling any regional or national debates on the subject of race would be a deep misinterpretation of history. In 1964, at least one article on race relations appeared in Norfolk's *Virginian-Pilot* newspaper every single day of the Old Dominion Monarchs baseball season. In some cases, nonviolent civil rights protests or demonstrations were reported—in Tallahassee, Indianapolis, San Francisco, New York City, and, closer to Norfolk, in Suffolk and in Petersburg. But some of the demonstrations took a violent turn, as well: three days of violence in Jacksonville, 285 arrested in St. Augustine, a civil rights demonstrator's death in Cleveland touching off "rock-throwing, car-smashing disorders,"[25] "club-swinging policemen" breaking up "antisegregation demonstrations by Negro teenagers" in Nashville,[26] and a suspected arson in the burning of a recently desegregated school in Alabama.

As such events and protest unfolded across the country, the Civil Rights bill submitted to Congress by slain President John F. Kennedy was under debate in the United States Senate. As Old Dominion's 1964 baseball team first took the field for a practice game on March 25, the government of the United States was in the process of considering legislation that would do no less than truly define America in terms of its treatment of all citizens. Would the United States of America legally accept discrimination based on race, color, religion, or national origin? Segregated schools? Unequal application of voter registration requirements? The answer, ultimately, was "no." Less than two weeks after the Monarchs' 1964 season ended, the United States Senate passed "the most sweeping civil rights legislation in the nation's history," according to the Senate's website. The law remains "one of the most significant legislative achievements in American history."[27]

VIETNAM

While not an everyday occurrence during the 1964 baseball season, the *Virginian-Pilot* very routinely covered events in Vietnam as well, as United States involvement in Southeast Asia began to ramp up in earnest. The first combat missions by US forces against the Viet Cong had occurred in 1962, and between April and June of 1964, American air power in Vietnam was on a steady increase. With military conscription a real and ever-present possibility between the years 1948 and 1973, members of the 1964 Monarch baseball team could read such *Pilot* headlines in April 1964 as "Vietnam Stepup Hinted" (April 19), "Stepup By U.S. Forecast" (April 24), and "Widening the War in Vietnam" (April 26).

On the Old Dominion campus, however, Vietnam didn't yet register with great impact in 1964, perhaps partly because the college was mainly a commuter school. Frank Zadell remembers of the time, "I went to school, and you don't live there in those days. I went home, I commuted from my parents' home in Norview. I wasn't at school on weekends, when all that kind of stuff [protests] may be going on."[28] Tom Harrell, too, remembers, "There were not any kind of protests going on; there was not any kind of talk about it. It was just not in Norfolk. I might have been out of the loop as far as news was concerned, but I don't remember anything back then."[29]

The first article in Old Dominion's school newspaper *The Mace and Crown* pertaining to Vietnam did not appear until October 4, 1965. On that day, the paper published an account of an address to the History Club by Old Dominion professor Dr. William Schellings, comparing and contrasting the European policy of appeasement during Germany's annexations in the 1930s to the developing policy towards Vietnam. (In an incidental side note, Dr. Schellings was also a favorite of Old Dominion ballplayers and History majors Frank and Jimmy Zadell. Jimmy Zadell recalls Dr. Schellings as "a great supporter of Old Dominion baseball. He loved it, he cherished it; he cherished baseball. I'll never forget him, he was such a supporter for us, and he's the reason that Frank and I graduated." Of course, it didn't hurt that Jimmy Zadell also remembers springtime encouragement from Dr. Schellings such as, "Hey, you Zadells! If either of you hit a home run, I'm going to give you an A.")[30]

Demonstrating a general and continuing lack of interest in the affairs of Southeast Asia on campus, the paper attributed to Dr. Schellings the sentiment that "students at Old Dominion are not truly interested as a whole in the problems of Southeast Asia. He [Dr. Schellings] cited as his reason for this conclusion the fact that on two separate occasions, in two semesters, he had offered a course dealing with the problems and history of this part of the world. Lack of interest forced the termination of this offer, he said, proving the emptiness of true student interest in the affairs of Southeast Asia."[31] Yet, over the next year and a half, the subject of Vietnam *did* become an important and regular feature in the school newspaper, as United States involvement became an important issue to students. On March 3, 1967, the *Mace and Crown* reported the first demonstration on campus against Vietnam involvement, in which an approximate eighteen protesters were "pelted with raw eggs and were subjected to harsh reprimands by several bystanders throughout the march."[32]

Still, in 1964, the prospect of service in Vietnam was a very real one to the members of the baseball team. Several eventually received deferments: Fred Edmonds received a student deferment, Mel Renn and John Ingram teaching deferments, and Tom Harrell received a marriage deferment. At the same time, even at this early stage of the United States' involvement in the conflict, several of Bud Metheny's young men served in Vietnam. Frank Zadell, citing the influence of his father, himself a Navy man, went to Officer Candidate School in the Navy, and served at the American Naval Base at Cam Ranh Bay, among other places. Boyd Nix, pitcher on the 1963 team, recalls, "Immediately after graduation, I joined the Air Force, got my commission and attended pilot training. Later I was assigned to Thailand,

and had 100 missions flying at night in Laos in support of the U.S. air war effort. After thirty-one years in the Air Force, I retired as a Full Colonel. Frazier O'Leary [catcher on the 1963 Old Dominion team] served as a U.S. Army enlisted soldier on the ground in Vietnam, and he had it much worse than I did."[33] Additionally, although pitcher Bill Yeargan's whereabouts after college are unknown to the author, available records suggest strongly (although don't prove) that he, too, served, as a member of the United States Air Force between the years 1965 and 1969.[34]

COLLEGE GROWTH

The college itself was growing, too, a fact which began to define the campus tenor, as evidenced by how students wrote about the institution; the 1963 *Troubadour* yearbook is replete with references to the "growth" and "expansion" in Norfolk. At the very beginning of that yearbook, the Foreword refers to Old Dominion as a "dynamic and expanding institution, surging forward under youthful leadership to meet the needs, of education today." Just one page later, "Striving to meet the demands of higher education, the College is now in the midst of a building program greater than any since its founding. At present many millions of dollars are being put to work building classrooms, laboratories, and the many other facilities essential to a growing College." Summarizing four years' worth of changes, the senior class write-up states (possibly erroneously, as the author's research does not reveal that "Norfolk College" was ever a formal designation) that "1963 graduates have seen the coming of many buildings and changes in policies and procedures around Old Dominion. Four years ago our seniors entered Norfolk Division of William & Mary. They have since attended Norfolk College of William & Mary, Norfolk College, and now Old Dominion College. This is the last class to graduate that has attended the college under its four names. The class has witnessed the addition of three new buildings, the Hughes Library, the Fine Arts Building, and the Physics and Business Administration Building."[35]

The growth of the college did not stop with the addition of these three new buildings. According to newspaper reports of early 1964, the construction start of a $1.75 million Student Union was anticipated in the summer of that year; a new classroom building was anticipated for September of 1965, and, in something of a milestone which would make the school more than a commuter school for the first time, construction on a 304-resident dormitory began in spring 1964.[36]

Lewis Webb, Bud Metheny, and the City of Norfolk had grand visions for the school by significantly raising its athletic profile, too. On February 23, 1964, *Virginian-Pilot* sportswriter Russell Borjes began a five-part series that outlined that vision, and its goals. With Metheny as the "architect of the program," Borjes described plans for a $2.5 million, 6,000–10,000 seat arena. "Perhaps there has never been a more propitious time for athletic expansion at the college," he wrote in the February 23rd edition. "Tidewater and ODC are growing at an unprecedented rate. Furthermore, the area needs a larger coliseum-type facility as much as the college. The school is willing to share the auditorium with Tidewater for various entertainment, cultural, civic and commercial events." This willingness to proceed as a joint venture highlighted the close relationship with Old Dominion and Norfolk. Mayor Roy B. Martin Jr. noted in the series that "a good athletic program at Old Dominion is good business for Norfolk and the area." Not insignificant in this newspaper series is also the treatment of the new and groundbreaking Intercollegiate Foundation, which would begin providing official athletic scholarships at ODC.

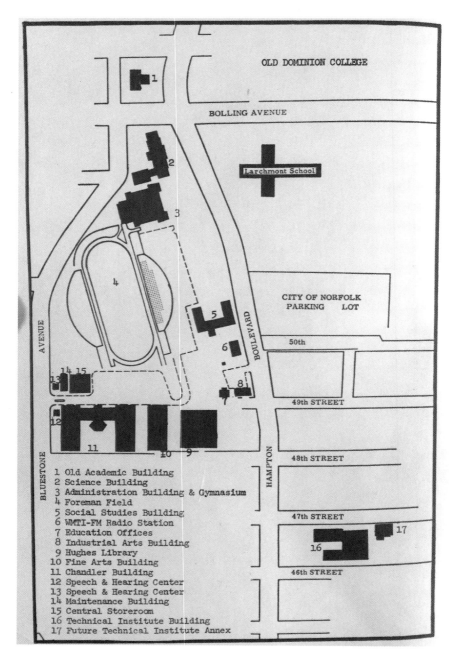

OLD DOMINION COLLEGE

BOLLING AVENUE

Larchmont School

CITY OF NORFOLK
PARKING   LOT

50th

49th STREET

48th STREET

47th STREET

46th STREET

BOULEVARD

HAMPTON

AVENUE

BLUESTONE

1 Old Academic Building
2 Science Building
3 Administration Building & Gymnasium
4 Foreman Field
5 Social Studies Building
6 WMTI-FM Radio Station
7 Education Offices
8 Industrial Arts Building
9 Hughes Library
10 Fine Arts Building
11 Chandler Building
12 Speech & Hearing Center
13 Speech & Hearing Center
14 Maintenance Building
15 Central Storeroom
16 Technical Institute Building
17 Future Technical Institute Annex

*Old Dominion College campus map, reproduced from the College's "1963-1964 General Catalogue."
Courtesy of Special Collections and University Archives, Old Dominion University.*

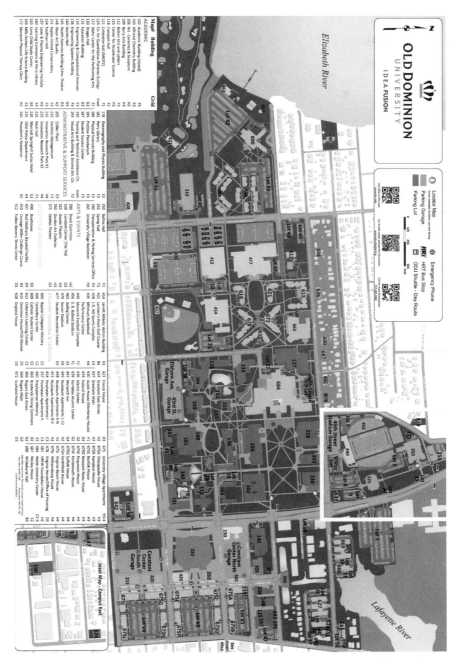

Old Dominion University's 2021 campus map, presented only for comparison purposes. The area shown boxed in white represents almost the entire 1964 campus. Courtesy of Special Collections and University Archives, Old Dominion University.

CHAPTER EIGHT

1964
Pinnacle

*This season could be the best ever
under Metheny's direction.*

—ED HEWITT, *in the* Virginian-Pilot, *March 22, 1964*

[Author's Note: Coverage of the 1964 season is somewhat condensed here for flow of the main text; it is covered game-by-game in the Appendix.]

THE REGULAR SEASON

In March 1964, in the midst of these fundamental shifts in national culture and politics, and the changes associated with the growth of the college, baseball, like "hope," still sprang eternal. Coming off the program's most successful season to date in 1963, the Monarchs were still loaded with talent, and well-prepared for another successful campaign. Coach Metheny had laid the groundwork for his team's

1964 season over the course of fifteen years at the college, from his earliest squads playing against Navy teams and freshman teams, to later teams playing in the Little Eight and then the Mason-Dixon Conference. During those fifteen years, Metheny had also simultaneously improved his winning percentages while upgrading the quality of his scheduled competition.

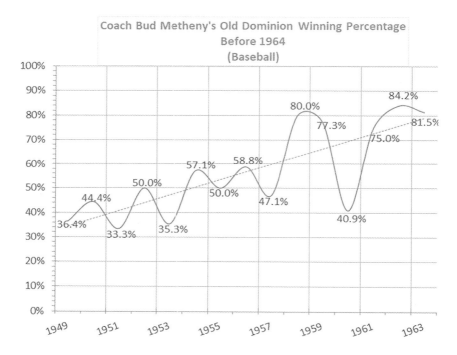

Sportswriter Ed Hewitt had noticed the upward trend. On March 13, 1964, twelve days before the start of the season, he had proclaimed 1964 to be "THE Year for ODC Baseball" in the school's *Mace and Crown* newspaper (and had then published almost the same story nine days later for Norfolk's *Virginian-Pilot*, saying generally the same thing, but going to the effort of rewriting the article entirely). In Hewitt's reckoning, Bud Metheny had built such a powerhouse in Norfolk that a 1964 season without a loss was a real possibility:

This is THE Year for ODC Baseball

This is THE year! The year of the presidential race; the year of the Olympics; the year of the New York's World Fair; the year that Richard Burton may or may not become Mr. Elizabeth Taylor; and the year of the opening of the Chesapeake-Bay Bridge Tunnel.

But to the Old Dominion College athletic program, this is THE year for the Monarch baseball team. This is the year that all the wildest dreams of success are supposed to become reality. And the exciting thing is that it will!

For some schools, the record of last year's team would have been enough to content most coaches, faculties, and administrations for years to come.

What did the Monarchs do? As usual, they won the imaginary Little Eight title with a perfect 8–0 mark. Then, in their first year in the Mason-Dixon Conference the Monarchs took the Championship. Moving on, ODC won the only small college baseball tournament in the country by defeating the Coast Guard Academy and whipping Buffalo. Old Dominion finished its year with a 22–5 record. Including its 1961–62 record of 16–3, ODC is 38–8 for the past two years.

By most standards, after two very successful years, this should be a rebuilding year. But, on last year's championship team there was only one senior . . .

The Old Dominion outfield should be one of the strongest in college baseball . . . Joining the Zadells in the outfield is Fred Kovner. One of the most exciting players on the squad, Kovner batted .331 last season and led the Monarchs in homeruns (7), stolen bases, runs scored, and was among the leaders in doubles, triple, and runs batted in . . . Anyone who has attended an ODC game knows who the third baseman is. Co-captain Wayne Parks is one of the finest players on the team . . . The pitching staff is one of the brightest spots on the team. Led by All-American first-team choice Bob Walton and fire-balling Freddy Edmonds, the Monarch hurlers did a magnificent job last season. Edmonds, a strong hurler (with either brown or blond hair), has a blazing fast ball that the batters sometimes fail to see . . .

This is the lineup. Add to this the expert knowledge that Bud Metheny, a former New York Yankee outfielder, can offer and you have a powerful presentation on the baseball field. For his coaching ability last season, Bud was named Coach of the Year in District III by the American Association of College baseball Coaches. This district includes Virginia, North Carolina, South Carolina, Maryland, and West Virginia . . .

The 1964 season begins March 25 with a practice game against Penn State. A 24-game season concludes on May 14–16 with the Mason-Dixon Conference Tournament. And after that tournament, who knows where they will go.

An undefeated season is not out of the question. This is THE year![1]

THE year began on the fifth day of spring, a beautiful March 25th in Norfolk that saw the high temperature reach sixty-nine degrees. In a practice contest, the Monarchs took the field against Penn State in a game that would not count in either team's final record. The Nittany Lions had participated in several College World Series in the 1950s, and, in fact, had been a participant just the year before, and represented the finest collegiate baseball competition to ever come to the Norfolk area.

It is tempting to think of Old Dominion, the defending NCAA East Regional champions from the College Division, playing against a University Division team fresh from a College World Series appearance, as a classic David versus Goliath, or a Jets versus Colts in Super Bowl III, moment. The *Virginian-Pilot* noticed, and wrote on game day that "The Old Dominion College baseball team will play a nationally ranked Penn State team today at noon on the Larchmont field . . . Penn State was ranked one of the top 10 schools in the country last year. The Nittany Lions, working out at Ft. Eustis, arrived Sunday night . . .

Although billed as a practice game, ODC coach Bud Metheny will use his first-string players. 'We intend to play it as a regular game, going the full nine innings,' Metheny said."[2] But if Penn State's credentials struck any awe in the Old Dominion players, such sentiment is distinctly muted fifty years later in the memories of those Monarchs. Reminded of Penn State's sterling 1964 résumé in 2016, Wayne Parks noted, "I didn't remember all that about them, at this time. But, yeah, they had a real good team."[3] Fred Kovner doesn't recall the Penn State résumé at all, and was unimpressed enough with them that in 2016 he didn't even remember taking the field against them, commenting, "They were just teams. If you say we beat some team named Penn or Penn State, I don't know it . . . Did we beat a Penn team? I don't know the answer to that."[4]

Maybe this Monarch team had such confidence that it simply and collectively did not care who was in the opposite dugout. Collectively, they *knew* they were good. They had proved it the year before and had the titles to show for it, and were ready to do it again, no matter who took the field against them. And Penn State coach Chuck Medlar didn't hold back in his selection of pitcher, starting Richard Rhine, who would be selected by the Baltimore Orioles in the 1965 MLB draft. Bud Metheny countered with Fred Edmonds to start the game, and then gave John Ingram and Bob Walton three innings apiece, too.

Old Dominion's College Division pitchers, authors of a collective 2.59 ERA the year before, held up against their University Division foes. In three innings of work apiece, Edmonds, Ingram, and Walton gave up only one hit each and no earned runs, and set down eleven Nittany Lions by strikeout. A couple of unearned runs allowed, however, left the score tied at two going into the bottom of the ninth, when Frank Zadell ended the affair with a one-out double that plated Mel Renn. Asked in 2016 if he recalled that game-winning RBI against such top-flight competition, Zadell said with a laugh, "No. Sorry . . . You sure it was me?"[5]

EARLY-SEASON SURPRISES

Dartmouth returned to Norfolk in late March for games that had been a fixture in the Old Dominion early-season schedule since 1960. Since that year, the Monarchs had gone 7–3 against the Big Green, owned a six-game winning streak against their Ivy League opponents, and came into the three scheduled games with a lot of confidence—and as much hype as the local newspaper and the school's newspaper could muster.

Then, on March 27, 1964, the Monarchs faced Dartmouth's Ted Friel, a future St. Louis Cardinal draftee. In a game scheduled for seven innings, Friel no-hit Old Dominion (a team that had batted .322 cumulatively the year before) through seven innings, then eight, and then nine. Fred Edmonds was blanking Dartmouth at the same time, however, and so the first game of the season entered the tenth inning tied at zero. Dartmouth scored one in the top of that inning, and while Fred Balmer did collect the Monarchs' first hit in the bottom half against Friel's relief help, no further damage was done, and the undefeated season that Hewitt had felt was not out of the question was already out of the question, after just one game.

In the second game of the doubleheader, Metheny sent his other workhorse, All-American Bob Walton, to the hill—and Walton turned in what would be his worst performance of the year. Lasting only into the fifth, Walton gave up five of the Big Green's seven total runs in a 7–4 loss, and the mighty Monarchs, almost incredibly, were winless after their first two games. In the first game, the bats that had been so prolific the season before were silent; as a team, Old Dominion batters went one-for-thirty-two. In the second game, it was the pitching, as Bob Walton, who had recorded a 1.42 ERA and sub-1.00 WHIP in 1963 (and had not given up more than three earned runs in any start), was charged with five earned runs in four official innings, equating to an 11.25 ERA.

Sportswriter Ed Hewitt was not impressed, and Hewitt's opinion mattered. As the Norfolk Division of William & Mary became Old Dominion College, Hewitt was the primary voice covering Monarch baseball fortunes in those early years, thereby shaping both campus and regional knowledge and opinion about the baseball program. He effectively married "town and gown," writing for Old Dominion's student publication, the *Mace and Crown*, but also simultaneously for Norfolk's *Virginian-Pilot*. In the *Virginian-Pilot's* 1963 coverage of Old Dominion baseball, another young writer, Dan Richards, published more attributed articles about ODC baseball than did Hewitt (and, forty years later, Richards still recalled Bud Metheny and the Larchmont field, noting in his memoirs that "Bud was fun for a young writer to be with," and that "the baseball team played across the road of Larchmont Park, where the chill winds came right off the nearby waters at Hampton Roads in March and April . . . when it was cold, we huddled together under parkas, coats and blankets and double headers went on until halted by darkness. Thank goodness, the field didn't have lights, or we might have frozen to death.")[6] Richards contributed about two *Pilot* articles to each of Hewitt's in 1963, but by 1964, no single article about Monarch baseball appeared in the *Virginian-Pilot* (or *Mace and Crown*) that wasn't attributed to Hewitt. He was ingrained with the baseball team, and as John Ingram recalled, "He traveled with us . . . Best of my knowledge, you know, wrote truthful, comprehensive articles about the team . . . he hung around with us, and basically a good guy."[7] As much as any single player, Hewitt's role in spreading the message about what Bud Metheny and Old Dominion baseball were doing in Norfolk was essential to raising the developing program's profile.

But even after a convincing win over Washington and Lee that followed the Dartmouth series, Hewitt wasn't impressed with the early returns in 1964. In his April 10th *Mace and Crown* article, Hewitt wrote that "The 1964 baseball team opened here March 27, but it was a full week later before our team decided to start playing. The

Monarchs, who roared like Lions last season, played the wounded Lion on opening day as they got stuck by an Ivy League thorn called Dartmouth College . . . The Monarchs were saved by a rainy day as nature won the third game of the Dartmouth series. The weather appeared to be giving our boys as much trouble as their opponents."[8] Three games into the season, Hewitt still retained a sense of optimism, but it was cautious, and much tempered from how he had written about the team less than a month before. "The team can still have the brilliant year that is so very possible," he wrote. "Perhaps Dartmouth did the Monarchs a favor. There's nothing like a couple of losses to remedy false contentment."[9]

The weather certainly did present a difficulty and had not allowed the team to get into the rhythm of the season. After the practice game against Penn State on March 25, Norfolk experienced nine days with precipitation out of the next fourteen, and the "chill winds" that Dan Richards describes in his memoirs were certainly at play as well, as the mean wind speed in Norfolk was in double digits in eight of those fourteen. Norfolk high temperatures averaged only fifty-eight degrees in that two-week

Monarch Story: Still Wet

NORFOLK—The weather won its third decision of the season over Old Dominion College Tuesday as the Monarchs' baseball game with Richmond Professional Institute was rained out. The game has been rescheduled for April 20 at Larchmont Field.

With the season almost a third over, ODC has one victory, two losses, and three rained out games. And not only has nature canceled the games, it has also stopped outdoor practice and sent the Monarchs inside.

Consequently, when most teams at this point of the season are finally rounding into shape, ODC is still trying to get the wrinkles out of the hitting and pitching.

Part of the April 8, 1964, Virginian-Pilot article. ©Virginian-Pilot. All rights reserved. Distributed by Tribune Content Agency, LLC.

stretch, failing four times to even get out of the forties. Consequently, one practice game and three regular-season games had already been washed out by the time the Monarchs faced Hampden-Sydney on April 11.

Hewitt's piece had come out before the April 11th game at Hampden-Sydney College. The last time Old Dominion had played on the HSC field was the previous May, when they had beaten Buffalo to win the NCAA College Division East Regional championship. But the last time they had played *Hampden-Sydney* on this field was three weeks before that, and the Monarchs had delivered a morale-crushing defeat to their Mason-Dixon rivals. In that game, Old Dominion had stormed back from a five-run deficit after four innings to take a late lead, and then after Hampden-Sydney had tied it again, Wayne Parks broke Farmville hearts with a two-out, two-run single to seal an Old Dominion win. In 1964, the Tigers certainly had revenge in mind, and they got it early, as Fred Edmonds delivered his worst performance in what would be an otherwise stellar year. Four of the first five Tigers to bat scored, as eight men came to bat in the home half of the first inning. Edmonds lasted into the fifth inning, but in that frame, he faced five hitters, and all five reached base—four with singles, and one on Edmonds' own error. Monarch bats offered no answer this time, submitting a four-for-thirty performance that plated only one run for the contest, against the Tigers' eight. For his part, Edmonds' four official innings pitched represented only 6.1 percent of his 1964 workload, but 35 percent of all runs he allowed for the season (and 30 percent of the *earned* runs he allowed) crossed the plate in this brief window. As a team, the vaunted 1964 Monarchs stood at one win against three losses, with a batting average of .187.

THE ROAD TO RECOVERY

If the Monarchs believed Ed Hewitt's early-season hype, then the first four games of the 1964 season certainly offered a hard dose of reality, but despite the weather and the disappointing results to date, Old Dominion was loaded with big-game experience and senior leadership. Seven players had returned from the starting lineup of the 1963 team that had won the NCAA Regional crown, and five seniors led the 1964 team, in the persons of catcher John Ward, outfielder Frank Zadell, pitcher John Ingram, and the co-captains, third baseman Wayne Parks and pitcher Bob Walton. The team had a returning first-team All-American in Walton, and a second-team All-American in outfielder Jimmy Zadell. The team had the steadying leadership of Bud Metheny, and the team, as a unit, had *confidence*, a quality recalled very clearly by team members even fifty years later.

After the embarrassing loss to Hampden-Sydney left the Monarchs with one win in four tries, something special started to happen. Over the next several weeks, Old Dominion won thirteen straight games, but incredibly, did so in their final at-bat in *eight* of those thirteen games, by breaking ties six times, and by coming from behind twice. The team's cumulative batting average continued to rise after the early-season slump, and while it would not approach 1963's unbelievable .322 team average, by year's end it would sit at .278. While paling, to a degree, beside the 1963 mark, it could nevertheless be noted for comparison's sake that only five major league teams exceeded a team batting average of .278 between the decade of 2011–2020[10]—and no major league team in that span exceeded the Monarchs' 1964 high-water mark of .288, where it stood at the end of the regular season.

Where the 1964 team truly stood out, though, was on the mound and in the field. The 1963 pitching staff had put together a very impressive season statistically, turning in a season with a 2.59 ERA and 1.27 WHIP—in fact, the team's cumulative ERA never got above 3.00. The 1964 Monarchs, however, improved significantly even on those tidy numbers. Despite the early-season 7–4 and 8–1 losses, the 1964 Monarchs pitching staff compiled a superb 2.27 ERA for the year, with an improved WHIP rate and slightly improved strikeout rate over the year before. Improved defensive play, however, accentuated these results, because the Monarchs also cut the number of unearned runs allowed in 1964 by more than half from the previous year, from thirty-nine to nineteen. While offensive production had declined from the year before, improved pitching and defense meant that Old Dominion gave up almost a full run less than in 1963, as only 2.84 total runs per game crossed the plate in 1964 against the Monarchs.

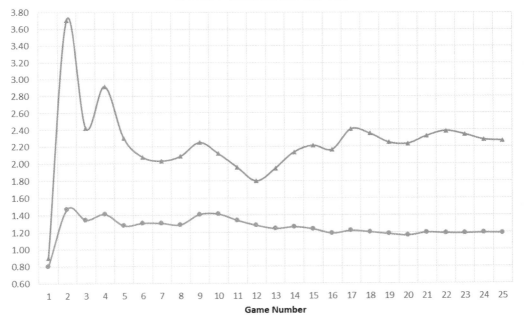

1964 ODC Cumulative ERA and WHIP

"A ray of hope that began on April 13 has brightened the entire outlook of the Old Dominion College baseball team and now has the Monarchs basking in the glorious sunshine of victory," Ed Hewitt opined later in the April 24 edition of the *Mace and Crown*.[11] The weather cooperated on that 13th day of April in Norfolk, and Old Dominion faced another Mason-Dixon rival, Randolph-Macon College, at 2:30 p.m. on a seventy-one-degree day, while President Lyndon Baines Johnson was inaugurating the start of the major league season with the ceremonial first pitch in Washington. With the civil rights bill still in hot debate and in the news daily, Johnson "displayed a strong right arm and a zest for popcorn," as an Associated Press story reported in multiple outlets the next day, before a public address announcement called all his Senate friends back from the game for a "quorum call in the civil rights debate . . . Sen. Hubert H. Humphrey, D-Minn., sitting behind Johnson, threw his hands in the air in a gesture of resignation and headed for the exit. Dirksen, Mansfield, and Sens. George A. Smathers, D-Fla., and George D. Aiken, R-Vt., followed. Johnson stood, grinning, and sped them on their way with a handshake."[12]

On the same day in Norfolk, Bob Walton, who had already lost the only game he would lose all year on the season's opening day, took the mound against Randolph-Macon and pitched nine innings, allowing no runs while striking out seven and walking two. Hard-luck loser Jim Garwood was nearly as effective for the Yellow Jackets, but the Monarchs began a long winning streak when Frank Zadell reached base on an error in the bottom of the ninth inning, stole second base, and came around to score the game's only run on shortstop Mel Renn's clutch, two-out single.

As the team began winning games, the momentous global, national, and local events that have shaped modern history swirled around their baseball season. The civil rights bill entered its fiftieth day of Senate debate on May 7, and newspaper reports of demonstrations that turned violent were common throughout the season, most typically with the one-sided tone expressed by a United Press International article on March 25 (the day of Old Dominion's opening baseball game), when it was reported that in Jacksonville, Florida, "Fifteen hundred screaming Negro youths attacked police with rocks, set fire to an automobile and a school and beat a newsman Tuesday in a continuation of a bloody, two-day uprising."[13] As United States involvement in Vietnam continued to escalate, the *Daily Press* on May 2 noted student demonstrations against American involvement in New York's Times Square, in San Francisco, and in Boston, Seattle, and Madison, Wisconsin. The same outlet carried news on May 17 that US casualties in Vietnam had reached 1,000 since American involvement in 1961. On May 19, the *Daily Press* reported that Lyndon Johnson had requested another $125 million for efforts in that country. The *Daily Press* reported a heightening of Cold War tensions on May 20, when "more than 40 secret microphones were found in the U. S. Embassy in Moscow when U. S. security men tore into walls of the building in April."[14] On May 31, an article noted that the Warren Commission had begun writing its report after investigations into the murder of John F. Kennedy. Closer to home, the Chesapeake Bay Bridge-Tunnel opened on April 15, connecting Norfolk to the Eastern Shore and ending ferry service. On April 11, while the baseball Monarchs were playing at Hampden-Sydney, celebrated General Douglas MacArthur was laid to rest in Norfolk, where more than 61,000 people viewed his body. However, amid such significant historical events occurring simultaneously during the baseball season, there was also apparently still room in the newspapers for frivolities; the same May 14, 1964, edition of the *Daily Press* that reported on air power in Vietnam, amendments to the civil rights bill, and violent civil strife in Cuba also headlined a page-two story out of eastern North Carolina, "Seven-Foot, 250-Pound Monster Scares Tarheels at Hope's Pond." A search party of one hundred people evidently "failed to turn up a trace of the man or monster reported terrorizing the neighborhood."[15]

The baseball Monarchs were able to block out all the noise and concentrate on the work at hand. On April 15 in Lexington, John Ingram beat the VMI Keydets despite seven walks, evening the Monarchs' record at three wins and three losses. The next day in Ashland, Old Dominion victimized Randolph-Macon's Jim Garwood again, this time scoring the two winning runs against him in the top of the tenth inning, giving Bill Yeargan a win in relief of Fred Edmonds.

The team played in temperatures above eighty degrees for the first time in Norfolk on April 18, as the thermometer hit eighty-five. As the air began to warm, so too did the Old Dominion offense, in an unfortunate turn for the visiting Baltimore Bees, the same team that had ended ODC's twenty-four-game win streak with a doubleheader sweep the year before. Baltimore pitching shut down the Monarch offense in the bottom of the first inning of the first game, but that was as good as it would get for Baltimore coach "Otts" Bosley, who would get a grand total of five outs from his two starting pitchers, Dick Mitchell and Ron Mather. In the bottom of the second inning of the first game, Old Dominion batted around and scored five times, to begin the onslaught. On the day, the Monarchs batted around three separate times, scored twenty-six runs in just twelve offensive half-innings, and took their team batting average from .211 all the way up to .260, with a combined twenty-seven-for-sixty performance. Individually, Fred Kovner went six-for-eight with a home run and brought his average up to .353 from .231 (and it would not dip below .345 for the rest of the season); Fred Balmer went five-for-eight with four RBI. The champion Monarchs, it seemed, were finally, and fully, back.

And not just back, but back as a *team*. "Many teams would choke were they to go into the seventh or eighth inning some three runs behind," according to Hewitt's *Mace and Crown* analysis of May 8. "But it never seems to bother this year's team. They just seem to know that they are going to win. There is no pressure."[16] Although the second Baltimore game had been a laugher in its final 14–7 reckoning, the score was actually 7–6 in Baltimore's favor as the contest entered the home half of the sixth inning, in a game scheduled for seven. But in their sixth inning, Old Dominion batted around and plated eight runs after two men were already out, with the tiebreaking runs scoring on a two-run double by Wayne Parks. The victory was part of a remarkable nine-game stretch that would see Old Dominion score the winning runs in their last at-bat six separate times, with a different clutch performer in five of them:

- April 18 vs. Baltimore: A two-out, two-run double by Wayne Parks gave the Monarchs the lead in the bottom of the sixth inning (of seven).

- April 21 vs. Atlantic Christian (Game 2): A one-out sacrifice fly by Tom Harrell in extra innings scored Fred Kovner, and gave ODC a 1–0 win.

- April 25 vs. Bridgewater (Game 1): A two-out single by Frank Zadell in extra innings scored Lee McDaniel, for a 5–4 win.

- April 25 vs. Bridgewater (Game 2): A two-out double by Lee McDaniel in the bottom of the sixth inning (of seven) knocked in the winning runs in a 7–5 comeback victory.

- May 1 at Lynchburg (Game 1): A one-out triple by Fred Balmer broke a tie in extra innings, and a two-run home run from Frank Zadell that followed gave Old Dominion a 6–3 win.

- May 2 at Washington and Lee: A two-out single by Wayne Parks scored Jimmy Walker in the top of the ninth, as the Monarchs won 7–6.

As the spring marched on, the victories continued to accumulate one after another for the Monarchs. The doubleheader sweep of Bridgewater in Norfolk on April 25 made it ten straight victories going into the season's May stretch run, and repeat Little Eight and Mason-Dixon championships began to come into view. Hampden-Sydney continued to lurk close behind in both races, but May did nothing to slow the Monarchs. On May 1, they took two from Lynchburg on the road: a close one that took an extra frame, and then an easy fifteen-run win that included a thirteen-batter inning and the statistical anomaly of each of the first five Monarch batters (Fred Kovner, Wayne Parks, Jimmy Zadell, Lee McDaniel, and Fred Balmer) recording a triple during the game, accounting for 45 percent of all ODC triples in 1964.

The Lynchburg sweep ran the Monarch Little Eight record to 7–1 and their Mason-Dixon ledger to 8–1. Hampden-Sydney's Tigers, however, could not keep pace, and dropped a game to Randolph-Macon College the following day, giving the Mason-Dixon's South Division title to the stampeding Monarchs for the second year in a row. The Little Eight remained yet in doubt, although with odds stacked strongly in the Monarchs' favor. A hard-fought Old Dominion victory over Washington and Lee, and then a pair of wins over a tough Pembroke State College team (which had only lost one game against college competition the entire year), ran the Monarch win streak to fifteen games, but did nothing to improve their Little Eight mark. Not until May 7 would the team have the opportunity to salt the Little Eight title away too, and it came against Richmond Professional Institute on a calm, eighty-degree day in Norfolk.

The Monarchs only had to win one of their final two Little Eight games to clinch the title. Hampden-Sydney, with an early-season victory against Old Dominion already in hand, would have to win their remaining three and pair that with two Old Dominion losses. In light of these facts, senior left-hander John Ingram took the mound against the RPI Rams before the home fans and offered his cleanest performance of the year, starting with six shutout innings blemished only by four hits and no walks. Ingram found some trouble in the seventh and gave up a pair of runs that the official scorekeeper called earned runs, although the second runner to score had officially reached by an error by first baseman Fred Balmer, and the first runner would probably not have scored without that error. But the official scorekeeper called the runs earned, and the official scorekeeper was Coach Bud Metheny, and there is no arguing that decision fifty-five years later. However, had Metheny scored those runs as unearned, Ingram's season ERA would have been almost a full run lower, and the Monarch team ERA for 1964 would have dropped from an already incredible 2.27 to 2.18.[17]

That scoring decision was, of course, irrelevant. The Monarchs were on a fifteen-game winning streak, and they knew how to win. In the third inning of this game, Fred Kovner had smashed a three-run home run after catcher John Ward and Ingram had delivered singles, and that was all Old Dominion needed. This game didn't require offensive heroics in the team's last at-bat; it required clutch performances from the pitching staff. Ingram stranded a man on third in the seventh, and reliever Bill Yeargan stranded men on first and third in the eighth, before closing out the 3–2 victory with a one-two-three ninth. The Old Dominion Monarchs, for the third straight year, were Virginia's Little Eight champions.

The final game of the regular season, then, was for nothing but pride, the continuation of a sixteen-game win streak, and of course, some amount of revenge for the 8–1 shellacking that Hampden-Sydney had given Old Dominion on April 11. Bob Walton, the winning pitcher in his last six starting assignments, opposed the Tigers' Hal Blythe, and Walton uncharacteristically began the game by allowing three straight hits, followed by a walk. An assist at the plate from center fielder Fred Kovner helped limit the damage to a single run in the Tiger first, but Walton was never his typically masterful self, as he allowed a season-high fourteen hits and two walks against only one strikeout over his 8⅓ innings.

Neither was Hal Blythe masterful, however. In the second inning, Blythe surrendered four straight hits and a walk, as the Monarchs gained a 4–1 advantage. Fred Balmer continued to put the pressure on the Tiger starter with solo home runs in the third and sixth innings, before Hampden-Sydney Coach Bill Pegram relieved the beleaguered Blythe with Mark Chinn, who threw a little extra fuel on the Monarch fire by giving up two more runs in two innings.

In this final regular season contest of the year, and with only pride on the line, Bill Yeargan offered one more clutch Monarch performance for the books. With his team winning by an 8–3 score going into the ninth, Bob Walton had allowed two runs to score, and then departed with only one out and runners on second and third, and the potential tying run at the plate. Yeargan immediately got the all-important second out by retiring first baseman Jeff Bowker by strikeout, and then Lee McDaniel recorded a putout of third baseman Wayne Tennent to end the game. Whether it was the pitching, defense, or offense, the Monarchs had again demonstrated that they knew how to perform under pressure, and that Old Dominion College was truly the king of the baseball hill in the "Old Dominion." With the regular season over, the team's batting average at its season high of .288, and with all the confidence that comes with a seventeen-game winning streak, the Monarchs awaited a best-of-three matchup with Mason-Dixon North Division champions Washington College, who remained undefeated in conference play.

THE MASON-DIXON CHAMPIONSHIP

Looking to repeat the previous year's success in the Mason-Dixon Conference championship series, Metheny's Monarchs faced Washington College of Chestertown, Maryland, in the first-ever meeting between the two schools. Washington College, a small school that graduated only 113 seniors in 1964, has a similar historical background to Washington and Lee University, at least in that George Washington was a major early benefactor. In 1782, Washington "gave the 'College at Chester' a founding gift of fifty guineas, agreed to serve on the Board, and gave us his permission to use his name," according to the school's website. A guinea approximates an English pound, and while that may not sound like an excessive gift, the school claims that gift as the largest of the time. And while Washington and Lee claims to be the "ninth oldest institution of higher learning in the nation," Washington College claims to be the "tenth oldest college in the nation and the first chartered under the new Republic."[18]

Baseball at the school dates all the way back to 1871, when an unknown coach guided them to a 2–0 record. However, records don't show an annual team until 1889; since that time, the school has fielded teams every year except possibly 1931, 1932, and 1951, years for which there are no records.[19]

In 1964, the Shoremen (familiarly, "Sho'men") were coached by 1956 alumnus and former Marine Ron Sisk, a member of the Washington College sports Hall of Fame for his basketball and baseball exploits while in school. Sisk was familiar with Mason-Dixon championship games; he authored one of two shutouts by Washington pitching in the 1954 title doubleheader,[20] earning the college its first and only Mason-Dixon championship to that point, even though

ODC Seeks 2nd M-D Title

By ED HEWITT
Virginian-Pilot Sports Writer

NORFOLK — The streaking Old Dominion Monarchs will seek their second straight Mason-Dixon Conference baseball championship this w e e k e n d against Washington College on Larchmont Field.

A doubleheader is scheduled for Friday and a single game Saturday if needed in the best-of-three series. If it rains Friday, a single contest Saturday will decide the winner.

The Monarchs, coached by Bud Metheny, will come into the tournament with an 18-3 overall record and winners of their last 17 games. They are 9-1 in the Mason-Dixon.

The Sho'men from Chestertown, Md. are 13-2 overall and 7-0 in the M-D. Washington won the Northern Division title and Old Dominion the Southern Division.

Pitching has been the main reason for the Sho'men's success. Bill Bates has won seven against no losses this season and defeated Loyola last Saturday with a two-hitter. Chuck Meding, another Washington ace hurler, stopped Loyola in the nightcap of Saturday's doubleheader on one hit

From the Virginian-Pilot, May 11, 1964.

the school had been a charter member in 1940. In his fourth year as coach, his teams to date had only enjoyed mild success, but 1964 was different.

The 1964 team romped through its Mason-Dixon schedule unmolested, logging eight league victories against no defeats as part of an overall 13–2 record, according to results published in the school's yearbook. The Sho'men weren't doing it with offense, although the 4.7 runs they scored per game was passable. Primarily, it was the pitching staff that carried the team, as Washington allowed an average of only 1.9 runs per contest.[21] Their pitching had, moreover, improved as the season progressed. In the last eight games they had played, representing approximately half the season, Sho'men pitching had spun four shutouts and given up only seven total runs, for an average of just .9 per game.[22]

Chief among Washington pitchers was Bill Bates, just a freshman. In the March 4, 1964, edition of the school newspaper *The Elm*, an overview of the upcoming baseball season referred to Bates as "also fighting for a regular spot as a hurler." But by the April 15th edition, "Coach Sisk rates Bates as a fine college pitcher and feels that he should develop into one of the best in Washington's history." According to a 1964 memo sent to Mason-Dixon baseball coaches soliciting their votes for the conference All-Star team, Bates was 7–0, had pitched sixty innings, struck out seventy-one, and only given up eighteen hits, although he had walked thirty-three batters.[23]

As for Sisk's assessment of his championship series opponent, *The Elm* wrote on May 16, "According to Sho'men Coach Ron Sisk, Old Dominion is a hard hitting, fairly good fielding ball club. Sisk stated that the boys from the South have one good pitcher and one adequate pitcher."[24] In retrospect, it would be difficult to tell which "good" pitcher Sisk had in mind. Coming into the best-of-three conference championship, Fred Edmonds carried a 1.28 ERA with four wins, Denny Riddleberger had a 1.72 ERA, and Bill Yeargan carried a 1.15 mark. The staff leader,

All-American Bob Walton, had won seven games to go with his 2.57 ERA, and his ERA was actually almost a quarter of a run *higher* than the team's overall 2.33 ERA before the game. No matter which pitcher Sisk referred to as "good" and which as "adequate," his ball club would only have to face two from the Monarch stable.

Game One

It was no surprise when Metheny saw Bates' name penciled in to start the first game, and Metheny countered with either his "good" or his "adequate" pitcher, Bob Walton. In the top half of the Sho'men lineup were three future Washington College athletic Hall of Fame members in shortstop and leadoff hitter Tom Finnegan (also later a Chicago Cubs farmhand), left fielder John Sloan, and the cleanup man, second baseman Al Eisel. The first inning passed without incident for either team, but Walton ran into a little trouble in the second, as a one-out walk to right fielder Glen Shipway turned into the first run of the game. In the third, Finnegan led off with a single, and two outs later, consecutive base hits by Eisel and Shipway plated two more, to put the Sho'men up by three.

Metheny had seen this act before. Members of this Old Dominion team consistently point to the faith they had in each other, and the confidence they had as a team. Metheny himself had given voice to that same thinking in an article published just a week before in the *Progress-Index* of Petersburg: "These kids have forgotten how to lose," he told Associated Press writer Ed Young. "They think they can't be beat. It's like we felt in the old days when I played with the New York Yankees. We figured we weren't supposed to lose, didn't know how, and couldn't. We have that kind of team down here in Norfolk."[25]

In the fourth inning, the Monarchs started climbing back into the game. Cleanup hitter Lee McDaniel reached on a two-out error by the left fielder, Sloan, and Fred Balmer reached on an error by third baseman

Bill Morgan—the first of three for the game by the team captain. Frank Zadell took advantage of the opportunity and delivered a clutch double to deliver them both home, and bring the team within a run.

In the bottom of the fifth, catcher John Ward worked Bates for a walk, the first free pass Bates had issued. Metheny knew he had Fred Kovner, batting .384, and Wayne Parks, at .354, waiting for their turn at the top of the lineup, and stayed by the book, calling for Walton to move Ward over with a bunt. After the successful sacrifice, Kovner lined out to shortstop and Parks walked, but Tom Harrell, batting .432 at that point, didn't mind getting his chance at it, and delivered a two-out, game-tying single.

The game stayed tied until the bottom of the seventh (of seven), as Walton faced only one batter above the minimum in his last four innings of work. In the home half of the last inning, Walton led off and drew a walk from Bates, and advanced to second on an error committed by the Washington catcher. Fred Kovner brought the winning run home with a ground-rule double, and for the ninth time, the 1964 Monarchs had won a game in their last at-bat. In this one, it was really the patience of Old Dominion batters that won the game; Bud Metheny had seen the stats, and he knew that Bates walked .55 batters per inning. It took seven innings, but ultimately, the tying and winning runs for Metheny's squad came via the bane of every pitching coach's existence—the base on balls.

Game Two

Trying to even the series and push it to a deciding third game on Saturday, Sisk turned to sophomore Chuck Meding, who had battled arm problems both in his freshman year and in the current season. Bud Metheny countered with his other "good" or "adequate" co-ace, Fred Edmonds, whose last four appearances had been about as good as it will ever get for a pitcher: 22⅔ innings pitched, eleven hits, two walks, thirty-four strikeouts, and just a single earned run, resulting in three wins and, if the stat had existed then, one save.

Edmonds didn't disappoint, recording the first six outs all by strikeout. Meding, however, was done after one. Fred Kovner led off the game with a walk, stole second, and took third on a passed ball. Wayne Parks waited Meding out and drew another walk. With one out, Meding hit Lee McDaniel to load the bases. Fred Balmer's single drove Kovner home, opening the scoring, and Frank Zadell plated Parks with a fielder's choice—and a rout was on.

Meding moved out to center field, and freshman Sonny Wunderlich came in to offer scant better mound results, recording only six outs while permitting four hits and four walks. Another freshman, Dick Carrington, relieved Wunderlich, and with catcher Buddy Harrington behind the plate, formed a poetic Carrington-Harrington battery. But Carrington inherited a bases-loaded situation, and the first batter he faced, Lee McDaniel, cleared them with a double, closing the book on Wunderlich with five earned runs and putting Old Dominion up 7–0.

The Sho'men pushed a pride run across in the bottom of the fourth (although the games were in Norfolk, the teams alternated as the "home" team). Al Eisel led off with a double and scored on a two-out John Sloan single, but with the way Edmonds was pitching, the outcome was not in doubt. Edmonds matched his season high with twelve strikeouts and marked his fourth consecutive start with double-digit strikeouts, even though none of them were nine-inning games. For the fourth time on the season, Walton and Edmonds had also won both ends of a doubleheader. In the first doubleheader of the season, against Dartmouth, Metheny had started Edmonds first and Walton second, and both had lost. Knowing he had two different kinds of pitchers, Metheny went to school on that, and in every subsequent doubleheader, started the softer-tossing Walton first, softening the opposition up for the fastballs to follow. Metheny's strategy worked; in the four games in which he pitched right after Walton, Edmonds went 4–0, with a 0.62 ERA and forty-five strikeouts in twenty-nine innings.

With the Mason-Dixon crown defended, and Virginia's "Little Eight" title in hand for the third consecutive year, all that was left to do was to wait for the call from the NCAA to see who would put the nineteen-game winning streak to the test.

THE NCAA TOURNAMENT

In May 1963, Old Dominion had accepted a bid to participate in an NCAA postseason tournament, in what *Virginian-Pilot* sports writer George McClelland referred to as a "surprise move" in the title of his article. A surprise move, maybe—but only if the deciding factors were only short-term considerations. In fact, despite freshman unavailability, the decision should have been no real surprise at all, aligning as perfectly as it did with Bud Metheny's long-term vision for his baseball team and school. As McClelland had written on May 22, 1963, "The glittering baseball season at Old Dominion is not a memory after all. Arthur (Bud) Metheny, the head coach and athletic director, announced Tuesday at the college honors convocation, acceptance of a bid to the 2nd annual Atlantic Coast Regional NCAA College Division tournament . . . The decision to make this first bid to broaden Old Dominion athletic horizons was greeted with sustained applause. It came as a surprise, for Metheny had indicated earlier that an NCAA tournament rule forbidding [sic] use of freshmen would cripple Monarch chances . . . Dates of the tournament—not to be confused with the University Division regional at Gastonia for which Old Dominion was also mentioned—are May 30th and 31st. The site is Hampden-Sydney College."[26]

A year later, in the May 22, 1964, *Mace and Crown*, Sports Editor Ed Hewitt wrote of defending the small-college tournament championship, to be held this year in New York: "Old Dominion, understandably, would like to skip the Long Island trip and instead travel to Gastonia, N.C. where the NCAA university division tournament is held. Four teams are invited for the May 28–29 regionals. The Atlantic Coast Conference, the Southern Conference, and the Southeastern Conference will join an at-large team in the tournament. The selections, however, had not been announced as yet for this tournament at press time. . . . An Associated Press sports writer told this reporter that he had seen most of the ACC and Southern Conference teams play and that he was sure that the Monarchs could defeat them. The writer also said he saw no reason why ODC shouldn't be invited."[27]

Were these Old Dominion teams that good? Could this group of local boys, recruited by Bud Metheny with an offer of practically nothing—no scholarship money from the school, not even a campus that that had any housing—represent Old Dominion College successfully on the baseball diamond against such schools as the University of North Carolina, the University of Florida, Louisiana State University, or West Virginia University, in a University Division regional? Consider that on the 1964 ODC team were a future major leaguer in Denny Riddleberger, a second-round selection in the 1965 Major League Baseball draft in Fred Kovner (right after Johnny Bench, and right before Larry Hisle), and three other players who were College Division All-Americans, in outfielder Jimmy Zadell, and pitchers Bob Walton and Fred Edmonds. Consider that the 1965 team would have only three games on the schedule from the University Division conferences represented above, but won all three—one against the ACC's University of Virginia, and two against the Southern Conference's William & Mary, and by a combined score of 26–11. Even though it was a practice game, consider that the 1964 team beat Penn State, a College World Series participant the year before. If pitching wins championships, the 1964 Old Dominion staff, with its 2.27 staff ERA, offered shining credentials.

But it is impossible to know. Conventional wisdom, as expressed by the two sportswriters quoted above, may have suggested that the

Monarchs should have been considered as an at-large selection for the NCAA University Division tournament. And maybe they could have beaten the best of the Southeastern, the ACC, or the Southern Conferences. But it simply was not possible, as Bud Metheny made clear in a May 1975 interview: "I believe that there was some lack of communication here because there is no way possible that a College Division team could go to a University Division team [sic]. Now, we do have in a couple of sports like wrestling, where if a boy finished in, I believe it's in the top three in the College Division tournament, then he automatically went to the University Division, if he so desired. But you can't do that in team sports. They won't accept it. Individual sports they accepted in some areas. But I believe there was just lack of communication when this came out."[28]

The 1964 Monarchs accepted the NCAA's bid to defend their NCAA College Division regional tournament crown, and traveled to New York to join the University at Buffalo, Central Connecticut State College, and host school Long Island University, as the "Final Four" of the NCAA Regional. At the time, the regional tournament was both the pinnacle and the terminal, with no further advancement into any kind of national tournament available. For Bud Metheny, it also meant a return to Yankee Stadium, where the tournament would be held. This time, he would be wearing his Old Dominion pinstripes, which had been inspired by those he had worn as a member of a Yankees World Series championship team.

If the Monarchs had felt their chances for success in 1963 were hurt by the unavailability of their freshmen, it was also an acute pain in 1964. Freshman catcher Jimmy Walker, sharing time with John Ward behind the plate, had batted .353 for the season, and if Walker's RBI per at-bat was extrapolated over a season with 500 at-bats, he had been on a pace for 118. But Ward had finished the season over .300 as well, so the real concern was pitching. Only seven pitchers had logged innings for the Monarchs over the entire year, and now the team was going to travel without freshman Denny Riddleberger. Of the remaining six to pitch in 1964, Ray Corson had only thrown two innings before leaving school, and senior left-hander John Ingram, with the chance to pitch in the home park of his baseball idols, had contracted an ancient disease known as the mumps, and was unable to travel with the team (before the inception of the mumps vaccination program three years later in 1967, there were about 186,000 cases in the United States per year; after 1967, that number has been reduced by more than 99 percent).[29] Tom Harrell had pitched, but only six innings, and none since April 20.

Although Walton and Edmonds had accounted for an astounding 71.8 percent of innings pitched by Old Dominion in 1964 (148 out of 206), what was left to win two more games was a very thin pitching staff of Bob Walton, Fred Edmonds, and Bill Yeargan. Coach Bud Metheny, in a letter dated June 1, 1964, sent notice to the Reservation Manager of the Concourse Plaza Hotel (three blocks from Yankee Stadium), naming the mere sixteen players with whom he intended to win another championship—just twelve position players, three pitchers, and one who was actually out with the mumps.

Old Dominion made the trip to the tournament in a bus, which was a very rare occasion, as third baseman Wayne Parks recalled. In fact, to his memory, that only happened for the two NCAA Regional appearances, and every other time it was either travel by personal cars or school-owned station wagons.[30] But there were more people for this trip, and so a bus made sense. Accommodations were at the Concourse Plaza, once a grand dame of the Bronx, although no longer as opulent and luxurious as it had been in the decades following its 1923 opening (although it was still a much more viable enterprise than in the decade to follow 1964, during which it would become a welfare hotel, and then transfer to the city and re-open as a senior citizen home). But the hotel was rich with New York history, especially for the sports fan. Since it was walking distance to Yankee Stadium, the Yankees had for a time kept apartments rented for younger players, and the hotel had hosted

Mickey Mantle, Roger Maris, and Babe Ruth, as well as football star Frank Gifford, not to mention visiting teams as well.[31]

Most, if not all, of the boys from Norfolk had never seen anything like New York, and they took it all in—and perhaps with some trepidation. Jimmy Zadell remembers of his father, "He gave us ten bucks. He says, 'I'm going to give you a safety pin. Use safety pins anytime you go out anywhere. If you take money with you, you safety pin it to the inside of your pants pocket,' so I'm not pickpocketed. We did that and so

June 1, 1964

Reservation Manager
Concourse Plaza Hotel
Grand Concourse & 161st. Street
New York, New York

Dear Sir:

The following people will be with the Old Dominion College Baseball team Thursday and Friday nights, June 4th and 5th.

Fred Balmer	A. B. Metheny
William Bigger	John Metheny
Fred Edmonds	Hart Slater
Tom Harrell	David Slater
John Ingram	L. G. Plummer
Gene Johnson	J. H. McGinnis
Fred Kovner	
Lee McDaniel	
Ray Nelson	
Wayne Parks	
Melvin Renn	
Robert Walton	
John Ward	
Bill Yeargan	
Frank Zadell	
James Zadell	
John Young	

Very truly yours,

A. B. Metheny
Coach

From Bud Metheny's papers. Courtesy of Special Collections and University Archives, Patricia W. and J. Douglas Perry Library, Old Dominion University Libraries, Norfolk, Virginia.

we went places—I, of course, took it out before we went into the store, didn't want to feel embarrassed taking ten dollars out of my pocket, for crying out loud!...I'm talking about myself and my brother Frank, we only went on vacation to Wheeling, West Virginia!"[32]

While there was little time allotted for sightseeing, there was still one incredible perk to traveling to Yankee Stadium with Coach Bud Metheny: Bud's old friend, Yankee clubhouse manager Pete Sheehy, a fixture at the Stadium from 1927 until his death in 1985, was still there. Sheehy, the "Keeper of the Pinstripes" according to a Yankee dugout plaque, and the man for whom the Yankee clubhouse is named, was there from Lou Gehrig to Don Mattingly, and remembered Bud Metheny well. As dominant as the New York teams were in those years, there were many Yankees fans on the Old Dominion team, and the personal connection between Metheny and Sheehy opened the door to a unique opportunity for the Monarchs. As Wayne Parks remembers, "Bud got him to open up the Yankees dressing room just for the Old Dominion team. We were the only ones that got a private tour of the Yankees dressing room. This was when Mickey Mantle was playing, Whitey Ford, Bill Skowron, Yogi Berra—not Yogi, but Elston Howard was catching then—and all those guys. So that was quite a thrill."[33] Walking the sacred halls of Yankee Stadium with his coach, Jimmy Zadell recalled, "Team pictures up on the wall, in the hallway. There's number three ... not Babe Ruth, but Bud Metheny. He's the last man to wear number three, as you know. What an exciting thing to see. I think Bud was standing there with a lot of the players, looking at that picture. The pride that man had to be in that picture, to be a part of that environment."[34] John Ward II, son of the Old Dominion catcher, remembers a favorite story of his father's from this experience: Bud Metheny lining the players up in the outfield with baseballs and fungo bats, and telling them, "I want all of you to be able to say you hit a baseball out of Yankee Stadium."[35]

In one sense, it could be said that here was a group of young ball-players having fun and enjoying the thrill of a lifetime—tourists, so to speak, who see Machu Picchu or the Leaning Tower of Pisa once, never to return. But in another sense that was just as real, this was mightily significant. Old Dominion had been an independent college for only two years and was less than a decade removed from the relative infancy of its baseball program, when Navy teams, junior colleges, and non-four-year schools dotted the schedule. Now, players from this same growing institution would be representing their school on the single most hallowed baseball diamond on Earth. Fun, yes; a thrill, sure—but also an opportunity perfectly in line with Bud Metheny's grander vision for Old Dominion.

Staff Photo by Ray Dolwick

Off To Yankee Stadium
Bus Carrying the Old Dominion Baseball Team Leaves for New York and the NCAA Tourney After Student Pep Rally

From Norfolk's Ledger-Star, *June 5, 1964.* ©Ledger-Star. *All rights reserved. Distributed by Tribune Content Agency, LLC.*

What rivalry? John Ward, splitting time with Jimmy Walker behind the plate all year, still thought enough of his ineligible freshman teammate and friend to send this postcard from the Bronx.

"Jim, Stadium is beautiful. Wish you were here. The city is screwed up. We are going to win-win-win just for you. John, Mel, Bob, & team."

Monarchs Defend Title Today In Yankee Stadium

By ED HEWITT
MACE AND CROWN SPORTS EDITOR

NEW YORK — The Old Dominion Monarchs open defense of their NCAA small-college eastern regional championship today against the University of Buffalo, the team they defeated last year for the title.

The tournament, held in the hallowed Yankee Stadium, gets underway this morning at 10:30 when host team, Long Island University, meets Central Connecticut. The ODC-Buffalo game begins one hour after the first contest ends.

Old Dominion and Long Island come into the tournament with identical 20-3 records. ODC won its second straight Mason-Dixon Conference title and its third consecutive Little Eight championship. The Monarchs have won their last 19 games in a row.

The Blackbirds from Brooklyn captured their seventh Knickerbocker Conference title in a row this year. They are led by Sal Campisi, a 6-2, 205-pounder, who is 11-1 this year with an amazing 0.29 earned run average.

Buffalo returns to the tournament with what the coach calls a "better defense" and John Stoffa (.393), Dan Kraft (.365), and Linn Johnson (.349). Larry Gergley, who lost to the Monarchs in last year's finals, is 3-1 and heads a strong pitching staff.

Connecticut, which won the NAIA championship this year, appears to be a one-man team. Gene Reilly is a sophomore pitcher with a perfect 9-0 record and a 1.89 earned run average. When not on the mound, Reilly plays first base and carries a .400 average.

Coach Bud Metheny will pitch either Bob Walton (8-1, 2.67 era) or Fred Edmonds (5-2, 1.28). Should the Monarchs run into any trouble, relief artist Bill Yeargan is 4-0 and has been most effective this season.

Leading the power brigade is Tommy Harrell (.419), Fred Kovner (.380), and Wayne Parks (.357). Freshmen are not allowed to play in the tournament and so Metheny had to leave behind catcher Jimmy Walker and his .354 average.

ODC won last year's tournament with victories over the Coast Guard Academy and Buffalo. Walton, chosen the outstanding player on this year's team, hurled a five-hit shutout in the finals.

From the Mace and Crown, June 5, 1964. Courtesy of Special Collections and University Archives, Old Dominion University.

Semifinals: *Old Dominion College vs. the State University of New York at Buffalo*

The semifinal game of the 1964 NCAA tournament was a chance for some further revenge for the Monarchs, although revenge in a series that historically has been very one-sided. Just one year prior, Old Dominion had won the NCAA Regional title at Hampden-Sydney College by defeating the Bulls of the University at Buffalo by a 9–0 score. But prior to that game, the Buffalo coach, Jim Peelle, had offered an uncomplimentary assessment of the appearance of the

Norfolkians that had drawn the ire of some of the Monarchs, and with so many returning ballplayers who had been part of the 1963 team, these comments had surely not been forgotten just one year later.

The University at Buffalo had been founded in 1846 as a private school by Millard Fillmore four years before he would become the thirteenth United States President, but in 1962, the school had become part of the State University system. The name of the school today is the "State University of New York *at* Buffalo," although prior to the annexation, it had been known as the "University of Buffalo." The difference that an "of" or an "at" makes would seem to be a relatively small one, but it remains problematic (or irritating) enough for the university that the authors of the 2015 baseball media guide were compelled, even fifty-three years later, to still add the following disclaimer.[36]

> PLEASE NOTE: The proper school name is the University *at* Buffalo, NOT the University *of* Buffalo. Please make all references to the school name as the University at Buffalo, Buffalo, or UB.

Buffalo was a huge school, in comparison to the relatively small commuter school in Norfolk. The 1965 yearbook, *The Buffalonian*, cited an enrollment approximating 19,000[37]—more, by a large margin, than Old Dominion, or for that matter, all schools Old Dominion played that year except Penn State. In its baseball history, Buffalo had fielded a few teams starting at least as far back as 1894, but the sport had been dropped in 1904 (along with all other sports) due to "lack of financial support, personnel and leadership,"[38] reinstated in 1914, dropped again in 1920, and restarted again only after the World War II years.

In 1949, as Bud Metheny's first Norfolk Division teams were taking the field, Buffalo was also reviving baseball under head coach and athletic director Jim Peelle. Peelle had been a three-year letter winner as a quarterback at Purdue in the early 1930s, and had also served as the

Buffalo football coach, beginning in 1936 and continuing for a dozen years until 1948, when several newspapers reported that he had been relieved of those duties.[39] The same sources, however, noted that he retained the position of athletic director, begging the question of who, then, had relieved him of his football coaching responsibilities?

Coach Peelle's baseball teams were successful from the start, and, although interrupted by two seasons after his initial one in 1949, his tenure lasted seventeen seasons, marred by only one losing campaign. Prior to the 1964 game against Old Dominion, the Bulls had gone 140–58 under coach Peelle, for a winning percentage of 70.7 percent—and, depending on which source is to be believed, had won either six or ten consecutive Western New York Intercollegiate Conference titles.[40]

The Bulls' media guide gives pretty clear indication of just how good the 1964 team was. The team was led by All-American Bill Barto and future professional Earl Tomkins, who coincidentally would be on the same 1967 short-season single-A Batavia team as ODC pitcher Denny Riddleberger. The Bulls batted .295 as a team, but the team's pitching statistics are incredible—a 1.67 ERA *as a team*, and 1.12 strikeouts per inning over a 13–5 campaign.[41] The math in the guide doesn't exactly work out, as only starter Larry Gergley's 1.88 ERA from 1964 registers among the top-ten all-time Buffalo seasonal bests, and if there was no other pitcher in 1964 to come in under 1.88, it's hard to see how the team ERA could have been less than that. Mathematically, it's also hard to see how Gergley could have the third-best career ERA at Buffalo (1.39), if the only time he appears in the seasonal top-10 list was his 1.88 in 1964.[42] He may not have met the minimums for other years, or some records may be incomplete, so despite the apparent mathematical inconsistencies, it will be assumed here only that Gergley, a member of Buffalo's sports Hall of Fame, was *good*.

The Monarchs, however, had seen Gergley in the 1963 NCAA Regional final at Hampden-Sydney. On that day, the Monarchs had taken six walks and tagged Gergley for ten hits en route to scoring nine runs, while ODC starter Bob Walton held the Bulls to four hits and no runs. The 1964 rematch featured almost the same two teams: Old Dominion's lineup retained seven of nine players from the year before, having lost only shortstop Jerry Hammer and second baseman Ron Killmon, but replacing them with Lee McDaniel and Fred Balmer, who turned out to be the top two RBI men for the season. The Bulls lost just three players from their 1963 lineup, but among their 1964 replacements was first-team All-American Bill Barto and his .338 average.

Long Island University defeated Central Connecticut in the first semifinal to start the action in Yankee Stadium. Bill Hoodzow, who would also later in his career call games in the College World Series, donned the mask to call balls and strikes in the second game, while John F. Mackin, who would later get the proverbial "cup of coffee" as a major league umpire, took the bases. Bob Walton got the starting pitching assignment for Old Dominion, opposed, again, by Larry Gergley.

"Before the game I never said a word to my boys, but they were so high that I think that if I had said anything to them at all that they would have blown a fuse. And all I said to them was 'Go get 'em,'" Bud Metheny recalled in 1975. "It happened that we beat Buffalo the year before, Bobby Walton pitching, and so when we were paired against Buffalo this year in the Yankee Stadium I also pitched Bobby against them. And this was the same team that won the year before, and they just felt that they could win. But I will say this, that for the first time for them to play in a stadium such as Yankee Stadium the tension was extremely high, probably higher than I'd ever seen it . . . it was a tremendous amount of tension on the athletes because once they walked into Yankee Stadium you could sense that they felt that they were playing in the ultimate."[43]

Old Dominion was the "away" team, and at the top of the Monarchs' lineup, Fred Kovner, Wayne Parks, and Tom Harrell went relatively quietly in a 1–2–3 top of the first inning. Walton, a control pitcher who issued only 1.74 walks per game in 1964, started the bottom half by issuing a walk to second baseman Earl Tomkins, perhaps as he tried to calm a bout of nerves while throwing from future Hall of Famer Whitey Ford's mound. After Walton struck out third baseman Steve Wasula for the first out, shortstop Barto ripped a double for the first of his four hits on the day, and Old Dominion was in early trouble, with runners on second and third with one out, and the cleanup hitter due. Right fielder John Stofa, however, couldn't get it out of the infield, putting a ball in play that was caught by Monarch third baseman Wayne Parks, and then Lynn Johnson ended the early threat with an out to left field.

The top of the second inning got off to a good start for Old Dominion, with cleanup hitter and second baseman Lee McDaniel reaching first with a single. Fred Balmer flied out to center field, but then Frank Zadell also contributed a single, ramping up the pressure on Gergley and his defense. The very next hitter, Mel Renn, hit one that Tomkins booted at second for the first of his two errors on the day, allowing McDaniel to score the opening run of the contest. With two runners still on, Larry Gergley started to get wild, and as he was in the process of walking ODC catcher John Ward, catcher Gerald Montemarano let one by that scored Zadell and put the Monarchs up 2–0.

Gergley righted the ship, though, setting down eight of the next nine hitters, including three strikeouts in a row in the fourth inning. For his part, Walton was laboring but making the big pitches when he needed them most. In the third, consecutive singles by Wasula and Barto again put two men on base with one out, but again Walton retired Stofa and Johnson to keep the Bulls scoreless. In the top of the fourth, consecutive singles by Montemarano and center fielder Dan Kraft opened the inning, and a sacrifice by first baseman Dale DelBello moved them to second and third. But Lee McDaniel cut down the lead runner at home on a fielder's choice, and Walton got Tomkins on another fielder's choice, and the Bulls had left seven men on base through four innings, without scoring a run.

The top of the fifth started slowly for the Monarch offense, as Walton and center fielder Fred Kovner recorded back-to-back ground-outs. But an absolutely disastrous seven-batter stretch followed for the Bulls, as Gergley got wild, the defense got tight, and Monarch batters patiently let it play out in front of them. Tom Harrell, Fred Balmer, Mel Renn, and John Ward all took walks in that stretch. Steve Wasula made two errors at third, and Tomkins booted one at second. Montemarano allowed a passed ball. Mel Renn and Frank Zadell executed a double steal of second and home, respectively. Only two of the seven batters in that stretch reached base on hits, including Lee McDaniel's two-run triple and Zadell's run-scoring single, but by the time the inning was complete, the game was well in hand and Old Dominion held a 7–0 lead.

It remained that way until the bottom of the seventh, when Gergley tripled, and one batter later, finally scored the Bulls' first run on a Wasula groundout to second. In the Buffalo eighth, a pair of errors by ODC shortstop Mel Renn put two men on with two out, and a Gergley single plated the second run for the Bulls. With two men still on and the tying run in the hole, there was some faint hope for the Bulls, but Walton retired Tomkins on a foul out to first to eliminate that possibility, and the game would end by the final score of 7–2. Rather than the dominating Monarch win the score might suggest, it was more a case of a patient approach, applying pressure to the defense, and letting their opponent beat themselves. Buffalo had actually outhit Old Dominion 11–6, but Gergley had also walked nine batters and threw a wild pitch, the Bulls' defense had committed four errors and allowed two passed balls, while their offense had stranded twelve runners. The opportunistic Monarchs had scored seven runs on only six hits, taken what Gergley had given them, and applied pressure on the basepaths by stealing three bases. Even third baseman Wayne Parks had stolen a base, doubling his season total to two. When asked whether it was a thrill to steal second base in Yankee Stadium, the admittedly slow-footed Parks recalled with a laugh, "*Any* time I stole a base it was a thrill. I must have been going on a hit and run or something, and the catcher let the ball get by him, or something . . . Yeah, any time I stole a base it was a thrill, that's for sure."[44]

The still-fresh memory of Coach Peelle's 1963 comments doubt-lessly made the semifinal win even sweeter, but the tough talk didn't exactly inspire a lasting back-and-forth rivalry. Historically, the 7–2 Monarch victory is the closest Buffalo has ever come to a win in the all-time series. The two schools have met three other times since 1964: as Division I competitors, ODU won a pair in 1982 by scores of 10–2 and 10–3, and by a 17–0 score in 1984, behind a one-hitter pitched by Brian Rice.

More important than payback for any perceived slight, however, the 7–2 victory vaulted the Monarchs into the next day's champion-ship game against the Long Island Blackbirds.

Finals: *Old Dominion College vs. Long Island University*

To capture the NCAA East Regional for the second consecutive year, and to extend a twenty-game winning streak for the 1965 squad, the Norfolkians squared off against Long Island University, which came in with an equal 21–3 mark on the season, and which was in the middle of a wildly successful decade and a half. Like many college teams, the Long Island program had starts and stops in the first half of the twentieth century, fielding teams between 1929 and 1931, and then again from 1934 to 1940, before fielding a team in 1949 that began an unbroken annual edition to the present. Beginning with that 1949 team, and up to the 1964 NCAA Regional tournament, the Blackbirds had totaled 200 wins, sixty-seven losses, and two ties, and had won their Knickerbocker Conference title nine times including, with 1964, seven consecutively.[45]

The Blackbirds were coached by twenty-nine-year-old former Detroit Tiger farmhand Anthony Russo, already in his third season in Brooklyn and boasting a 50–9–1 record coming into the 1964 championship game.[46] Although Russo's Hall of Fame entry for Kingsborough Community College (where he would serve for almost twenty-five years after his stint at Long Island) describes his professional experience as getting "all the way to the AAA affiliate of the Detroit Tigers before he blew out his arm and was no longer able to pitch,"[47] available records don't quite support that rosy recollection. According to minor league records, Russo's professional career included stops in Class-C and Class-D circuits during the 1955 and 1956 seasons. In Idaho Falls, he played for the Russets; in Kokomo, Indiana, he was a teammate of seventeen-year-old Orlando Cepeda; in Hazlehurst, Georgia, he played in the same place where Old Dominion's Bud Metheny had played before coming to the Norfolk Division.[48]

Russo had some talented ballplayers on his 1964 Blackbird edition, and a particularly deep pitching staff. Future major leaguer Sal Campisi had completed a 12–1 season with a 0.27 ERA and logged an incredible 101⅔ innings over twenty-four games, which is still the highest seasonal total ever recorded by a Blackbird. His ninety-eight strikeouts in 1964 is still the fifth-highest season total in Long Island's record book, and his career total of 209 over three seasons is still the third highest total, even though today's teams play more than twice as many games. Campisi's 0.27 is easily the best seasonal ERA ever recorded at LIU, topping his own 1963 mark of 0.87. The Blackbirds also had their fourth and fifth-best ever seasonal ERAs *on the same staff* in 1964, with Denis Murphy's 1.01, and Michael Couch's 1.05. Couch, in fact, is the school's all-time career ERA leader, with a published 0.87 mark, although Long Island may have learned some mathematical tricks from Buffalo, because somehow none of his season ERAs are below that number.[49]

As for position players, second baseman and leadoff man Tony Napolitano still holds the third-best Long Island seasonal stolen-base mark with his twenty-one in 1963, even though the team only played seventeen games. Third baseman Neal Baskin and center fielder Richard Small were future major league draftees. Right fielder Ernest Defilippis, another future MLB draftee, knocked in twenty-eight runs in twenty-four games in 1964. And first baseman George Kalafatis, a .533 hitter in 1963, hit fourteen home runs in forty-two games over the 1963 and 1964 seasons, a pace for fifty-four over 162 games. All told, four of the eleven members of the LIU Sports Hall of Fame elected for baseball played on the same 1964 squad.[50]

But the Monarchs' 1964 roster could also boast five future members of the school's Hall of Fame, four past or future All-Americans, two future major league draftees (although Denny Riddleberger, a freshman, had not traveled for this series), and a former New York Yankee leading the charge from the Yankee Stadium dugout. The former Yankee handed the ball to Fred Edmonds, charging him with the task of completing Old Dominion's most successful baseball season ever.

The day was cool for that time of the year, staying in the mid-sixties, and the action began with the consolation game, as Central Connecticut beat Jim Peelle's Buffalo Bulls by a 4–2 score. The championship game followed immediately. Behind the plate was veteran minor league umpire Sam Van Hook, and minding the bases was umpire Henry C. "Hank" Morgenweck, a future major league umpire who would call balls and strikes for two no-hitters (one by Dick Bosman in 1974 and one by Nolan Ryan in 1975).

At 1:37 p.m., Van Hook exclaimed "Play Ball!" Long Island, despite its status as the nominal host school, batted as the visiting team, and Edmonds took the hill on an incredible hot streak that had seen him throw 29⅔ innings with a 0.61 ERA, four wins, and forty-six strikeouts over his previous five appearances. Despite pitching from the mound in the center of the baseball universe, and despite the intimidating Blackbird lineup, Edmonds started solidly, recording two strikeouts and a fly to center in a 1–2–3 top of the first.

In the previous day's semifinal, Coach Russo had sent Sal Campisi out for the final game of his collegiate career, and Campisi had responded with a two-hit, ten-strikeout gem in a 1–0 victory over Central Connecticut. That left Denis Murphy and Michael Couch, both with ERAs around one, as possible starters for the championship affair—and Russo picked Murphy. In the top of the first, it seemed like Murphy was no more awed by the setting than Edmonds was, as he set down Fred Kovner on strikes, and then Wayne Parks and Jimmy Zadell on balls in play, to match Edmonds.

In the top of the second, only a two-out walk to center fielder Richard Small marred Edmonds' inning, and Small did not advance beyond first. In the bottom half, however, Monarch batsmen demonstrated the patience that had seen them walk ninety-two times in twenty-four prior contests, good for an average of almost four per game, and a full thirty beyond what Monarch pitching had permitted, giving Old Dominion 1.25 baserunners more per game than their opponents. Cleanup batter Lee McDaniel led off with a walk and was followed by first baseman Fred Balmer's single. Left fielder Frank Zadell struck out, and shortstop Mel Renn followed with a flyout to right field to leave two on and two out for catcher John Ward. Ward had been a little shaky behind the plate to start the game, as he had dropped two of Edmonds' third strikes and had to secure the putouts on throws to first. But there were no such jitters at the plate, as Ward took a ball four to load the bases for his pitcher's turn at the plate.

With the limited number of at-bats that a pitcher sees over the course of the season, Fred Edmonds came to the plate at only .240 for the year on six-for-twenty-five hitting, and only two RBI on the ledger. But after the Penn State practice game, sportswriter Dave Lewis had quoted Edmonds in Norfolk's *Ledger-Star* as saying, "If I had a choice, I'd rather be a shortstop. I enjoy playing, not watching from the bench . . . And I enjoy hitting, too. I had a fairly good average in high school. A pitcher doesn't get much of a chance to hit and hardly ever gets batting practice."[51]

But if this team knew patience at the plate, it also knew confidence, and, up and down the lineup, it knew the "big hit." Edmonds stepped to the plate and delivered a three-run double, plating McDaniel, Balmer, and Ward—increasing his season RBI total to five in the biggest game of the year, on the biggest stage of his life, and against a pitcher with an ERA less than 1.00. That hit ended Murphy's day, and reliever Michael Couch came on to retire Fred Kovner on a strikeout to end the inning.

But the one big hit didn't take the life out of the Blackbirds or put them on their heels, as Lee McDaniel's two-run triple had seemed to do against Buffalo the day before. Second baseman Ed Schwal led off the top of the third by drawing a walk against Edmonds, and after relief pitcher Couch struck out, leadoff hitter Tony Napolitano also worked a walk. Third baseman Neal Baskin followed with a run-scoring single, and George Kalafatis reached on an error by Frank Zadell, which also plated Napolitano, cutting the lead to 3–2 and still leaving a lot of danger on the basepaths. Cleanup hitter Larry Wassermann drew the third walk issued by Edmonds in the inning to load the bases with just one out, bringing top RBI man Ernest Defilippis (whose 1964 RBI pace would have extrapolated to 189 over 162 games) to the plate. But Edmonds won this battle in the war; Defilippis grounded back to the pitcher, who began a pitcher-to-catcher-to-first double play and preserved the lead.

In the fourth, a leadoff single by Small turned into the tying run without the benefit of either another hit or walk, as two Monarch miscues allowed him to advance around the bases, leaving the score at 3–3 after four innings. A pitcher's duel ensued from there; over the next four innings, Edmonds faced only one batter more than the minimum twelve, and Couch faced only two more than the minimum, while only one runner from either side in that stretch got as far as second base.

Ninth inning, tie ball game, Yankee Stadium, NCAA Regional title on the line. Despite a twenty-game winning streak, this situation wasn't as nerve-wracking to the Old Dominion squad as might be expected. The Monarchs had scored the winning runs in their last bat in nine of those twenty wins, and three times in extra innings. And they had won close games in pressurized situations, such as the first game in the Mason-Dixon Conference championship series against Washington College. This team had confidence on their side, and they knew how to win the close ones because they had done it, and had *been* doing it, for twenty straight games.

Edmonds ran into difficulty in the top of the ninth with consecutive hits, as Richard Small doubled and was followed by a single from catcher Joe Matrone. But Edmonds bore down and recorded the all-important second out via strikeout of Ed Schwal, advancing no runners and allowing the half-inning to pass harmlessly when Couch flied out to center field.

Couch had been masterful on the mound in his six innings of work, permitting just one base hit—an infield single by Fred Edmonds in the seventh. The bottom of the ninth in a tie game, though, belonged to Old Dominion in 1964. Fred Balmer led it off with a double, putting Couch in early trouble in the frame. But consecutive batters failed to advance Balmer and brought John Ward up with a chance to win the game. Ward was zero-for-two on the day and had allowed the tying run to score on a passed ball in the fourth. His defense may have been shaky for the game, but his confidence wasn't shaken, and he delivered a single that advanced Balmer to third.

Now with runners on first and third with two outs, Fred Edmonds was the batter. With a two-for-three performance so far, he had raised his season average to .286, and now had the chance to go over .300 for the year, while driving in the run that would win the NCAA Regional, and make himself the winning pitcher. In Yankee Stadium. What pressure? Edmonds drove Balmer in with a game-winning single, a "shot that soared over the shortstop's head with plenty to spare," as the *New York Times* reported the next day.[52]

With that swing, Edmonds brought the season to a close (and raised his 1964 average to .310). Old Dominion had won the Little Eight, Mason-Dixon, and NCAA Regional Championships, and carried an intact twenty-one-game winning streak. The overall season record stood at 22–3, for a winning percentage of .880. And this day's NCAA Regional championship was not hidden in rural Virginia in Hampden-Sydney's "Death Valley"; this one was at the center of the baseball universe, for anyone to see. The following day, to Coach Bud Metheny's certain enjoyment, the name "Old Dominion" made newspapers as far removed as Philadelphia, Rochester, Chicago, Phoenix, Reno, and, of course, New York City.

The 1964 NCAA East Regional Champion Monarchs in "The House that Ruth Built." Courtesy of Special Collections and University Archives, Patricia W. and J. Douglas Perry Library, Old Dominion University Libraries, Norfolk, Virginia. Back row, left to right: Tom Harrell, Lee McDaniel, John Ward, Jim Zadell. Kneeling, left to right: Bill Bigger, Bob Walton, Fred Balmer, Ray Nelson, Mel Renn, Gene Johnson, Fred Edmonds, Frank Zadell, Fred Kovner, Bill Yeargan, Wayne Parks.

The photo is taken in center field at the old Yankee Stadium in New York, when there were only three monuments, Miller Huggins (whose 1929 death sparked the tradition), Lou Gehrig, and Babe Ruth, and two plaques, for former owner Jacob Ruppert and former General Manager Ed Barrow. The monuments have been moved to the new Yankee Stadium, and are housed in "Monument Park," which now holds more than thirty plaques and monuments and is accessible to fans. In 1964, the monuments and the base of the flagpole were in play.

Above: *Wayne Parks in front of Yankee Stadium monuments for Lou Gehrig, Miller Huggins, and Babe Ruth.*

Below: *Parks with a backdrop of the 1964 Yankee Stadium scoreboard and right-field porch.*

Above: *The 1964 Old Dominion Monarchs in the New York Yankees dugout, led by Fred Balmer, foreground.*

Below: *Old Dominion celebrates a repeat championship in Yankee Stadium.*

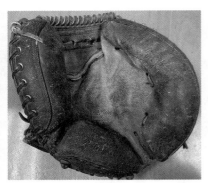

Catcher's mitt used by John Ward in the NCAA title game. In possession of John Ward II.

EDMONDS IS STAR OF VIRGINIA NINE

Pitches 3-Hitter and Bats In 4 Runs—Buffalo Bows in 3d-Place Game, 4-2

By MICHAEL STRAUSS

Fred Edmonds, a well-built right-handed pitcher, turned in a one-man show yesterday in leading his Old Dominion teammates to a 4-3 victory over Long Island University at the Yankee Stadium.

The victory gave the Norfolk, Va., college its second straight National Collegiate Athletic Association Atlantic Coast College Division crown.

Edmonds, yielding only three hits, rounded out his performance by driving in all of his team runs. His key contribution was a line single with two out in the last of the ninth to win the game.

Faced by Mike Couch, L.I.U.'s right-hander who had done an air-tight job in relief since the second inning, Edmonds connected with Couch's third offering. It sent Fred Balmer home with the payoff run.

The victory was the 21st in a row for the Old Dominion nine.

In the program opener for third place in the tournament—Central Connecticut of New Britain turned back the University of Buffalo, 4—2. A big four-run eighth inning won the game for the Blue Devils.

Edmonds, experiencing difficulty with his control in the early stages, settled down after the fourth inning and parted with only one safety the rest of the way. He gave up only three hits in all while striking out eight.

The end came suddenly. Couch, who had relieved Denis Murphy with two out in the third, had little difficulty in checking the visitors. Going into the final frame, he had held the Virginians to only a scratch infield single. Only two balls had been sent to the outfield during his six-and-one-third-inning stint.

Hurler Puts Team Ahead

But Balmer opened the inning with a line double to left field. Couch got the next two men on a strike-out and a pop fly, but then John Ward lofted a single over short to send Balmer to third.

Edmonds, who previously had lashed out a two-bagger and beat out an infield hit, connected solidly. It was a shot that soared over the shortstop's head with plenty to spare.

In the second inning, Edmonds sent the team out in front with a hard-hit double to right with the bases filled. Scoring were Lee McDaniel, Balmer and Ward. Balmer had singled while McDaniel and Ward had walked.

Couch came to the rescue and was effective from the start. His teammates came on to tally twice in the third inning on three bases on balls, an error, a passed ball and Neal Baskin's single.

Then in the fourth, the Blackbirds evened matters when Ed Schwal doubled to left, raced to third on a field with Joyce and registered on a passed ball. Edmonds was in trouble only once thereafter—in the ninth when Schwal doubled again and Joe Matrone singled before he could retire the side without a run.

Schwal looked particularly impressive at the plate and did a fine job at shortstop. In addition to his two doubles, the L.I.U. infielder blasted a long drive to right field that was caught on the warning track.

```
Central Conn. ..0 0 0  0 0 0  0 4 0--4  5  0
Buffalo ........0 0 0  0 1 0  0 1 0--2  6  0
  Batteries: Newfield and McGrath; Wianacki,
Whalen (8) and Montemarrano.
```

```
                                    R. H. E.
L. I. U.........0 0 2  1 0 0  0 0 0--3  3  1
Old Dominion ..0 3 0  0 0 0  0 0 1--4  6  2
  Batteries: Murphy, Couch (2), and Ma-
trone; Edmonds and Ward.
```

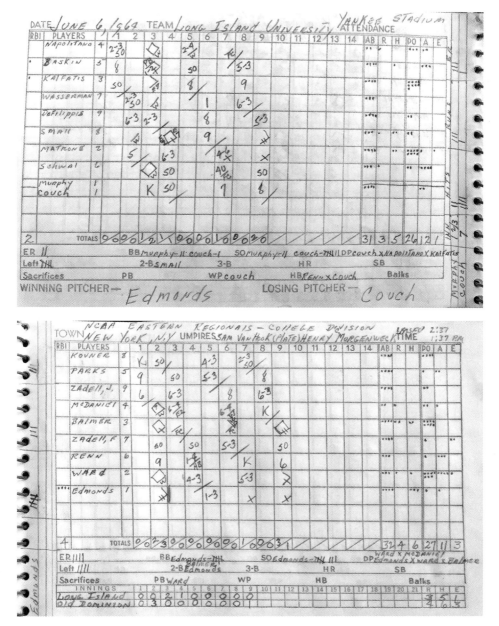

The NCAA Championship scorebook entry, in Bud Metheny's own hand. Courtesy of Special Collections and University Archives, Patricia W. and J. Douglas Perry Library, Old Dominion University Libraries, Norfolk, Virginia.

The hardware. The plaque above celebrates the three titles the 1964 team won. The medal shown below left is inscribed simply "O. D. C. 64" on the back, and the medals below center and below right are the 1964 NCAA medal (center) and 1963 NCAA medal (right), shown side-by-side since they are the same except for the inscription.

1964
NCAA EASTERN REGIONAL CHAMPIONS
MASON-DIXON CONFERENCE CHAMPIONS
VIRGINIA LITTLE EIGHT CHAMPIONS

Back Row: (L to R) Larry Watson, Fred Edmonds, Jim Walker, Lee McDaniel,
                    Dennis Riddleberger, Ray Nelson, Jim Zadell
Middle Row: A. B. Metheny (Coach), Fred Balmer, John Ward, Melvin
                    Renn, Bill Yeargan, Frank Zadell, Fred Kovner, John Young
                    (Manager)
Front Row: Al Baker, Bill Bigger, Gene Johnson, Tom Harrell, John
                    Ingram, Bob Walton (Co-Capt.), Wayne Parks (Co-Capt.),
                    Bob Demille, Joe Grandy (Bat Boy)

May 9, 2015, 50th anniversary at "The Bud." Left to right: Frazier O'Leary, Fred Kovner, Ron Killmon, Boyd Nix, Frank Zadell, Fred Edmonds, John Ingram, Don Strickland, Wayne Parks, Lee McDaniel, Tommy Harrell, Tony Zontini, Jimmy Walker, Mel Renn.

1964 OLD DOMINION MONARCHS TEAM LEADERS

(Collated from records in Bud Metheny's scorebook, including postseason)

	AB		R		RBI		2B	
1.	W PARKS	93	F KOVNER	26	L McDANIEL	23	F BALMER	8
2.	F ZADELL	90	F BALMER	22	F BALMER	20	L McDANIEL	6
3.	F BALMER	88	W PARKS	22	F ZADELL	19	F ZADELL	5
4.	F KOVNER	87	L McDANIEL	17	F KOVNER	13	T HARRELL	3
5.	L McDANIEL	69	F ZADELL	14	W PARKS	11	F KOVNER	3
6.	J ZADELL	67	T HARRELL	12	M RENN	9	M RENN	3
7.	M RENN	58	M RENN	10	J ZADELL	8	F EDMONDS	2
8.	T HARRELL	47	J ZADELL	9	WALKER	8	W PARKS	2
9.	J WARD	42	J WALKER	6	T HARRELL	7	J WALKER	2
10.	J WALKER	34	2 tied with	5	F EDMONDS	6	3 tied with	1

	3B		HR		SB		AVG	
1.	W PARKS	2	F KOVNER	3	F KOVNER	11	B DEMILLE	0.500
2.	J WARD	2	F ZADELL	3	F ZADELL	8	T HARRELL	0.383
3.	F BALMER	2	F BALMER	3	M RENN	3	J WALKER	0.353
4.	L McDANIEL	2	L McDANIEL	1	J ZADELL	2	F KOVNER	0.345
5.	F ZADELL	1	J WALKER	1	W PARKS	2	W PARKS	0.333
6.	J ZADELL	1	8 tied with	0	F BALMER	1	F EDMONDS	0.310
7.	T HARRELL	1			L McDANIEL	1	J WARD	0.310
8.	6 tied with	0			B WALTON	1	F BALMER	0.295
9.					5 tied with	0	M RENN	0.293
10.							F ZADELL	0.267

	IP		K		K/9	
1.	B WALTON	82.67	F EDMONDS	75	F EDMONDS	10.33
2.	F EDMONDS	65.33	B WALTON	38	J INGRAM	9.65
3.	J INGRAM	18.67	J INGRAM	20	B YEARGAN	6.89
4.	B YEARGAN	15.67	B YEARGAN	12	D RIDDLEBERGER	5.17
5.	D RIDDLEBERGER	15.67	D RIDDLEBERGER	9	T HARRELL	4.50
6.	T HARRELL	6	T HARRELL	3	B WALTON	4.14
7.	R CORSON	2	R CORSON	0	R CORSON	0.00

	BB		BB/9		W	
1.	R CORSON	1	B YEARGAN	1.72	B WALTON	9
2.	T HARRELL	2	B WALTON	1.74	F EDMONDS	6
3.	B YEARGAN	3	T HARRELL	3.00	B YEARGAN	4
4.	D RIDDLEBERGER	8	F EDMONDS	3.03	J INGRAM	2
5.	J INGRAM	15	R CORSON	4.50	D RIDDLEBERGER	1
6.	B WALTON	16	D RIDDLEBERGER	4.60	R CORSON	0
7.	F EDMONDS	22	J INGRAM	7.23	T HARRELL	0

	L		ERA		WHIP	
1.	F EDMONDS	2	B YEARGAN	1.15	B WALTON	1.05
2.	B WALTON	1	F EDMONDS	1.38	F EDMONDS	1.06
3.	R CORSON	0	D RIDDLEBERGER	1.72	B YEARGAN	1.08
4.	J INGRAM	0	B WALTON	2.50	D RIDDLEBERGER	1.21
5.	T HARRELL	0	T HARRELL	3.00	J INGRAM	1.88
6.	B YEARGAN	0	R CORSON	4.50	T HARRELL	2.00
7.	D RIDDLEBERGER	0	J INGRAM	5.31	R CORSON	3.00

CHAPTER NINE

Epilogue

"Jimmy, let me tell you something." And he pulled his pocket out and he turned it upside down. He says, "We've got our hands on millions." I didn't know what he was talking about. He had nothing in it but the inside of his pocket, and he says, "Jimmy, we've got our hands on millions." And he was right.

—**JIMMY ZADELL,** *referring to Bud Metheny in a December 14, 2016, interview*

1965 AND BEYOND

On January 9, 1965, Coach Bud Metheny was named as the first recipient of the College Division Baseball Coach of the Year award from a nationwide pool of candidates, and this fact was reported across the country, in cities and towns large and small. The *Baltimore Sun* reported it in Maryland, the *Daily Press* in Newport News, and the *Progress-Index*

BUD METHENY GETS AWARD FOR COACHING

NORFOLK (AP) — A. B. (Bud) Metheny of Old Dominion College will be honored today as baseball coach-of-the-year (small college) by the NCAA. Metheny, athletic director as well as basketball and baseball coach at ODC, led his team to the NCAA small college Atlantic Regional championship last June.

Jim Watley of Georgia confirmed Metheny's award Saturday. Watley, a spokesman for the American Association of College Baseball Coaches, said Metheny was selected for "an outstanding job of coaching last season."

Metheny's Monarchs finished with a 22-3 record and won the Mason-Dixon Conference championship for the second time.

The small college award was initiated this year. It covers NCAA small colleges coast to coast and embraces eight districts.

From the January 10, 1965, Daily Press (Newport News). Copyrighted 1943–1965. Associated Press.

in Petersburg, Virginia. Beyond these relatively local outlets, Metheny's selection was reported in Montgomery, Alabama; Lincoln, Nebraska; and Tucson, Arizona, and in less populous places, such as Bryan, Texas; Twin Falls, Idaho; and Mexia, Texas. The news traveled as far as Honolulu, Hawaii. Personal letters and telegrams to Coach Metheny acknowledged the award, such as one from Old Dominion history professor Stanley Pliska, who congratulated Metheny with the words, "Hail to the Coach of the Year! Good for you, good for Old Dominion College. Whenever the 'Society for Telling of Jokes, Especially Spicy Ones' meets I shall recommend you for the Joke Teller of the Year. I am sure you would win there also." Metheny's cousin Gloria Godfrey Yates spoke for the maternal side of the family with a telegram sent to the awards banquet at the Conrad Hilton Hotel in Chicago, saying "Congratulations from the Godfreys. It's good to have a celebrity in the family."[1]

Additionally, Old Dominion College's *Mace and Crown* faithfully reported the news on January 15, in words that no doubt gave Coach

Metheny the greatest satisfaction: "Old Dominion College shares in Mr. Metheny's award. Just as there was national recognition for Mr. Metheny, there was national recognition for Old Dominion College. If the first question was who was the Coach of the Year, then the second question surely was where is he from? The 1964 baseball team and the college received recognition by winning the Eastern Regional championship in Yankee Stadium. And now the coach has received his well-desired [sic] honor . . . We are quite sure that when Mr. Metheny received his honor, foremost in his thoughts was the recognition the college received. This is the caliber of professor we need at Old Dominion College; this is the caliber of coach we need at Old Dominion College."[2] Perhaps in a nod to the school's rising profile, the college's name was again in national newspaper outlets across the country just a few weeks later, when on March 1, Old Dominion athletic director Bud Metheny named Sonny Allen as his successor as basketball coach.

The pinnacle of team success achieved by the 1964 baseball Monarchs also included many individual successes. When the Mason-Dixon Conference all-star team was announced in June, Old Dominion had three players on the first team, namely third baseman Wayne Parks, outfielder Fred Kovner, and pitcher Bob Walton.[3] First baseman Fred Balmer made the second team, and Fred Edmonds also garnered honorable mention. In terms of national recognition, Fred Kovner was named a first-team All-American, and Bob Walton as a second-teamer. A full five players from this team went on to be enshrined in Old Dominion's athletic Hall of Fame, along with their coach. So good was the 1964 pitching that the team remains very well-represented in the Old Dominion record book for several statistics: three of the pitchers with the best career ERAs were on the 1964 team: Bill Yeargan (first, 1.25), Fred Edmonds Jr. (third, 2.02), and Bob Walton (fourth, 2.38); only Brett Wheeler (1.50), from the mid-1990s, breaks this trio up. Behind only Wheeler, Edmonds also has the second-best win percentage ever at the school, with his cumulative 24–3 record, or 88.9 percent. In terms of shutouts, Bob Walton is still the all-time leader with eight, Edmonds is fourth with five, and Yeargan tied for fifth with four, and none of these statistics even include Denny Riddleberger, the future major leaguer who was also on the 1964 staff. As for team accomplishments, the group was part of the two longest winning streaks in Old Dominion baseball history (twenty-three and twenty-six games) and in 1964 established the best seasonal win percentage ever at the school, with an incredible 88 percent.[4]

Despite such achievements, Bud Metheny did not consider his mission complete, and he came into 1965 with another stacked roster that still included Kovner, Edmonds, and former second-team All-American Jimmy Zadell, to go with the returning Denny Riddleberger, Jimmy Walker, Lee McDaniel, Mel Renn, Tom Harrell, and Fred Balmer. True to form, Metheny continued to try to improve the quality of his baseball schedule, and with a twenty-one-game winning streak still alive, the Monarchs started the year strong with two resounding wins over the University of Rochester, by scores of 16–8 and 10–4. After a sweep of two games against Dartmouth, the Monarchs then hammered the Cavaliers of "Mr. Jefferson's University" in Charlottesville, by a 9–1 count.

But all good things come to an end, and Ithaca College finally ended the win streak at twenty-six games with a pair of one-run victories over the Norfolkians. By the end of the regular season, however, the 1965 Monarchs had again turned in an exceptional campaign, not necessarily matching the winning percentage of the 1964 squad but certainly putting itself in the same category statistically. During the 19–5 regular season campaign, Old Dominion had recorded eight victories to go with one inexplicable 17–2 defeat to Bridgewater in the Mason-Dixon Conference, qualifying again for the best-of-three championship tournament, this time against Western Maryland. In Little Eight play, their record stood at 6–2, good enough to win the mythical title again.

Statistically, the team still shone brightly. Extrapolating his 1965 season numbers over the entire twenty-eight-game schedule (including postseason) to 162 games, Fred Kovner was on pace for a season with a .415 batting average, twenty-three home runs, ninety-three stolen bases, 174 runs batted in, and 179 runs scored. Jimmy Zadell, returning to All-American form, was on pace for a 162-game season with a .327 batting average, ninety runs batted in, forty-one stolen bases, 133 runs scored, and 208 hits. Fred Balmer set a pace for 127 runs batted in, and Mel Renn and Tom Harrell were both on pace to score more than 100 runs. The pitching was outstanding again, led by Bill Yeargan with an ERA of less than one, and workhorse Fred Edmonds.[5] Newcomer Fred Carlson also proved a welcome addition, contributing forty-one innings with a minuscule ERA of 1.32, as part of a staff that held their opposition to a skimpy .212 batting average for the entire year. As a team, according to statistics that Coach Metheny signed and returned to the National Collegiate Athletic Bureau accounting for the full twenty-eight games played, the Monarchs doubled their opponents' run totals (165–82), stole .89 more bases per game than their opponents (39–14 total), had a batting average eighty-seven points higher (.299-.212), and committed .93 errors per game less than their opponents (46–72 total).[6]

After sweeping two games from Western Maryland to win the 1965 Mason-Dixon Conference crown for the third straight year, the Monarchs had the chance to make it three straight in the NCAA regional tournament, as well. The tournament was again held in New York's Yankee Stadium, and the 1965 field featured Le Moyne College of Syracuse, Colby College of Maine, and Union College of Schenectady, New York. Coach Metheny gave the starting nod in the semifinal game against Le Moyne to the hero of 1964's title game, Fred Edmonds, and was rewarded with a complete game by his starter, in which Edmonds allowed just eight hits and one run, while his Monarch teammates were scoring five times. By the accounting of Le Moyne's hometown newspaper, though, the *Post-Standard* of Syracuse, Le Moyne probably would have won if it just hadn't been so darn *hot*. "LeMoyne [sic] College bowed to the heat and the righthanded slants of Fred Edmonds, as Old Dominion beat the Dolphins 5–1, in the opening game of the Atlantic Coast regionals of the

NCAA College Division baseball tournament at Yankee Stadium," as the reporter described the events of the day. Further, "Gary DeYulia, a junior right-hander, had pitched a nifty two-hitter for LeMoyne [sic] until the 92-degree heat helped wilt him in the fifth inning, during which the winners scored three runs."[7]

Denny Riddleberger got the start on the following day, but a third consecutive NCAA title was not in the cards for the Monarchs. Old Dominion maintained a tight 1–0 lead going into the seventh inning, but two Union runs in that inning, and one more in the eighth, was all that Union starter Gary Brown needed. The Old Dominion team that had shown the capacity for such late-inning magic in recent years didn't have enough left for the bottom of the ninth and bowed by the 3–1 score.

Colby Defeats Old Dominion For NCAA Title

NEW YORK (AP) — Union College won the Atlantic Coast tournament of the NCAA college division championships Wednesday with a 3-1 upset over Old Domination at Yankee Stadium.

Gary Brown pitched a three-hitter for Union, striking out seven and walking two. The winners scored twice for a 2-1 lead in the seventh inning on singles by Bob McAdams and Rick Erdoes, a passed ball, force play and Bruce Fike's double. Union's insurance run came in the eighth.

Old Dominion, which had won the tourney the past two years, collected its lone run in the fourth when Fred Kovner socked a 410-foot triple to center field and continued home when Greg Olson bobbled the ball.

Union finished its season with a 15-2 record and Old Dominion wound up 22-6.

Colby won third place over Lemoyne 5-0 as Roger Valliere pitched a five-hit shutout.

Union	000 000 210—3	10 2
Old Dom'n	000 100 000—1	3 0

Brown and Marshall. Riddleberger, Yeargan (8), Edmonds (9) and Walker.

Lemoyne	000 000 000—0	5 3
Colby	010 002 11x—5	9 1

Volz, Wallace (6), Frawley (8) and Sisk. Valliere and Haigis, Thomas (9).

From Burlington, Vermont's Free Press, June 10, 1965: notable for naming the wrong team champion, as well as for "Old Dominion" becoming "Old Domination." Copyrighted 1943–1965. Associated Press.

Bud Metheny's 1966 team fell off to a 9–12 overall record, and his Monarchs would never again have success in the College Division comparable to that of the 1963–1965 teams. However, the growth of the school and its athletic program that Metheny had helped engineer, and the visibility that these baseball teams had provided, continued to open doors for Old Dominion. For his baseball team, Coach Metheny began to be able to recruit the highest caliber of baseball player, and from places other than Norfolk—not only did Denny Riddleberger make the major leagues, but from some of Metheny's following teams, so did Paul Mitchell of Worcester, Massachusetts, and John Montague of Newport News, Virginia. Of his 1974 class, Metheny recalled that he had recruited players of such caliber that they were signed by major league teams just three days before classes were to start at Old Dominion: Massachusetts' Mark "The Bird" Fidrych by the Detroit Tigers and Virginia Beach's Joseph Kwasny by the New York Yankees.[8] In more recent years, the most obvious example of Old Dominion's ability to appeal to the highest caliber of talent is provided by Justin Verlander, the Old Dominion career strikeout leader (and second-place holder in games started and innings pitched), who has gone on to a certain Hall of Fame major league career, including a Rookie of the Year Award, two Cy Young Awards, an MVP award, eight All-Star nods, and a 2017 World Series title with the Houston Astros.

As Old Dominion continued to grow, it wasn't long before the athletic affiliation with the Mason-Dixon Conference, so important as recently as 1962, began to feel restrictive. In March 1969, it was reported in newspapers that two proposals threatened to divide the league. As the *Progress-Index* of Petersburg, Virginia, reported on March 14:

> *The controversial proposal, to be offered by Western Maryland and Washington College, would require that all athletic grants-in-aid given in the future by conference colleges be based solely on need.*

It is certain to be opposed with some heat by several Mason-Dixon institutions—among them Old Dominion, Roanoke, and Mount St. Mary's—which have ambitious programs in basketball.

Should the proposal win approval—which appears unlikely—some members quite probably would withdraw from the conference, which includes colleges in Virginia, Maryland, West Virginia, and Washington, D. C. Another thorny problem to be faced is the proposal by Lynchburg College that transfer students be made eligible for varsity competition after one semester instead of one year.

Lynchburg also belongs to the Dixie Conference, in which transfers are eligible after a single semester, and deliberately broke Mason-Dixon bylaws this winter by allowing transfer students to play against MDC foes on the one-semester basis. No one protested—but Lynchburg beat no one.[9]

Only two months before, Old Dominion basketball coach Sonny Allen had tipped the college's hand, at least to a degree, as he provided a sound bite to a *Daily Press* reporter, sounding very much like Bud Metheny in his desire for improved competition. Allen indicated that eventually "we'll have to get out of the Mason-Dixon Conference . . . We're not worrying. Getting out of the league will take care of itself. We want to play good opposition."[10] Both of the controversial measures introduced in March 1969 were defeated by conference vote, but tension between the larger institutions and smaller schools within the group remained, and on June 1 of that year, Bud Metheny pulled the plug. In a terse press release, the Old Dominion athletic director announced that "Old Dominion College, as of June 1, 1969, will resign as a member of the Mason-Dixon Conference and enter into the Collegiate Independent category. The Old Dominion University will be a member of the NCAA College Division (small college) in competition."[11] The distinction made in this brief release between "Old Dominion College" and "Old Dominion University" was neither an oversight, nor unintentional. Further signaling both the growth and the continued ambition of the school, Old Dominion College's Board of Visitors had voted in 1968 to change the name of the school to Old Dominion University on September 1, 1969. Bud Metheny knew that for the athletic program to continue to be a prime driver for Old Dominion, the school must leave the Mason-Dixon Conference.

In 1978, the Mason-Dixon Conference itself, unable to meet the competing goals and demands of its members, officially disbanded.[12] By that time, its demise appears to have been a foregone conclusion, as the league was already unrecognizable as its former self. Randolph-Macon, Hampden-Sydney, Lynchburg, and Bridgewater left to join the Division III Old Dominion Athletic Conference in 1976, and by 1978, some of the remaining Mason-Dixon schools wanted to elevate their programs to Division I status, while one (Frostburg State) wanted to de-emphasize athletics to Division III. Only one, Mount St. Mary's, remained as a Division II competitor. While Commissioner "Lefty" Reitz still sounded the hopeful note that "It's not out of the realm of possibility that the conference might be formed again as a split conference or a Division I conference,"[13] in 1978 the Mason-Dixon Conference was done.

In 1976, seven years after becoming a university, Old Dominion's athletic programs joined Division I competition and sought and gained admission to the East Coast Athletic Conference (ECAC). The *Daily Press* described this conference, incredibly, as a "sprawling . . . 212-member league with 58 NCAA Division I schools," and noted that "affiliation with the ECAC would in no way affect ODU's petition to join the Southern Conference."[14] After five years with ECAC affiliation, Old Dominion started to look elsewhere again. On February 2, 1982, Newport News' *Daily Press* wrote that "Old Dominion Athletic Director Jim Jarrett emphatically denies printed claims that ODU has agreed to join the Sun Belt Conference. 'Absolutely no decision has been made. We still have several avenues open.'"[15] Yet barely more than two months later, on April 6, the *St. Petersburg Times*, along with many other national outlets, announced Old Dominion's inclusion in the Sun Belt: "Athletic officials at Old Dominion University unveiled their worst-kept secret Monday—the school will join the Tampa-based Sun Belt Conference. Athletic director Jim Jarrett said the affiliation provides a 'great marriage' of television coverage and the cities in which the circuit plays will enhance recruiting."[16]

Sun Belt affiliation lasted only until June 1991, when Old Dominion joined the Colonial Athletic Conference (the evolution of the ECAC South), which included more local programs and natural rivalries, such as William & Mary, East Carolina, Richmond, and James Madison. Progress has continued to the present, without slowdown. As a prime example, in 2009, Old Dominion revived football after a nearly 70-year absence. Playing in the lower-division FCS (formerly I-AA), the Monarchs sold out every game and finished with a 9–2 record in their return to the gridiron. This success paved the way for the future, too; in 2013, Old Dominion joined Conference USA, and in 2014 began competing in the FBS division (formerly I-A). In 2016 they won a bowl game (the Bahamas Bowl, by a score of 24–20 over Eastern Michigan), and in 2018 they shocked #13 Virginia Tech, with a 49–35 victory over the Hokies in Norfolk.

In 2019, Old Dominion continued to modernize, replacing the eighty-two-year-old Foreman Field with a contemporary facility. "Old Dominion University's old Foreman Field has been replaced with a modern upgrade. S.B. Ballard Construction Company was proud to announce the grand opening of the new S.B. Ballard Football Stadium at Old Dominion University on Saturday, August 31, 2019," Ballard's website says of the project. "The goal was to make this facility more fan-friendly and with seat back chairs, bench back seating, elevators, better concessions, more restrooms, improved audio and video components and more . . . virtually all of the original stadium was demolished to make way for new seating and new amenities."[17]

Even as the growth of the school and its athletic program are easy to trace today with the hindsight of fifty years, Bud Metheny had actually already begun fielding questions about Old Dominion's stay in the Mason-Dixon Conference as early as 1965. In January of that year, he denied any intention to leave that conference, stating that "Our philosophy is to win our own conference and then let the chips fall their own way. At present we are in an era of transformation. We want a chance of an Ivy League basis and we'll get it soon."[18] Still, despite these protestations, the athletic director was one to envision positive change and to drive it, not one to let chips fall as they may. In 1965, the Intercollegiate Foundation provided a means to help take the next step in Old Dominion's athletic progress.

As Metheny recalled in an interview with Dr. James Sweeney in 1975:

> The Old Dominion College Intercollegiate Foundation came about through the interest of a student and automobile dealer Jack Wilkins. And to this day he's constantly taking classes here. And Jack, being quite a promoter and very interested in the university, got together with Jimmy Howard, a lawyer here in town, and we talked it over. And then we got together with the coaching staff, and we decided to put all our eggs in one basket, which would be basketball, because it was the one sport that we could take in money at the gate. And so, we felt that this was the avenue to go. And so, Jack Wilkins and James A. Howard helped us to do this. And, by the way, Mr. Howard was on our Board of Visitors at the time. So, we had the sanction of this possible program all the way from the Board of Visitors.[19]

At its inception, Metheny commented that the foundation's goal for 1965 would be to raise $50,000, and that the next goal would be to reach $100,000 annually. A December 1964 kickoff dinner for the new foundation reserved fifty seats for local businessmen, and Metheny proudly announced that "Forty-nine of those seats were filled. This shows the enthusiasm and support we're getting from the community."[20] The initial fundraising goals would fund four basketball scholarships per year, and, therefore, create an incredibly more advantageous recruiting position. Metheny, however, wasn't ready to adopt a "win at all costs" mentality that required any ethical compromise, as the *Mace and Crown* reported on January 15, 1965. "The college wants four 'quality' boys a year," the paper declared. "Aid they will receive will go through the same channels as any other scholarship at the college. The only restriction for the scholarship is that the boy maintain [*sic*] a 'C' average each semester. Coach Metheny stressed that the college will support no college bums."[21]

In an ironic turn, the coach who had been unfairly at the center of a racial controversy in 1957 (when Shepherd College had not been permitted to use any African-American players in a basketball contest against the Norfolk Division) presided as Old Dominion athletic director when one of the first scholarships available through the Intercollegiate Foundation was awarded to Arthur "Buttons" Speakes of Huntington, West Virginia. The June 17, 1965, edition of the Danville (Virginia) *Register* reported the event:

> The first Negro athlete recruited by a predominantly white college in Virginia was granted a scholarship Wednesday by Old Dominion College.
>
> He is Buttons Speakes, a 6–0, 170-pounder from Huntington, West Va., who will play basketball and baseball for Old Dominion.
>
> Speakes was recruited by Sonny Allen, the new head basketball coach at Old Dominion and former freshman coach at Marshall University in Huntington.
>
> 'I have watched Speakes' athletic progress since he was in junior high,' Allen said. 'He is an excellent athlete. He has unusual ability in the basketball phases of speed, shooting and ball-handling. He was also a fine football and baseball player in high school.'

A. B. (Bud) Metheny, athletic director at Old Dominion, said the way has been cleared for Speakes to attend ODC on a scholarship provided by the Old Dominion Intercollegiate Athletic Foundation.

Old Dominion, a state-supported college with a day-night enrollment of just over 6,000, numbers several Negroes in its student body but Speakes will be the first Negro to compete in varsity athletics at ODC.

No other white college in Virginia has yet recruited a Negro athlete, although Bridgewater, like ODC a member of the Mason-Dixon Conference, played non-recruited Negro athletes in both football and track several years ago.[22]

In 1975, Bud Metheny noted the impact of the Intercollegiate Foundation, with the perspective of a decade: "Without the Foundation we couldn't have gotten underway, because they were the group that solicited moneys for athletic scholarships, primarily for basketball. And, as I say, this was to be done with the expectation that in the future, by developing basketball, it would help our entire athletic program, and then the money would come down to our other sports. The Intercollegiate Foundation is still here today, and they have helped us tremendously in the securing of funds."[23]

"THE BUD"

The 1980 baseball season would be Coach Bud Metheny's last. Even though his schedule now featured such schools as Michigan, Missouri, North Carolina State, and St. John's, the coach's final baseball tour included a tip of the cap to his program's past, featuring two games with Dartmouth (a series which would be abandoned after his retirement), four games against his alma mater, William & Mary, and seven games with Virginia Commonwealth University, a school that Metheny-coached teams had battled for the first time in his very first year of 1949, when it was known as the Richmond Professional Institute.

A 1–8 start to the season took the shine off any nostalgia tour, but the team steadily improved over the year and finished Coach Metheny's final season by winning ten of their last fifteen games. Despite an overall 20–22 record, the late-season push enabled the team to win the Virginia Division I East title against Richmond. Following that, Metheny's Monarchs won the Tidewater Invitational Tournament at Norfolk's Met Park, at that time the home field of the New York Mets' Triple-A team, the Tidewater Tides. On April 30, 1980, in what would be Coach Metheny's final game, his Monarchs took to their home field in Larchmont and faced the Cavaliers of the University of Virginia. Old Dominion's Mark Wasinger, a future major leaguer, belted two home runs and, fittingly, gave Metheny the gift of a Virginia State Division I Championship to finish his career.

Barely more than a month later, Old Dominion gave Metheny an even greater gift, in recognition of his years of service to the school, and central role in its growth. In front of many of his former athletes, the school named the planned new baseball facilities in his honor. As the *Daily Press* reported on June 7:

> The pursuit of hits, runs—no errors—and victories was supposed to have ended Friday night for Arthur B. 'Bud' Metheny. It didn't.
>
> A testimonial banquet, marking his retirement as baseball coach and 32 years of service to Old Dominion University, turned out to be a big rally before over 200—and Metheny scored heavily.
>
> Ten 'designated hitters' delivered awards and two thrills perhaps equal to Metheny's 1943 World Series appearance with the New York Yankees.
>
> Eight of the DHs (from various school departments) presented the ex-Yankee (1938–47) with plaques, fishing equipment, honor certificates and even a cord of wood for his home fireplace, but it was ODU's

Board of Visitors and the Yankees who cut loose with the thunderous, clutch hits.

Elston Howard, former catcher and an all-time great, represented the Yankees and came through with a 'double' in his DH role.

On behalf of Club President George Steinbrenner, Howard invited Metheny to play in the Yankees' famed Old-Timers' game, June 21, then added that ODU's pioneer baseball-basketball mentor will be the first recipient of a 'Yankee Family Award.'

Howard noted that 'this will not necessarily be an annual award, but rather something special to recognize the achievements of a former Yankee who has dedicated the better part of his life to the old adage that 'it's better to build boys than to mend men.'

A standing ovation greeted the ODU Visitors' gift of appreciation for Metheny's long service to ODU, including seven years as athletic director (1963–70).

The university's new baseball stadium, to be completed by the Spring of 1982, is to be named 'The Bud Metheny Baseball Complex,' announced Robert Fodrey, who read a resolution to that effect.

Fodrey good-humoredly added that Metheny had not yet fully earned this honor. He reminded Metheny that he is being retained on the staff as advisor to Athletic Director Jim Jarrett—and to assist in the fund-raising needed to bring the project to fruition.[24]

On August 19, 1982, the official "groundbreaking" was held, and "The Bud" opened for business in the 1983 season with a 7–2 ODU victory over Millersville University. The following season, the biggest crowd ever recorded to date at the facility (2,125) came out for the dedication of the field named for the legendary coach.[25] The move from Larchmont Field to the brand new, 2,500-spectator facility was demonstrative of progress on the baseball front and was a fitting tribute to an Old Dominion leader, but it was also part of the bigger vision for the school. The same period saw expenditures of funds approved to renovate Foreman Field, install artificial turf for the soccer and field hockey fields, and develop a new sports complex including basketball and soccer facilities, to go along with the baseball improvements.

And progress has not stopped. As the 2019 Old Dominion Baseball Media Guide says, "The Bud, as its [sic] often referred to in Monarch Nation, received a bevy of renovations prior to the 2018 season. New additions included the Rally Alley Patio, a video-based Daktronics scoreboard and turf baselines. The Rally Alley Patio is an elevated viewing deck on the right-field foul line that features an outdoor bar, a grilling station and a three-tiered deck of tables and bar stands. The new scoreboard offers fans a more in-depth viewing experience due to its ability to play video replays, post advanced stats and player information and engage fans with cheer prompts. The turf baselines (which include home plate, the first base line and the third base line) provides easier maintenance of the playing surface and will now blend in with the all-turf backstop. Overall, the 2018 renovations cost nearly a million dollars. During Chris Finwood's tenure as the head coach, over two million dollars have been put into the facility, most of which has been privately funded."[26] And displayed on the outfield wall is a retired pinstriped number "3" jersey, so familiar to baseball fans as the uniform worn by Babe Ruth, but this one bearing the last name of another old Yankee: "Metheny."

In April of 1980, Ken Samet, now president and CEO of MedStar Health, was, in his own words, a "cub reporter" for Old Dominion's *Mace and Crown* newspaper, and had the honor of summarizing Coach Bud Metheny's career for the paper:

> Sure, coaches, like aging college sports editors, have to hang it up eventually. But with Bud Metheny it goes a lot deeper than that. The man has been part of the ODU athletic scene for the past 32 years, serving in capacities from coach, to teacher, to athletic director. To say he is

one of the major reasons why the athletic teams at ODU have grown so fast would be touching on just the tip of the iceberg.

'Bud has provided great and consistent leadership for our baseball program for the past three decades. As our former athletic director he set the foundation for the present success our teams are now enjoying,' commented present ODU Athletic Director Dr. Jim Jarrett.

'But an even greater contribution than his athletic leadership and baseball coaching has been the tremendous job he has done in building character in his players and students,' continued Jarrett. 'Bud has always represented the university with class, and would accept no less from the members of his teams.'

. . .

'But anyway,' continued Metheny, 'I'm looking forward to the day in the near future when I can sit in the stands and watch us play for the national championship.'

The national championship? Old Dominion baseball? Is that a realistic dream, coach?

'You're doggone right it is,' concluded Metheny, in such a tone as to make even the most skeptical of followers believe.

And as I left his office and walked through the back halls of the field house, I thought that if that day ever does become a reality, Bud Metheny would have to get a doff of the cap for a job well done.[27]

Bud Metheny was a tireless advocate for Old Dominion, not only in the classroom or the field of competition, but also in the community as well. He could be found regularly speaking at a Peninsula Sports Club event, presenting awards at a local high school league banquet, attending a Norfolk Sports Club meeting, or talking to a coach at a local high school game. The success that he and his early-1960s baseball teams brought to Old Dominion in its infancy as an independent institution of higher learning, and the visibility they created for the school, provided a foundation that the little commuter school with fewer students and faculty than the surrounding high schools could use to become one of the largest employers in Hampton Roads and to contribute more than two billion dollars annually to Virginia's economy today.

That foundational impact and influence is immeasurable, and in some ways intangible, but certainly goes even beyond the school and into the surrounding community it serves. Virginia Beach, for example, became an independent city during Bud Metheny's Old Dominion career, and as the Tidewater area as a whole grew, the college in Norfolk sent more and more graduates into that community every year, and Bud Metheny sent more and more of his former baseball and basketball players into the community in the same way. From the 1964 baseball team, Bob Walton and John Ingram went into high school coaching locally, and Lee McDaniel helped coach Greenbrier Christian Academy in Virginia Beach; from the 1963 team, Frazier O'Leary went on to teach and coach at a school in a disadvantaged area of Washington, DC. The list would be far too long to include all such examples, but notably, Leo Anthony coached high school basketball, cross country, and golf, winning four state golf titles with Princess Anne High School in Virginia Beach. The captain of Bud Metheny's first basketball team, Ted Bacalis, went on to a long and successful basketball coaching tenure at Maury High School in Norfolk. Baseball player Buddy Denton went on to coach high school baseball on the Peninsula, winning 365 games in a career of almost thirty years at Kecoughtan High School, where the baseball field is named for him.

Old Dominion University and Norfolk can and should be proud and thankful for this coach, and his protégés who took his lessons into the community. When Kirkie Harrison '62, baseball and basketball player for Bud Metheny at Old Dominion and subsequently high school coach in Norfolk and Chesapeake, was welcomed into to the ODU sports Hall of Fame, he invoked a most Methenian thought: "My biggest satisfaction has been the growth of my athletes as people. I'm proud that I have been able to help others the way I was helped."[28]

AFTER COLLEGE

I think they are the high points of my career in that I've got doctors, lawyers, bank presidents, teachers, principals. They've all gone out, and for them to come back and say that the things that they learned in baseball have stood them in good stead, I think those are the high points. The development of the university—I came here when there was, I guess, between 200 and 250 students; now there's over 11,000. To be able to grow up with the university, the athletic program, to see it go from nothing to something is just pleasing to me. And to know that things have progressed in the manner that they have, I think that that's what we're here for, and that's what makes me feel good. Disappointments—I haven't had many. I don't even talk about them.

—BUD METHENY, 1975

The following section is not intended to be all-inclusive. It includes post-college career and family highlights only from those who chose to participate and is in most cases in their own words. Some additional posthumous entries were added by the author.

Fred Edmonds Jr.: A pitcher on the 1964 Monarch baseball team, Fred taught school in Virginia Beach for thirty years. In 1987, Fred was honored to be selected into the Old Dominion Hall of Fame. He followed in the footsteps of his father, Fred Edmonds Sr., to be the only father-son in the ODU Hall of Fame. In 2006, Fred was selected as part of the twenty-member all-time baseball squad as voted by the fans on the ODU website. Since retiring, Fred enjoys spending his time fishing and being around the water. He and his wife, Lisa, live in Virginia Beach.

Tom Harrell: The 1964 team leader in batting average (.383), Tom moved to Palm City, Florida, in 1973, where he owned and operated a floor covering business for eighteen years. He stayed involved with baseball by coaching Little League and at the high school level, and played golf professionally after turning 50, including competing in three PGA Senior Tour events. Tom is retired and lives in Lenoir, North Carolina, and Palm City, Florida. Tom and his wife Sue have two children (Cathy and Tim).

John Ingram: A senior pitcher on the 1964 Monarch baseball team, John went into teaching and coaching after Old Dominion, and coached baseball at several junior high and high schools in Virginia Beach after his graduation. In 1996, his Cox High School Falcons won the Virginia State baseball championship. John and his wife Arlene retired in Virginia Beach, and had two children, one son (Jay) and one daughter (Allison). John Ingram passed away on October 16, 2020, in Virginia Beach.

Fred Kovner: Fred left Old Dominion as a two-time first team All-American. He was drafted by the Chicago White Sox in the second round in 1965, playing three seasons in Single-A and Double-A baseball, with one season in spring training with the big club, where he appeared in thirteen preseason games. Among others, he played against Reggie Jackson, Rollie Fingers, and Rod Carew in the minors, and against Mickey Mantle in spring training. A back injury ended his baseball career, and he began a data processing career in 1968, retiring from Sentara Healthcare in 2006. Fred also played cello in the Norfolk Symphony, and retired after twenty-five years with emeritus status. He has been married to his wife, Bunny, for twenty-six years, and has two children and two grandchildren. Fred was inducted into the Old Dominion Sports Hall of Fame in 1981, and into the Tidewater Softball Hall of Fame for his postgraduation play with the F&M Bankers fast-pitch team.

Lee McDaniel: Lee McDaniel furthered his education after Old Dominion, receiving a Master of Business Administration degree, but always retained a passion for athletics. Lee worked as a football official and referee with the Southeastern Football Officials' Association for forty-one years, as his obituary notes. Lee was very active in both his church and his community. He was a member and servant of the Kings Grant Baptist Church, and served as president of the Princess Anne Plaza Civic League. Lee and his wife, Shirley, had three daughters (Ashley, Courtney, and Megan). Lee McDaniel passed away on September 30, 2016.

Arthur B. "Bud" Metheny: Bud Metheny passed away in Virginia Beach on January 2, 2003, within hours of his beloved wife Frances, leaving one son (John) and one daughter (Eileen). Mr. Metheny is a member of the Virginia Sports Hall of Fame, American Association of College Baseball Coaches Hall of Fame, the Tidewater Baseball Shrine, the William & Mary Hall of Fame, the Old Dominion Hall of Fame, the Hampton Roads Sports Hall of Fame, and doubtlessly several others. Mr. Metheny was a lifelong and dedicated servant of Old Dominion University, and lends his name to the Bud Metheny Award, given annually by the university.

Boyd Nix: Colonel Boyd Nix, USAF (Ret.) graduated from ODU in 1968, and later that year, received his commission from Officer Training School at Lackland (TX) Air Force Base. Between 1971 and 1972, he flew one hundred combat missions in support of the air and ground campaign in Laos, with only one of those missions occurring during daytime hours. Boyd retired from the Air Force in 1999, and then spent eight years working as a contractor on the Air Force Predator and Global Hawk (UAV) programs. Boyd is married to the former Sharon Marie Chauret, and they have three daughters (Michelle, Laura, and Melissa).

Frazier O'Leary: Dr. Frazier L. O'Leary Jr. taught AP English Literature and Language at Cardozo High School in Washington, DC. He taught English in the DC public schools for forty-seven years and is also an adjunct professor at the University of the District of Columbia. He taught A.P. Literature and Language for twenty years and is a Table Leader in English Literature and a consultant for the College Board in English Language and Literature. He has a bachelor's in English from American University, a master's from St. John's College, and a PhD from St. Mary's College. He is the vice president of the PEN/Faulkner Foundation and a member of the board of the Toni Morrison Society and The School Club. He is a member of the District of Columbia Board of Education representing Ward 4.

Wayne Parks: Wayne Parks, a third baseman and co-captain with pitcher Bob Walton on the 1962–1964 teams, made a career in food sales and management in the Southeast United States. Wayne has a daughter (Shelly) and two stepdaughters (Amy and Rebecca) with his wife, Linda.

Mel Renn: Mel Renn was a third baseman and shortstop at Old Dominion. After graduation, he taught school and coached football, baseball, and basketball at Thorpe Junior High School. After teaching, he went on to work for the ILA and retired from there after thirty years. After graduating from ODU, Mel continued playing fastpitch softball at Fox Hill for fifteen years, where he was the all-time home run hitter. Mel is married to Marsha Renn, and he has two sons (Mel Jr. and Bubba), who both played baseball for the Newport News Apprentice School. He also has two stepsons (Steve and Sean), five grandchildren, and one great-grandchild.

Denny Riddleberger: Denny Riddleberger went on to a professional baseball career after playing for Bud Metheny at Old Dominion. He began his professional career in 1967 with stops playing for the Pirates of Gastonia, North Carolina, and the Trojans of Batavia, New York. Denny compiled 24 wins and a 3.18 ERA in the minor leagues, and debuted in the major leagues for the Washington Senators on September 15, 1970, with one clean inning pitched against the Baltimore Orioles. Denny's career major league stats included four wins against four losses, a 2.77 ERA, and a 1.316 WHIP.

Bob Walton: All-American pitcher Bob Walton went on to a coaching career after his time at Old Dominion. Bob coached football in Galax and Waynesboro, Virginia, and had been the head baseball coach and an assistant football coach at Norfolk's Granby High School before his untimely death on July 6, 1993. Bob left his wife (Karen), two daughters, and one son.

John Ward: John Ward graduated from Old Dominion in 1964, but returned later for graduate work at that institution, and in 1974 earned a master of education degree. John had a varied career, spending more than a decade teaching and coaching at the high school level, more than fifteen years in agriculture management, and then more than a decade in insurance before his retirement. John demonstrated his commitment to education by serving as the chairman of the Board of Education in Gates County, North Carolina, for several of his thirteen years on that board, and by teaching GED classes to prison inmates in his retirement. John married Joan Alexander of Richmond, and they had two children, John II and Beth. John Ward passed away on December 1, 2003, in Suffolk, Virginia.

Frank Zadell: After ODU baseball, Frank went to Officer Candidate School in Newport, Rhode Island. Upon receiving his commission in the US Navy, he served on the USS *St. Paul* and the USS *Henrico*, on which he deployed to Vietnam. In 1965, he and Miss Gail Lynch, a 1967 ODU graduate, were married in Coronado, California. After the Navy, Frank and Gail headed to New York, where Frank joined IBM and worked as a computer programmer. In 1970, they relocated to North Carolina with IBM, and he retired from IBM in 1997. Frank and Gail reside in Apex, North Carolina. They have three children and five grandchildren. Frank has found that hitting a curve ball was a lot easier than fixing a nasty slice on the golf course, where he now spends most of his leisure time.

APPENDIX

A GAME-BY-GAME ACCOUNT OF THE 1964 OLD DOMINION MONARCH BASEBALL SEASON

Practice Game: *3/25/1964—Norfolk—Penn State*

According to Penn State's 2018 baseball yearbook, the Nittany Lions' baseball team has faced Old Dominion twelve times—winning five and losing seven, all in Norfolk. The book states that the series between the schools didn't begin until a doubleheader on March 13, 1988. But the Nittany Lions *did* play the Monarchs at least once before that, in Norfolk on March 25, 1964, in what Bud Metheny described as a "practice game" in his scorebook—twelve days before Penn State's official April 6 opener against Gettysburg.[1] When Penn State took the field that day in Norfolk, they represented the best college talent with whom Old Dominion had ever shared a baseball diamond and offered an early-season litmus test for the 1964 Monarchs.

Penn State's 1963 team, under first-year coach Chuck Medlar, had played in the College World Series, with losses in the double-elimination tournament coming to traditional powerhouses Arizona and Texas, sandwiching a win over Western Michigan. 1963, in fact, was the fourth year of the previous eleven in which Penn State had advanced to that tournament, with appearances in 1952, 1957, 1959, and 1963. The 1964 team that came to Norfolk did not advance as far, but would still compile a 15–6–1 record, comparing favorably to 1963's 14–6 mark.[2]

When Old Dominion starter Fred Edmonds took the hill, he immediately met the Penn State challenge by striking out the first two Nittany Lions he faced, and went on to pitch three complete innings, striking out five, walking one, and surrendering just one hit while allowing no runs. The Monarchs plated a single run in the second, when Old Dominion left fielder Frank Zadell singled, advanced on an error, and came home on shortstop Ray Nelson's single.

Edmonds turned the ball over to senior left-hander John Ingram after three innings, and Ingram pitched another two clean innings, but a walk, a passed ball, and an error allowed the tying run to cross in the sixth. In the bottom half of the inning, consecutive singles by right fielder Jimmy Zadell and second baseman Mel Renn, helped by an error by the Penn State pitcher, Elmer Praul, allowed Old Dominion to retake the one-run advantage.

Senior right-hander Bob Walton took his turn on the mound to start the top of the seventh, and was as effective as Edmonds and Ingram had been, but two walks and an error in the top half of the eighth left the Lions and Monarchs tied again going into the ninth inning. Penn State's leadoff man, Don Tokash, reached on a two-out error, but third baseman Wayne Parks gloved the next ball that was put in play, ending the Penn State ninth. In the bottom half, Mel Renn led off with a single and took second on a passed ball. After Fred Balmer struck out, Frank Zadell then stood in and capped a three-for-four day with a game-winning double.

Even though it was only a practice game, the Virginians had tested themselves against the stiffest competition they had faced on the field since games against the professional Norfolk Tars, and they had won the game, both in score and statistically. Old Dominion pitching had held Penn State to just three hits and two unearned runs, while striking out eleven batters. Monarch batters recorded seven hits in thirty-two at-bats, only a .219 pace—but for a team that had finished sixth in the College Division in batting average the year before (.322 as a team), and lost only one starter, hitting wasn't a concern. Maybe this was to be "THE year," after all, as *Mace and Crown* writer Ed Hewitt had posited in the preseason!

Game One: *March 27, 1964—Norfolk—Dartmouth College*

The first game the Norfolk Division Braves had ever played against a major college varsity was the contest against Dartmouth in 1953, a 7–3 win authored by starting pitcher Jack Smart. Although Dartmouth doesn't appear on the official Norfolk Division schedule and results again between 1953 and 1960 (when it became an official annual affair again), the two schools likely continued to play practice games, as Coach Metheny recalled playing them every year from that first game. The results published by the official website of Dartmouth College varsity athletics do seem to support that likelihood, as they show that Dartmouth's baseball team visited Virginia in March every year between 1953 and 1959[3] (although they describe the game in 1953 as a loss to "William and Mary"). Interviewed by Dr. James Sweeney in 1975, Bud Metheny recalled the history of the series with Dartmouth:

> *Sweeney: On April 2, 1953, the Norfolk Division's Braves baseball team played a varsity major college team, Dartmouth College, for the first time. I was wondering how this came about and what you recall of the 7–3 victory by the Braves pitched by Jack Smart?*

Metheny: *Well, you know, this moving up in caliber of athletics, that's part of my philosophy, and I knew the coach; he was a former professional, Tony Lupien. He was a graduate of the Harvard School of Business, but he lives up there at Hanover, Mass., so as a result he was coaching there. And they wanted to come South so he called me, and from that day on of 1953 we have played every year anywhere from two to five games with Dartmouth. They wonder how we got these large universities and colleges to come here to play. They came here and they played for nothing. They got no room and board, no guarantee of anything. They just came here to play us, and they helped us along, and that's one way that we have developed. And to this day Dartmouth never accepts a penny. So, it's unique in that sense.*[4]

As noted previously in this work, the Dartmouth coach in 1953 was Bob Shawkey, who led the team from 1952–56. While Bud Metheny mentioned in the 1975 interview that he knew Coach Lupien, he also knew Coach Shawkey, at least for playing in Old-Timers' Games in New York City with him. Like Metheny, Shawkey was also a former Yankee, and was a fifteen-year major league veteran, finishing with a career that included 195 wins, a 3.09 ERA, and, in his final season, a roster spot on the famed 1927 Yankee team. According to the Bio Project of the Society for American Baseball Research (SABR), "Shawkey returned to Yankee Stadium for many special events and old-timers' games. He was present in 1939 when Lou Gehrig gave his farewell speech and in 1948 when Babe Ruth made his final appearance. Shawkey pitched the first game ever played at Yankee Stadium, and in 1973, he threw the ceremonial first pitch at the stadium's 50th anniversary celebration, using the same ball that Governor Smith threw in 1923. In 1976, the 85-year-old Shawkey again threw out the first pitch when the stadium reopened after a two-year renovation."[5] Whether this Yankee connection is what originally started the Norfolk Division-Dartmouth series would be a matter for speculation, but in retrospect, the beginning of the series certainly must be viewed as a seminal event for the Old Dominion University baseball program.

However the series began, when Harvard's Ulysses John "Tony" Lupien assumed the reins of Dartmouth baseball beginning with the 1957 season, he and Bud Metheny were already used to competing against one another. In 1941, both had played in the Double-A American Association—Metheny had played the full season for the Blues of Kansas City, while Lupien, a five foot ten, 185-pound first baseman, had been with the Colonels of Louisville for the whole year.[6] In 1943, both spent the entire year in the major leagues, experiencing one of the most storied rivalries in baseball firsthand and from opposite sides of the field—Bud Metheny in the Yankees dugout, and Tony Lupien in the Red Sox. Their collegiate rivalry continued for many years as well, as Lupien coached Dartmouth to 313 wins over a twenty-one-year career.[7]

There were very few similarities between Dartmouth and Old Dominion off the baseball field in 1964. While Old Dominion had been an independent institution for two years, Dartmouth was only five years away from celebrating its bicentennial. Dartmouth had the academic respect that goes with the Ivy League; Old Dominion could fairly be described as a community college. Dartmouth had ice hockey, squash, and ski teams that competed at an intercollegiate level.[8] Their first baseball competition had been in 1866, almost a hundred years before.[9] For that matter, Dartmouth even had dormitories. But on the baseball field, Bud Metheny's Monarchs came into their first official game of 1964 with a five-game winning streak against Dartmouth and an overall 7–3 mark against their opponent.

Old Dominion's expectations were sky-high as they took Larchmont Field at noon on Friday, March 27, in a pitching matchup featuring Dartmouth's Ted Friel against the Monarchs' junior Fred Edmonds. Friel was one of two players in the Dartmouth lineup to later be selected in Major League Baseball's inaugural draft in 1965, going in the ninth round to the St. Louis Cardinals. Teammate and cleanup hitter, catcher Dick Horton, was also selected that year, going to the Orioles in the second round with the 35th overall pick. The Reds had the next pick after the Orioles, and also sensing a need for a catcher, selected Johnny Bench. And with the 37th overall pick, the White Sox selected Old Dominion center fielder Fred Kovner.

Neither Horton nor Friel would play above Double-A, but Friel established a career mark of eighteen wins against eight losses that left him tied as the lifetime leader in wins at Dartmouth for twenty-two years, until future major leaguer Mike Remlinger broke the mark in 1987.[10] As of 2020, Friel remained tied for third in career wins, and just out of the top ten in career winning percentage, at .692.[11]

Friel was part of an impressive staff that would compile an ERA under 3.00 in 1964, but Edmonds came into the game with sterling credentials as well. An All-Mason-Dixon Conference performer the year before, Edmonds established an 8–0 record with sixty-four strikeouts in sixty-six innings in 1963, to go with a 3.00 ERA—and, in fact, is still credited with the third-lowest career ERA of any Old Dominion starter, at 2.02.

Edmonds started the game hot, striking out three of the first four hitters, and didn't allow a hit until the fourth inning. But the Monarchs' offense—almost the same squad that had been potent to the tune of a .322 average in 1963—was also putting up zeroes. While Edmonds pitched out of some amount of trouble and left six runners stranded through nine shutout innings, Friel had set the Monarchs down in order in seven out of eight frames. The only exception was a pair of walks in the third to shortstop Ray Nelson and center fielder Fred Kovner, neither of whom scored.

To the bottom of the ninth inning in a game that had been scheduled for seven, the score remained tied at zero. After an Edmonds flyout to right field and a Kovner groundout to second, third baseman Wayne Parks reached on an error by the Dartmouth second baseman.

But when Old Dominion right fielder Jimmy Zadell put a ball in play that was caught by the center fielder, the Monarchs had compiled zero hits in twenty-eight at-bats through nine innings. Friel, though, still didn't have a no-hitter—or even a win—to his credit, as the game remained deadlocked.

Fred Edmonds was back on the hill to start the tenth and began the inning with a walk to first baseman Douglas Hayes. After a sacrifice by Michael Bloom, Dartmouth removed Friel from the game for pinch-hitter Bill Dubocq, who became the second out of the inning with a groundout to short. Leadoff hitter and third baseman William Bower, 0-for-4 to this point in the game, followed with the two-out, run-scoring single that gave Dartmouth the lead.

Shortstop Mel Renn, in a pinch-hitting role, began the bottom of the tenth by reaching on the second error in two innings by Dartmouth second baseman Michael Bloom, and Fred Balmer followed with a single. As Ed Hewitt would describe the game's conclusion in the next day's *Virginian-Pilot*, "Fred Balmer, ODC first baseman, got the only Monarch hit in the first game, in the tenth inning off reliever Bill Caterino. His single followed an error on Mel Renn's grounder and placed men on second and third with no outs. But loose base-running resulted in two Monarchs racing to the same base, killing a possible rally."

No runs scored, Ted Friel did get the win, and Peter Barber would have gotten a save, if such a statistic had existed at the time. After one game in THE year, the Monarchs were 0–1, and the one-for-thirty-two day at the plate left them with a team average of .031.

Game Two: *March 27, 1964—Norfolk—Dartmouth College*

Game Two of the doubleheader featured a starting pitching matchup of Dartmouth's Bob MacArthur against Old Dominion's senior right-hander Bob Walton, and the Monarchs' fortunes figured to change with this game, as Walton had put together an impressive 1963 season: a 7–2 record, a .95 WHIP, and a minuscule 1.42 ERA. These numbers had led to Walton's selection as a 1963 first-team All-American, and had included a pair of shutouts, one of which happened to be in the deciding game of the 1963 NCAA Eastern Region College Division championship.

In the May 22, 1964, *Mace and Crown*, Ed Hewitt wrote, "All-America status is the highest and most treasured reward for an athlete. Bob was named to the first team in small college circles in 1963. This accomplishment has been the most pleasing to Walton during his career. And proud he should be for this recognition was deserved. Last season, Walton won seven of nine games and established a brilliant 1.42 earned run average. His control was superb as he only walked five men in over 70 innings. His five-hitter in the final game of the NCAA small-college tournament against the University of Buffalo gave the Monarchs the championship. 'The game against Buffalo ranks with the All-American selection as my biggest thrills in baseball,' Bob said. At that game in Hampden-Sydney, Bob's mother saw him pitch for the first time since he was 12."[12]

Walton is remembered for that control, and his ability to get outs with location and changes of speed. While Edmonds had struck out .97 batters per inning in 1963, Walton's similar statistic was only .62. As Walton's former Old Dominion battery mate Jimmy Walker recalls, "He had a curveball. His fastball wasn't nearly as fast as Edmonds', but he could put it where he wanted to. If you wanted to call it low inside, that's where he put it. High outside, that's where he put it. He had command of the mound, he really did." And Walton was a team leader, especially as a senior in 1964. Walker recalls, "He was like Bud's right-hand man, he was like a coach on the field. He was an amazing player and he knew the game. Everybody looked up to Walton."[13]

On March 27, 1964, the past was the past, and the accolades of 1963 weren't going to help beat Dartmouth. Dartmouth opened the top of the first with a single by third baseman William Bower, and star catcher Dick Horton, the cleanup hitter who had been held to a relatively benign one-for-four in the first game, doubled him home two outs later. But the Monarchs answered in their half, with a walk to Kovner, who moved to third on a single by senior third baseman Wayne Parks. After Parks was picked off first, Jimmy Zadell brought Kovner in on a sacrifice fly to left, plating Old Dominion's first run of the year and tying the score.

Walton worked around a pair of errors in the second but ran into more trouble in the third. After consecutive singles by speedy center fielder Stephen Dichter and Horton, left fielder Kenneth Lapine delivered a one-out, two-run triple to put the Big Green (also known at that time, interchangeably, as the Indians) up 3–1. An RBI groundout from Fred Kovner scored Jimmy Walker in the bottom half of the frame to halve the lead, but the fifth and sixth innings were harmful to the Monarch chances. Dartmouth batted around in the fifth and sent another seven men to the plate in the sixth. The innings both started in unusually repetitive fashion; in both innings, Dichter led off and singled, stole second, Horton singled, Kenneth McGruther recorded an out, and then Lapine walked. All told, four runs crossed in the two frames, leaving Old Dominion down 7–2 going into the bottom of the seventh inning, in a game only scheduled for seven.

Old Dominion had only managed four hits off MacArthur through six innings, and so coach Lupien left him in for the seventh. The Monarchs still had some fight left, however—a one-out single by Bob DeMille, pinch-hitting for Ray Nelson, and a base on balls to freshman catcher Jimmy Walker put the tying run in the hole. John Ogletree, in his only at-bat of the season, struck out pinch-hitting, but consecutive RBI singles by Fred Kovner and Wayne Parks put the tying run at bat with two outs. Lupien brought in new closer Bill Dubocq to face Monarch right fielder Jimmy Zadell, and a groundout back to the pitcher doused the threat.

After two games in the books, the team was 0–2, and Bob Walton, after a third of an inning in relief in the first game followed by what would be his least effective start of the year, carried a 10.39 ERA. The team batting average stood at .136, and star pitchers Walton and Edmonds had been the losing pitchers on both ends of a doubleheader, which was quite an unusual result in a year which would see the exact opposite result no less than four times. Worse, the team would have to wait until 1965 to avenge the losses, as the single game scheduled for Saturday, March 28, was rained out in the top of the first inning.

Practice Game: *April 2, 1964—Norfolk—Rensselaer Polytechnic Institute*

A practice game was scheduled for April 2, against the team from Rensselaer Polytechnic Institute of Troy, New York. The Engineers, no doubt, were on the Southern swing typical of Northern college baseball teams when they arrived for a Thursday game in Norfolk.

As a practice game, it didn't have much relevance, as the 13–2 Monarch victory didn't count. The game doesn't show up in the mimeographed sheets of the 1964 schedule that can be found in Bud Metheny's papers in the ODU library. It didn't show up when the *Mace and Crown* published the upcoming season's schedule on March 13 of that year. As far as the Old Dominion baseball record book goes, ODU has no record against Rensselaer. The only place the game shows up is in Bud Metheny's 1964 scorebook.

Yet, the game did have significance. Considering the Penn State game even though it didn't count in the standings, Old Dominion had collected just fifteen hits in ninety-one at-bats in their first three contests, for a .165 average. Defensively, those first three games had included eight Monarch errors, a pair of passed balls, and a pair of wild pitches. The team needed work, and the team needed confidence.

Metheny did not start any of the pitchers that he knew he'd be relying on as the season progressed. Instead, he put eighteen-year-old Denny Riddleberger, a freshman left-hander out of Churchland High School in Portsmouth, Virginia, on the mound. This choice gave the practice game another significance. On September 15, 1970, Riddleberger, with one clean inning pitched for the Washington Senators, would become the first Old Dominion player ever to compete in the major leagues. His career numbers are good, but sparse: in three years, two with the Senators and one with the Cleveland Indians, Riddleberger logged 133 innings in 103 games, with a 2.77 ERA, 1.32 WHIP, ninety-five strikeouts, four wins, and one save. Jimmy Walker, a freshman at ODC the same year as Riddleberger, recalls catching him: "He did not have the speed that Edmonds had, but he was left-handed, and lean and tall. He kind of slung the ball in there, and I'll tell you, he was hard to catch. His balls *moved*; they moved a lot, and that's what you need. Some pitches are just straight pitches, but those balls that move, they're hard to hit, and he did really good."[14]

Riddleberger's Old Dominion debut came in this Rensselaer game, in three innings of work that included one hit, no runs, and four strikeouts. Bill Yeargan relieved Riddleberger in the fourth, and pitched another three innings of shutout ball (and if these innings had counted, Yeargan would have lowered what was already the best career ERA ever at Old Dominion—an incredible 1.25). Tom Harrell closed it out for the Monarchs, allowing just two unearned runs over three innings. While the pitching was strong, the defense was still stuck in March; Old Dominion committed six errors and two passed balls.

While the Old Dominion mound work was solid, the offense started to show some signs of life, as well. Nineteen different batters came to the plate for the Monarchs, who scored thirteen runs on thirteen hits. The only surprise may have come in the fifth inning, when Bill Bigger stood in to bat for ODC's version of "Iron Man" Cal Ripken Jr., senior co-captain Wayne Parks. Aside from Bigger's three at-bats, which were not taken in a game that counted, Parks started and finished every game at third base in 1964, hit in the second spot every game, and did not at any time come out of a game. Reminded of this fact in 2016, Parks recalled, "When I got there my freshman year, the third baseman had graduated the year before I got there. Back then freshman could play, so once I got the third base, I loved it. I didn't want to move the next year, and Bud just left me at third base, for all four years. I had pitched at Maury, and in my freshman year we were a little short on relief pitchers. I pitched a few innings of relief, not a whole lot, my freshman year. After that, I never pitched anymore. I just played third base all the time . . . I liked hitting second, because I was a right-handed batter, and I loved to hit to right field behind the runner. Felt like I could put the bat on the ball, at least hit it somewhere."[15]

Game Three: *April 3, 1964—Norfolk—Washington and Lee University*

On Friday, April 3, the Monarchs squared off in Norfolk against another venerable institution: Washington and Lee University. Tracing its history back to 1749, Washington and Lee claims to be the ninth-oldest institute of higher learning in the United States and the second-oldest in Virginia (behind William & Mary). The school had previously been known as Augusta Academy, and after the revolutionary events of 1776, Liberty Hall, but had been renamed in 1796 to honor George Washington, who had endowed Liberty Hall with James River Canal stock valued at $20,000. At the end of the Civil War—just 117 days after the surrender at Appomattox, in fact—General Robert E. Lee was elected president of Washington College, and according to the brief historical synopsis on W&L's website, "Far more than serving as a figurehead, Lee proved a creative educator whose innovations laid the groundwork for both a curriculum and a sense of honor that remain distinctive to this day." Upon Lee's death in 1870, he was buried beneath Lee Chapel on campus, as were many of his family members, including his famous father, "Light Horse" Harry Lee, and if a horse may be described as family, Lee's beloved Traveller. Very shortly after General Lee's death in 1870, school trustees added the name "Lee" to go with "Washington."[16]

Washington and Lee's pride in honor, history, and tradition did not extend to the baseball field. As Pete Heumann (W&L '67) recalled, "Other than playing baseball in high school, there was no reason for any athlete to choose W&L. There was no history of baseball success. Our baseball team was not very good to say the least . . . [As a pitcher,] I won nine of the eleven games we won in four years and I accounted for one of the other two wins with a pinch hit single in the bottom of the ninth."[17] Although the Division III Generals of 2019 compete in the Old Dominion Athletic Conference, as do many of the former Mason-Dixon Conference member schools, in 1964 they competed in the College Athletic Conference, which included schools such as Washington of Saint Louis, Sewanee, Southwestern and Centre, to Heumann's recollection. As such, the Monarchs and the Generals had faced each other only five times previously, and never twice in a season until 1964. Still, starting in 1960, the series had become an annual affair, and would remain so until the 1974 season.

1964 had started with some amount of optimism for Washington and Lee. On March 3, *The Ring-tum Phi*, school newspaper of Washington and Lee, had published a generally upbeat season preview under the title, "Baseball Outlook Bright," and continued on the next page as "General Nine Shows Potential."[18] "The success of Washington and Lee's baseball team appears to hinge on one position, catching. Give the Generals a solid defensive catcher, and they should win a few games this season," read the first paragraph. "The pitching looks pretty solid with star left-handers Chris Wigert and Brice Gamber returning." But for a program remembered by Heumann for "no history of baseball success," the remainder of the article told the fuller tale of a program accustomed to some hard knocks. The cautious optimism of the first few paragraphs of the 1964 Generals preview gave way to these closing paragraphs:[19]

Coach Lyles summed up his needs which he seems to think are many, in one sentence. He is looking for a catcher, a third baseman, a shortstop, and two outfielders. He also wants another right handed pitcher.

Lyles also seems upset at the fact that the team must play seven games in eight days on the Spring Trip. He hopes to have his pitching staff ready by then.

He also commented that anyone who is interested in a tryout may still come out. The team will work out in the gym from 4 to 6 p.m. Monday through Friday until he feels that they are ready to go out onto the field. As of now, there are only 25 men on the roster.

From the Washington and Lee student newspaper Ring Tum Phi. Courtesy of Washington and Lee University Special Collections and Archives Department.

Gamber drew the starting assignment for the 0–2–1 Generals, opposed by Fred Edmonds, 0–1 but with a 0.93 ERA after one start. While Edmonds worked a relatively clean first two innings, Gamber was in trouble from the start, and at many points until his exit in the fourth.

Fred Kovner, the Monarchs' star center fielder, led off the bottom of the first. Kovner had hit .330 the previous season and led Old Dominion in stolen bases and runs, as well as home runs, with seven. Fifty-two years later, Kovner's teammates still remember with some degree of awe his prowess on the diamond. A well-rounded player, his athleticism and defensive skills still earn as much praise as his bat from those former teammates, just as they did in contemporary newspaper articles. "He was the best player I played with at Old Dominion . . . And he had a fantastic arm, great fielder out in the field. He hit for average, had speed,"[20] recalled Wayne Parks, who hit behind Kovner in the second spot in the order in 1964. Catcher Jimmy Walker remembers Kovner as "the greatest player I've ever seen . . . He was unbelievable, I always looked up to him."[21]

After two games against Dartmouth pitching, Kovner was only one-for-seven with two walks and a run scored, but he started this game by drawing a base on balls. After a single by Parks, consecutive walks to right fielder Jimmy Zadell and second baseman Lee McDaniel plated the first run of the day. The Monarchs left the bases loaded without scoring again in that frame, but continued the attack in the bottom of the second, pushing three more runs across, as Edmonds, Kovner, and Parks singled in succession, and Generals' first baseman Jim Crothers assisted the Monarch cause with his first two errors of the day.

Edmonds ran into the only trouble of his relatively short day's work in the top of the third. After retiring the first two batters, a walk and an error by catcher John Ward permitted the inning to continue, and the heart of the Generals' order responded with consecutive singles and then a double, pushing three unearned runs across and turning it back into a competitive game. Going into the sixth, the score stood at 5–3, Old Dominion.

The game would get no closer. Bob Walton relieved Edmonds in the top of the sixth and shut the Generals down on one hit the rest of the way. Monarch bats, meanwhile, took aim on a couple of new pitchers. According to Bud Metheny's scorebook, "Heumsas" relieved Gamber in the bottom of the fourth inning (although one must assume that Metheny referred either to Pete Heumann or Terry Herman, since no "Heumsas" pitched for Washington and Lee), and in the bottom of the eighth, "Heumsas" was relieved by Roy Powell for an inning of work. The last three offensive half-innings for ODC yielded four walks, five hits, and three errors—including the third of the day by Jim Crothers, which prompted his removal from the contest by Coach Joe Lyles. Capped by first baseman Fred Balmer's home run in the bottom of the eighth, the Monarch outburst resulted in five more runs, and a 10–3 victory. As the calendar had turned to April, the bats appeared to have awakened, and the eleven-for-thirty-four performance as a team brought the cumulative batting average up from .136 to .204 after three games.

Game Four: *April 11, 1964 — Farmville — Hampden-Sydney College*

No sooner had the Monarch offense put together a performance representative of expectations than they had to take an eight-day break, due to spring rains. For Old Dominion, three out of six games thus far had been washed out, including a home game against Dartmouth, and in the week before the Hampden-Sydney game, contests against Richmond Professional Institute and Randolph-Macon. The Tigers of HSC were having no better luck with Mother Nature, however, and entered the game with a 4–3 record and five washouts.

For the Monarchs, a trip to Hampden-Sydney meant a return to the field where they had achieved the greatest athletic success the new college had ever seen, less than a year prior. The NCAA College Division regional tournament, a four-team season-ending tournament won by the Monarchs, had been held at Hampden-Sydney in late May 1963. Somehow, the 10–13 Hampden-Sydney Tigers had also been invited to the tournament (perhaps because they agreed to host it) and finished third, after a consolation win against the Coast Guard Academy.

Coach Bill Pegram was at first unsure what to make of his 1964 team. The Hampden-Sydney *Tiger* published its season preview on April 3, 1964, as the team already stood at 2–2 (with three rainouts). Under the headline "Tigers Just Hope," the paper described the coming season as more or less a blank canvas. "'Question mark' is the phrase used by head baseball coach Bill Pegram when asked about the 1964 version of the Hampden-Sydney diamond men. With ten men on the roster that have never put on the Tiger uniform before and only seven returning lettermen, question mark seems to be a mild phrase indeed. 'We will give all twenty men a shot at a position. With a lack of experience and such a heavy schedule, desire will have a great deal to do with our success this season,' explained Pegram, who is starting his fourth year as baseball coach as well as being head basketball coach."[22]

Among the returning lettermen, however, were some solid talents, especially Travis "Ty" Tysinger. Tysinger, an outfielder (as well president of his sophomore and junior classes), had hit .396 the year before, and, including the NCAA tournament, had scored twenty-two times, knocked in twenty-four runs, walked thirteen times, and stolen ten bases in twenty-five games. Extrapolated to a 162-game schedule, that would equate to 143 runs, 155 RBI, and sixty-five steals. For his efforts, Tysinger had been named a second-team College Division All-American in 1963, as he would again in 1964. Returnees Dave Trickler ("Clown Prince," as the 1965 HSC yearbook referred to him) and Mike Crone gave the Tigers two more players in the lineup with double-digit steals the year before.[23]

Even though they did not play in the same conference until 1963, the series between Old Dominion and Hampden-Sydney had started with a single game in 1955 and had been on the schedule for at least two games every year since. The late 1950s—in which HSC won four straight Mason-Dixon Conference championships from 1956–1959— had seen some pretty severe beatings applied by the Tigers, by such scores as 19–7 in 1956, 21–6 in 1957, and 13–2 in 1958. But the Monarchs had reversed the trend and held a 10–8 series edge and a six-game winning streak after season-series sweeps of both games in 1961, 1962, and 1963.

Junior right-hander Fred Edmonds returned to the hill for Old Dominion, with a 1–1 record and 0.61 ERA after two starts. In his last appearance on the Hampden-Sydney diamond, Edmonds had beaten the Coast Guard Academy in the NCAA semifinals, and had launched a homer for good measure. His mound opponent was Harold "Hal" Urquhart Blythe, who had yet no pitching statistics for the 1963 Tigers. But Blythe began the game sharply, retiring the first three Monarchs on groundouts to shortstop Jim Rosenstock, and he continued to pitch a total of three fairly clean innings, giving up only a run-scoring double to Edmonds in the third.

The bottom of the first, however, had an ominous start for ODC. Edmonds struck out leadoff man Dave Trickler, but an error by catcher John Ward allowed Trickler to reach first. A single, a walk, and another error around a putout brought right fielder Mike Crone to the plate, and Crone (oddly, the only player listed with a first name in Metheny's scorekeeping, and erroneously called "Ray") delivered a triple. The following day, the *Virginian-Pilot* would inaccurately describe this triple as an impossible "two-run triple in the big first inning with the bases loaded."[24] Edmonds stranded Crone on third with consecutive strikeouts to end the inning, but ODC was in a 4–0 hole after just one inning.

The Monarchs had their best chance to stage a rally in the top of the fourth inning, when cleanup hitter Lee McDaniel led off with a walk, and Fred Balmer and Frank Zadell walked in succession to load the bases with none out. Blythe was removed from the game in favor of Mark Chinn, whose 1963 freshman season had ended with thirty-five innings pitched that included forty hits and thirty walks, for a 2.00 WHIP and a 7.20 ERA, although he had managed to win two out of six decisions.[25] Despite those inflated numbers, Chinn recorded two strikeouts and a force at first to retire the Monarchs with no damage done and would complete and win the game for the Tigers, pitching a total of six innings of one-hit ball, with six strikeouts.

It didn't get better for ODC in the field. In the bottom of the fifth, the first six Tiger batters reached base, including five by singles and one by error, resulting in three more runs. While the relief corps of Ingram, Harrell, and finally Riddleberger provided a pretty solid four innings and allowed just one run, the defense still showed what an eight-day layoff could do, with four errors and a passed ball. As a result, while Edmonds allowed seven runs in what would prove to be his least effective start of the season, only three of them were earned. As a team, the Monarchs were four-for-thirty on the day, and after four games, the team's batting average dropped back down to .187, and the team's won-loss record to 1–3.

Game Five: *April 13, 1964—Norfolk—Randolph-Macon College*

The fifth official game of the season was a makeup of a previously rained-out game against Randolph-Macon College, at 2:30 on a spring afternoon in Norfolk. The Monarch nine appeared to be struggling under the weight of high expectations thus far, although the inability to play games (or even practice outside) due to the weather certainly had something to do with the early-season performance. The ODC pitching staff had compiled a respectable 2.65 ERA, but the team was actually giving up an average of 4.50 runs per game, when eight unearned runs allowed were also considered. Combined with a .187 team batting mark, that had led to just a single win in four tries.

Randolph-Macon, located near Richmond in Ashland, Virginia, was founded in 1830 by the Methodist Church as an all-male institution in the Virginia town of Boydton, a tiny southside outpost on Route 58. After the Civil War, operations moved to Ashland, where the school flourished. Today, it is a co-educational school of approximately 1,400 undergraduate students, but in 1964, as former RMC pitcher Jim Garwood recalls, there were about 800 students—still mostly male, although Garwood recalls some women as day students.[26] To put this enrollment in perspective, in 2016 the average number of students enrolled at each of the five Norfolk, Virginia, high schools is 1,573, or nearly twice Randolph-Macon's 1964 number.

The rivalry between Old Dominion and Randolph-Macon had begun with a pair of games in 1946, during the Dark Ages of Old Dominion baseball. While there is no record of the two teams meeting again until 1955, after that year the series had become an annual affair. Although the series record stood at nine wins apiece, the more recent success had belonged to the Monarchs, as Randolph-Macon had won the first six encounters. In 1963, the intensity of the rivalry had begun to heat up, as the two schools had become competitors within the same South Division of the Mason-Dixon Conference.

Old Dominion must have looked at RMC as the gold standard upon entering the conference in 1963. The Yellow Jackets, since Coach Hugh Stephens' first year in 1950, had completed a winning season every year, which included three Mason-Dixon Conference titles,[27] two Little Six and, after expansion, three Little Eight championships.[28] In fact, Randolph-Macon was the reigning Mason-Dixon champion when ODC entered the conference in 1963 and supplanted RMC as champions on the strength of two head-to-head wins.

The Yellow Jackets of 1964 looked strong again, returning nine lettermen from the year before, as well as one who had lettered in 1962. Included in that number were Vic "The Golden Greek" Sakellarios, an All-Mason-Dixon performer from the year before who had put up a .324 average and seventeen RBI in twenty games, which would equate to 138 RBI if extrapolated to a 162-game schedule. Returning moundsmen Jim Garwood and Archer Rose had accounted for more than half of RMC's innings pitched in 1963, completing the season with three wins apiece, and 2.03 and 2.27 ERAs, respectively.

The RMC student newspaper, *The Yellow Jacket*, covered the baseball team faithfully. From these pages are gleaned such nicknames as "The Golden Greek," John "Country" Faulconer, and Boyce "Elf" Reid. *Yellow Jacket* sportswriter Jay Pace offered what must be one of the more colorful pieces of baseball writing in the April 10th edition, describing an RMC loss to Delaware: "Grabbing the toss from Reid as if it were a gold nugget, bespeckled [sic] catcher Paul McLaughlin stood like Stonewall did at Bull Run and killed the charging titan. Both players crumbled [sic] to the ground, but McLaughlin won the race for the Jackets by holding tightly to the missile which had just been put through a rapid series of test flights."[29] As if he could have done anything else, Pace went on to become a writer, then editor, and finally owner of Ashland's *Herald-Progress* newspaper.

In this first game of a home-and-home series with the Yellow Jackets, Coach Bud Metheny gave the ball to Bob Walton, to oppose the Yellow

Jackets' Jim Garwood. To date, Walton had only logged 8⅓ innings in one start and two relief appearances, and carried a 5.40 ERA and 0–1 record. Walton started strong, allowing no hits to the Yellow Jackets through four innings. The only baserunner, Hampton's Stan Trimble, had reached base with a first-inning walk but had been erased when he was picked off first, and so Walton had faced the minimum of twelve batters.

Garwood was putting up zeroes as well and was getting good defense in the field. The Monarchs didn't get a hit until the third inning and mounted no serious threat until the fourth. In that inning, Frank Zadell walked with one out and moved to second on a Gene Johnson groundout. A Mel Renn single put runners at the corners, but Renn was cut down on the basepaths in a 1–3–6 putout.

Walton gave up the first Yellow Jacket hit in the fifth to the cleanup man, Skip D'Alessandro, but worked out of a two-on, one-out jam in that inning, and worked out of a two-on, two-out jam in the seventh, although at no point in the game would any RMC runner reach third base against him. Garwood, however, continued to match the pace, setting down ten consecutive Monarchs between the fifth and eighth innings, relying heavily on his defense in a complete-game performance that included only one strikeout.

With a quick ninth, Walton completed what should have been a complete-game, seven-strikeout shutout, but the Monarchs had still failed to score. In the bottom half, Garwood retired Fred Balmer on a flyout to left field—the third time in the game that Balmer's old Hampton High School and American Legion teammate Stan Trimble recorded the putout on him. But five-foot-six shortstop Norris "Squirrel" Strickland then committed the first error by either team in an otherwise clean defensive game, putting Frank Zadell on first. Monarch chances started to look good when Zadell took advantage of the opportunity and stole second, putting a runner in scoring position with one out. Garwood responded by recording his first and only strikeout of the day for the second out, but sophomore Mel Renn

By ED HEWITT

Virginian-Pilot Sports Writer

NORFOLK — A brilliant five-hitter by Bob Walton and a two-out run-producing s i n g l e in the ninth inning by Mel Renn gave Old Dominion College a 1-0 victory over Randolph-Macon Monday afternoon at Larchmont Field.

The victory was the first of the season in the Mason-Dixon Conference for the defending champions. The monarchs lost last Saturday to Hampden-Sydney. They are 2-3 overall.

With one out in the bottom of the ninth, Frank Zadell was safe on a throwing error by shortstop Norris Strickland and stole second. After Gene Johnson struck out, Renn, a stocky shortstop from Newport News, lined his second hit of the game to center to score Zadell.

A pitching duel between the Yellow Jackets' Jim Garwood and Walton highlighted t h e game, a contest originally scheduled for last week but which had been rained out.

Garwood, a lanky sophomore lefthander, lost a tough game. He allowed only six hits and in one stretch retired 10 batters in a row.

Walton, who evened his record at 1-1, put down the first 12 men he faced. He walked one of these but picked him off first. The senior co-captain walked two and struck out seven in becoming the first Monarch hurler to pitch a full game.

Still in a batting slump which has lasted the entire season, Old Dominion managed only six hits. The Monarchs, who won 22 of 27 games last year, have gotten only 29 hits in five games.

Of the five hits that Randolph-Macon got off Walton, three of them went to Skip D'Alessando. The sophomore first baseman singled his last three trips to the plate.

Old Dominion threatened in the third, fourth and eighth innings but Garwood bore down and stopped the rallies.

The Monarchs play at VMI Wednesday and meet Randolph-Macon again Thursday in Ashland.

R-M	ab	r	h	bi	OLD DOMINION	ab	r	h	bi
Strick'd, ss	4	0	1	0	Kovner, cf	4	0	1	0
M'L'gh'n, c	4	0	0	0	Parks, 3b	4	0	1	0
Trimble, lf	3	0	0	0	L. Zadell, rf	3	0	0	0
D'Al'do, 1b	4	0	3	0	Balmer, 1b	4	0	0	0
Sakel'ris, rf	4	0	0	0	F. Zadell, lf	3	1	0	0
M'Con'el, cf	4	0	1	0	Johnson, 2b	4	0	0	0
Falc'v'r, 3b	2	0	0	0	Renn, ss	4	0	2	1
Reid, 2b	3	0	0	0	Ward, c	3	0	1	0
Garw'od, p	3	0	0	0	Walton, p	3	0	1	0
Totals	31	0	5	0	Totals	32	1	6	1

```
Randolph-Macon ....... 000 000 000—0
Old   Dominion   ...... 000 000 001—1
E—Strickland. PO-A—R-M, 26-7, (2 outs
when winning run scored); ODC—27-12.
LOB—R-M, 5; ODC, 6. SB—Strickland,
Sakelforis, F. Zadell.
                   IP  H  R ER BB SO
Walton (W)          9  5  0  0  2  7
Garwood (L)      8 2-3  6  1  0  2  1
U—Archer, Zeb. T—1:55.
```

then delivered a clutch, game-winning single, making a winner out of Walton and a tough-luck loser out of Garwood. Randolph-Macon's "Golden Greek?" Zero-for-four with a stolen base.

The shutout lowered the Old Dominion team ERA to an outstanding 2.30, and Bob Walton's own ERA from 5.40 to 2.60. The defense showed flawless form. But the offense still needed to find the rhythm of 1963, if the success of the previous year was to be repeated. The six-for-thirty-two, or .188, against Garwood did not move team's batting average from where it had started, at .187.

Game Six: *April 15, 1964—Lexington—Virginia Military Institute*

Looking to even the season ledger at three wins against three losses, the Monarchs traveled to Lexington for a Wednesday afternoon game against the Keydets of the Virginia Military Institute. Only twice before had the schools met on the diamond, both Old Dominion wins, by scores of 14–7 in 1954 and 6–1 in the 1963 season.

VMI is an iconic and proud Virginia school. Founded in 1839, it is the oldest state-supported military college in the United States, and, somewhat unlike its cross-town Lexington neighbor Washington and Lee, retains a distinct Virginia character, at least as evidenced in microcosm by the baseball rosters. In 2016, the VMI team counted thirty-five Virginians among its thirty-six players; in 2020, that number was twenty-nine out of thirty-four.[30] VMI has also been notable on a national stage several times, such as the 1938 film *Brother Rat* (and its sequel, *Brother Rat and a Baby*), starring Ronald Reagan and Jane Wyman, and VMI's battle in the 1990s to maintain all-male status, a case that ultimately went all the way to the United States Supreme Court before resulting in the 1997 admission of women. But the singular event in VMI history is the Civil War's Battle of New Market, in which the 257-man enrollment of the Corps of Cadets served as a unit, losing ten men but helping to repel, at least temporarily, a Union advance.

The event is marked every year at VMI, but in no year more so than 1964. Just a month after the Monarchs completed their 1964 baseball invasion of Lexington, VMI celebrated the centennial of the May 15, 1864, engagement at New Market.

Baseball, too, is a long-standing part of Keydet tradition. According to the media guide's retelling of baseball's beginnings at VMI, the sport got its start on campus in 1866, as the rebuilding of the school continued after it was burned by Union troops in the summer of 1864. As one Hugh Fry recalled the time for the 1914 school yearbook:

> *I remember that fall that Sam had returned to the Institute from Richmond, where he had been spending his vacation. The day after his arrival he asked me to accompany him to the Parade Ground. Once there he instructed me to stand off from him about fifty feet. I did so.*
>
> *Sam twirled his arm around two or three times and let fly an object at me. Instinctively I was in the act of dodging, but Sam cried, 'Catch it, you clodhopper!' So, I caught it. Not knowing what the missile was, I asked Sam, 'What in tarnation is this thing?' Sam replied, 'You stupe, it's a baseball.' By that time, a crowd of cadets gathered around, and we formed a circle. For some time, we were carried away with the sport of passing the ball from one to the other.*[31]

Actual baseball *success* is another story. VMI records are available starting in 1950, and since that time, of those who have coached the team for a minimum of four seasons, only one, Charles Meriwether McGinnis, can boast a win percentage better than .500. McGinnis coached the squad from 1962–1965, and finished his legendary four-year run with a record of 48–39–1, a relatively spare win total which still leaves him eighth all-time at the Institute. His 15–9 team in 1965 was the last winning team the Keydets would have until 2006, a span that included 1988 VMI product and current ODU coach Chris Finwood's 1992–1994 tenure (which included fifty-two wins, still good in 2020 for fifth all-time at VMI).[32] Finwood, incidentally, took over at Old Dominion in 2012, and through 2021, has led the Monarchs to six thirty-win seasons, 287 wins overall, a 2014 NCAA Regional appearance, and a 2021 NCAA Regional appearance and Conference USA championship.

VMI teams of the 1960s featured the best pitching the school has known; eight years in that decade are in the schools' top ten all-time seasonal ERAs. The 1964 team particularly featured Percy Sensabaugh, author of "the greatest season on the mound in VMI baseball history," according to VMI's 2016 baseball prospectus.[33] In 1964, Sensabaugh struck out twenty batters in one game against West Virginia, and, in an eleven-inning affair, another twenty-one against The Citadel. His final numbers in 1964 included a 0.67 ERA, a 14.17 K/9 rate, and a total of 106 strikeouts, which is still second all-time at VMI for a single season, even though the 1964 team only played twenty-four games.

But it was Don Reed who took the hill for Coach McGinnis against the Monarchs on April 15, 1964. Reed merely "completed the pitching staff" after Jeff Gausepohl, Jim Maurer, and Sensabaugh, according to the 1964 yearbook, hardly a ringing endorsement of his skill set.[34] For the Monarchs, Bud Metheny sent lefty John Ingram to the hill. To this point in the season, Ingram had logged no official starts, with his only starting assignment (March 28 against Dartmouth) washed out after the top of the first. Not counting three innings of the practice game against Penn State, Ingram's official line showed only two relief innings to his credit thus far, in the loss to Hampden-Sydney four days prior.

VMI came in to the game with a 6–4–1 overall mark as members of the Southern Conference, the once-mighty conference that had spawned the SEC in 1933, and then the ACC in 1953. In 1964, membership consisted of such schools as William & Mary, Davidson, Furman, George Washington, and Richmond. West Virginia University was also a member, and with two games against the Mountaineers (both losses), and two games against the Bulldogs of Georgia (also losses), VMI had already faced some major competition.

Coach McGinnis may have figured to save his "big three" for University Division competition, and so chose to start Reed against the College Division Monarchs. Reed started strong, pitching a 1–2–3 first that included a popup to third by Fred Kovner, and consecutive groundouts to shortstop by Wayne Parks and Jimmy Zadell. Ingram had a rougher start to the game, beginning with a leadoff walk to second-team All-Southern Conference center fielder Joe Bush. A groundout to second by shortstop Duane Conques was then followed by consecutive walks to Tracy Hunter and Billy Loughbridge, leaving the bases loaded with one out. A sacrifice fly by third baseman Ricky Parker plated one run, but then Ingram doused the threat with a big strikeout of "Diamond Jim" Workman, leaving runners on second and third.

The Monarchs answered immediately. Mel Renn, making the second of only three 1964 starts he would have in the cleanup role, and Fred Balmer, batting in his typical five spot, both drew walks. A single by catcher Jimmy Walker scored Renn, and a single by Frank Zadell loaded the bases with still none out. The prospects looked good for an extended rally, but Ray Nelson's grounder to short turned into a 6–2–3 double play, and a following strikeout limited the damage to the single run.

Ingram worked around two hits with a pair of strikeouts in the second, and the Monarchs took the lead in the top of the third, when Fred Kovner singled, and advanced twice by way of passed balls. A Jimmy Zadell single brought him in, giving Old Dominion a 2–1 advantage. It would stay that way until the fifth, when the Monarchs plated two on just one hit—an Ingram single—to go with the assistance of four errors from the VMI infield, one by "Diamond Jim" at first, one by Billy Loughbridge at second, and two by shortstop Duane Conques, typically a third baseman who was playing out of position due to the injury absence of All-Southern Conference shortstop and 1963 national stolen base runner-up Donnie White.[35]

These two runs gave Old Dominion a 4–1 lead and ended the scoring. Ingram lasted one out into the sixth, and after two walks in that frame increased his game total to seven (to go along with five strikeouts), Coach Metheny turned to Bill Yeargan to close the door. Yeargan contributed $3\frac{2}{3}$ scoreless innings, and with consecutive wins, the Monarchs had evened their record at 3–3.

The early-season trend continued for Old Dominion: strong pitching, but an offense still stuck in February. Ingram and Yeargan had combined for nine innings of six-hit, one-run ball to go with nine strikeouts. With the seven baserunners also allowed by way of walks, Old Dominion hurlers had made the pitches when they mattered most, stranding eleven Keydets on base while permitting just the single run. For the season, the effort dropped the already stellar 2.30 team ERA to 2.08.

Reed, meanwhile, had gone the distance for VMI, allowing only seven singles in thirty-five at-bats, or a .200 average, which actually raised the Old Dominion team average to .189 after six games.

Game Seven: *April 16, 1964—Ashland—Randolph-Macon*

A day after the VMI affair, Old Dominion was in Ashland, Virginia, to face Coach Hugh Stephens' Randolph-Macon Yellow Jackets for the second time in four days. The game pitted two coaches who would both become legendary at their respective institutions.

Hugh Stephens, a 1941 graduate of Randolph-Macon and a member of the US Armed Forces during the war years of 1942–45, had assumed head baseball coaching duties at RMC in 1950, a year after Bud Metheny had done the same at the Norfolk Division. Like Metheny, Stephens coached the basketball team for a time as well (although never concurrently with his baseball duties) and served as athletic director for his school. Over a career as baseball coach that lasted from 1950 to 1982, the "Silver Fox," as he came to be known, registered 451 wins against just 212 losses and five ties, leaving him the all-time winningest baseball coach at the school.[36] The parallels between Stephens' and Coach Metheny's Old Dominion career are remarkable. By comparison, Metheny coached Old Dominion's baseball team from 1949 to 1980 (with a one-year break in 1970), and compiled 423 wins, the most ever at Old Dominion. Both coaches have been inducted into the Virginia Sports Hall of Fame, Metheny in 1979 and Stephens in 1994. And the baseball fields at both Randolph-Macon (Hugh Stephens Field at Estes Park) and Old Dominion (the Bud Metheny Baseball Complex) have both been named for these legendary coaches.

Stephens and Metheny were alike in one other major way as well, in that both dedicated the whole of their professional lives to the advancement of their respective institutions. In a 1975 interview, Metheny recalled the many hats he had worn for Old Dominion over the years. Among his final comments in that interview was, "To be able to grow up with the university, the athletic program, to see it go from nothing to something is just pleasing to me. And to know that things have progressed in the manner that they have, I think that that's what we're here for, and that's what makes me feel good."[37] For his dedication to Randolph-Macon that paralleled Metheny's to Old Dominion, Hugh Stephens in 1990 received an honorary Doctorate of Humane Letters from the school, for "unwavering devotion to Randolph-Macon, to its students, and to the athletic program."[38]

Coming into the April 16, 1964, contest, Bud Metheny had ten head-to-head wins to Hugh Stephens' nine, and Metheny's teams had won four straight in the series. Metheny gave the starting nod to Fred Edmonds, who had seen his ERA go from 0.61 to 1.93 after the April 11 loss to Hampden-Sydney. Still, Edmonds' fastball would provide a good change-of-pace to Yellow Jacket hitters who had been kept off balance four days before by Bob Walton's slower style. Freshman Dave Brown of Poquoson, Virginia, opposed Edmonds, as a member of the Randolph-Macon pitching staff that would ultimately compile a 1.74 ERA for the season.

The Yellow Jackets were used to diamond success, if not always against Old Dominion. In fourteen years as head coach, Stephens had never suffered through a losing campaign, and, in fact, would only suffer one in thirty-three years at the helm.[39] His 1964 team, with many freshmen contributing, had started only 3–3 amid the rainouts, but had proved in the last game that they could compete with the Monarchs. Dave Brown started relatively cleanly on the mound, stranding four Monarch baserunners in three scoreless innings, while Edmonds was uncharacteristically inefficient, permitting three hits, three walks, and two stolen bases over the first third of the game. Still, only one of those runners scored, as Dave Brown plated third baseman "Country" Faulconer with a two-out single in the second.

Trailing 1–0, the Monarchs batted in the top of the fourth. With one away, Frank Zadell stood in against Brown, and launched only the second home run of the year for Old Dominion. But this one was different. In the longer view, this one seemed to be a shot that roused a slumbering Monarch offense that had struggled through the first six games of the season. The blast tied the score at one, but eight Yellow Jackets then batted in the bottom half of the inning, which included three errors by Old Dominion, and two unearned runs.

Old Dominion then proceeded to knock Brown out in the top of the next inning. A leadoff single by Fred Edmonds turned into a run on the strength of three walks, although the damage stopped there, as the Monarchs left the bags loaded. Still trailing 3–2, Edmonds had settled in, retiring eleven in a row from the end of the fourth through the seventh. Jackets reliever Bob Stearns, who would compile a 0.86 ERA in 41⅔ innings for RMC in 1964, ran into trouble in the eighth, as Mel Renn started the frame by reaching on an error. Base hits by

Fred Balmer and Frank Zadell followed. After a timely sacrifice fly by catcher John Ward, the Monarchs had the lead again and went into the bottom of the frame up 4–3.

Center fielder Bob McConnell of Williamsburg opened the bottom half with a single but was gunned down by John Ward in a failed attempt at a theft of second base. The out on the basepaths proved costly, as consecutive doubles by Faulconer and freshman Don Smiley proceeded to tie the score at four heading into the ninth.

Neither side scored in the ninth, as Bill Yeargan relieved Fred Edmonds, and Jim Garwood, who had lost a heartbreaker to Old Dominion despite a masterful complete game four days prior, relieved Stearns. But the Monarchs had the measure of Garwood, and in the top of the tenth inning, pushed two runs across on a Mel Renn double, a run-scoring single by Fred Balmer, and one batter later, a clutch single by Jimmy Walker, batting for John Ward. Yeargan completed the extra-inning win, inducing three consecutive flyouts to end the game and hand Garwood his second loss in a week. The Monarchs finished the game twelve-for-thirty-eight at the plate, for a .316 average on the day, led by Fred Balmer (three-for-four with a walk, one run, and three RBI) and Frank Zadell (three-for-four with a walk, a home run, two runs scored, an RBI, and a steal). The six runs scored by the Monarchs in the contest represented 12.2 percent of all the runs the Yellow Jacket pitching staff would give up in their entire sixteen-game season.

Randolph-Macon went on to finish 10–6 in 1964, their fifteenth consecutive winning season to begin Coach Stephens' tenure. The respect that Bud Metheny had for the athletes of his conference rival is clear. On May 14, 1964, Metheny submitted his All-Opponent first and second team nominations to Mason-Dixon Conference Commissioner Paul Menton. Yellow Jackets Stan Trimble, Skip D'Alessandro, and Jim Garwood made his first team ballot, while Paul McLaughlin, Dave Brown, and Vic "The Golden Greek" Sakellarios (despite his

0-for-8 performance against Monarch pitching) appeared on the second-team list. On May 29, when Metheny submitted his Mason-Dixon All-Star nominations, he included RMC's John "Country" Faulconer on his first team.[40]

The rivalry between Old Dominion and Randolph-Macon ended in 1974 with a 7–6 Monarch win. Old Dominion claims a close 21–16 all-time edge in the series, and except for one lone contest in 1970, every single one of those games paired legendary coaches Bud Metheny and Hugh Stephens.

Game Eight: *April 18, 1964—Norfolk—University of Baltimore*

On a modest three-game winning streak, the Monarchs welcomed Coach Arthur "Otts" Bosley and the University of Baltimore Bees to Norfolk for a Saturday doubleheader, on an unusual 86-degree spring day that was sure to warm the bats up. The two teams had met just five times prior, with Baltimore holding a 3–2 series advantage—but in a single afternoon during Old Dominion's 1963 championship season, the Bees had handed them two of only five losses they would suffer that entire season with a doubleheader sweep in Baltimore, doubtlessly leaving the homestanding Monarchs with payback in mind on this day.

Coach Bosley was the athletic director of the school, as well as its baseball coach, roles that he assumed in 1961 after spending the previous seven years serving in the high school ranks. Bosley had played varsity baseball, basketball, and soccer at the University of Maryland, during which time he may also have gotten some professional baseball experience, since professional records show that an Arthur Bosley played nineteen games for the Wilmington Pirates in the Class-D Tobacco State League in 1949.[41] As Baltimore A.D., Bosley oversaw the five Bee teams that competed on an intercollegiate level: wrestling, basketball, golf, lacrosse, and baseball. Despite the small number of teams the school fielded, they had a fair degree of success: the undefeated 1963 soccer team won the NCAA small college championship, and in 1964, the wrestling team had finished first or second in the Mason-Dixon for four straight years.[42] In baseball, the Bees had won the 1961 conference championship, and in 1963, had finished second to Loyola in the North Division, with a 14–5 overall record that had included the pair of one-run victories over Old Dominion.[43]

The 1964 version of the Bees came into Norfolk with a 4–2 record, averaging six runs per contest. The team had several key performers back from the previous year and could put a very competent lineup on the field—one that would ultimately finish with an 11–6 mark on the season. This team featured four players who would eventually enter the University of Baltimore athletic Hall of Fame in Ron Mather, James Cassaday, James Rafferty, and Joe Binder, and also featured several who were 1964 All-Mason-Dixon performers in Steve Nieberding (First Team), Binder (Second Team), and Rafferty and Jim Scagg (Honorable Mention). Leading the pitchers were the senior Mather and junior right-hander Paul Nicholson, credited by Baltimore's *Reporter* yearbook with a 4–1 record and 1.71 ERA for the 1964 season. The yearbook stats can be taken with at least a small grain of salt, however; the *Reporter* also states that center fielder Al Mank "batted .301 and played errorless defense,"[44] but Coach Metheny's 1964 scorebook charges Mank with committing an error.

Coach Bosley decided to start sophomore Dick Mitchell against the Monarchs in the first game of the afternoon, while Bud Metheny went with Bob Walton, five days removed from his five-hit shutout of Randolph-Macon. For an inning, Bosley's decision looked sound. In the top of the first, a single by cleanup hitter Steven Nieberding pushed an opening run across for the Bees, and Mitchell stymied the top of the Monarch lineup on three groundouts in the bottom of the inning. But Old Dominion got the bats going in the second—after Walton worked around a walk and a hit in the top half, the Monarchs batted around in their turn. A walk to cleanup man Lee McDaniel started the frame, and he was followed in order by a Fred Balmer single, a run-scoring fielder's choice by Frank Zadell, and then a three-run home run by catcher Jimmy Walker. With the bases cleared, Gene Johnson worked a walk, and came around to score on a Fred Kovner double one batter later, closing the book on Mitchell after $1\frac{1}{3}$ innings pitched, two walks, three hits, and five earned runs.

The two teams traded single runs in the bottom of the third and the top of the fourth, but Walton settled in after that, retiring nine of the last ten batters he would face in the seven-inning contest. Baltimore reliever John Trimp, the 1964 strikeout leader for the Bees, did not fare so well. Trimp had relieved Mitchell with only one out in the second and had stayed in trouble for the remainder of the game. Although he had doused the second-inning Old Dominion rally with no further damage than the five runs, the Monarchs would have runners in scoring position in each of the four full innings Trimp would pitch, and would score in three of them, including consecutive three-run outbursts in the fifth and sixth innings. For his final line, Trimp presented the unenviable stat line of $4\frac{2}{3}$ innings pitched, eight hits, three walks, and seven earned runs, good for a 13.50 ERA and 2.36 WHIP.

By game's end, to go along with error-free defense and Walton's complete game, the Monarchs had gone eleven-for-twenty-seven (.407) and plated twelve runs, including the home run by Walker and a three-run fifth inning shot by Frank Zadell. Balmer, Zadell, and Walker, hitting in the five through seven spots in the lineup, had combined to go six-for-eleven, with five runs scored and nine runs batted in.

Game Nine: *April 18, 1964 — Norfolk — University of Baltimore*

In the second game of the twin bill, Coach Bosley elected to start senior Ron Mather against Old Dominion's senior left-hander John Ingram, who had earned a win in his start against VMI just three days prior.

The doubleheader turned out to be a breakout affair for junior center fielder and cellist Fred Kovner. Going into the day's games, Kovner was hitting .231, with six hits in twenty-six at-bats to go along with four walks, six runs scored, three runs batted in, and a stolen base. But the six-for-eight day against Baltimore, which added a home run, two runs batted in, four runs, and a steal to his season totals, helped kick-start an amazing season that would culminate in his selection as a first-team All-American.

The story of this baseball team, which is in a sense also a microcosm of the coming-of-age of Old Dominion University, must necessarily also include mention of Kovner's father, Professor Edgar A. Kovner. Beginning a 43-year association with the Norfolk Division of William & Mary in 1946, the elder Kovner embarked on a long career of service to the school in much the same vein as Lewis Webb and Bud Metheny, who dedicated the entirety of their professional careers to furthering the school and its mission during formative years. Kovner was an engineering technology professor, Dean of the Technical Institute, coached the school's lacrosse team for a time, and even endowed, with a personal $75,000 donation, the "Edgar and Kathleen Kovner Endowed Scholarship Fund," intended to help up to twenty students in the School of Engineering annually.[45]

In an April 1975 interview, Edgar Kovner recalled his All-American son's sports and academic career to University Archivist Dr. James Sweeney: "I had always contended that you can mix sports and music, so Fred had to, as a youngster . . . participate in both sports and music. He is to this day a cellist in the Norfolk Symphony. He played baseball all through his growing period, and when he came to Old Dominion he set his heart on a professional career. So, he neglected his studies, we might say. He was the second choice of the first baseball draft for the White Sox and a very high bonus, exceptionally high. It was way up in the five figures, which made me the poor father of a rich son."[46]

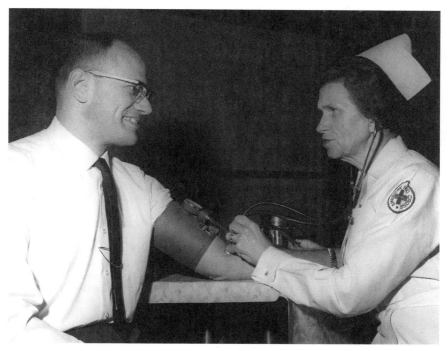

"May 1, 1964. Professor passes the five-gallon mark. Mr. Edgar A. Kovner, Director, Technical Institute Program, School of Engineering, passes the five-gallon mark as a blood donor." Courtesy of Special Collections and University Archives, Patricia W. and J. Douglas Perry Library, Old Dominion University Libraries, Norfolk, Virginia.

For his part, Fred in 2016 recalled the decision to attend the Norfolk Division through the prism of the family finances, in that his father wouldn't pay to send him anywhere else. "That's the only option," Fred recalled. "You know, people talk about, 'Oh, I need to apply to this school,' stuff like that. I went over there the first day, and registered. I never 'applied' to go to Old Dominion. You just went over there, and you paid your tuition, and you signed up for classes. That's where we were going . . . Of course, school was cheap in those days. $200 a semester was tuition. Being the son of a professor, it was half price. So, I went to school for $100 a semester, rather than $200 a semester."[47]

In the bottom half of the first inning in the second game of the doubleheader, Kovner, Wayne Parks, and Jimmy Zadell initiated the assault with consecutive singles. After Lee McDaniel grounded out to second base, Fred Balmer and Tom Harrell also singled, putting the Monarchs up by an early 3–0 score. Gene Johnson, starting at second base and batting seventh, contributed a two-run double, to put Old Dominion up by five and knock Mather out of the game after only a third of an inning pitched, six hits, and five earned runs.

Old Dominion starter John Ingram flirted with danger in the first two innings but came up with big strikeouts to end scoreless first and second innings with two runners on base. Protecting an early five-run lead with a starter on three days' rest, however, Coach Metheny's leash was short, and when four out of five Bee batters reached base to start the third inning, Metheny was quick to bring in left-handed freshman Denny Riddleberger for only his second official appearance of the year. Riddleberger allowed one inherited run to score, but save for a Fred Kovner home run in the fourth—his third of four hits on the day—the game quieted offensively, and entered the top of the sixth inning with the Monarchs holding a comfortable 6–2 cushion.

The sixth inning was a rare treat for those baseball fans who like to see a lot of runs scored, but don't necessarily want to see a lot of good pitching and defense. The Baltimore start to the inning was innocuous enough, as Riddleberger retired the first two batters, but then Baltimore's Joe Binder, Jim Scagg, and Steve Nieberding—the 2-3-4 hitters—ran off consecutive two-out singles, plating one run. Lee McDaniel's error at shortstop allowed another run to score, and knocked Riddleberger from the game in favor of relief artist Bill Yeargan, with Old Dominion still up by two. Third baseman Wayne Parks was next to have a defensive chance to stop the rally, but after that chance was misplayed, and then light-hitting Baltimore catcher Bill Henderson stroked a triple, the Bees' improbable two-out, five-run uprising had given them a 7–6 lead.

But as Bud Metheny often said when talking about this team, they had skill, drive, confidence, and, most importantly, they just didn't know how to lose. Down by one, Frank Zadell entered the game in an atypical role as a pinch hitter and drew a leadoff walk, but was promptly erased when catcher Jimmy Walker rapped into a 5–4–3 double play. With two outs and nobody on, remaining prospects for the bottom of the sixth looked bleak. Analysis available at Baseball Prospectus demonstrates statistically that in this situation, a major league offense can expect to score approximately 0.10 runs on average, or only a single run every tenth time.[48] The odds of proceeding to score *eight* runs in that situation are infinitesimally small. But the Old Dominion batters were known for their ability to score runs, not ponder advanced statistics, and they immediately set about defying those odds.

Mel Renn, batting for Yeargan, started things with a single and a steal of second base. Fred Kovner's single that followed put two men on base, and then Wayne Parks made up for the error with a two-run double, reclaiming the lead for the Monarchs. Paul Nicholson, the author of 5⅓ strong innings in relief of Mather before the rally started, issued an ensuing walk to Jimmy Zadell, and Coach Bosley brought in John Trimp (already with 4⅔ innings and seven earned runs on his ledger from the day's first game) to keep the score where it was.

Trimp stoked the proverbial fire, however, giving up consecutive base hits to Lee McDaniel, Fred Balmer, and Tom Harrell, before his own removal with a stat line of zero innings pitched, three hits, and, ultimately, two earned runs recorded by Coach Metheny. So, who was left in the bullpen? No one that shows up in the Baltimore team picture in either 1964 or 1965, or in the yearbook write-ups for either year. Metheny recorded the incoming fireman as "Peroni," although the closest evident name to that was a lightly used first baseman named Farone. Peroni/Farone gave up an RBI double to Frank Zadell and an RBI single to Jimmy Walker, before, mercifully, Mel Renn hit an inning-ending ground ball to the shortstop. The Monarchs had scored eight runs starting with nobody on base and two outs; altogether, the sixth inning had seen thirteen runs score on twelve base hits, three bases on balls, three errors, two passed balls, and two stolen bases. Twenty-two batters had come to the plate, and the inning had even caused Bud Metheny to demonstrate some little-used artistic skill in his scorebook, as he had to write on the *inside* of the spiral binding!

From Coach Bud Metheny's 1964 scorebook. Courtesy of Special Collections and University Archives, Patricia W. and J. Douglas Perry Library, Old Dominion University Libraries, Norfolk, Virginia.

The breakout offensive day for the Monarchs, which included twenty-six hits in sixty official at-bats over both games, raised the Old Dominion team average forty-nine points, from .211 before the day started to .260 at day's end. To put the numbers in perspective from Baltimore's side, the Bees only gave up eighty-two runs over seventeen contests in 1964; the twenty-six runs given up in these two games alone represented 31.7 percent of the total given up *all year*.[49]

The Monarchs would meet the Bees nine more times after 1964, winning seven of those contests in a series that ended in 1970. Resumption of the rivalry is, unfortunately, an impossibility. On Tuesday, April 19, 1983, the *Baltimore Sun* published the decision of University President Halcott Mebane Turner to discontinue all intercollegiate athletic programs.[50] Academically, the school seems to have thrived during the thirty-three-year service of Turner, a former University of Virginia varsity football player. "The greatest expansion of the University and its programs occurred during his tenure," the school's website notes, and "UB's transformation from a private institution to a public institution to its inclusion in the University System of Maryland all occurred during Turner's tenure."[51] The ability to maintain an athletic program at the commuter school, obviously, was a different story, yet despite serving as the program's executioner, former President H. Mebane Turner was still granted 2007 entry as a "Special Contributor" when the school began a posthumous athletic Hall of Fame!

Game Ten: *April 20, 1964—Norfolk—Richmond Professional Institute*

On a five-game winning streak, Old Dominion welcomed Richmond Professional Institute to Norfolk for a Monday afternoon game, the first of two games between the two teams scheduled for the 1964 season. The series with RPI had begun in Bud Metheny's first year, 1949, and had continued annually since that time, with all but three seasons in that period featuring two recorded games between the schools.

Historically, the two schools shared remarkable similarities, including their very date of birth as independent state institutions. Originally the "Richmond School of Social Economy," RPI had existed since 1917 and had begun offering extension classes from The College of William & Mary in 1920, a year after W&M had taken the same step in Norfolk. In 1925, five years before the *Norfolk* Division of the College of William & Mary officially began, RPI had added permanence to their relationship with Williamsburg, becoming the *Richmond* Division of the College of William & Mary, and would become the Richmond Professional Institute of the College of William & Mary in 1939.[52]

Similarities between the two schools continued with the relationship RPI began with Virginia Polytechnic Institute in 1946, offering VPI's freshman- and sophomore-level engineering coursework in Richmond, as Norfolk had done since 1931. And although RPI had previously purchased older apartment buildings for the purpose, both schools even opened their first new dormitories within four years of each other—Old Dominion with Rogers Hall in 1964, and RPI (which had become Virginia Commonwealth University a few months prior) with Rhoads Hall in September 1968. Operation under the umbrella of the William & Mary system, the tie that had most obviously bound the sister schools together, had only recently been severed, with Virginia Governor Albertis Harrison's February 16, 1962, signature on legislation that dissolved the system and made both schools independent.

But similarities ended on the diamond; the baseball series had been owned by Old Dominion, which had won twenty-four straight games. In fact, ODC had won twenty-six out of the twenty-seven total meetings, by a combined score of 259–123, or an average score of 9.6–4.6 per contest. The most recent meetings, in 1963, had gone Old Dominion's way by scores of 16–6 and 22–6, helping the Green Devils along to what RPI's school newspaper, *The Proscript*, termed a "most disastrous season"[53] that concluded with a single win (vs. Randolph-Macon College) against nineteen losses.

Before the start of the 1964 season, the *Proscript* had quoted RPI Coach Ed Allen as saying "We can't do any worse than we did last season . . . I guess I should retract that, because we could lose that one game. We averaged six or more errors a game last season. Our fielding and pitching were bad, but we had good hitting. I hope this year we'll be able to field and pitch like our hitting and then we'll be all set to go."[54] Among the changes Coach Allen brought with him to Norfolk in 1964 was a new brand: the team known as the Green Devils since 1948 had a new name—the Rams—and a new color scheme, blue and gray, intended to portray Richmond as a melding of North and South[55] (incidentally, due to the name change, the school newspaper also stopped referring to the women's sports teams as the "Devilettes," and instead began calling them the "Ewes").

By April 20, 1964, the Rams had already quadrupled 1963's win total. They had gotten some of the pitching Coach Allen had hoped for, as freshman right-hander Milt Woody stood at 2–0 with a 0.50 ERA and a nine-strikeout game against Mount Union College already to his credit. As a team, in fact, the Rams had yet to lose, with four victories in four tries, although in the wet spring of 1964, only these four out of the first nine scheduled had been played. And, since this game was a make-up of a washed-out contest from April 7, it meant that Bud Metheny had to find pitching for this middle game of five contests in four days.

Tom Harrell got the start for Old Dominion, with only 1⅔ official innings on the books so far in the season, and a 5.40 ERA, three hits, and two walks to go with those five recorded outs. Opposing Harrell was RPI's Milt Woody, looking to extend his team's hot start and stop the Rams' twenty-four-game losing streak to the Monarchs.

Harrell worked the first three innings relatively unscathed, notching three strikeouts to work around an error and two hits—a pair of singles from the Rams' corners, third baseman Billy Gordon and first baseman Stan Barrack. Offensively, it must have felt just like old times against RPI right from the start for Old Dominion. Fred Kovner led off the bottom of the first with a single and followed that with his first of four steals on the day. Two batters later, shortstop Lee McDaniel plated him with a run-scoring single. In the third, Kovner again led off an inning with a single, and after Wayne Parks walked, the two executed a double steal. Although Kovner was later out at home on a fielder's choice, Wayne Parks and Jimmy Zadell crossed the plate in the inning, leaving Old Dominion up 3–0 after three innings.

However, the Rams weren't ready to give up, as the Green Devils of old might have done. A double by catcher and cleanup hitter Bill Schwartz, an error, and then a two-run triple by center fielder Eddie Coffman cut the lead to one in the fourth, and then a single run on back-to-back doubles by shortstop Nubby Thomas and Billy Gordon tied the game in the fifth. But ODC relief specialist Bill Yeargan had also taken over on the mound in the fifth, and the Rams would not score again. Old Dominion pushed two runs across in the seventh, when Jimmy Walker singled and later scored on an error, and when Fred Kovner singled again, stole second again, and scored on a Wayne Parks single, for a 5–3 lead. RPI got two-out singles in the ninth from Jerry Harding and Stan Barrack to bring the potential go-ahead run to the plate, but Coffman, already three-for-four with two RBI, hit into a fielder's choice to end the game.

Coach Allen got the pitching he had desired with an eight-inning complete game out of Milt Woody, who surrendered four earned runs. His team even outhit the Monarchs, 12–8, according to *Proscript* writer Sam Shield, but 11–7 according to Bud Metheny's obviously more rigorous scorekeeping. Still, the defense that had concerned Allen before the season led to the Ram's first loss of the year, as they committed five errors in eight defensive innings.

Game Eleven: *April 21, 1964–Norfolk–Atlantic Christian College*

After the RPI game, the Monarchs had strung six victories in a row together. The team batting average, which had languished at just .189 after the VMI game, had been raised sixty-eight points to .257 in just six days, while the team ERA had remained mostly unchanged, at a stellar 2.12. The Bulldogs of Atlantic Christian College, in Norfolk to play two, seemed like the perfect victim to run the win streak to eight.

Atlantic Christian, founded in 1902, is a small liberal-arts school located in Wilson, North Carolina. The school began with, and maintains, an affiliation with the Christian Church (Disciples of Christ), and in fact changed the name of the institution in 1990 to Barton College to honor one of the founders of that denomination, Barton Warren Stone. In 1964, by count of the yearbook photos, the college only had 782 students: 187 seniors, 144 juniors, 197 sophomores, 249 freshmen, and five "special students," a designation which went unexplained in that source.[56] Despite the 1990 name change, Barton College has changed relatively little since the Bulldogs visited Larchmont Field in 1964. The total of 782 students enrolled that year has grown only to 1,051 in the fall of 2016, the Bulldogs still compete in NCAA Division II (the "College Division" of 1964), and, in fact, they still compete in the Conference Carolinas, as they have since 1930.

One major change, however, is the racial makeup of the school. In 1964, Atlantic Christian College was attempting to navigate some of the same racially-based turmoil that Norfolk had seen since the late 1950s, and which was playing out in many places across the South at that time. Prior to 1964, the Atlantic Christian College charter had opened the school to white applicants only, but in April of that year, times were changing. The college trustees had already approved a proposed change to the college's charter that would allow black students, but the resolution had not been introduced to, or approved by, the college's governing body, the Christian Churches of North Carolina. In the spring of 1964, several articles appeared in the student newspaper, *The Collegiate*, treating the topic from different angles. One discussed a resolution to "give more serious consideration in allowing student Negro entertainers to eat in the campus cafeteria"[57] after a musical group called The Dynamics was refused service. Another noted that the easiest integration might be on the athletic field, partly following the logic of an unnamed "student leader" who had mentioned that integration "would help us have a winning basketball team," a point with which the author evidently agreed, by writing "This point is not questioned."[58] On April 25, 1964, only four days after the Bulldog baseball team visited Norfolk, the resolution to change the charter of the college to allow black students went before the North Carolina Convention of Christian Churches, and was passed unanimously.[59]

In 1964, the Atlantic Christian baseball team may not exactly have been an afterthought, but the Bulldog nine certainly didn't seem to be generating headlines, either. Other than publication of the upcoming schedule, the spring issues of the student newspaper contained no articles about the baseball team, yet featured articles about the golf, tennis, and track teams, and even two about the intramural basketball tournament. The yearbook contains no better coverage, exemplified by the 1964 *Pine Knot*, which has only the single word "Baseball" with a photo of the team above it, although the book also contained a three-page spread with individualized pictures of the basketball team, and a two-page feature of the Bulldog cheerleaders.

Prior to the 1964 games, Old Dominion owned a record of eight wins and four losses against Atlantic Christian, in a series that had started in 1956 and had continued intermittently since. But the Monarchs had won the last six in the series, highlighted by consecutive seven-inning shutouts in a doubleheader in Wilson the year before, including a five-hitter authored by ODC starter Bill Yeargan, and a three-hit, eight-strikeout gem by Bob Walton. And the 1964 season had not been off to a great start for the Bulldogs, either. They had already dropped both ends of a doubleheader twice, including one in which Elon pitchers had thrown a perfect game against them, and then followed it with a one-hitter.

Bud Metheny chose to start Bob Walton on the mound in the first game, in the hope that he could repeat his success from the year before, while Bulldog coach Jack McComas opted to oppose the defending NCAA East Regional champion Monarchs with freshman Larry Poore. The weather was chilly; the high for the day reached only fifty-one degrees, although the Monarchs had played in eighty-degree weather as recently as three days prior, against Baltimore. The chill didn't seem to affect Walton, nor did it appear to affect the ODC bats in the first game.

Walton shut down the Bulldogs in a 1–2–3 top of the first, and then the Monarch batsmen proceeded to provide a rude Norfolk welcome to Larry Poore. Fred Kovner started the bottom half of the first with a single, and Wayne Parks followed with a single. Right fielder Jimmy Zadell, hitting third, notched the third straight Monarch single, to load the bases and set the stage for a two-run double by cleanup man and second baseman Lee McDaniel. Consecutive RBI singles by first baseman Fred Balmer and left fielder Frank Zadell brought the run total to four before the first out was even recorded. The Monarchs would plate one more on a Ray Nelson fielder's choice, bringing the total to five, in a first inning that had opened with six consecutive ODC hits and saw the Monarchs bat around.

The second looked a lot like the first. The Bulldogs recorded a hit in their half, but a fielder's choice and then a Walton-McDaniel-Balmer double play quickly ended any Atlantic Christian hopes. In the bottom of the second, Fred Kovner started with a single again and was again followed by a Wayne Parks single. After Jimmy Zadell struck out, Lee McDaniel blasted a three-run home run and was again followed by consecutive singles by Fred Balmer and Frank Zadell. ODC batted around again and led 8–0 after just two innings, knocking Larry Poore out of the game with a less-than-stellar pitching line of two innings pitched, eleven hits, one walk, and eight earned runs.

The onslaught continued, although at a somewhat abated pace, as a pitcher named Sakas came in to try his hand. Sakas gave up another seven hits and four runs in his four innings on the mound, although he had some small consolation in that none of the runs was earned. But Walton had only needed the very first one, anyway. Just as the year before, he again spun a three-hit shutout against the Bulldogs, allowing just one runner to safely advance past first base. By the end of the game, Old Dominion had scored twelve times on eighteen hits, Lee McDaniel had gone two-for-four with three runs and five RBI, and co-star Frank Zadell had knocked in four and scored one, as part of his four-for-four day. The offensive output also added twenty-four points to the team batting average, bringing it to the season's high-water mark to date at .281.

Game Twelve: *April 21, 1964—Norfolk—Atlantic Christian College*

Bulldog coach Jack McComas, of Shelbyville, Indiana, had originally come to North Carolina as one of N.C. State basketball coach Everett Case's "Hoosier Hotshots," six players with Indiana roots who came to Raleigh in 1946 to play for Case in his first year, and helped begin a decade of twenty-win seasons, after four consecutive losing ones. But while his athletic fame was related mainly to his basketball skills, McComas was also a fair collegiate baseball player. As late as May 12 in 1948, his season average for the Wolfpack was still at .500,[60] and he was named to the Southern Conference (to which N.C. State belonged in 1948) writer's association's "most outstanding players" list later that season.[61] He went on to play professionally for a few seasons beginning in 1949, starting in the Boston Braves organization with the Denver Bears of the single-A Western League, before spending 1950 with the Class-B Raleigh Capitals in the Carolina League. The following season, he found a home with the Wilson "Tobs" (short for Tobacconists) in the Class-D Coastal Plain League. According to statistics published in Atlantic Christian College's school newspaper *The Collegiate*, McComas led the league with twenty-two home runs and ninety-four RBI that year, the same year in which he also later joined the staff at Atlantic Christian as head basketball and baseball coach.[62] He gave professional baseball one last run in 1952, functioning as player-manager for part of the Wilson Tobs' season, while at the same time coaching baseball at Atlantic Christian, a capacity in which he would serve until 1964.

But on April 16, 1964, just five days before the games against Old Dominion in Norfolk, McComas announced a career change, to become golf pro and manager at Wedgewood Country Club in Wilson, effective June 1, two weeks after the Bulldogs' last scheduled baseball game. As further evidence of the relative importance of baseball at Atlantic Christian, when McComas announced his career change, the Asheville *Citizen-Times* and the Atlantic Christian school newspaper were both among publications announcing that the "basketball coach" was resigning.[63]

Whether the lame-duck status of their coach affected the play of the Bulldogs would be impossible to know, but while their 1964 won-loss record didn't turn out as they would have hoped, they certainly made the second game in Norfolk an exciting one. Fred Edmonds, pitching on five days' rest and putting his 2.02 ERA on the line, took the hill for the Monarchs, against a pitcher Bud Metheny named as "Stead" in the scorebook. Edmonds started the top of the first with a pair of strikeouts, setting the tone for his day, and quickly got the third out on a fly ball to right fielder Frank Zadell. In the bottom half, Fred Kovner started the hit parade again with a single, and a steal of second. But then, as hot as the Monarch bats had been in the first game, they went quiet. Wayne Parks reached on an error following Kovner's hit, but Stead set down ten Monarch batters in a row after that, until a Lee McDaniel single in the fourth inning. Edmonds also had a hot hand for Old Dominion, and had recorded seven strikeouts through four innings, punctuated by stranding a leadoff triple in the top of the third by striking out three consecutive batters.

Despite recording only a single strikeout, Stead remained effective all day long. Through six innings, the score was still deadlocked at zero, with only six total hits for either side. In the seventh inning, Edmonds got into some two-out trouble by allowing consecutive singles but closed it out with his twelfth strikeout of the game. Stead, unfazed by the pressure of the bottom of the last scheduled inning of a tie game on enemy turf, answered by retiring Frank Zadell, Jimmy Walker, and Mel Renn in order.

Edmonds stayed in the game for the eighth and completed another scoreless frame, allowing a leadoff single but nothing else. But McComas replaced Stead with Elliott, a move which played well for only one batter. After Edmonds had flied out to center field, Fred Kovner then came through with his second single and then second steal of the game, and Wayne Parks followed by drawing the only base on balls by either side in the game. A passed ball had moved Kovner to third, allowing Tom Harrell the chance to play hero. Playing in only their twelfth game of the year, the Monarchs had already three times scored the winning runs in their final at-bat, and this game followed the script. With Kovner ready to run at third, Harrell delivered the sacrifice fly to center field that scored him, running the win streak to eight and pushing the overall season record to nine wins against three losses.

Game Thirteen: *April 25, 1964—Norfolk—Bridgewater College*

After four days to enjoy the exciting win, the Monarchs were back to work for a Saturday twin bill in Norfolk against Bridgewater College, in a Mason-Dixon Conference South Division matchup. Despite the conference affiliation, to say that the two schools were rivals would be an overstatement. Historically, thirteen contests had been played between the two schools in a continuous series between 1955 and 1961, with the Norfolk Division Braves winning nine of them. The series had been dormant since that time, however, and so Bridgewater had never faced the "Monarchs" of "Old Dominion College," and none of the previous meetings had been inter-conference affairs.

Bridgewater College, a small school in the Shenandoah Valley of Virginia, began operations in 1880. The school, while taking care on its website to note that all faiths are welcome, is historically affiliated with the Church of the Brethren and at present still claims 9 percent of their student body as members of that faith.[64] From humble beginnings of just six students, the school flourished, and before the turn of the century, began fielding its first baseball team, and competing at an intercollegiate level by 1900. Besides a seven-year hiatus from intercollegiate competitions from 1909–1916 "for unknown reasons aside from 'mismanagement'," according to the 1993 Bridgewater baseball media guide, and a one-year break in 1918 due to World War I, the school has fielded a team since 1898, and with a fair degree of success. In the years between 1950 and 1964, according to the book *Bridgewater College: The First Hundred Years*, Bridgewater played 246 games of baseball and "gained victories in about 52 percent of all of those contests."[65] In that time, Coach Danny Geiser, patrolling the dugout for all of those years except for 1957, also saw six of his charges go on to the professional ranks.[66]

In 1960, the Eagles of Bridgewater had shared the Little Eight title with Hampden-Sydney and Randolph-Macon, and had shared the title again in 1962, on that occasion with the Norfolk Division. The Bridgewater College history also claims that Bridgewater won the 1963 Mason-Dixon Championship; that, however, is either wishful thinking, or revisionist history. The Eagles had a very successful 1963 season, finishing with a 13–7 mark, but Old Dominion's Monarchs won the Mason-Dixon, attested by the game ball still in the possession of the family of winning pitcher John Ingram, signed by Bud Metheny and the team after the 9–3 win over Loyola in the championship game that year.

In 1964, Coach Geiser's Eagles came into their first conference meeting with Coach Metheny's Monarchs carrying a 7–6 overall record and a 3–3 mark in the Mason-Dixon after their most recent games, a doubleheader sweep of Lynchburg College in which the Eagles had put twenty-nine runs on the board. The Monarchs stood at 9–3, with a 4–1 Mason-Dixon record, making the day's games critical to Bridgewater's hopes. Old Dominion starter Bob Walton began the game with a sterling 1.95 ERA after his dismantling of Atlantic Christian four days before, but Walton got off to a rough start against the Eagles in the first game. After the leadoff man struck out, third baseman Roger Seale ripped a one-out double. The center fielder, eventual Bridgewater sports Hall of Fame member Yager Marks, couldn't bring Seale home, but cleanup man Wayne Shifflett did with an RBI single to open the scoring. One batter later, first baseman Guy Stull, also an eventual Bridgewater Hall inductee, made it an early 3–0 lead with a home run.

The Monarchs' half of the first looked promising to start. Leadoff hitter Fred Kovner drew a walk from starter Al Morrow. A single by Wayne Parks followed, but Kovner was thrown out on the front end of a double steal, and Old Dominion couldn't sustain the rally.

Walton began to settle down, retiring seven men in a row after Stull's blast, but in the fourth inning Shifflett came up for a second time and led off with a solo home run. Stull followed with a double, which may have started Coach Metheny thinking about his bullpen, but Walton stranded Stull right where he was by inducing a popup to catcher John Ward, and then consecutive flyouts to Jimmy Zadell in right field.

Behind 4–0, the Old Dominion batters had some work to do. But this team had won, in blowouts and in close games, and knew *how* to win. As third baseman Wayne Parks recalled in 2016, "I don't care what the score was. We were behind, we just never felt like we were going to lose that game. We just . . . our team had unbelievable confidence."[67] The team also had patience, taking 103 walks over a twenty-five-game season, or an average of 4.12 per game. As Fred Kovner recalled the simple philosophy: "We want to get on, we want to get around, and we want to score."[68] Al Morrow lost the strike zone in the bottom of the fourth and fell victim to Monarch patience. Second baseman Lee McDaniel, batting cleanup, drew a walk to start the inning. First baseman Fred Balmer waited Morrow out and pushed McDaniel to second with a walk. Frank Zadell followed by accepting another free pass, which knocked Morrow from the game. Freshman Mike Jacobs came on to provide relief but was immediately greeted by a two-run single off the bat of shortstop Mel Renn, halving the Eagle lead.

Bob Walton had found his groove after Stull's double, retiring fifteen of the next sixteen batters he faced and allowing only a harmless single in the top of the seventh. Old Dominion scratched one run back in the sixth when Mel Renn drew a walk and scored on John Ward's triple, cutting the lead to one. In the bottom of the seventh in a game only scheduled for seven, the Monarchs tied it with another run, manufacturing it in classic small-ball style and without the benefit of a hit: Wayne Parks reached on an error by third baseman Seale, Jimmy Zadell sacrificed him over, Lee McDaniel grounded out but moved the runner to third by hitting to the right side, and after a Fred Balmer walk, Jacobs balked the tying run home.

No runs were scored in the eighth, ninth, or tenth innings, and Walton was still on the mound. In the eleventh, Walton again permitted no runs. In the bottom of that inning, the Monarchs put an end to it with a Lee McDaniel single, and then one batter later, a two-out, game-winning single by Frank Zadell. For a second straight game, Old Dominion had won a game in their last at-bat, while winning pitcher Bob Walton ran his record to 4–1 with the eleven-inning complete game, in which he had faced a total of forty-two batters.

Game Fourteen: *April 25, 1964 — Norfolk — Bridgewater College*

In the second game of the day, Metheny decided to use Denny Riddleberger on the hill instead of Fred Edmonds, who was probably ready after four days of rest since his shutout of Atlantic Christian. Riddleberger had never started a college game to that point, but had logged 4⅓ relief innings thus far in the season with a solid 2.08 ERA, although he was also allowing 1.85 baserunners per inning, in contrast to Edmonds' 1.56 ERA and 1.24 WHIP. But Metheny knew that a tough stretch for his pitching staff was ahead, with games scheduled (but never played) on April 28 at Loyola and April 29 at Mount St. Mary's, followed by two at Lynchburg on May 1 that *were* played. Plus, he undoubtedly wanted to see what his freshman pitcher could do in a starting role.

Coach Danny Geiser, thin on pitching already anyway, decided to start Jim Matheson. Geiser at that time was already in his 18th season at the baseball helm, and he is a member of Bridgewater's athletic Hall of Fame for that service—as well as many years leading the basketball team and the football team, which he is credited with reviving on a mere five-hundred dollar budget after the World War II years.[69] Geiser was a graduate of Juniata College, another institution historically affiliated with the Church of the Brethren, where he had earned thirteen letters during his four years. He never played professional baseball after college, but that may be because he was otherwise engaged: During World War II, he was a Navy pilot and earned the Distinguished Flying Cross decoration given for "heroism or extraordinary achievement while participating in an aerial flight," as well as eight service ribbons and six combat stars.[70] To add to his impressive military resume, Geiser had also received a doctorate from Columbia University, and had been named as the president of the Mason-Dixon Conference only the previous September.

None of those accomplishments, however, helped his pitching depth on April 25, 1964. As one Chuck Moore had prophetically reported in his "About Sports" column, appearing on April 17, 1964, in the *B.C. Bee*, "Kidding aside we look at the business side of the Eagle Nine and see several strong points but some weaknesses as well. To put it bluntly we need more, experienced pitchers. Al Morrow, Mike Jacobs, and Jim Strayer do all right but you can't expect them to carry the whole load."[71]

Jim Matheson's pitching, though, wasn't the early concern for the Eagles; the defense was. In the first inning, left fielder Lee Dellinger contributed two errors behind Matheson, the first allowing Fred Kovner to reach and later score, and the second allowing Tom Harrell to advance into scoring position after a single, to be later driven in by Fred Balmer's sacrifice fly. The Monarch offense kept the pressure on Bridgewater all game—a steal, a wild pitch, a passed ball, five walks, not to mention five Bridgewater errors by four different players. But bunches of runs weren't crossing the plate. At the end of the game, Metheny had recorded eleven Monarchs left on base in the six innings that they batted. Matheson labored, but after allowing two runs in the first, still put up three zeroes through the fourth inning, despite all five of the errors, the passed ball, two of the walks, and a Fred Kovner steal occurring in those first four.

Denny Riddleberger was sharp for Old Dominion early, striking out two in three scoreless innings to start. Bridgewater, however, didn't lack for offense, and averaged 7.1 runs per contest in the 1964 season. In the fourth, the Eagles drew three consecutive walks and tied the game when Dellinger knocked in two with a single, and the go-ahead run scored on a Monarch miscue charged to right fielder Tom Harrell. Bill Yeargan took over on the mound for the fifth inning and got two quick outs, but then consecutive singles by Yager Marks and Wayne Shifflett, followed by Guy Stull's double, pushed the Eagle lead to three, 5–2.

Old Dominion trimmed the lead to two in the fifth when Tom Harrell knocked in Fred Kovner with a one-out single, but the Monarchs again failed to get the big hit, stranding both Harrell and Fred Balmer (who had walked), and so the game went to the sixth with Bridgewater clinging to a two-run lead in a must-win game. Yeargan permitted no runs in his second inning of work, pitching around a single and an error. In the bottom half of the inning, Matheson retired the first two ODC batters in shortstop Mel Renn and catcher Jimmy Walker, but his pitch count was up, and the top of the order had already seen him three times. Al Baker, in his only plate appearance of the season, hit for Yeargan with only four outs remaining to continue the nine-game winning streak.

With two out, Baker walked. Fred Kovner followed with his third single of the day, and Wayne Parks singled for his first hit. Tom Harrell singled for the third time, but even with blood in the water,

Geiser left Matheson on the hill. Big Lee McDaniel took advantage with a critical double, plating the tiebreaking third and the go-ahead fourth runs of the inning. Matheson stayed in; Balmer walked and Frank Zadell singled, making it seven straight batters to reach base with two outs, and loading the bases. Mel Renn ended the rally with his second flyout to left field of the inning, but for the second time on the day, Bridgewater couldn't stop the late-inning heroics. The Monarchs took a two-run lead into the top of the seventh and final inning.

Reliever John Ingram came in to wrap it up and retired Yager Marks on a groundout to second, but then put the potential tying runs on first and second base with a walk to Shifflett and a beaning of Stull. Fred Edmonds, in his only relief appearance of the season, took over and retired catcher Carlton Cox on a flyout to Tom Harrell in right field, but then walked second baseman Jim Benson to load the bases. With the tying run on second, Edmonds struck out Lee Dellinger, ending the game. For the third time in as many games — and for the sixth time in fourteen games — Metheny's cardiac kids had won the game in their last at-bat. Yeargan got his fourth win to stay tied with Bob Walton for the team lead, although Yeargan was winning games without the benefit of starting a single one all season. Offensively, the two games dropped the Old Dominion batting average one point, to .273. Along with the eighteen hits on the day, the patient Monarch nine had taken sixteen walks in seventeen innings, although they had also left twenty-five runners on base.

Game Fifteen: *May 1, 1964 — Lynchburg — Lynchburg College*

After the Bridgewater doubleheader, the Old Dominion team faced its first real road test of the season. Five games were scheduled in five days, including a pair in the Baltimore area and then three in the western part of Virginia. The 1964 team already had the benefit of a home-heavy schedule, since fifteen of twenty-four slated games were in Norfolk. But rain had forced cancellation of one contest in Norfolk on March 28, and when the single games on Tuesday, April 28 (at Loyola) and Wednesday, April 29 (at Mount St. Mary's) were also cancelled due to weather, it meant that the 1964 Monarchs had the advantage of a regular season in which a full 67 percent of the games were played on Larchmont Field in Norfolk. Relying as he had on so few pitchers to get through the season, Coach Bud Metheny probably didn't view the rainouts in Baltimore as the worst thing that could have happened to his ballclub, as it meant that every pitcher on his staff would get at least six days of rest, particularly Bob Walton, who had pitched eleven innings in his start six days prior.

The day's opponent was Lynchburg College, a coeducational institution affiliated with the Christian Church (Disciples of Christ). Founded in 1903, the school had first been formed as Virginia Christian College, but had taken the name of "Lynchburg College" in 1919 and would continue to be known that way for almost a century, until becoming "Lynchburg University" in 2018.[72] In the Spring 2021 semester, Lynchburg University boasted 2,660 undergraduate and graduate students representing forty-eight states,[73] but in 1964, the Lynchburg yearbook reveals that only 274 students had entered school as the Class of 1964, of which approximately forty did not finish.[74] Despite its small size, sports played a prominent part of the experience at the college. In its early incarnation as Virginia Christian College, baseball predominated. According to a passage in one edition of the school's *Argonaut* yearbook, "Baseball . . . being our national game, should be encouraged by parents, schools, and colleges. Few people have an adequate conception of the importance it has assumed. Baseball is played in large cities, small towns and country places, from juvenile to the professional. It is a manly sport and as such appeals to the higher nature of the youth of our land. It is healthful and invigorating to mind and body alike, and is deservingly encouraged in all of our higher institutions of learning.

Much time should be devoted to the promotion of this game."[75] In fact, in keeping with this stated mission of developing young minds along with young bodies, an early VCC baseball game against Milligan College was followed immediately by a debate in the school chapel between the two teams on the subject of "Does nature or education have the greater influence in the formation of character?"[76] While there is no record that Old Dominion's Bud Metheny ever sponsored such intellectual affairs for his charges, certain impromptu debates, such as the 1963 difference of opinion with Buffalo coach Jim Peelle, could never be ruled out as spontaneous "development opportunities."

In 1964, Lynchburg College could not fairly be described as a Little Eight or Mason-Dixon powerhouse, but could still challenge the conference elite, as evidenced by a victory earlier in the season over traditional power Randolph-Macon. The Hornets also won the unofficial 1964 championship in the Dixie Conference, another league in which they competed, as the *Daily Press* reported on May 8.[77] Lynchburg had played to an 11–10 record in 1963, and despite heavy losses to the starting lineup for 1964 ("an all-conference catcher, two outfielders who batted .370 and .390, our starting third baseman, shortstop, and the mainstay of the pitching staff," according to the school newspaper),[78] six lettermen had returned in 1964 and continued to have the team around the .500 mark, with five wins against six losses coming into the May 1 doubleheader.

The 1964 Hornets were led by the man for whom their field has been named since 1979, James C. "Jimmy" Fox. Fox had served the school since 1946, and in 1964, led not only the baseball program, but also the entire Lynchburg College athletic program, as athletic director. Fox, a native of Coburg, Oregon, held a Doctorate in Education from the University of Virginia, and served in the Pacific Theater as a member of the US Naval Reserve in World War II. His thirty-three years of dedicated service to the college would not only result in the naming of the current baseball complex in his honor, but also in his induction as a "Special Citation" in the inaugural 1978 class of the

Lynchburg College Sports Hall of Fame,[79] recognition of his service with a 1989 "Honorary Alumni Award,"[80] and an annual academic award in his name at the school.

Recent returns in this baseball rivalry had been squarely in favor of Old Dominion. The Monarchs' ledger against Lynchburg had begun with a 14–8 loss in 1948, and included a 9–7 overall mark; in more recent history, however, Old Dominion had won five of the six contests from 1961 to 1963, scoring at nearly double the rate of the Lynchburg offense, with an average game score of 6.3–3.5 in that span. In the 1963 meetings, the Monarchs had swept a doubleheader from the Hornets in Norfolk in April, by scores of 4–3 and 7–2. The starting Lynchburg pitcher in the second of those two losses was Len Frady, and the Monarchs had tagged him with ten hits and five earned runs over a six-inning complete-game effort. As the starting pitcher in this day's game, he doubtlessly took the hill on his home field with payback in mind, while Coach Metheny, with his well-rested stable, turned to a familiar strategy: control artist Bob Walton in the first game, fireballer Fred Edmonds in the second.

The first game started slowly for both offenses, possibly in part due to the unusually cool weather in Lynchburg, which didn't get above fifty-nine degrees for the day. Despite hitting Wayne Parks with a pitched ball, Frady faced the minimum six batters through the first two innings, after Parks was caught stealing by the Lynchburg catcher. Walton, too, was strong early. Despite a shaky first which included a single and an uncharacteristic walk, Walton proceeded to run off four consecutive three-up, three-down innings.

Not until the top of the sixth inning (in a game scheduled for seven) did either team push a run across. Old Dominion had runners in scoring position in each of the three previous offensive frames but hadn't been able to come up with the big hit. In the sixth, though, the heart of the Monarch lineup came up for the third time against Frady, and had measured the opposing pitcher. Tom Harrell, batting third, started the rally with a one-out triple, and was immediately followed by a run-scoring triple off the bat of cleanup man Lee McDaniel. First baseman Fred Balmer brought McDaniel home with a single, and after a strikeout, Mel Renn completed the outburst with a two-out RBI single, leaving Old Dominion up 3–0.

Tasked with holding a three-run lead with only six outs to go, Walton permitted a single run on a two-out double by Hornet third baseman Jerry Dillon in the sixth, but still held the two-run advantage going into the bottom of the seventh. Lynchburg catcher Ronnie Cox started that inning with a single, and one out later, a double by shortstop Sewell Rowley put the tying runs on second and third. A groundout to Old Dominion shortstop Mel Renn plated the first of those runs, but left the task of completing the comeback to pinch-hitter Doug Craddock, batting for Frady. Craddock didn't disappoint the home fans, delivering a two-out single to tie the score.

With Frady gone from the game, the Hornets sent Dave Layman to the mound for the extra innings. But the heart of the Old Dominion lineup was due up again, and again Tom Harrell started things with an extra-base hit, doubling to lead off the frame. After Lee McDaniel grounded out to shortstop, Fred Balmer gave the Monarchs the lead again with a run-scoring triple, and Frank Zadell followed with a two-run home run, completing the scoring. Walton set Lynchburg down in order in the bottom half, securing his second straight extra-inning complete-game win, and the eleventh in a row for the team.

Game Sixteen: *May 1, 1964 — Lynchburg — Lynchburg College*

In the second game, Coach Fox decided to start Dale Donovan against Metheny's selection of Fred Edmonds. Whether the emotional letdown of the first game played into the outcome of the second game, or whether the fact that this was the only doubleheader Lynchburg had scheduled all year while Old Dominion had already played four, the second game was simply not a contest. Fred Kovner opened the top of the first with a triple, and the Monarchs never looked back. Of the next three batters, Wayne Parks walked, Jimmy Zadell contributed a sacrifice fly, and Lee McDaniel tripled, leading to a 3–0 advantage after one inning. In the Monarch second, Parks and Fred Balmer both contributed triples, while Fred Kovner and Jimmy Zadell both contributed singles and steals of second base, and Old Dominion led 7–0 after two frames. The teams traded single runs in the fifth, but the top of the sixth, with Donovan still on the hill, was another disaster for Lynchburg—three errors, a walk allowed, and eight Old Dominion hits paved the way for thirteen batters to come to the plate and eight runs to score, tying the Monarchs' season high for an inning, set on April 18 against Baltimore. Donovan, mercifully, exited during the inning, and Ed White came on to get the final four outs in the eventual 16–1 Hornet loss.

The final box score was overpowering. Eight of nine hitters in the Monarch lineup had at least one hit, and the one who didn't, Jimmy Walker, still reached base four times. Seven Monarchs had at least one run batted in, paced by Jimmy Zadell's three. Eight of nine Monarchs had scored at least one run, and six of those scored at least twice, led by Fred Kovner, who scored four times. The Monarchs had recorded five triples and stole four bases. And despite this output, Old Dominion *still* left seven runners on base, compared to Lynchburg's one. As for pitching? Fred Edmonds struck out ten, walked none, and allowed only two hits, which happened to be back-to-back, creating the lone Hornet run of the day.

On the other side of the ledger, the Hornet stats were as unimpressive as Old Dominion's were outstanding. Donovan had completed 5⅔ innings, allowing fourteen hits, three walks, and *sixteen runs*—although only seven of them were earned, because the Hornet defense also committed nine errors. At the plate, the Hornet offense contributed two hits in twenty-one at-bats, for an .087 average on the day.

The seventeen-for-forty offensive performance in the second game, when combined with nine-for-twenty-nine in the first contest, had the effect of raising the Old Dominion team batting average to the highest point of the season, up a full fourteen points from the start of the day, from .273 to .287. Team pitching numbers also improved; while the team ERA stayed steady at a minuscule 2.17, the average number of baserunners allowed per inning by hit or walk dropped to 1.19, the lowest number since the beginning of the season.

Game Seventeen: *May 2, 1964—Lexington—Washington and Lee University*

In 1964, although they were in different conferences, the Monarchs played Washington and Lee in a home-and-home series for the first time, with the second game scheduled for Lexington, about an hour's drive from the previous day's doubleheader sweep in Lynchburg. As John Ingram recalled the Monarchs' mode of travel: "We spent a lot of time in station wagons. Basically, the guys who were older, the juniors and seniors rode in one station wagon. Freshmen rode with Bud and sophomores and/or juniors kind of rode in the other station wagon." Why did the freshmen have to ride with Bud? "Who wants to ride with the coach? I mean, that's just normal."[81]

Washington and Lee Coach Joe Lyles, like ODC's Bud Metheny, had been born in St. Louis, although the two were not contemporaries; Lyles was fourteen years younger than Metheny. But like Metheny, Lyles also pursued a career in professional baseball, as a member of the St. Louis Browns organization. His career as a player, which spanned 1949 to 1954, was not as fruitful as Metheny's, as he never rose above Class-C, but he did play for some colorful-sounding teams: the Pittsburg Browns of the Kansas-Oklahoma-Missouri League, the Muskogee Reds of the Western Association, the Paducah Chiefs of the Mississippi-Ohio Valley League, and the Lexington Colts of the Mountain States League.[82] None of these low-level leagues survived beyond the mid-1950s, in a general national trend often attributed to the growing availability of televised major league baseball. But if Lyles didn't find his professional baseball career satisfying, he also played professional basketball, and perhaps his most enduring athletic fame comes from his role as a member of the United States All-Stars, for which he played games in forty-four countries in 1952, as the foil to the Harlem Globetrotters.[83]

Lyles assumed head coaching duties at Washington and Lee in 1959 and became a well-known and beloved baseball and soccer coach for the university. His career baseball record of 108–229–3, compiled from 1959 to 1978, is probably not what endeared him to the community, but, along with his fifty-year dedication to the school, his "Lylesisms" may have helped. "Members of the W&L community relished his sense of humor and what they called his Lylesisms, such as 'I want the left-handers over here, right-handers over there, and the rest of you come with me,' and 'This year, all our home games are going to be here'," according to a story in the 2013 W&L Alumni magazine.[84] In fact, *Cincinnati Enquirer* sports columnist Paul Daugherty, himself a W&L alum, evidently believed that the liberties Joe Lyles took with the English language were notable enough to be worthy of the legendary Yogi Berra and Casey Stengel, and in 2015, published a fictional conversation among the three.[85]

In 1999, The Generals opened "Cap'n Dick Smith Field" on campus—a great Division III facility—but in 1964 the conditions were much different. "The field was the worst I've ever played on . . . Our field was a 'sawed off' top of a mountain with a backstop and a bench for both teams. If you hit a hard line drive between the outfielders, it was a home run since there was no fence,"[86] as former player Pete Heumann recalled. Possibly, such conditions led to the six errors the Generals would commit in this game.

Heumann was the starter for Washington and Lee, going against ODC left-hander John Ingram, who came into the game with ten innings under his belt, a 1–0 record, and a 2.70 ERA. Both pitchers worked out of some early trouble in the first, stranding two runners apiece. But while Heumann pitched a scoreless second, the Generals sent ten men to the plate in their half, nine of them against Ingram. Skip Chase, starting at first base instead of Jim Crothers, who had made three errors at that position in the previous meeting, began the rally with a single, and second baseman Mike Saunders followed with another single. After a strikeout, Heumann and leadoff man Richard Brown delivered run-scoring singles, and shortstop Dave Kirkpatrick walked to load the bases. Ingram recorded a strikeout to put the Monarchs an out away from minimizing the damage to two runs, but consecutive bases-loaded walks ended his day. Denny Riddleberger came in and was immediately greeted by a two-run single from Skip Chase, and the inning only ended when center fielder Tom Harrell caught Chase off the bag at first, assisting on an 8–3–6 putout. All told, six runs crossed the plate.

With a twelve-game win streak on the line, as well as a modest three-game win streak against Washington and Lee, the Monarchs knew there were plenty of outs left to make up the ground. As Jimmy Walker recalls the team mindset at the time, "We did not think that anybody could beat us. During that winning streak—two of them— we were behind in quite a few of the games, and came back and won them, to keep the streak going. As a matter of fact, it became where the visiting team knew about it. I think it put more pressure on them than it did us. Once we were down, and we'd start hitting in the late innings or something like that, and it was 'Here we go, here we go!', 'Getting ready to come on now,' and stuff like that. They'd choke up or something, we'd come back and win. We won a lot of games coming from behind. Didn't think we could lose."[87]

Whether it was the nervous play described by Walker, or bad field conditions, or simply an outfit that wasn't that good, the defense began to let Heumann down as he tried to hold the six-run lead. ODC began battling back in the top of the third with a leadoff single by center fielder Tom Harrell, playing in the first of only two games all year he would start at that position in place of Fred Kovner. After singles by Wayne Parks and Jimmy Zadell loaded the bases, Heumann struck out second baseman Gene Johnson, but Fred Balmer started the comeback with a statistical rarity: a run-scoring sacrifice fly to shortstop Dave Kirkpatrick. Denny Riddleberger scored another single run in the top of the fourth to cut the lead to 6–2.

Riddleberger was effective over 7⅓ innings, and the Monarch defense was strong, recording three outs on the basepaths, including a pickoff, a caught-stealing, and an outfield assist. Despite eight walks, Heumann was actually effective for the Generals as well, pitching seven innings and giving up only two earned runs while striking out nine, the most strikeouts any opposing pitcher would record against

ODC all season. But the top of the fifth for the Generals' defense included three errors by three different players, two walks, a passed ball, a wild pitch, and three runs scored. Another single run scored by Jimmy Zadell in the top of the sixth made four straight innings in which the Monarchs had scored, and the game was tied.

It went to the ninth that way. In the top of that frame, seventh-spot hitter Jimmy Walker led off with a single—his second hit of the day, to go with two walks. Mel Renn, who had relieved Ray Nelson at shortstop, advanced Walker with another single, but Riddleberger and Harrell both recorded outs that didn't advance either. Wayne Parks, however, already one-for-three with a pair of walks on the day, delivered the tie-breaking, two-out single that brought Walker around. In the home half, the Generals could only muster a harmless walk, and a 7–6 victory kept the ODC win streak alive.

The recap of the Washington and Lee season, printed in the 1965 *Calyx* yearbook, described a baseball team that came into the year "loaded with talent and seasoned competitors from the surprising '63 team, 5–8 over-all and second in the CAC tournament," and described 1964 as "the year that should have been."[88] But for Coach Lyles, the missed opportunity against the Monarchs in Lexington was one disappointment in a season that ended up filled with many, as Washington and Lee went on to a 2–10–1 overall mark, with the only two wins coming against Lynchburg College. The Monarchs went back to Norfolk to put a thirteen-game win streak on the line against Pembroke State.

Game Eighteen: *May 5, 1964—Norfolk—Pembroke State College*

In 1964, Pembroke State College was the second school on the Old Dominion schedule, along with Dartmouth, that had opened to serve Native Americans. Pembroke State, started originally as the Croatan Normal School, began in 1888 with fifteen students and just a single instructor for the purpose of training teachers, and stayed much truer to its charter mission of specifically educating Native Americans than did Dartmouth, which only graduated a total of nineteen Native American students in 200 years.[89] In fact, the college located in Pembroke, North Carolina, was specifically focused enough that until 1945, it had only welcomed those from Robeson County to Pembroke, which the Lumbees call "the economic, cultural and political center" of their tribe.[90] In that year, the school began allowing any Native American from a federally recognized tribe, but not until 1954, after a Supreme Court decision on desegregation, was the school fully opened to all races.[91]

The school remained fairly small for many years, comparable in enrollment to many high schools. Part of the University of North Carolina system now, it is home to approximately 6,500 students, but when Old Dominion played them in 1964, there were only 642.[92] As it evolved and grew, Pembroke State (then known as the "Cherokee Indian Normal School of Robeson County") granted its first four-year degrees in 1940, the same year that its intercollegiate baseball program started.

The story of Pembroke State baseball is one of success. Through the 1974 season, only four losing seasons can be found in the annals of Braves' baseball. The seasons leading up to 1964 were particularly successful, with records of 18–7 and 16–8 in 1962 and 1963, respectively.[93] As Wayne Parks, Old Dominion senior third baseman in 1964, recalls, "There was a Pembroke College, and man, they always had strong baseball teams. We played them two or three years. That was one of the toughest teams, year in and year out, that we played on a regular basis."[94]

The overall series had begun in 1961, and the teams had squared off seven times in three seasons, with Old Dominion winning five, by an average 7.9–6.7 score. One of those Pembroke victories, in 1963, had victimized Parks' Little Eight, Mason-Dixon, and NCAA Regional champion Monarchs team. Despite the loss of some productive seniors from the year before, Bud Metheny knew that this

Pembroke edition was not in rebuilding mode, at least not offensively, with returnees such as future Pembroke athletic Hall of Famers Tecumseh "Tee" Brayboy and Tim Brayboy ("most athletic" at the school in 1964), as well as 1963 NAIA all-district performer Linwood Hedgepeth. Going into the season, Coach Raymond Pennington did have some concern about the pitching staff, as writer Tommy Thompson of *The Robesonian* wrote on March 3: "Pennington sights [sic] pitching as the weakest part of the squad because there are only two returning hurlers from last season's roster."[95]

Those two returning starting pitchers, Richard "Cooter" Powell and Mackie Hoffman, had certainly shouldered their share of the load during the 1964 season. For statistics immediately preceding the Old Dominion games, *The Robesonian* reported a 7–0 record for Cooter Powell with an earned run average of zero, which the paper called "one of the best in the state."[96] Hoffman was reported at 4–1 with a 0.60 ERA, and the pair had accounted for all Pembroke's wins, as the team's record stood at 11–1 on the season against college competition.

Metheny tabbed Bob Walton to start the first game of the day against the visiting Braves, and Walton drew the difficult assignment of facing a lineup with five hitters over .300—the Brayboys, Hedgepeth, William "Cuffy" Contreras, and third baseman and leading hitter Roland Deaton, at .459. Cooter Powell, to no one's surprise, started for Pembroke State, and a pitcher's duel immediately began in Norfolk. Despite the offensive punch on both sides, the two teams would combine to go seven-for-forty-seven for the game, or .149.

Walton only allowed one baserunner to reach, by way of an error, through the first two innings, but the Monarchs plated an important run in the bottom of that inning, as Mel Renn singled, moved over when catcher John Ward walked, and then came home when Walton reached first on an error by first baseman Al Costa. Not until the fifth would either side score again, when Wayne Parks reached on an error by the third baseman Deaton, and then scored on another error by Deaton, after a Jimmy Zadell single and a walk issued to Lee McDaniel.

Leading by two going into the seventh and final inning, Walton had been cruising, giving up no runs, and only two hits and one walk. But the seventh was shakier. To start the inning, Contreras walked and was followed by a Tee Brayboy single, putting the tying runs on base with no outs. Right fielder Robert Dondero executed a successful sacrifice to move them both into scoring position, and then Roland Deaton walked to load the bases. But the senior Walton had pitched three consecutive complete games before this start, and Metheny had seen him work out of trouble before and left him in the game. B. W. Holt came in to pinch-hit for Costa and broke up the shutout by delivering a run with a groundout to second, earning the only RBI for either side in the entire game, but also costing the Braves an out. With Brayboy standing on third and Deaton on second, Walton struck out Cooter Powell to preserve the 2–1 Monarch victory. This one had come down to defense, since Powell had struck out none and Walton had struck out only two; the Braves had tallied five errors, two of which allowed runs to score, and the Monarchs just one error. On the positive side for the Braves, Powell, although taking the loss, maintained an ERA that was still one of the best in the state (and even the nation), since it had not moved from 0.00.

Game Nineteen: *May 5, 1964—Norfolk—Pembroke State College*

Coach Pennington had an easy decision to make for his starter in the second game, with Mackie Hoffman and his 0.60 ERA ready to go. Pennington, in his first season as head baseball coach, was a 1957 graduate of East Carolina, where he had lettered in both baseball and football all four years, and where he enjoys membership in the athletic Hall of Fame. In 1964, the rookie coach was taking over after a successful run by Dick Lauffer, who had guided the team to an 88–62 (.587) mark from 1957 to 1963. Coach Pennington would do even better. During his run in the 1960s, his teams won 114 games and lostthirty-two, for a winning percentage of 78.1 percent; no coach at the school that served more than one year has ever done better. Although he didn't coach the Braves after 1969, he continued to serve the school for many years as professor, chair of the Health and Physical Education Department, and athletic director. Around age sixty, when most people would be starting to think about retirement, he even ran for, and won, the mayor's job in Lumberton, North Carolina, a position that he held for another twenty years until his 2015 retirement at age eighty.[97]

Pennington's 1964 team ultimately finished at 13–7, still a .650 winning percentage, but that season would actually be the worst, by far, of Pennington's career. And the second game against Old Dominion in 1964, judging from available scores from the year, may have been the worst defeat within his worst season.

Metheny countered Pennington's Hoffman with Fred Edmonds, who retired the first seven batters he faced, four by strikeout. Hoffman struggled against the Monarchs from the very first inning. He retired center fielder and leadoff man Tom Harrell on a groundout to shortstop, but that may have been the highlight of the afternoon for the Braves' staff. Wayne Parks singled for the first of four hits he would get in the game, and Jimmy Zadell and Lee McDaniel both singled to load the bases. First baseman Fred Balmer contributed a productive out with a run-scoring fielder's choice, and then a double by Frank Zadell plated his brother.

The bottom of the third was more of the same. A flyout to left off the bat of Jimmy Walker opened the frame, but consecutive singles by Edmonds, Harrell, and Parks loaded the bases. Center fielder Jimmy Zadell brought the first one in with a sacrifice fly, and then cleanup hitter Lee McDaniel picked up the other two with a two-out double. In the fourth, a Harrell single, a Parks triple, and a run-scoring groundout by McDaniel continued the scoring, and the game was out of reach at 7–0. All of the runs were earned, and all of them were charged to Mackie Hoffman.

Pennington let Hoffman stay in to finish the fourth, but then pulled him in favor of freshman Bobby Johnson, who performed slightly better, although he still gave up one run in his two innings of work. Metheny needed to make no such decision when it came to his starter. In seven innings, Fred Edmonds gave up only four hits, one walk, and struck out eleven in a complete-game shutout. Monarch batters went thirteen-for-thirty in the second game and actually raised the team's average from .285 to .288 over the doubleheader, despite the ineffective showing in the first game. The five .300 hitters in Pembroke's lineup? They had combined to go four-for-twenty-six (.154), with six strikeouts, no runs batted in, and a single run scored, proving in part the old Casey Stengel adage, "Good pitching will always stop good hitting and vice-versa."

Game Twenty: *May 7, 1964—Norfolk—Richmond Professional Institute*

On the seventh of May, the 16–3 Monarchs, riding a fifteen-game winning streak overall and a twenty-five-game winning streak against the day's opponent, traveled to Richmond to square off for the second time in 1964 against the Rams of Richmond Professional Institute. RPI had moved their mark to 5–3 with a victory against Newport News Apprentice two days before, and gave the ball to Tee Alphin to oppose the Monarchs' John Ingram. Ingram's ERA had moved to 6.95 in the small sample size of $11\frac{2}{3}$ innings that included the six earned runs at Washington and Lee five days prior, but also had a somewhat unusual 16:15 K/BB ratio—or 12.3 strikeouts per nine innings and 11.57 walks per nine. Bud Metheny didn't use the typical scorebook notation of "K" for a swinging strikeout, and "backwards K" for a caught-looking; he used

"K" and "SO," and so working on the assumption that "K" retained its meaning as a swinging strike, Ingram had caught thirteen of his victims looking, or more than one "caught-looking" per inning.

The Rams liked to swing the bat. The *Proscript's* preview of RPI's 1964 squad reported that despite the 1–19 record from 1963, they had batted .289 as a team,[98] and they had only walked twice in the April 20, 1964, meeting. On this day neither Ingram, over seven innings of work, or Bill Yeargan, over two innings of work, walked a single Ram batter. Ingram struck out four and permitted just six hits and two earned runs over seven innings, but was largely matched by Alphin, who pitched a complete game, giving up three earned runs while striking out eight.

The deciding moment in the game came in the top of the third. After catcher John Ward and later Ingram had reached base with singles, Fred Kovner took one of Alphin's offerings deep to center field for a one-out, three-run home run, his second of the year. No Monarch would advance any further than first base the rest of the way, but the pitching did its job after that. Ingram gave up a pair of runs in the seventh on second baseman Roland Wheeler's double, and Bill Yeargan kept it interesting by allowing a pair of two-out singles in the bottom of the eighth, but finished the game off in the ninth with a strikeout of Wheeler, clinching another Little Eight title for the Monarchs.

The twenty-six-game Monarch win streak over the Rams would come to an end in the 1965 season with a 9–8 loss, but the Monarchs would win three out of the remaining four games they would play with RPI, for an all-time record of thirty-one wins versus three losses. On July 1, 1968, Virginia Commonwealth University was formed by the merging of RPI and the Medical College of Virginia (also a former Norfolk Division opponent, as the two played seven times between 1939 and 1953, with the Norfolk Division winning four); therefore, the series between Old Dominion College and Richmond Professional Institute, as such, is over. But the similarities and the natural athletic rivalry between the schools continued, and continues; as VCU formed in 1968, so too did Old Dominion College officially become Old Dominion University a year later. Many schools on Old Dominion's 1964 schedule no longer compete at the same level as ODU does, but VCU has paralleled the growth and success of Old Dominion, and their baseball rivalry has lasted largely unbroken through ODU's rise to university status and 1976 transition to Division I athletic competition. In fact, the two schools can even both claim the same standout coach—Tony Guzzo compiled a 329–300–1 mark at VCU between 1983 and 1994, and then moved to ODU, where he enjoyed a 303–252 mark over ten years. Even current ODU coach Chris Finwood was part of the VCU staff between 1995 and 2000, first as an assistant and then associate head coach, helping lead the Rams to 219 wins in that time.[99]

The most recent publication of ODU's official baseball "History and Records" at the time of this writing (released prior to the 2019 season) gives all-time won-loss records against collegiate opponents, and the record shows that the two schools have met 152 times, by far the most of any Monarch opponent. The published record is 91–61 in Old Dominion's favor, but it improved to 93–61 after the Monarchs took the Rams down by a 6–5 final on April 9, 2019, and 7–5 on April 16.

Game Twenty-One: *May 9, 1964—Norfolk—Hampden-Sydney College*

The win streak, which had reached sixteen games, was alive and well as ODC welcomed Hampden-Sydney back to Larchmont for a 2 p.m. Saturday game. The Tigers had dealt the Monarchs a surprising 8–1 defeat almost a month before, and without doubt, it was not soon forgotten by Old Dominion players.

Hampden-Sydney is another of several schools on Old Dominion's 1964 schedule that enjoyed a long and rich history that stood in contrast to the relatively new ODC. Hampden-Sydney, in fact, slightly predates the United States of America, and even takes its name from the simmering revolutionary sentiment. John Hampden and Algernon Sydney were 17th-century Englishmen who fought for the same ideals that drove the Revolutionaries in America. In Hampden-Sydney's synopsis of their own history on their website, they state, "Indeed, the original students eagerly committed themselves to the revolutionary effort, organized a militia-company, drilled regularly, and went off to the defenses of Williamsburg, and of Petersburg, in 1777 and 1778 respectively. Their uniform of hunting-shirts—dyed purple with the juice of pokeberries—and grey trousers justifies the College's traditional colors, garnet and grey."[100] Hampden-Sydney College is also one of very few remaining undergraduate colleges to retain its all-male status. As of 2016, there were only three others: Wabash College, Morehouse College, and Saint John's University in Minnesota, although the latter two have separate women's-college peer institutions.

Despite the lack of historical commonalities, Old Dominion had begun to develop an athletic rivalry with Hampden-Sydney with the Monarchs' inclusion in the "Little Eight" in the fall of 1955. The rivalry was strengthened in 1963, when Old Dominion, a new member of the Mason-Dixon Conference, was added to the South Division with Randolph-Macon, Bridgewater, Catholic, American, Hampden-Sydney, and Lynchburg, although conference play was scheduled somewhat differently than today, since ODC would not play Catholic or American as Mason-Dixon Conference members until 1966.

Coach Bill Pegram had had success with Hal Blythe as his starter before, and decided to put him on the hill against ODC's Bob Walton, who was riding a personal six-game winning streak. Despite the motivation of payback, the top of the first didn't start easily for the Monarchs. Second baseman Dave Trickler led off the game for the Tigers with a double, which was followed by singles from Jim Rosenstock and Travis Tysinger, and then a walk to cleanup man Mike Crone. Strong Monarch defense held the resulting damage to a single run, however: an outfield assist from center fielder Fred Kovner cut down Trickler at the plate, and catcher John Sartain ended the threat by hitting into a Parks-McDaniel-Balmer double play, one of two twin killings the Monarchs would turn.

Blythe tossed one tidy inning but got into trouble quickly in the bottom of the second. Sophomore first baseman Fred Balmer of Hampton started his big day against Tiger pitching with a one-out single in the second. Frank Zadell followed with a double, and Mel Renn brought them both home with a big two-run single. The next two also reached base, as John Ward singled and Bob Walton walked, making five consecutive batters to reach base against Blythe, four of whom ultimately scored in the inning. Balmer accounted for the next two Monarch runs with solo home runs in consecutive at-bats against Blythe in the third and sixth innings.

Going into the seventh, the Monarchs were in good position, leading 6–1. The teams traded single runs in the seventh and eighth, with Monarch runs coming as McDaniel doubled home Wayne Parks in the seventh, and Ward tripled home Renn in the eighth. Bob Walton, by the scorebook, didn't have his best game, and allowed fourteen hits in 8⅓ innings, but still took an 8–3 lead into the top of the ninth.

A two-run single by Sartain plated Rosenstock and Tysinger in that frame, and Bud Metheny had seen enough; Bill Yeargan came in for two quick outs, and saved the Monarch win. As Ed Hewitt had reported in the *Mace and Crown* the day before the game, however, "The best record the Tigers could have, should they win their remaining two games, is 6–2. Should the Monarchs lose to H-S their record would be 8–2. The team with the best percentage is the champion. Thus, the expected showdown between ODC and H-S tomorrow, failed to materialize."[101] This Monarch victory, save for the motivations of revenge and preparation for the championship series against Mason-Dixon North Division champion Washington College, did not decide either the Mason-Dixon or Little Eight races, since Old Dominion had already won both. Despite the loss, Hampden-Sydney still completed a

10–6 season, for what the *Farmville Herald* called a "banner year for the Tiger baseballers"[102] (even though they did not actually capture any banner), as it was the "most winning team in five years." Certainly, the payback win was a nice feather for the Monarch cap, and prepared Old Dominion to fight for the conference championship, still riding a win streak that had reached seventeen.

ENDNOTES

BEGINNINGS

1 "History & Traditions | William & Mary," accessed March 2, 2021, www.wm.edu/about/history/index.php.

2 "Norfolk and vicinity : March 1921 | Library of Congress (loc.gov)", accessed July 1, 2021, www.loc.gov/resource/g3884n.ct009373 /?r=0.175,-0.018,0.299,0.19,0.

3 Dr. James Sweeney, *Old Dominion University: A Half Century of Service* (Norfolk: ODU Office of Printing and Publications, 1980), 4.

4 "William Moseley Brown Will Head New University At Virginia Beach," *The Bristol (TN) Herald Courier*, April 13, 1930, 1. www.newspapers.com/ image/585708924/.

5 "3 William-Mary Professors Will Be Faculty Members At Atlantic University," *Daily Press* (Newport News, VA), May 31, 1930, 10. www. newspapers.com/image/230182128/.

6 "Board of Visitors to Take Action on College Saturday," *Daily Press* (Newport News, VA), May 31, 1930, 10. www.newspapers.com/ image/230182128/.

7 "Abandon Plans For College At Virginia Beach," *Chicago Daily Tribune*, January 5, 1931, 6. www.newspapers.com/image/354963858/.

8 "Alleged Psychic Healer Arrested," *The Baltimore Sun*, November 9, 1931, 1. www.newspapers.com/image/373439632/.

9 Dr. James Sweeney, *Old Dominion University: A Half Century of Service* (Norfolk: ODU Office of Printing and Publications, 1980), 5.

10   "Board Of Visitors To Take Action On College Saturday," *Daily Press* (Newport News, VA), May 31, 1930, 10. www.newspapers.com/image/230182128/.

11   "Enrollment Office for Norfolk School to be Opened Here," *Daily Press* (Newport News, VA), June 15, 1930, 22. www.newspapers.com/image/230186864/.

12   "William and Mary Junior College at Norfolk to Open," *Daily Press* (Newport News, VA), September 5, 1930, 11. www.newspapers.com/image/231222809/.

13   "AN EXPLANATION OF THE HONOR SYSTEM," *The High Hat*, November, 1930.

14   "The Football Season," *The High Hat*, November, 1930, 1.

15   *The High Hat*, November, 1930.

16   "University Facts & Figures—Old Dominion University," accessed March 2, 2021, www.odu.edu/about/facts-and-figures.

17   Ibid.

CHAPTER ONE

1   "Baseball Team Organized," *The High Hat*, March 21, 1931, 4.

2   "College Baseball Scholarship Requirements and Facts," accessed March 1, 2021, www.ncsasports.org/baseball/scholarships.

3   "Thomas L. Scott—Virginia Sports Hall of Fame," accessed March 1, 2021, vasportshof.com/inductee/thomas-l-scott/.

4   "Braves Trim Deep Creek by 8–3 Score," *The High Hat*, April 2, 1931, 4.

5   "Prospects for Nine Appear Very Bright," *The High Hat*, March 4, 1932, 1.

6   "Braves Face Tough Battle To Retain Tidewater Flag," *The High Hat*, March 24, 1933, 4.

7   "Baseball Squad To Hold First Workout Monday," *The High Hat*, Mach 13, 1937.

8   Clay Shampoe and Thomas R. Garrett, *Baseball in Norfolk, Virginia* (Charleston, SC: Arcadia Publishing, 2003), 51.

9   Tony Zontini, *The History of Baseball at Old Dominion University* (Norfolk, VA, 1978). Master of Education Thesis, available at Old Dominion University's Patricia W. and J. Douglas Perry Library, Norfolk, Virginia. Note: Mr. Zontini's thesis reflects two consecutive 8–2 losses to the Naval Training Station in 1938, but based on a *Virginian-Pilot* article of May

6, 1938, the author believes one of those losses to be a 6–5 victory, and counts wins and losses accordingly.

10   Marlowe, "Tars Rout Braves; Caldwell Gets Four Hits," *The Virginian-Pilot*, April 5, 1939.

CHAPTER TWO

1   "Expanded Intra-Mural Program In Prospect," *The High Hat*, February 16, 1940, 3.

2   "Sports Will Not Be Discontinued During Spring," *The High Hat*, December 14, 1934.

3   George Wright, "Daily Pressings," *Daily Press* (Newport News, VA), August 3, 1941, 1C. www.newspapers.com/image/230609164/.

4   Ibid.

5   Tony Zontini, *The History of Baseball at Old Dominion University* (Norfolk, VA, 1978), 84. Master of Education Thesis, available at Old Dominion University's Patricia W. and J. Douglas Perry Library, Norfolk, Virginia.

6   M. Doyle, "High Hatting The World," *The High Hat*, March 10, 1933, 1.

7   "High Hat Forum," *The High Hat*, March 9, 1934, 2.

8   Dr. James Sweeney, *Old Dominion University: A Half Century of Service* (Norfolk: ODU Office of Printing and Publications, 1980), 32–33.

9   "Former W. & M.—V. P. I. Students In Armed Forces," *The High Hat*, May 19, 1943.

10   "Division Athletes Now In Uniform," *The High Hat*, May 19, 1943.

11   "Airmen Shutout Braves, 8 to 0, As 3 Twirlers Hurl No-Hitter," *The Virginian-Pilot*, April 15, 1942.

12   Clay Shampoe and Thomas R. Garrett, *Baseball in Norfolk, Virginia* (Charleston, SC: Arcadia Publishing, 2003), 52.

13   Martha and Johnny, "Around the Gym," *The High Hat*, May 23, 1944, 3.

14   Norfolk Division of the College of William & Mary *The Voyager 1946*, ed. Regina O'Brien (Norfolk, VA: Burke & Gregory, Inc., 1946). digitalcommons.odu.edu/scua_yearbooks/1/.

15   Dr. Ernest Gray, "Comments From Gray," *The High Hat*, February 27, 1946.

16   "Norfolk Division Rolls Hit All-Time High Mark," *The High Hat*, September 23, 1946, 1.

17   Old Dominion University, *Old Dominion Baseball 2019 Media Guide* (Norfolk, VA: 2019). static.odusports.com/custompages/2018–19/baseball/2019%20media%20guide.pdf.

18   "Everett Whips Division, 4–1," *The Virginian-Pilot*, May 12, 1946.

19   Joseph C. "Scrap" Chandler, "Interview with Mr. Joseph C. Chandler," Interview by Dr. James R. Sweeney. October 28, 1975. dc.lib.odu.edu/digital/collection/oralhistory/id/23/rec/1.

CHAPTER THREE

1   Bud Metheny file, National Baseball Hall of Fame, Cooperstown, New York. File received by author via e-mail message from Matt Rothenberg (Manager of the Giamatti Research Center, Cooperstown), June 8, 2016. Note: Collection includes 21 pages of newspaper clippings, unindexed.

2   This information is gleaned from analysis of the census returns for the family in 1920 and 1930, available at www.ancestry.com.

3   "ODU's Metheny To Quit After Baseball Campaign," *Daily Press* (Newport News, VA), December 9, 1979, D10. www.newspapers.com/image/234190174/.

4   Bob Broeg, "Old Dominion Gets New Look," *St. Louis Post-Dispatch*, September 6, 1966, 5C. www.newspapers.com/image/142249293.

5   Arthur B. "Bud" Metheny, "Oral History Interview with Arthur B. Metheny (Part One)," Interview by Dr. James R. Sweeney. May 22, 1975. dc.lib.odu.edu/digital/collection/oralhistory/id/561/.

6   "Directory | Valley League Baseball," accessed March 2, 2021, www.valleyleaguebaseball.com/view/valleyleaguebaseball/directory-5.

7   "1989 Inductees—Hampden-Sydney College," accessed March 2, 2021, hscathletics.com/sports/2020/6/22/information-Hall-of-Fame-Hall-of-Fames-Classes-1989.aspx.

8   Arthur B. "Bud" Metheny, "Oral History Interview with Arthur B. Metheny (Part One)," Interview by Dr. James R. Sweeney. May 22, 1975. dc.lib.odu.edu/digital/collection/oralhistory/id/561/.

9   Ibid.

10   Ibid.

11   College of William & Mary *Colonial Echo 1937*, ed. Roger B. Child (Nashville: Benson Printing Co., 1937), 170.

12   College of William & Mary *Colonial Echo 1936* (Nashville: Benson Printing Co., 1937), 160.

13   College of William & Mary *Colonial Echo 1937*, ed. Roger B. Child (Nashville: Benson Printing Co., 1937), 175.

14 College of William & Mary *Colonial Echo 1939*, ed. Frank Damrosch III (Nashville: Benson Printing Co., 1937), 121–122.

15 Marc Z. Aaron and Bill Nowlin, eds. *Who's On First: Replacement Players in World War II* (Phoenix: Society for American Baseball Research Inc., 2015), 293.

16 Bud Metheny file, National Baseball Hall of Fame, Cooperstown, New York. File received by author via e-mail message from Matt Rothenberg (Manager of the Giamatti Research Center, Cooperstown), June 8, 2016. Note: Collection includes 21 pages of newspaper clippings, unindexed.

17 "Wives Superstitious Too," *Asbury Park (NJ) Evening Press*, April 8, 1943, 12. www.newspapers.com/image/143935782/.

18 Bud Metheny file, National Baseball Hall of Fame, Cooperstown, New York. File received by author via e-mail message from Matt Rothenberg (Manager of the Giamatti Research Center, Cooperstown), June 8, 2016. Note: Collection includes 21 pages of newspaper clippings, unindexed.

19 "1943 New York Yankees Lineups and Defense," accessed March 2, 2021, www.baseball-reference.com/teams/NYY/1943-lineups.shtml.

20 "1944 Major League Baseball Right Field," accessed March 2, 2021, www.baseball-reference.com/leagues/MLB/1944-specialpos_rf-fielding.shtml.

21 Bud Metheny file, National Baseball Hall of Fame, Cooperstown, New York. File received by author via e-mail message from Matt Rothenberg (Manager of the Giamatti Research Center, Cooperstown), June 8, 2016. Note: Collection includes 21 pages of newspaper clippings, unindexed.

22 Ibid.

23 Arthur Daley, "Red Jones Recollects: Metheny Won on 'Strike-Ball' Call," The Times Dispatch (Richmond, VA), February 1, 1962, 39. www.newspapers.com/image/616233400/ Note: This article was written for the New York Times News Service, and appeared in many more newspaper outlets across the country.

24 "1944 Major League Baseball Standard Batting," accessed March 2, 2021, www.baseball-reference.com/leagues/MLB/1944-standard-batting.shtml. Note: This is an extrapolation. The league average was 59 RBI, but based on 600 plate appearances, Metheny had 592.

25 "1945 Major League baseball Right Field," accessed March 2, 2021, www.baseball-reference.com/leagues/MLB/1945-specialpos_rf-fielding.shtml.

26 "Bud Metheny—Society for American Baseball Research," accessed March 2, 2021, sabr.org/bioproj/person/bud-metheny/. The note of seven

additional home runs comes from his professional statistics: www.
baseball-reference.com/register/player.fcgi?id=metheno01art.

27   Marc Z. Aaron and Bill Nowlin, eds. *Who's On First: Replacement Players
      in World War II* (Phoenix: Society for American Baseball Research Inc.,
      2015), 294.

28   "Coast Hurler Sold," *Arizona Republic*, December 5, 1943, sec. 4, p. 1. www.
      newspapers.com/image/117592138/.

29   Joseph C. "Scrap" Chandler, "Interview with Mr. Joseph C. Chandler,"
      Interview by Dr. James R. Sweeney. October 28, 1975. dc.lib.odu.edu/
      digital/collection/oralhistory/id/23/rec/1.

30   "Well-Cushioned Cochrane, Trout Collide, Decide Old-Timers'
      Game," *St. Louis Post-Dispatch*, July 28, 1957, 2E. www.newspapers.com/
      image/140101432/.

CHAPTER FOUR

1   Arthur B. "Bud" Metheny, "Oral History Interview with Arthur B.
      Metheny (Part One)," Interview by Dr. James R. Sweeney. May 22, 1975.
      dc.lib.odu.edu/digital/collection/oralhistory/id/561/.

2   Old Dominion University, *2019–20 ODU Basketball Guide*
      (Norfolk, VA: 2019), 108. s3.amazonaws.com/odusports.com/
      documents/2019/11/13/2019_20_ODU_MBB_Guide.pdf.

3   Thomas R. Garrett and Clay Shampoe, *Old Dominion University Men's
      Basketball* (Charleston, SC: Arcadia Publishing, 2007), 17–18.

4   Old Dominion University, *2019–20 ODU Basketball Guide*
      (Norfolk, VA: 2019), 108. s3.amazonaws.com/odusports.com/
      documents/2019/11/13/2019_20_ODU_MBB_Guide.pdf.

5   Norfolk Division of the College of William & Mary *The Voyager 1947*,
      ed. Margaret Knight (Norfolk, VA: Burke & Gregory, Inc., 1947), 62.
      digitalcommons.odu.edu/scua_yearbooks/2/.

6   Thomas R. Garrett and Clay Shampoe, *Old Dominion University Men's
      Basketball* (Charleston, SC: Arcadia Publishing, 2007), 23.

7   Arthur B. "Bud" Metheny, "Oral History Interview with Arthur B.
      Metheny (Part One)," Interview by Dr. James R. Sweeney. May 22, 1975.
      dc.lib.odu.edu/digital/collection/oralhistory/id/561/.

8   Norfolk Division of the College of William & Mary *The Voyager 1949*, ed.
      Bessie Theodore Hatzopolous (Norfolk, VA: Burke & Gregory, Inc., 1949),
      72. digitalcommons.odu.edu/scua_yearbooks/3/.

9   "Bud Metheny Award Recipients—Old Dominion University," accessed March 1, 2021, odusports.com/news/2017/12/1/211687995.aspx.

10   "Bluejackets Rout Division, 21 to 1," *The Virginian-Pilot*, May 11, 1949.

11   "Flyers Crush Braves, 16–1," *The Virginian-Pilot*, May 21, 1949.

12   "1949 Piedmont League," accessed March 1,2021, www.baseball-reference.com/register/league.cgi?id=e1b84fe0.

13   "The Sports Roundup," *The Daily Mail* (Hagerstown, MD), August 31, 1949, 15. www.newspapers.com/image/22058898/.
     Note: This blurb may have been an Associated Press release, as it appeared in several other newspaper outlets across the country.

14   Charles Karmosky, "Bud Metheny Replaces Campanis As Manager of Newport News Dodgers," *Daily Press* (Newport News, VA), July 21, 1950, 8. www.newspapers.com/image/231024787.

15   "1950 Newport News Dodgers Statistics," accessed March 1, 2021, www.baseball-reference.com/register/team.cgi?id=40f55ea1.

16   Julian Rice, "Metheny Leads Dodgers To 7–5 Win Over Colts," *Daily Press* (Newport News, VA), July 23, 1950, 1C. www.newspapers.com/image/231025118/.

17   "Newport News Dodgers—BR Bullpen," accessed March 1, 2021, www.baseball-reference.com/bullpen/Newport_News_Dodgers.

18   "Cubs Down Baby Dodgers, 3–1," *Daily Press* (Newport News, VA), August 31, 1950, 9. www.newspapers.com/image/231027451/. Note: The *Daily Press* printed Dodgers box scores daily.

19   Arthur B. "Bud" Metheny, "Oral History Interview with Arthur B. Metheny (Part One)," Interview by Dr. James R. Sweeney. May 22, 1975. dc.lib.odu.edu/digital/collection/oralhistory/id/561/.

20   "Percy Dawson Takes Job As Phillies' Scout," *Daily Press* (Newport News, VA), February 9, 1957, 11. www.newspapers.com/image/231103688/.

21   Joe Pierce, "Watching the Play . . . ," *Daily Press* (Newport News, VA), November 20, 1950, 8. www.newspapers.com/image/231234420.

22   "Yearbooks," accessed March 2, 2021, digitalcommons.odu.edu/scua_yearbooks/. This information comes from a review of several yearbooks from the Norfolk Division of the College of William & Mary, available at the link shown, or at the Patricia W. and J. Douglas Perry Library, Norfolk, Virginia.

23   Arthur B. "Bud" Metheny, "Oral History Interview with Arthur B. Metheny (Part One)," Interview by Dr. James R. Sweeney. May 22, 1975. dc.lib.odu.edu/digital/collection/oralhistory/id/561/.

24 Ibid.

25 "Pitching Talent No Problem To Division Baseball Coach," *The Virginian-Pilot*, March 22, 1950.

26 Frank Zadell, in phone interview with the author, December 11, 2016.

27 Boyd Nix, in phone interview with the author, February 28, 2016.

28 "1955 Major League Baseball Standard Fielding"; accessed March 1, 2021, www.baseball-reference.com/leagues/MLB/1955-standard-fielding.shtml.

29 Bill Harrison, "Home Of The Braves," *The Virginian-Pilot*, April 13, 1959.

30 *Arthur "Bud" Metheny Papers, 1930–1991*, Series II, Box 4. Special Collections of Old Dominion's Patricia W. and J. Douglas Perry Library, Norfolk, Virginia. Collection includes Metheny's baseball scorebooks from 1952–1980.

31 Note: a 9–8 record does not align with the 8–8 record shown in Tony Zontini's research in this case; the *Virginian-Pilot* reported a 13–3 victory over the "Fleet Marines" that does not appear in Zontini's thesis.

32 Bernie Weiss, "Pitching Is Big Question Mark of '53 Division Diamonders," *The High Hat*, March 13, 1953, 3.

33 "Diamond Dust," *The Virginian-Pilot*, April 3, 1953.

34 Arthur B. "Bud" Metheny, "Oral History Interview with Arthur B. Metheny (Part Two)," Interview by Dr. James R. Sweeney. May 29, 1975. dc.lib.odu.edu/digital/collection/oralhistory/id/563/rec/7.

35 "Diamond Dust," *The Virginian-Pilot*, April 3, 1953.

36 Arthur B. "Bud" Metheny, "Oral History Interview with Arthur B. Metheny (Part One)," Interview by Dr. James R. Sweeney. May 22, 1975. dc.lib.odu.edu/digital/collection/oralhistory/id/561/.

37 Ibid.

38 Tony Zontini, *The History of Baseball at Old Dominion University* (Norfolk, VA, 1978). Master of Education Thesis, available at Old Dominion University's Patricia W. and J. Douglas Perry Library, Norfolk, Virginia.

39 *The College of William and Mary in Norfolk General Catalogue 1955–1956,* (Norfolk, VA: 1955), 104. Available in the Special Collections of Old Dominion's Patricia W. and J. Douglas Perry Library, Norfolk, Virginia. Note: An article entitled "Division Enters Its Twenty Fifth Year" on the front page of the September 30, 1954, *High Hat* cites a total enrollment of 1,968, with 805 Day College students.

40 Tony Zontini, *The History of Baseball at Old Dominion University* (Norfolk, VA, 1978), 27. Master of Education Thesis, available at Old Dominion University's Patricia W. and J. Douglas Perry Library, Norfolk, Virginia.

41 "Plebes Rout Braves, 13–1," *The Virginian-Pilot*, April 17, 1955.

42 Norfolk Division of the College of William & Mary *The Chieftain 1954* (Norfolk, VA: Crowder Offset Printing Company, 1954), ~45 (pages not numbered). Note: The *Virginian-Pilot* article is reproduced in this yearbook, I did not go back and look for the *V-P* microfilm.

43 Norfolk Division of the College of William & Mary *The Chieftain 1956*, ed. Aimi Kuun (Norfolk, VA: 1956).

44 *The College of William and Mary Norfolk Division 1960 General Catalogue* (Norfolk, VA: 1960). Available in the Special Collections of Old Dominion's Patricia W. and J. Douglas Perry Library, Norfolk, Virginia.

45 Arthur B. "Bud" Metheny, "Oral History Interview with Arthur B. Metheny (Part One)," Interview by Dr. James R. Sweeney. May 22, 1975. dc.lib.odu.edu/digital/collection/oralhistory/id/561/.

46 Ibid.

47 "Schools Rejected By Mason-Dixon," *The Baltimore Sun*, March 28, 1955, 16. www.newspapers.com/image/374905163/.

48 Arthur B. "Bud" Metheny, "Oral History Interview with Arthur B. Metheny (Part One)," Interview by Dr. James R. Sweeney. May 22, 1975. dc.lib.odu.edu/digital/collection/oralhistory/id/561/.

49 Fred Edmonds Jr., in phone interview with the author, January 23, 2017.

50 Arthur B. "Bud" Metheny, "Oral History Interview with Arthur B. Metheny (Part One)," Interview by Dr. James R. Sweeney. May 22, 1975. dc.lib.odu.edu/digital/collection/oralhistory/id/561/.

51 Ibid.

52 "Baseball Turnout at W. and M. Largest Yet," *The High Hat*, March 15, 1956, 5 and John Hightower, "Eleven Lettermen Lead Diamonders," *The High Hat*, March 14, 1957, 7.

53 Cal Rosenthal, "Braves Open Baseball Season," *The High Hat*, March 17, 1958, 6.

54 "College Nines Set for Busy Schedule But Little Cooperation Is Expected from Weather This Week," *The Progress-Index* (Petersburg, VA), May 7, 1958, 9. www.newspapers.com/image/47721338/.

55 "Braves Open Baseball Season," *The High Hat*, March 17, 1958, 6.

56 "Wm & Mary Braves Remain Undefeated," *The High Hat*, May 1, 1958, 8.

57 Arthur B. "Bud" Metheny, "Oral History Interview with Arthur B. Metheny (Part One)," Interview by Dr. James R. Sweeney. May 22, 1975. dc.lib.odu.edu/digital/collection/oralhistory/id/561/.

58 "Braves Down R-M, Take Little Eight Crown," *The High Hat*, May 23, 1958, 7.

59 Ibid., 8.

60 Bill Harrison, "Home Of The Braves," *The Virginian-Pilot*, March 16, 1959.

61 Bob Ainsworth, "Diamond Round-Up," *The High Hat*, May 22, 1959, 7. Note: In contradiction, Bill Harrison's May 11, 1959, "Home Of the Braves" column in the *Virginian-Pilot* says there were five .300 hitters, led by Bert Harrell at .380, with Palumbo and Marshall at .364 and .333, respectively.

62 "Braves, H-S Vie Monday for Little 8 Title," *The Virginian-Pilot*, May 7, 1959, and "Brave Nine Wallops Towson," *The Virginian-Pilot*, May 9, 1959.

63 Bill Harrison, "Home of the BRAVES," *The Virginian-Pilot*, May 11, 1959.

64 "Crewe, Virginia," accessed March 2, 2021, en.wikipedia.org/wiki/Crewe,_Virginia#cite_note-DecennialCensus-7.

65 "NCAA Accepts Norfolk W-M," *The Virginian-Pilot*, April 29, 1959.

66 "Braves Open Today," *The Virginian-Pilot*, March 19, 1960.

67 "Elon Nine Blasts Norfolk W-M, 16–2," *The Virginian-Pilot*, April 19, 1960.

68 Mel Renn, in phone interview with the author, January 22, 2017.

69 *Arthur "Bud" Metheny Papers, 1930–1991*, Series II, Box 4. Special Collections of Old Dominion's Patricia W. and J. Douglas Perry Library, Norfolk, Virginia. Collection includes Metheny's baseball scorebooks from 1952–1980. Note: The "year-by-year" files in the Series II collection includes some manual calculations, which put the rates at 2.95 errors per game in 1960, and 1.29 in 1961. The primary source data from Metheny's own scorebook is preferred here.

70 Ibid.

71 Bill Harrison, "Braves End Best Season With Win," *The Virginian-Pilot*, May 19, 1961.

72 "Monarch Nine Loses 2 Stars," *The Virginian-Pilot*, March 27, 1962.

73 "1962 New York Mets Batting Splits," accessed March 2, 2021, www.baseball-reference.com/teams/split.cgi?t=b&team=NYM&year=1962.

74 Dan Richards, "Boyce Theme: 'Fence Me In,'" *The Virginian-Pilot*, May 12, 1962.

75 "Students Favor Keeping Name of William and Mary," *The High Hat*, April 1960, 11.

76 Charles Baldwin, "Athlete's Feats," *The Mace and Crown*, November 1961, 20.

77 Arthur B. "Bud" Metheny, "Oral History Interview with Arthur B. Metheny (Part One)," Interview by Dr. James R. Sweeney. May 22, 1975. dc.lib.odu.edu/digital/collection/oralhistory/id/561/.

78   Ibid.

79   "Delaware One Of Nine schools in Conference," *Wilmington (DE) Morning News*, April 22, 1940, 15. www.newspapers.com/image/160641557.

80   "Mason-Dixon Conference To Hold Annual Meeting And Election Today," *The Baltimore Sun*, December 7, 1941, 4*. Note: The asterisk refers to nothing; that's how the paper numbers it. www.newspapers.com/image/373657303/.

81   "Mason-Dixon Conference Rejects Membership Bids," *Wilmington (DE) Morning News*, March 28, 1955, 19. www.newspapers.com/image/155548479/.

82   "Cage Tourney Switch Made In Conference," *The Gettysburg (PA) Times*, September 17, 1963, 12. www.newspapers.com/image/46883338/.

83   *Arthur "Bud" Metheny Papers, 1930–1991*, Series II, Box 5. Special Collections of Old Dominion's Patricia W. and J. Douglas Perry Library, Norfolk, Virginia.

84   "Mason-Dixon Transfer Rule Not Changed," *The Danville (VA) Bee*, March 26, 1956, 7. www.newspapers.com/image/46922541/.

85   Charles Baldwin, "Who Said it Couldn't be Done?," *The Mace and Crown*, May 1962, 16.

86   Arthur B. "Bud" Metheny, "Oral History Interview with Arthur B. Metheny (Part One)," Interview by Dr. James R. Sweeney. May 22, 1975. dc.lib.odu.edu/digital/collection/oralhistory/id/561/.

87   Dick Welsh, "Crabbers Run Over Cradock By 75–50, Gain Tie For District Lead," *Daily Press* (Newport News, VA), February 12, 1954, 6. www.newspapers.com/image/231237463/.

88   Arthur B. "Bud" Metheny, "Oral History Interview with Arthur B. Metheny (Part One)," Interview by Dr. James R. Sweeney. May 22, 1975. dc.lib.odu.edu/digital/collection/oralhistory/id/561/.

89   Old Dominion University, *2018–19 ODU Basketball Guide* (Norfolk, VA: 2018). static.odusports.com/custompages/2018–19/mbb/2018–19%20odu%20mbb%20guide%20use.pdf.

90   Thomas R. Garrett and Clay Shampoe, *Old Dominion University Men's Basketball* (Charleston, SC: Arcadia Publishing, 2007), 24.

91   Norfolk Division of the College of William & Mary *The Chieftain 1961*, ed. Nancy Winfree (Norfolk, VA: 1961).

92   "Leo Anthony—Old Dominion University," accessed March 2, 2021, odusports.com/sports/2019/9/16/208421987.aspx.

93   Arthur B. "Bud" Metheny, "Oral History Interview with Arthur B. Metheny (Part One)," Interview by Dr. James R. Sweeney. May 22, 1975. dc.lib.odu.edu/digital/collection/oralhistory/id/561/.

94   Thomas R. Garrett and Clay Shampoe, *Old Dominion University Men's Basketball* (Charleston, SC: Arcadia Publishing, 2007), 23.

95   Arthur B. "Bud" Metheny, "Oral History Interview with Arthur B. Metheny (Part Two)," Interview by Dr. James R. Sweeney. May 29, 1975. dc.lib.odu.edu/digital/collection/oralhistory/id/563/rec/7.

96   Old Dominion University, *2018-19 ODU Basketball Guide* (Norfolk, VA: 2018), 85. static.odusports.com/custompages/2018-19/mbb/2018-19%20 odu%20mbb%20guide%20use.pdf.

CHAPTER FIVE

1   Dr. James Sweeney, *Old Dominion University: A Half Century of Service* (Norfolk: ODU Office of Printing and Publications, 1980), 19.

2   Peggy Haile McPhillips, "Lafayette Park," accessed March 2, 2021, www. norfolkpubliclibrary.org/home/showdocument?id=320.

3   Rufus Tonelson, "Oral History Interview with A. Rufus Tonelson (Part Two)," Interview by Dr. James R. Sweeney. July 2, 1979. dc.lib.odu.edu/ digital/collection/oralhistory/id/579/rec/4.

4   Clay Shampoe and Thomas R. Garrett, *Baseball in Norfolk, Virginia* (Charleston, SC: Arcadia Publishing, 2003), 48.

5   "1931 Norfolk Tars Statistics," accessed March 2, 2021, www.baseball-reference.com/register/team.cgi?id=406ae5b1.

6   Mrs. Thomas Lawrence Scott, "Oral History Interview with Mrs. Thomas Lawrence Scott," Interview by Dr. James R. Sweeney. February 5, 1976. dc.lib.odu.edu/digital/collection/oralhistory/id/356/rec/1.

7   "Brave Batters Face Faculty Nine Today," *The High Hat*, April 6, 1934, 1.

8   "No Improvements To Scott Field Says Board," *The High Hat*, May 25, 1934, 1.

9   "Administration Plans New Baseball Diamond; Final Word Awaited," *The High Hat*, March 6, 1937.

10   Arthur B. "Bud" Metheny, "Oral History Interview with Arthur B. Metheny (Part One)," Interview by Dr. James R. Sweeney. May 22, 1975. dc.lib.odu.edu/digital/collection/oralhistory/id/561/.

11   *Arthur "Bud" Metheny Papers, 1930-1991*. Special Collections of Old Dominion's Patricia W. and J. Douglas Perry Library, Norfolk, Virginia.

12　"HISTORY | Tidewater Summer League," accessed March 2, 2021, tidewatersummerleague.com/history/.

13　Clyde "Ducky" Davis, in phone interview with the author, May 15, 2017.

14　Stephen Miller, "Al Gettel, 87, Pitcher For Yankees and Giants," *The New York Sun*, April 27, 2005. www.nysun.com/obituaries/al-gettel-87-pitcher-for-yankees-and-giants/12922/.

15　Fred Edmonds Jr., in phone interview with the author, January 23, 2017.

16　Clyde "Ducky" Davis, in phone interview with the author, May 15, 2017.

17　John Zeb, in phone interview with the author, August 1, 2016.

18　George McClelland, "City Baseball League Opens 18th Season on Sunday," *The Virginian-Pilot*, April 23, 1964, 52.

CHAPTER SIX

1　Jimmy Zadell, in phone interview with the author, December 14, 2016.

2　John Ingram, in phone interview with the author, January 25, 2016.

3　Jimmy Zadell, in phone interview with the author, December 14, 2016.

4　Fred Kovner, in phone interview with the author, February 29, 2016.

5　Mel Renn, in phone interview with the author, January 22, 2017.

6　Jimmy Walker, in phone interview with the author, March 10, 2016.

7　John Ingram, in phone interview with the author, January 25, 2016.

8　Jimmy Zadell, in phone interview with the author, December 14, 2016.

9　John Ingram, in phone interview with the author, January 25, 2016.

10　Fred Kovner, in phone interview with the author, February 29, 2016.

11　Wayne Parks, in phone interview with the author, February 28, 2016.

12　"Bud Metheny Builds Character, Also Top Old Dominion Clubs," *Daily Press* (Newport News, VA), April 1, 1963, 6. www.newspapers.com/image/231389636/.

13　National Collegiate Athletic Association, *Official Collegiate Baseball Guide 1964* (New York: The National Collegiate Athletic Bureau, 1964), 61.

14　Ibid.

15　"Loyola's Reitz dies at 82," *The Baltimore Sun*, April 4, 1992, 8C. www.newspapers.com/image/172672725/.

16　Loyola College *Evergreen 1963*, ed. James Burns et. al. (Baltimore, 1963), 88.

17　Ibid.

18　Ibid., 87.

19　John Ingram, in phone interview with the author, January 25, 2016.

20 Arthur B. "Bud" Metheny, "Oral History Interview with Arthur B. Metheny (Part One)," Interview by Dr. James R. Sweeney. May 22, 1975. dc.lib.odu.edu/digital/collection/oralhistory/id/561/.

21 Arlene Palmer Ingram, in phone interview with the author, February 3, 2016.

22 United States Coast Guard Academy *Tide Rips 1963*, ed. Karl Reichelt (New London, CT: 1963), 300. www.e-yearbook.com/sp/eybb?school=504&year=1963.

23 Accessed February 19, 2020. As of March 2, 2021, link is broken. www.dailyinterlake.com/archive/article-ea7bcdb0–81fe-59eb-8aeb-2a5e2b218ef9.html.

24 United States Coast Guard Academy *Tide Rips 1963*, ed. Karl Reichelt (New London, CT: 1963), 303. www.e-yearbook.com/sp/eybb?school=504&year=1963.

25 "Fine Hurling Is Expected In Tourney," *The Danville (VA) Bee*, May 29, 1963, 2D. www.newspapers.com/image/46685178/.

26 Arthur B. "Bud" Metheny, "Oral History Interview with Arthur B. Metheny (Part One)," Interview by Dr. James R. Sweeney. May 22, 1975. dc.lib.odu.edu/digital/collection/oralhistory/id/561/.

27 Tony Zontini, *The History of Baseball at Old Dominion University* (Norfolk, VA, 1978), 39. Master of Education Thesis, available at Old Dominion University's Patricia W. and J. Douglas Perry Library, Norfolk, Virginia.

28 "Fine Hurling Is Expected In Tourney," *The Danville (VA) Bee*, May 29, 1963, 2D. www.newspapers.com/image/46685178/.

29 State University of New York at Buffalo, *2017 UB Baseball Media Guide* (Buffalo: 2017), 36. issuu.com/buffalobulls/docs/2017_ub_baseball_media_guide.

30 Arthur B. "Bud" Metheny, "Oral History Interview with Arthur B. Metheny (Part One)," Interview by Dr. James R. Sweeney. May 22, 1975. dc.lib.odu.edu/digital/collection/oralhistory/id/561/.

31 Jimmy Zadell, in phone interview with the author, December 14, 2016.

CHAPTER SEVEN

1 "JFK: Jacqueline Kennedy Started 'Camelot,'" accessed March 2, 2021, www.wsj.com/articles/SB10001424052702304791704579212040151427918.

2 Boyd Nix, in phone interview with the author, February 28, 2016.

3 Fred Kovner, in phone interview with the author, February 29, 2016.

4   Arlene Palmer Ingram, in phone interview with the author, February 3, 2016.

5   "The Beatles—Ed Sullivan Show," accessed March 2, 2021, www.edsullivan.com/artists/the-beatles/.

6   Erskine Johnson, "Watch Out! The Beatles Are Invading the U. S.," *Lancaster (PA) New Era*, January 1, 1964, 14. www.newspapers.com/image/562518291/.

7   Warner Twyford, "Beatles Defy Reason," *The Virginian-Pilot*, February 11, 1964.

8   Mal Vincent, "For new movie critic Mal Vincent, "The Sound of Music" was his big chance," accessed March 2, 2021, www.pilotonline.com/entertainment/article_58db9f02-0ed9-5597-8b73-cd95dac48033.html.

9   "The Beatles Invade: Insecticides Useless," *The VMI Cadet*, February 14, 1964, 2. digitalcollections.vmi.edu/digital/collection/p15821coll8/id/12972/rec/1.

10   "We Shall Fight," RPI *Proscript*, February 14, 1964, 2. digital.library.vcu.edu/islandora/object/vcu%3Arps.

11   "Coed Hears Beatles Feels 'Happy Inside,'" RPI *Proscript*, February 21, 1964, 2. digital.library.vcu.edu/islandora/object/vcu%3A16454.

12   Frank Zadell, in phone interview with the author, December 11, 2016.

13   Mel Renn, in phone interview with the author, January 22, 2017.

14   Jimmy Walker, in phone interview with the author, March 10, 2016.

15   John Ingram, in phone interview with the author, January 25, 2016.

16   Wayne Parks, in phone interview with the author, February 28, 2016.

17   Tom Harrell, in phone interview with the author, February 6, 2017.

18   "Baptist church welcomes the Norfolk 17 home," *The Virginian-Pilot* online, July 7, 2008. www.pilotonline.com/news/article_11356ca6-2628-5eca-84b6-2e499ef466ed.html.

19   Fred Kovner, in phone interview with the author, February 29, 2016.

20   Frank Zadell, in phone interview with the author, December 11, 2016.

21   Tom Harrell, in phone interview with the author, February 6, 2017.

22   Arlene Palmer Ingram, in phone interview with the author, February 3, 2016.

23   "Racial Rift Costing Norfolk W&M Foe," *Daily Press* (Newport News, VA), January 12, 1957, 11. www.newspapers.com/image/231332867/.

24   Arthur B. "Bud" Metheny, "Oral History Interview with Arthur B. Metheny (Part One)," Interview by Dr. James R. Sweeney. May 22, 1975. dc.lib.odu.edu/digital/collection/oralhistory/id/561/.

25 "Rights Demonstrator Killed by Earthmover," *The Virginian-Pilot*, April 8, 1964.

26 "10 Negroes Jailed For Street Lie-Ins," *The Virginian-Pilot*, April 28, 1964.

27 "U.S. Senate: Landmark Legislation: The Civil Rights Act of 1964," accessed March 2, 2021, www.senate.gov/artandhistory/history/common/generic/CivilRightsAct1964.htm.

28 Frank Zadell, in phone interview with the author, December 11, 2016.

29 Tom Harrell, in phone interview with the author, February 6, 2017.

30 Jimmy Zadell, in phone interview with the author, December 14, 2016.

31 George A. Middleton, "Vietnam Meets History Club," *The Mace and Crown*, October 4, 1965, 1.

32 "Vietniks Protest at ODC," *The Mace and Crown*, March 3, 1967, 3.

33 Boyd Nix, in phone interview with the author, February 28, 2016.

34 Ancestry.com. *US, Department of Veterans Affairs BIRLS Death File, 1850–2010* [online database] (Provo, UT: Ancestry.com Operations, Inc., 2011).

35 Old Dominion College *Troubadour 1963*, ed. Betty Lou Parker et. al. (Norfolk, VA: 1963), 34. digitalcommons.odu.edu/scua_yearbooks/17/.

36 "1st Dormitory Opens; Only One-Third Filled," *The Mace and Crown*, September 8, 1964, 1.

CHAPTER EIGHT

1 Ed Hewitt, "This is THE Year for ODC Baseball," *The Mace and Crown*, March 13, 1964, 5.

2 "ODC Plays Penn State," *The Virginian-Pilot*, March 25, 1964, 24.

3 Wayne Parks, in phone interview with the author, February 28, 2016.

4 Fred Kovner, in phone interview with the author, February 29, 2016.

5 Frank Zadell, in phone interview with the author, December 11, 2016.

6 Dan Richards, *40 Years Behind the Sports Desk* (Lincoln, NE: iUniverse, Inc., 2002), 5–6. books.google.com/books/about/40_Years_Behind_the_Sports_Desk.html?id=SjpQsEoMPdkC.

7 John Ingram, in phone interview with the author, January 25, 2016.

8 Ed Hewitt, "Ed-iting Sports with Ed Hewitt," *The Mace and Crown*, April 10, 1964, 3.

9 Ibid.

10 "2020 MLB Team Batting Stats | ESPN," accessed March 2, 2021, www.espn.com/mlb/stats/team/_/view/batting.

11 Ed Hewitt, "Hitting, Fielding Improves; Baseball Team on Comeback," *The Mace and Crown*, April 24, 1964, 4.

12 "LBJ Enjoys Baseball, Popcorn," *Lansing (MI) State Journal*, April 14, 1964, C1. www.newspapers.com/image/208034682. Note: This article was released by the Associated Press and appeared in many newspaper outlets across the country.

13 "Jax Police Attacked By 1,500 Negroes," *The Orlando Sentinel*, March 25, 1964, 1. www.newspapers.com/image/223613289/. Note: This article was released by United Press International, and appeared in many newspaper outlets across the country, not necessarily under the same title.

14 "U. S. Discovers 40 Microphones In Walls Of Embassy In Moscow," *Daily Press* (Newport News, VA), May 20, 1964, 1. www.newspapers.com/image/232916019/.

15 "Seven-Foot, 250-Pound 'Monster' Scares Tarheels at Hope's Pond," *Daily Press* (Newport News, VA), May 14, 1964, 2. www.newspapers.com/image/232881760/.

16 Ed Hewitt, "ODC Wins M-D Southern Division Title," *The Mace and Crown*, May 8, 1964, 6.

17 *Arthur "Bud" Metheny Papers, 1930–1991*, Series II, Box 4. Special Collections of Old Dominion's Patricia W. and J. Douglas Perry Library, Norfolk, Virginia. Collection includes Metheny's baseball scorebooks from 1952–1980.

18 "Washington College Rises in Ranks of Top Institutions on Wall Street Journal/Times Higher Education and US News & World Report Lists," accessed March 2, 2021, www.washcoll.edu/live/news/WC-Rises-Ranks-on-Top-Education-Lists.php.

19 "Washington College," accessed March 2, 2021, washingtoncollegesports.com/sports/bsb/history/alltime_records.

20 "Shoremen Blank Randolph-Macon Nine Twice For Mason-Dixon Title," *The Baltimore Sun*, May 22, 1954, 15. www.newspapers.com/image/374830889/.

21 Washington College *Pegasus 1964*, ed. Frazer F. Jones (Buffalo: Wm. J. Keller, Inc., 1964), 97. archive.org/details/pegasusyearbook11964wash.

22 Ibid.

23 *Arthur "Bud" Metheny Papers, 1930–1991*, Series II, Box 5. Special Collections of Old Dominion's Patricia W. and J. Douglas Perry Library, Norfolk, Virginia.

24 "Sisk Sackers Take Northern Division," *The Washington Elm* (Washington College), May 16, 1964, 3. archive.org/details/elm196266wash.

25 Ed Young, "Metheny Explains OD Secrets For Success," *The Progress-Index* (Petersburg, VA), May 8, 1964, 16. www.newspapers.com/image/49134502/.

26 George McClelland, "ODC Accepts NCAA Berth," *The Virginian-Pilot,* May 22, 1963.

27 Ed Hewitt, "Monarchs Win Mason-Dixon Title For 2nd Season; Streak Hits 19," *The Mace and Crown,* May 22, 1964, 6.

28 Arthur B. "Bud" Metheny, "Oral History Interview with Arthur B. Metheny (Part Two)," Interview by Dr. James R. Sweeney. May 29, 1975. dc.lib.odu.edu/digital/collection/oralhistory/id/563/rec/7.

29 "Mumps | Cases and Outbreaks | CDC," accessed March 4, 2021, www.cdc.gov/mumps/outbreaks.html.

30 Wayne Parks, in phone interview with the author, February 28, 2016.

31 "THEN & NOW THE BRONX' GRAND HOTEL," accessed March 2, 2021, www.nydailynews.com/bronx-grand-hotel-article-1.788408.

32 Jimmy Zadell, in phone interview with the author, December 14, 2016.

33 Wayne Parks, in phone interview with the author, February 28, 2016.

34 Jimmy Zadell, in phone interview with the author, December 14, 2016.

35 Personal conversation between Jay Ingram and John Ward II, December 23, 2019.

36 State University of New York at Buffalo, *2015 UB Baseball Media Guide* (Buffalo: 2015), 2. issuu.com/buffalobulls/docs/2015_ub_baseball_media_guide.

37 State University of New York at Buffalo *Buffalonian 1965,* ed. Michael Donohoe (Buffalo: Wm. J. Keller Inc., 1965), 112. digital.lib.buffalo.edu/items/show/80418.

38 "Baseball—UB Sports University at Buffalo Libraries," accessed March 2, 2021, library.buffalo.edu/ub-sports/mens-sports/baseball/. Note: This information on the early history of the program is contradicted by Bulls media guides, which state that the 1949 team was the first in school history (issuu.com/buffalobulls/docs/2017_ub_baseball_media_guide).

39 "Peele Ends Duty as UB Grid Boss," *Rochester Democrat and Chronicle,* May 7, 1948, 35. www.newspapers.com/image/136143975/.

40 "1964 Buffalo Bulls Baseball," accessed March 2, 2021, library.buffalo.edu/ub-sports/mens-sports/baseball/1964-buffalo-baseball/ and State University of New York at Buffalo *Buffalonian 1965,* ed. Michael Donohoe (Buffalo: Wm. J. Keller Inc., 1965), 89. digital.lib.buffalo.edu/items/show/80418. Note: The first source says ten, the second says six.

41 State University of New York at Buffalo, *2017 UB Baseball Media Guide* (Buffalo: 2017), 32. issuu.com/buffalobulls/docs/2017_ub_baseball_media_guide.

42 Ibid., 36.

43 Arthur B. "Bud" Metheny, "Oral History Interview with Arthur B. Metheny (Part Two)," Interview by Dr. James R. Sweeney. May 29, 1975. dc.lib.odu.edu/digital/collection/oralhistory/id/563/rec/7.

44 Wayne Parks, in phone interview with the author, February 28, 2016.

45 Long Island University, *LIU Brooklyn Blackbirds Baseball Record Book* (New York: 2019), 11. s3.amazonaws.com/sidearm.sites/liuathletics.com/documents/2019/8/4/LIU_BK_Baseball_Record_Book.pdf.

46 Ibid., 12.

47 "Anthony Russo Sr (2014)—Hall of Fame," accessed March 2, 2021, kccathletics.com/hof.aspx?hof=2&path=hof&kiosk=.

48 "Anthony Russo Minor Leagues Statistics & History," accessed March 2, 2021, www.baseball-reference.com/register/player.fcgi?id=russo-003ant.

49 Long Island University, *LIU Brooklyn Blackbirds Baseball Record Book* (New York: 2019), 7–8. s3.amazonaws.com/sidearm.sites/liuathletics.com/documents/2019/8/4/LIU_BK_Baseball_Record_Book.pdf.

50 "LIU Brooklyn Blackbirds—Hall of Fame," accessed March 2, 2021, brooklyn.liuathletics.com/hof.aspx?type=sport&kiosk=.

51 Dave Lewis, "Edmonds Sharp in Debut," *The Ledger-Star* (Norfolk, VA), March 26, 1964.

52 "Old Dominion Beats L.I.U., 4–3, for Atlantic Coast N.C.A.A. Baseball Title," *The New York Times*, June 8, 1964. www.nytimes.com/1964/06/07/archives/old-dominion-beats-liu-43-for-atlantic-coast-n-c-a-a-baseball-title.html.

CHAPTER NINE

1 *Arthur "Bud" Metheny Papers, 1930–1991*. Special Collections of Old Dominion's Patricia W. and J. Douglas Perry Library, Norfolk, Virginia.

2 "The Coach of the Year," *The Mace and Crown*, January 15, 1965, 2.

3 *Arthur "Bud" Metheny Papers, 1930–1991*, Series II, Box 8. Special Collections of Old Dominion's Patricia W. and J. Douglas Perry Library, Norfolk, Virginia.

4 Old Dominion University, *Old Dominion Baseball 2019 Media Guide* (Norfolk, VA: 2019), 45. Note: The overall record is shown erroneously as 22–4, but the winning percentage is rightly specified as 88 percent, instead of 84.6

percent (which is what 22–4 would have been). static.odusports.com/
custompages/2018–19/baseball/2019%20media%20guide.pdf.

5   *Arthur "Bud" Metheny Papers, 1930–1991*, Series II, Box 5. Special Collections
    of Old Dominion's Patricia W. and J. Douglas Perry Library, Norfolk,
    Virginia. Note: statistics are taken from the 1965 folder, and extrapolated.

6   *Arthur "Bud" Metheny Papers, 1930–1991*, Series II, Box 5. Special
    Collections of Old Dominion's Patricia W. and J. Douglas Perry Library,
    Norfolk, Virginia.

7   "LeMoyne Loses NCAA Game To Old Dominion Nine, 5–1," *The Post-
    Standard* (Syracuse, NY), June 9, 1965, 20. www.newspapers.com/
    image/36481814/.

8   Arthur B. "Bud" Metheny, "Oral History Interview with Arthur B.
    Metheny (Part Two)," Interview by Dr. James R. Sweeney. May 29, 1975.
    dc.lib.odu.edu/digital/collection/oralhistory/id/563/rec/7.

9   "M-D Studies Aid Proposal," *The Progress-Index* (Petersburg, VA), March 14,
    1969, 6. www.newspapers.com/image/5923126/.

10 Bob Moskowitz, "The Way the Ball Bounces," *Daily Press* (Newport News,
    VA), January 19, 1969, C3. www.newspapers.com/image/230931861/.

11 "Old Dominion Quitting M-D," *Daily Press* (Newport News, VA), June 2,
    1969, 10. www.newspapers.com/image/230332824/.

12 "Mason-Dixon Conference Disbanded," *The Gettysburg (PA) Times*, October
    11, 1978, 16. www.newspapers.com/image/46295867/.

13 Ibid.

14 "ODU Seeks ECAC Pact," *Daily Press* (Newport News, VA), April 23, 1976, 35.
    www.newspapers.com/image/233682460/.

15 "Jarrett Denies Claim," *Daily Press* (Newport News, VA), February 2, 1982,
    20. www.newspapers.com/image/238177719/.

16 "Old Dominion makes it Sun Belt 8," *St. Petersburg (FL) Times*, April 6, 1982,
    6c. www.newspapers.com/image/332464594/.

17 "ODU S.B. Ballard Stadium Reconstruction," accessed March 2, 2021,
    www.sbballard.com/portfolios/odu-sb-ballard-stadium-updates/.

18 Jack Dorsey, "ODC Athletic Encouraging: Metheny," *The Mace and Crown*,
    January 15, 1965, 6.

19 Arthur B. "Bud" Metheny, "Oral History Interview with Arthur B.
    Metheny (Part Two)," Interview by Dr. James R. Sweeney. May 29, 1975.
    dc.lib.odu.edu/digital/collection/oralhistory/id/563/rec/7.

20 Jack Dorsey, "ODC Athletic Encouraging: Metheny," *The Mace and Crown*,
    January 15, 1965, 6.

21 Ibid.

22 "Buttons Speakes Given Scholarship at Old Dominion," *The Danville (VA) Register*, June 17, 1965, 1-D. www.newspapers.com/image/23418631.

23 Arthur B. "Bud" Metheny, "Oral History Interview with Arthur B. Metheny (Part Two)," Interview by Dr. James R. Sweeney. May 29, 1975. dc.lib.odu.edu/digital/collection/oralhistory/id/563/rec/7.

24 Charles Karmosky, "Metheny Turns Fete Into 'Rally,'" *Daily Press* (Newport News, VA), June 7, 1980, 21. www.newspapers.com/image/234199097/.

25 Old Dominion University, *Old Dominion Baseball 2019 Media Guide* (Norfolk, VA: 2019), 4. static.odusports.com/custompages/2018–19/baseball/2019%20media%20guide.pdf.

26 Ibid.

27 Ken Samet, "'Coach' Metheny," *The Mace and Crown*, April 28, 1980.

28 "Kirkie Harrison—Old Dominion University," accessed March 1, 2021, odusports.com/sports/2019/9/16/208421214.aspx.

APPENDIX

1 *Arthur "Bud" Metheny Papers, 1930–1991*, Series II, Box 4. Special Collections of Old Dominion's Patricia W. and J. Douglas Perry Library, Norfolk, Virginia. Collection includes Metheny's baseball scorebooks from 1952–1980.

2 Pennsylvania State University *La Vie 1965*, ed. Earl Lybarger (Williamsport, PA: Grit Publishing Co., 1965), 359. digital.libraries.psu.edu/digital/collection/lavie/id/39840/.

3 "All-Time Game-by-Game Results (1940–59)—Dartmouth College Athletics," accessed March 2, 2021, dartmouthsports.com/sports/2016/6/13/211016014.aspx.

4 Arthur B. "Bud" Metheny, "Oral History Interview with Arthur B. Metheny (Part One)," Interview by Dr. James R. Sweeney. May 22, 1975. dc.lib.odu.edu/digital/collection/oralhistory/id/561/.

5 "Bob Shawkey—Society for American Baseball Research," accessed March 1, 2021, sabr.org/bioproj/person/bob-shawkey/.

6 "MLB Stats, Scores, History, & Records," accessed March 2, 2021, www.baseball-reference.com/. Note: Player profiles for both Metheny and Lupien can be accessed from the main page.

7 "Tony Lupien—Society for American Baseball Research," accessed March 1, 2021, sabr.org/bioproj/person/tony-lupien/.

8 Dartmouth College *Aegis 1963*, ed. Jon Moscartolo et. al. (Hanover, NH: 1963). www.e-yearbook.com/sp/eybb?school=68&year=1963.

9   "All-Time Game-by-Game Results (1866–99)—Dartmouth College Athletics," accessed March 1, 2021, dartmouthsports.com/sports/2016/6/13/211016193.aspx.

10   "Individual Records—Dartmouth College Athletics," accessed March 1, 2021, dartmouthsports.com/sports/2018/7/3/589373.aspx?id=760.

11   "Top Ten Pitching Records—Dartmouth College Athletics," accessed March 1, 2021, dartmouthsports.com/sports/2018/7/3/589377.aspx?id=757.

12   Ed Hewitt, "Ed-iting Sports," *The Mace and Crown*, May 22, 1964, 7.

13   Jimmy Walker, in phone interview with the author, March 10, 2016.

14   Ibid.

15   Wayne Parks, in phone interview with the author, February 28, 2016.

16   "University History | Washington and Lee," accessed March 1, 2021, www.wlu.edu/the-w-l-story/university-history/.

17   Pete Heumann, e-mail message to author, March 8, 2016.

18   Tom Carpenter, "Baseball Outlook Bright," *The Ring-Tum Phi* (Washington and Lee), March 3, 1964, 3. dspace.wlu.edu/xmlui/bitstream/handle/11021/29201/RTP_19640303.pdf.

19   Ibid.

20   Wayne Parks, in phone interview with the author, February 28, 2016.

21   Jimmy Walker, in phone interview with the author, March 10, 2016.

22   "Tigers Just Hope," *The Tiger* (Hampden-Sydney College), April 3, 1964.

23   "It's Ancient, But Anyway...,". *The Tiger* (Hampden-Sydney College), April 10, 1964.

24   "Hampden-Sydney Nine Scores Early to Defeat ODC, 8–1," *The Virginian-Pilot*, April 12, 1964, D-2.

25   "It's Ancient, But Anyway...,". *The Tiger* (Hampden-Sydney College), April 10, 1964.

26   Jim Garwood, in phone interview with the author, March 2, 2016.

27   Randolph-Macon records in the school's Special Collections credits Randolph-Macon with winning the Mason-Dixon in 1960, but a sheet in Bud Metheny's papers in ODU's library says that Western Maryland won it that year. Newspaper accounts from 1960 confirm that Randolph-Macon won the South Division, but Western Maryland won the best-of-three championship series with a pair of 5–3 wins.

28   *Press Releases, March-April 1964*, Flavia Reed Owen Special Collections and Archives, McGraw-Page Library of Randolph-Macon College, Ashland, Virginia.

29 Jay Pace, "Sports Slants," *The Yellow Jacket* (Randolph-Macon College), April 10, 1964, 4.

30 "2020 Baseball Roster—Virginia Military Institute," accessed December 6, 2020, vmikeydets.com/sports/baseball/roster.

31 "VMI Baseball History & Records," accessed March 1, 2021, static. vmikeydets.com/custompages/interactiveguides/baseball/history/ baseball_history.html.

32 "2019 baseball end of season record book (PDF)—Virginia Military Institute," accessed March 1, 2021, vmikeydets.com/ documents/2019/12/17/2019_baseball_end_of_season_record_book. pdf?path=baseball.

33 "2016 baseball end of season record book_Layout 1," accessed July 10, 2021, s3.amazonaws.com/vmikeydets.com/documents/2016/8/1/4932507.pdf.

34 *1964 Bomb of the Virginia Military Institute*, ed. Lyman H. Goff (Roanoke, VA: Stone Printing and Manufacturing Company, 1964), ~230 (pages not numbered). archive.org/details/bomb1964virg.

35 National Collegiate Athletic Association, *Official Collegiate Baseball Guide 1964* (New York: The National Collegiate Athletic Bureau, 1964), 55. Note: The rankings were done in "Steals Per Game," and White stole 26 in 25 games (1.04 per game). He was shown as a member of the Virginia Tech team, rather than VMI, in the 1963 stats.

36 "Randolph-Macon," accessed March 1, 2021. www.rmcathletics.com/ sports/bsb/archive. Note: Other sources show a slightly different final tally, including Randolph-Macon's own Hall of Fame entry for Stephens, which reflects a 459–206–4 overall record (www.rmcathletics.com/Hall_ of_Fame/Hall_of_Fame_Bios/Hugh_Stephens).

37 Arthur B. "Bud" Metheny, "Oral History Interview with Arthur B. Metheny (Part Two)," Interview by Dr. James R. Sweeney. May 29, 1975. dc.lib.odu.edu/digital/collection/oralhistory/id/563/rec/7.

38 Randolph-Macon Closes out Hugh Stephens Field with 18–6 Win over Hampden-Sydney," accessed March 1, 2021, www.rmcathletics.com/ sports/bsb/2009-10/releases/20100417ihxn9k.

39 "Randolph-Macon," accessed March 1, 2021, www.rmcathletics.com/ sports/bsb/archive.

40 *Arthur "Bud" Metheny Papers, 1930–1991*, Series II, Box 5. Special Collections of Old Dominion's Patricia W. and J. Douglas Perry Library, Norfolk, Virginia.

41 "Arthur Bosley Minor League Statistics & History," accessed March 2, 2021, www.baseball-reference.com/register/player.fcgi?id=bosley001art.

42 University of Baltimore *Reporter 1964*, ed. Donald MacIntyre et. al. (Baltimore: Taylor Publishing Company, 1964), 93, 104. archives.ubalt.edu/ ub_archives/yearbooks/pdfs/UR0042_B02_F014.pdf.

43 University of Baltimore *Reporter 1963*, ed. Taylor Anderson and Kay Rodney Turner et. al. (Baltimore: 1963), 101. archives.ubalt.edu/ub_ archives/yearbooks/pdfs/UR0042_B02_F013.pdf.

44 University of Baltimore *Reporter 1964*, ed. Donald MacIntyre et. al. (Baltimore: Taylor Publishing Company, 1964), 114. archives.ubalt.edu/ ub_archives/yearbooks/pdfs/UR0042_B02_F014.pdf.

45 "Edgar Kovner, Retired Pioneering Engineering Technology Prof, Dies," accessed March 1, 2021, www.odu.edu/news/2013/6/edgar_kovner#. YD2oMGhKiUl.

46 Edgar A. Kovner, "Oral History Interview with Professor Edgar A. Kovner," Interview by Dr. James R. Sweeney. April 3, 1975. dc.lib.odu.edu/ digital/collection/oralhistory/id/206.

47 Fred Kovner, in phone interview with the author, February 29, 2016.

48 "Baseball Prospectus | Statistics | Custom Statistics Reports: Run Expectations," accessed March 1, 2021, legacy.baseballprospectus.com/ sortable/index.php?cid=1918829.

49 University of Baltimore *Reporter 1964*, ed. Donald MacIntyre et. al. (Baltimore: Taylor Publishing Company, 1964), 100. archives.ubalt.edu/ ub_archives/yearbooks/pdfs/UR0042_B02_F014.pdf.

50 John W. Stewart, "UB will discontinue its intercollegiate athletic program," *The Baltimore Sun*, April 19, 1983, B1. www.newspapers.com/ image/377510401/.

51 "Presidential History—University of Baltimore," accessed March 1, 2021, www.ubalt.edu/about-ub/offices-and-services/president/presidential-history.cfm.

52 Henry Horace Hibbs, *A History of the Richmond Professional Institute: from Its Beginning in 1917 to Its Consolidation with the Medical College of Virginia in 1968 to Form Virginia Commonwealth University* (Richmond, VA: Whittet and Shepperson, 1973), 44.

53 "Devils Conclude (1–19) season By Losing 2 to Pembroke State," RPI *Proscript*, May 24, 1963, 3. digital.library.vcu.edu/islandora/object/ vcu%3A16159.

54   Sam Shield, "Tomorrow Begins Ball Season; Alphin and Woody Are Starters," RPI *Proscript*, March 20, 1964, 3. digital.library.vcu.edu/islandora/object/vcu%3A16288.

55   "RPI Colors Changed to Grey and Blue," RPI *Proscript*, March 29, 1963, 4. Note: This edition also contains an editorial on the same subject on page 2. digital.library.vcu.edu/islandora/object/vcu%3A16174.

56   Atlantic Christian College *The Pine Knot 1964*, ed. Carolyn Cameron et. al. (Wilson, NC: 1964), 90. lib.digitalnc.org/record/32265.

57   "Consideration Pleaded For Negro Entertainers," *The Collegiate* (Atlantic Christian College), March 6, 1964, 1. newspapers.digitalnc.org/lccn/2014236903/1964-03-06/ed-1/seq-1/.

58   Jerry Elmore, "Sportscope," *The Collegiate* (Atlantic Christian College), March 13, 1964, 3. newspapers.digitalnc.org/lccn/2014236903/1964-03-13/ed-1/seq-3/.

59   "AC College Will Integrate," *The Collegiate* (Atlantic Christian College), May 1, 1964, 1. newspapers.digitalnc.org/lccn/2014236903/1964-05-01/ed-1/seq-1/.

60   "Duke Will Play Wolfpack Today," *The News and Observer* (Raleigh, NC), May 12, 1948, 10. www.newspapers.com/image/651668073/.

61   "Pitchers Win Six Places in Circuit Poll," *Asheville Citizen-Times*, May 23, 1948, 1D. www.newspapers.com/image/200917855.

62   "Jack McComas Is Named Manager Of Wilson Tobs For 1952 Season," *The Collegiate* (Atlantic Christian College), February 1, 1952, 5. newspapers.digitalnc.org/lccn/2014236903/1952-02-01/ed-1/seq-5/.

63   "McComas Resigns Position At ACC," *The Collegiate* (Atlantic Christian College), April 24, 1964, 1. newspapers.digitalnc.org/lccn/2014236903/1964-04-24/ed-1/seq-1/.

64   "Church Affiliation—Bridgewater College," accessed March 2, 2021, web.archive.org/web/20171024161912/http://www.bridgewater.edu/about-bc/church-affiliation. Note: This is an archived version; the current live page at www.bridgewater.edu has eliminated this information.

65   Francis Fry Wayland, *Bridgewater College: The First 100 Years, 1880–1980* (Lawrenceville, VA: Brunswick Publishing Company, 1993), 497.

66   Ibid., 499.

67   Wayne Parks, in phone interview with the author, February 28, 2016.

68   Fred Kovner, in phone interview with the author, February 29, 2016.

69   "Dr. Daniel Geiser—Bridgewater College," accessed March 1, 2021, www.bridgewatereagles.com/hallFame/98/Dan_Geiser?view=bio.

70 "Daniel Geiser Obituary—Death Notice and Service Information," accessed March 1, 2021, www.legacy.com/obituaries/name/daniel-geiser-obituary?pid=135733060.

71 Chuck Moore, "About Sports," *The B. C. Bee*, April 17, 1964, 3.

72 "College to University—University of Lynchburg," accessed March 1, 2021, www.lynchburg.edu/about/always-becoming/college-to-university/.

73 "Spring 2021 Student Profile," accessed July 11, 2021, www.lynchburg.edu/wp-content/uploads/lynchburg-by-the-numbers/spring-2021-student-profile-2–10–2020.pdf.

74 Lynchburg College *Argonaut 1964*, ed. Mary Joan Bentley et. al. (Lynchburg, VA: 1964), 25. www.e-yearbook.com/sp/eybb?school=110883&year=1964.

75 Michael Wayne Santos, *A Beacon Through the Years: A History of Lynchburg College 1090–2003* (Virginia Beach, VA: The Donning Company Publishers, 2005), 77.

76 Ibid., 78.

77 "Monarchs Trip Rams For Little Eight Crown,'" *Daily Press* (Newport News, VA), May 8, 1964, 31. www.newspapers.com/image/232846589.

78 "Six Lettermen To Lead Varsity '9,'" *Critograph* (Lynchburg College), March 13, 1964.

79 "Sports Hall of Fame Members—University of Lynchburg," accessed March 1, 2021, www.lynchburg.edu/alumni-friends/alumni/alumni-awards/sports-hall-of-fame-nomination-form/sports-hall-of-fame-members/. Note: The Fox family history webpage (foxfamilywebsite.com/james) says he was inducted in 1999, but Lynchburg's site states that he was awarded a special citation in 1978.

80 "Honorary Alumni Award Recipients—University of Lynchburg," accessed March 2, 2021, www.lynchburg.edu/alumni-friends/alumni/alumni-awards/honorary-alumni-award-nomination-form/honorary-alumni-award-recipients/.

81 John Ingram, in phone interview with the author, January 25, 2016.

82 "Joe Lyles Minor Leagues Statistics & History,," accessed March 1, 2021, www.baseball-reference.com/register/player.fcgi?id=lyles-001jos.

83 Julie Campbell, "Joe Lyles, Legendary W&L Coach, Dies at 83," accessed July 11, 2021, columns.wlu.edu/joe-lyles-legendary-wl-coach-dies-at-83/.

84 "Joe Lyles, Legendary Coach," *Washington and Lee University Alumni Magazine*, Winter 2013, 38. issuu.com/wlumag/docs/winter_mag_2013.

85 Paul Daugherty, "Doc talks baseball with the three wise men," accessed March 2, 2021, www.cincinnati.com/story/sports/columnists/

paul-daugherty/2015/05/12/paul-daugherty-yogi-berra-casey-stengel-joe-lyles/27179599/.

86   Pete Heumann, e-mail message to author, March 9, 2016.

87   Jimmy Walker, in phone interview with the author, March 10, 2016.

88   Washington and Lee University *The Calyx 1965*, ed. Arthur Sher and Dick Kreitler (Nashville: Benson Printing Co., 1965), 170. dspace.wlu.edu/handle/11021/27204.

89   "History—Native American Program," accessed July 11, 2021, students.dartmouth.edu/nap/about/history.

90   "History and Culture Backup | lumbee-tribe-of-nc," accessed March 1, 2021, www.lumbeetribe.com/history--culture.

91   "History | The University of North Carolina at Pembroke," accessed March 2, 2021, www.uncp.edu/about/history.

92   Pembroke State College *Indianhead 1964*, ed. Betty Braswell et. al. (Marceline, MO: Walsworth Publishing Co., 1964) lib.digitalnc.org/record/39196?ln=en#?c=0&m=0&s=0&cv=0&r=0&xywh=-1451%2C-153%2C5028%2C3055.

93   "Baseball—Year By Year Records—UNCP Athletics," accessed March 2, 2021, uncpbraves.com/sports/2018/5/31/baseball-year-by-year-records.aspx?id=1009.

94   Wayne Parks, in phone interview with the author, February 28, 2016.

95   Tommy Thompson, "PSC Baseball To Start May 13," *The Robesonian* (Lumberton, NC), March 3, 1964, 5. www.newspapers.com/image/42015261.

96   "Deaton Tops Pembroke Nine With .459 Batting Average," *The Robesonian* (Lumberton, NC), May 6, 1964, 9. www.newspapers.com/image/42019361/.

97   Roger Mullen, "Sunday Salute: Ray Pennington was a leader and mentor," *The Fayetteville (NC) Observer*, November 17, 2018. www.fayobserver.com/news/20181117/sunday-salute-ray-pennington-was-leader-and-mentor.

98   Sam Shield, "Tomorrow Begins Ball Season; Alphin and Woody Are Starters," RPI *Proscript*, March 20, 1964, 3. digital.library.vcu.edu/islandora/object/vcu%3A16288.

99   "Chris Finwood—Head Coach—Baseball Coaches—Old Dominion University," accessed March 2, 2021, odusports.com/sports/baseball/roster/coaches/chris-finwood/812. Note: The VCU Baseball Record Book at vcuathletics.com/documents/2020/5/21/VCU_Baseball_Record_Book.pdf cites the team's record at 215 wins and 137 losses, so the

additional wins and losses in the Old Dominion account likely include postseason games.

100   "History of H-SC (pdf)," accessed March 1, 2021, www.hsc.edu/documents/About H-SC/HistoryofHSC.pdf.

101   Ed Hewitt, "ODC Wins M-D Southern Division Title," *The Mace and Crown*, May 8, 1964, 6.

102   "Tigers End Season With 10–6 Record," *The Farmville (VA) Herald*, May 22, 1964, 3A.

BIBLIOGRAPHY

ARCHIVAL SOURCES

Arthur B. Metheny file, National Baseball Hall of Fame, Cooperstown, NY

Sargeant Memorial Collection, Slover Public Library, Norfolk, VA

Special Collections, Forrer Learning Commons, Bridgewater College, Bridgewater, VA

Hampden-Sydney College Archives and Special Collections, Walter M. Bortz III Library, Hampden-Sydney College, Hampden Sydney, VA

Special Collections and University Archives, Patricia W. and J. Douglas Perry Library, Old Dominion University, Norfolk, VA

Special Collections and Archives, McGraw-Page Library, Randolph-Macon College, Ashland, VA

Special Collections and Archives, Washington and Lee University Library, Lexington, VA

GOVERNMENT SOURCES

United States Federal Census returns, 1900–1940

Petro, Diane. "Brother, Can You Spare a Dime?", www.archives.gov/publications/prologue/2012/spring/1940.html

Virginia's Career and Workforce-Labor Market Information, virginiaworks.com/quarterly-census-of-employment-and-wages-qcew

Landmark Legislation: The Civil Rights Act of 1964, www.senate.gov/artandhistory/history/common/generic/CivilRightsAct1964.htm

Climate Data Online, www7.ncdc.noaa.gov/CDO/cdoselect.cmd?datasetabbv=GSOD&resolution=40

Mumps, www.cdc.gov/mumps/outbreaks.html

INTERVIEWS CONDUCTED PERSONALLY

Ingram, John A. Jr. Phone interview. 25 Jan. 2016

Ingram, Arlene. Phone interview. 23 Feb. 2016

Palmer, William A. Jr. Phone interview. 9 Feb. 2016

Nix, Boyd. Phone interview. 28 Feb. 2016

Parks, Wayne. Phone interview. 28 Feb. 2016

Kovner, Fred. Phone interview. 29 Feb. 2016

Garwood, Jim. Phone interview. 2 Mar. 2016

Heumann, Pete. Email Interview. 9 Mar. 2016

Walker, Jim. Phone interview. 10 Mar. 2016

Tysinger, Travis. Phone interview. 10 Mar. 2016

Zeb, John. Phone interview. 1 Aug. 2016

Zadell, Frank. Phone interview. 11 Dec. 2016

Zadell, Jim. Phone interview. 14 Dec. 2016

Renn, Mel. Phone interview. 22 Jan. 2017

Edmonds, Fred Jr. Phone interview. 23 Jan. 2017

Harrell, Tom. Phone interview. 16 Feb. 2017

Davis, Clyde "Ducky." Phone interview. 15 May 2017

Zontini, Tony. Phone interview. 12 June 2017

Whitehurst, G. William. Phone interview. 6 Aug. 2017

O'Leary, Frazier. Phone interview. 7 Aug. 2017

Killmon, Ron. Phone interview. 4 Oct. 2017

Ward, John Atwood II and Beth Ward Langston. Phone interview. 23 Dec. 2019

Fraim, Ed. In-person interview.

INTERVIEWS CONDUCTED BY DR. JAMES SWEENEY

(Note: former Archivist James Sweeney conducted many interviews with important figures in Norfolk and Old Dominion history. Transcriptions and audio files of these interviews can be found online via the Old Dominion University Libraries Digital Collections at dc.lib.odu.edu/digital/collection/oralhistory)

Chandler, Joseph C. "Scrap." 28 Oct. 1975

Kovner, Edgar. 3 Apr. 1975

Metheny, Arthur B. "Bud." Interview Part I. 22 May 1975

Metheny, Arthur B. "Bud." Interview Part II. 29 May 1975

Scott, Mrs. Thomas Lawrence. 5 Feb. 1976

Tonelson, Dr. A. Rufus. Interview Part I. 9 Dec. 1975

Tonelson, Dr. A. Rufus. Interview Part II. 2 July 1979

MEDIA GUIDES

State University of New York—Buffalo 2015 Baseball Media Guide. State University of New York at Buffalo, 2015

LIU Brooklyn Baseball 2015 Record Book. Long Island University—Brooklyn, 2015

2019-2020 ODU Monarch Basketball. Old Dominion University, 2019

Old Dominion Baseball 2019 Media Guide. Old Dominion University, 2019

Baseball 2018 Yearbook. Pennsylvania State University, 2018

2016 VMI Baseball Prospectus. Virginia Military Institute, 2016

2011 VMI Baseball. Virginia Military Institute, 2011

PERIODICALS

Alumni Newsletter, University of Baltimore (Baltimore, MD)

Asbury Park Evening Press (Asbury Park, NJ)

Asheville Citizen-Times (Asheville, NC)

The Baltimore Sun (Baltimore, MD)

The B.C. Bee (student newspaper of Bridgewater College, Bridgewater, VA)

The Cadet (student newspaper of Virginia Military Institute, Lexington, VA)

Chicago Tribune (Chicago, IL)

The Cincinnati Enquirer (Cincinnati, OH)

The Collegiate (student newspaper of Atlantic Christian College, Wilson, NC)

The Columns (Washington and Lee University Alumni Magazine, Lexington, VA)

The Critograph (student newspaper of Lynchburg College, Lynchburg, VA)

The Daily Inter Lake (Kalispell, MT)

Daily Press (Newport News, VA)

The Danville Bee (Danville, VA)

Danville Register (Danville, VA)

The Elm (student newspaper of Washington College, Chestertown, MD)

The Farmville Herald (Farmville, VA)

The Gettysburg Times (Gettysburg, PA)

The High Hat (student newspaper of the Norfolk Division of the College of William & Mary, Norfolk, VA)

Ledger-Star (Norfolk, VA)

The Mace and Crown (student newspaper of Old Dominion College and Old Dominion University, Norfolk, VA)

The New York Sun (New York, NY)

The New York Times (New York, NY)

The Petersburg Progress-Index (Petersburg, VA)

Proscript (student newspaper of Richmond Professional Institute, Richmond, VA)

Richmond Times-Dispatch (Richmond, VA)

Ring Tum Phi (student newspaper of Washington and Lee University, Lexington, VA)

The Robesonian (Lumberton. NC)

St. Louis Post-Dispatch (St. Louis, MO)

The Syracuse Post-Standard (Syracuse, NY)

The Tiger (student newspaper of Hampden-Sydney College, Hampden Sydney, VA)

Virginian-Pilot (Norfolk, VA)

Wilmington Morning News (Wilmington, DE)

St. Petersburg Times (St. Petersburg, FL)

Yellow Jacket (student newspaper of Randolph-Macon College, Ashland, VA)

PUBLISHED MATERIAL

Aaron, Marc Z. and Bill Nowlin. *Who's on First—Replacement Players in World War II*. The Society for American Baseball Research, 2015.

Borst, Bill. *Baseball Through a Knothole (A St. Louis History)*. St. Louis: Krank Press, 1980.

Bridgewater Baseball 1898–1993. Bridgewater, VA: Bridgewater College, 1993.

Brydges, Maggie, et al. *Old Dominion University, From the Great Depression to the New Millennium, 1930–2000*. Norfolk: Old Dominion University, 2000.

Crowley, Joseph N. *In The Arena: The NCAA's First Century*. Indianapolis: The NCAA, 2006.

Falla, Jack. *NCAA: The Voice of College Sports*. Mission, KS: National Collegiate Athletic Association, 1981.

Hibbs, Henry Horace. *A History of the Richmond Professional Institute: from Its Beginning in 1917 to Its Consolidation with the Medical College of Virginia in 1968 to Form Virginia Commonwealth University*. Richmond: Whittet and Shepperson, 1973.

Richards, Dan. *40 Years Behind the Sports Desk*. Writer's Showcase (an imprint of iUniverse, Inc.), 2002. Google Books.

Rutyna, Richard A. and John W. Kuehl. *Old Dominion University, Heritage and Horizons*. Norfolk: The Donning Company Publishers, 1987.

Santos, Michael Wayne. *A Beacon Through the Years: A History of Lynchburg College 1903-2003*. Virginia Beach: The Donning Company Publishers, 2005.

Sweeney, Dr. James R. *Old Dominion University: A Half Century of Service*. Norfolk: ODU Office of Printing and Publications, 1980.

Shampoe, Clay and Thomas R. Garrett. *Baseball in Norfolk, Virginia*. Charleston, SC: Arcadia Publishing, 2003.

Shampoe, Clay and Thomas R. Garrett. *Baseball in Portsmouth, Virginia*. Charleston, SC: Arcadia Publishing, 2004.

Shampoe, Clay and Thomas R. Garrett. *Old Dominion University Men's Basketball*. Charleston, SC: Arcadia Publishing, 2007.

Wayland, Francis Fry. *Bridgewater College: The First 100 Years, 1880-1980*. Lawrenceville, VA: Brunswick Publishing Company, 1993.

Zontini, Tony. *The History of Baseball at Old Dominion University*. Norfolk, VA: Old Dominion University Master's thesis, 1978. [not commercially published]

WEBSITES

Transpersonal Psychology & Mindful Leadership—Online Programs, www.atlanticuniv.edu

[University of Baltimore] Athletic Hall of Fame, www.ubalt.edu/alumni/hall-of-fame/index.cfm

Bridgewater College, www.bridgewater.edu

Bridgewater College [Athletics Hall of Fame], www.bridgewatereagles.com/hallFame/index

Ed Sullivan Show—Official Site, www.edsullivan.com

James Fox: Family Website, foxfamilywebsite.com/james

Hampden-Sydney College homepage, www.hsc.edu

LIU Brooklyn Blackbirds—Hall of Fame, brooklyn.liuathletics.com/hof.aspx

Sports Hall of Fame Members, www.lynchburg.edu/alumni-friends/alumni/alumni-awards/sports-hall-of-fame-nomination-form/sports-hall-of-fame-members/

MLB Stats, Scores, History, & Records, www.baseball-reference.com/

High Schools in Norfolk City Public Schools District, www.usnews.com/education/best-high-schools/virginia/districts/norfolk-city-public-schools-106692

[Map of] Norfolk and Vicinity: March 1921, www.loc.gov/resource/g3884n.ct00 9373/?r=-0.251,0.36,1.542,0.749,0

ODU—Old Dominion University, www.odu.edu

Old Dominion University Hall of Fame Members, odusports.com/sports/2016/2/19/210728289.aspx

Hall of Fame—UNCP Athletics, www.uncpbraves.com/honors/hall-of-fame

The University of North Carolina at Pembroke, www.uncp.edu

Dr. Raymond Pennington (1998)—ECU Athletics Hall of Fame, ecupirates.com/hof.aspx?hof=103

Home :: Randolph-Macon College, www.rmc.edu

Hall of Fame—Randolph-Macon, www.rmcathletics.com/information/hof/index

Anthony Russo Sr (2014)—Hall of Fame—Kingsborough Community College, kccathletics.com/hof.aspx?hof=2

Biography Project - Society for American Baseball Research, www.sabr.org/
bioproject

ODU S.B. Ballard Stadium Reconstruction, www.sbballard.com/portfolios/odu-
sb-ballard-stadium-updates/

[Shenandoah] Valley League Baseball, www.valleyleaguebaseball.com/view/
valleyleaguebaseball

Tidewater Summer League, www.tidewatersummerleague.com

Virginia Sports Hall of Fame, www.vasportshof.com

Washington College, www.washcoll.edu

The W&L Story – Washington and Lee, www.wlu.edu/the-w-l-story

2021 Baseball Roster—Washington and Lee University, www.generalssports.
com/sports/baseball/roster (includes historical rosters)

Weather History & Data Archive, www.wunderground.com/history

William & Mary, www.wm.edu

William & Mary Athletics—Hall of Fame, tribeathletics.com/hof.aspx

YEARBOOKS

Atlantic Christian College. *The Pine Knot*. Wilson, NC: 1964–1965

University of Baltimore. *Reporter*. Baltimore, MD: 1964–1965

Bridgewater College. *Ripples*. Bridgewater, VA: 1965

The State University of New York at Buffalo. *Buffalonian*. Buffalo, NY: 1962–1966

United States Coast Guard Academy. *Tide Rips*. New London, CT: 1963

Dartmouth College. *Aegis*. Hanover, NH: 1965

Hampden-Sydney College. *Kaleidoscope*. Hampden-Sydney, VA: 1964–1965

Loyola College. *Evergreen*. Baltimore, MD: 1963

Lynchburg College. *Argonaut*. Lynchburg, VA: 1964–1965

Maury High School. *The Commodore*. Norfolk, VA: 1931–1946

The Norfolk Division of the College of William & Mary. *The Voyager.* Norfolk, VA: 1946–1949

The Norfolk Division of the College of William & Mary. *Echolalia.* Norfolk, VA: 1950

The Norfolk Division of the College of William & Mary. *The Pow Wow.* Norfolk, VA: 1951–1952

The Norfolk Division of the College of William & Mary. *The Chieftain.* Norfolk, VA: 1954–1961

Old Dominion College. *Troubadour.* Norfolk, VA: 1962–1965

Pembroke State College. *Indianhead.* Pembroke, NC: 1964

Pennsylvania State University. *La Vie.* State College, PA: 1965

Richmond Professional Institute. *Cobblestone.* Richmond, VA: 1964–1965

South Norfolk High School. *The Tiger.* Norfolk, VA: 1940–1951

Virginia Military Institute. *The Bomb.* Lexington, VA: 1964–1965

Washington College. *Pegasus.* Chestertown, MD: 1964–1965

Washington and Lee University. *The Calyx.* Lexington, VA: 1965

The College of William & Mary. *The Colonial Echo.* Williamsburg, VA, 1935–1938

Woodrow Wilson High School. *The President.* Portsmouth, VA: 1931–1949

ACKNOWLEDGMENTS

This work would not have been possible without the help and contributions of many along the way. First and foremost, I would like to thank my parents, John and Arlene Ingram (both Old Dominion College '64), for support, providing the base of operations for Norfolk research, and for helping as "research assistants."

Particular thanks to Wayne Parks as well, for gaining support from the 1964 team and for helping to organize two separate gatherings of that championship team as part of that support.

Special thanks as well to my girlfriend, Ms. Amy Proffitt, for proofreading services rendered and for putting up with spending her 2016 spring break on a tour of Bridgewater College, Hampden-Sydney College, Washington and Lee University, Lynchburg College, and Randolph-Macon College libraries and baseball games.

Thanks to my uncle, William A. Palmer Jr. (Old Dominion College '63), for his support of the project by writing the Foreword and proofreading the almost-complete version.

Thanks to Dr. James R. Sweeney, former archivist of Old Dominion University and author of *Old Dominion University: A Half Century of Service*, for his advice and very detailed proofreading.

Finally, thanks to all the former Old Dominion College ballplayers who were willing to share their recollections in interviews: Fred Edmonds Jr., Tom Harrell, John Ingram, Ron Killmon, Fred Kovner, Boyd Nix, Frazier O'Leary, Wayne Parks, Mel Renn, Jimmy Walker, Frank Zadell, Jimmy Zadell, John Zeb, and Tony Zontini.

ABOUT THE AUTHOR

Jay Ingram grew up in Virginia Beach, Virginia. He attended college at Old Dominion's former parent school, William & Mary, where he received a bachelor of arts degree in history. His interest in the subject matter of this book stems from the fact that his father, John A. Ingram Jr., was a student at Old Dominion College, and a member of the baseball team from 1961-1964. Jay is currently employed by an electric utility in Roanoke, Virginia, as a director of transmission field services.

INDEX

Seelinger, Liz, 39

Selin, Carl, 156, 157, 158

Sensabaugh, Percy, 293

Sentara Healthcare, 265

Sewanee University, 281

Seward, William W. Jr., 20

Sewell's Point, 12

Shampoe, Clay, 29, 37, 64, 67, 119, 123, 128

Shawkey, Bob, 84, 85, 272

Sheehy, Pete, 217

Shelbyville, Indiana, 314

Shenandoah College, 64

Shenandoah Valley League, 45

Shepherd College, 91, 178, 179, 254

Shibley, Bob, 122

Shield, Sam, 310

Shifflett, Wayne, 317, 318, 321, 322

Shipway, Glen, 209

Shoop Park, 140

Sinatra, Frank, 171

Sisk, Ron, 207, 208, 209, 210

Skowron, Bill, 217

Sloan, John, 209, 211

Small, Richard, 228, 229, 230, 231

Smart, Jack, 85, 271

Smathers, George A., 200

Smiley, Don, 298

Smith, Jimmy, 97

Society for American Baseball Research, 272

South Carolina, 163, 192

South Norfolk High School, 17, 25, 27, 57, 60, 62, 64

Southeast Asia, 181, 182

Southeastern Conference, 213, 214

Southeastern Football Officials'

Association, 265

Southern Conference, 25, 32, 79, 108, 213, 214, 251, 293, 294, 295, 314

Southwestern University, 281

Speakes, "Buttons," 254, 255

Sportsman's Park, 44, 53

St. Augustine, Florida, 180

St. Helena Extension, 40, 66

St. John's College, 266

St. John's University, 255, 340

St. Joseph, Missouri, 117

St. Louis Browns, 56, 329

St. Louis Cardinals, 45, 53, 194, 274

St. Louis Hawks, 123

St. Louis Post-Dispatch, 44, 56, 58

St. Louis, Missouri, 13, 43, 44, 45, 53, 329

St. Mary's Academy, 117

St. Mary's College, 266

St. Petersburg Times, The, 251

Stanley, Bob, 102

Stanley, Rebecca Wilson, 267

Starr, Ringo, 171

State University of New York at Buffalo, 159, 160, 161, 191, 197, 214, 220, 221, 222, 223, 225, 226, 227, 228, 230, 276, 324

Staunton, Virginia, 89

Stearns, Bob, 297, 298

Steinbrenner, George, 257

Stengel, Casey, 330, 337

Stephens, Hugh, 91, 288, 295, 296, 297, 298, 299

Stephenson, Percy S., 13

Stewart, "Buckwheat," 25

Stirnweiss, George "Snuffy," 64, 65, 67

Stofa, John, 160, 224

United Press International, 201

United States, 11, 33, 56, 65, 168, 174, 180, 181, 182, 201, 215, 221, 280, 291, 339

University Division, NCAA, 192, 193, 212, 213, 214, 294

University of Arizona, 270

University of Baltimore, 94, 95, 115, 147, 202, 203, 299, 300, 301, 302, 304, 305, 306, 312, 327

University of Buffalo, 221

University of Delaware, 113, 288

University of Florida, 213

University of Georgia, 294

University of Kentucky, 123

University of Maryland, 48, 299, 307

University of Michigan, 255

University of Missouri, 255

University of North Carolina, 64, 213, 333

University of Richmond, 68, 71, 85, 252, 256, 293

University of Rochester, 85, 246

University of Texas, 270

University of Vermont, 48

University of Virginia, 85, 86, 87, 92, 106, 140, 213, 256, 306, 324

USS *Henrico*, 268

USS *New York*, 33

USS *St. Paul*, 268

Valentine, Ronnie, 120

Van Hook, Sam, 228

VanDaniker, Rel, 148, 152

Verlander, Justin, 249

Vermont, 49, 248

Viet Cong, 181

Vietnam, 2, 181, 182, 183, 201, 268

Vincent, Mal, 171

Virginia, 2, 10, 12, 17, 19, 21, 44, 45, 90, 92, 94, 96, 97, 112, 114, 117, 135, 161, 163, 174, 179, 192, 205, 212, 232, 250, 254, 255, 260, 264, 271, 280, 291, 322

Virginia Beach, Virginia, 3, 12, 13, 88, 89, 173, 174, 176, 249, 260, 264, 265

Virginia Christian College, 323

Virginia Commonwealth University, 255, 308, 338

Virginia General Assembly, 87, 174, 179

Virginia Military Institute, 17, 24, 25, 63, 85, 144, 171, 172, 173, 202, 291, 292, 293, 294, 295, 302, 310

Virginia Polytechnic Institute and State University, 20, 28, 63, 92, 252, 307

Virginia Sports Hall of Fame, 24, 25, 38, 265, 296

Virginia Wesleyan College, 140

Virginian, The, 135

Virginian-Pilot, The, 6, 20, 41, 72, 79, 81, 82, 83, 84, 86, 87, 97, 98, 99, 100, 101, 102, 103, 104, 107, 108, 137, 170, 171, 180, 181, 184, 190, 192, 195, 212, 275, 286

Vitasek, John, 70, 71, 119

VMI Cadet, The, 171

Voyager, The, 39, 63, 66, 69

Wabash College, 340

Wade, Gale, 74

Walker, Jimmy, 141, 173, 203, 214, 219, 239, 240, 246, 276, 277, 279, 282, 294, 298, 301, 305, 306, 310, 315, 321, 328, 331, 332, 336, 382

Walton, Bob, 9, 22, 105, 108, 134, 146, 149, 150, 151, 157, 158, 159, 160, 161,